MORE QUOTABLE CHESTERTON

MORE
QUOTABLE
CHESTERTON

A Topical Compilation of the Wit, Wisdom and
Satire of G. K. Chesterton

Edited by

GEORGE J. MARLIN, RICHARD P. RABATIN

and JOHN L. SWAN

With a Foreword by

GEORGE WILLIAM RUTLER

IGNATIUS PRESS   SAN FRANCISCO

Cover and jacket by Marcia Ryan

© 1988 Ignatius Press, San Francisco
All rights reserved
ISBN 0-89870-207-7 (HB)
0-89870-201-1 (SB)
Library of Congress catalogue number 88-80751
Printed in the United States of America

To Our Mothers

DOLORES MARLIN

ALICE RABATIN

FRANCES SWAN
(1897–1969)

The dates used in the citations in this volume are from the American edition of the *Illustrated London News,* which normally appeared two weeks later than those of the British edition.

CONTENTS

PREFACE

Gilbert Keith Chesterton was that rare specimen: an unassuming journalist. Even so, his influence was almost universal in scope. For example, for the philosopher Etienne Gilson, "Chesterton was one of the deepest thinkers who ever existed." For the common man—whenever G. K. C.'s column ran—the jump in circulation of The *Illustrated London News* attested to his catholicity. C. S. Lewis opines that for the scoffers or " . . . the critics who think Chesterton frivolous or paradoxical I have to work hard to feel even pity. Sympathy is out of the question." On *The Quotable Chesterton*, the *New York Times Book Review* (September 1986) conceded; "Chesterton was one of those indispensable writers whose job it was to keep modern art and life honest."

Chesterton enjoyed life. His delight was to be with his beloved common man whether in a pub, a chophouse or an omnibus. The result: hours of discussion over a bottle of port; a joyous interlude which may be observed in the columns quoted in this volume. Always, the quest was for truth and preservation of what Russell Kirk has called "the Permanent Things". His friend Belloc stated it best when he wrote of Chesterton:

> Truth had for him the immediate attraction of an appetite. He was hungry for reality. But what is much more, he could not conceive of himself except as satisfying that hunger; it was not possible for him to hesitate in the acceptance of each new parcel of truth; it was not possible for him to hold anything worth holding that was not connected with the truth as a whole.

Familiarity with Chesterton breeds not contempt, but awe; awe of a vision as wide as the heavens and as local as Fleet Street. G. K. C. knew what was in man, and with uncanny foresight and clairvoyance he alerted the common man and his world to the evils gathering over the twentieth century: Liberal theology and relaxed moral standards, feminism, homosexuality, divorce, eugenics, abortion, euthanasia; modern psychology, pseudo-science, Nazism and Communism— inevitably these would all lead to the desacralization of life, the annihilation of the family, and, ultimately the abandonment of God.

This volume represents passages from Chesterton's *Illustrated London News* columns published from 1905 until his death in 1936. Unlike some fellow journalists who journeyed to Moscow or accepted its handouts, and who were gulled into euphoria by the ongoing Bolshevist Experiment, G. K. C. wrote of communism:

"It is now both an ideal and a reality; and its name is slavery."

—November 12, 1921

9

"It looks as if Russia might remain for an indefinite time in the queer congested compromise of decayed communism and alien capitalism, and servile or conscript labour...."

—April 19, 1924

Of Hitler and Nazism, the second diabolic ideological perversion of the twentieth century, he foretold with his "uncanny clairvoyance":

"President Wilson eventually entered into the great war, remarking that it was a war to make the world safe for democracy. Herr Hitler is undoubtedly ready to wage another great war to make the world safe from democracy."

—December 3, 1933

"I am quite certain myself, for instance, that a great European war could be prevented tomorrow, if the British government had the moral courage to threaten Prussia with British support for France and Poland the moment they were attacked. I am equally certain that the last great war would not have happened at all, if we had done the same thing openly and from the beginning, instead of half secretly and too late."

—December 2, 1932

"We are already drifting horribly near to a new war, which will probably start on the Polish border. The young men have had eighteen years in which to learn how to avoid it. I wonder whether they do know much more about how to avoid it than the despised and driveling old men of 1914. How many of the young men, for instance, have made the smallest attempt to understand Poland? How many would have anything to say to Hitler, to dissuade him from setting all Christendom aflame by a raid on Poland? Or have the young men been thinking of nothing since 1914 except the senile depravity of the old men of that date?"

—September 24, 1932

Malcolm Muggeridge has observed:

When mortal men try to live without God, they infallibly succumb to megalomania or erotomania or both. The raised fist or raised phallus; Nietzsche or D. H. Lawrence.

Chesterton would agree but over and against this siege of despair, he would stand the Family—the *personification* of the children of God.

We pray that others may enjoy these Chestertonian samples half as much as the editors while putting them together. Even more, we hope this effort will lead many to approach and enjoy G. K. C.

As always, in a project of this nature, thanks are due to many for their material and moral support while any shortcomings must inevitably fall upon the editors. Particular recognition and gratitude are extended to Dr. Lawrence J. Clipper,

Frank Petta and the Mid-Western Chesterton Society whose dedication and labor have given us this cornucopia of Chesterton's thirty-one year output in the *Illustrated London News*. Very special thanks to Barbara Dyson Marlin and Donna Albertus Rabatin. Also, we wish to acknowledge the generosity and guidance of George William Rutler, S.T.D., Joseph Fessio, S.J., and the staff of Ignatius Press. Finally, heartfelt thanks to Larry and Pat Azar, Joseph Bierbauer, Msgr. Eugene V. Clark, Ph.D., Ronald Carolonza, John P. DeMaio, Esq., Andrew J. Donnelly, Anne H. Roberts, Thomas Walsh, Msgr. John G. Woolsey, and Charles G. Woram.

New York City   George J. Marlin
March, 1988   Richard P. Rabatin
                                                          John L. Swan

FOREWORD

On Snobbery

An Australian has served notice that he objects to ordinary people writing about Chesterton. He has said so in a scholarly journal, and so he must mean it. His particular complaint is against people other than scholars publishing studies of the great man. It seems hard for him to appreciate the substance of a thing done freely for the love of it and not as a professional function. I do not mean, by corollary, that professionals are pedants because they are required to write what others write freely. I do not even mean that there is anything wrong with doing a thing under duress or even as a punishment; consider the settlement of Australia. I suppose the Australian scholar is quite as justified in imagining himself "Up Over" as the rest of the world regards him "Down Under"; but it is inexcusable to look down upon the very people to whom Chesterton looked up. Chesterton would have considered himself vindicated in all his works to know that the "man in the street" responded to what he wrote. And he would have let loose a howl of delight like thunder from a cleft sky at the discomfort of an academician who had been thwarted in an attempt to lock him up in some tower of the academy.

Chesterton is to be observed as a fact; he cannot be taken apart as a theory. When a man is taken apart he quickly ceases to be alive; and there is a proprietary form of criticism which is very like a dissection, and sometimes less delicately like vivisection. Cain slew Abel; so far as we know, he did not compound his crime by drawing and quartering him. But Chesterton is very much alive—no thanks to the universities who neglected him for so long that he became a lacuna to young minds. And to perform an autopsy on a living thing is not scientific or in any way scholarly; it is morbid and murderous. Now a collection of quotations is tribute to the liveliness of the man; and to object that such a project makes Chesterton too accessible is to object to Chesterton himself. A quotable Chesterton is like a splashable ocean; he cannot be undone by being quoted. It is just hard to know where to begin and end. But not to begin anywhere is endless snobbery. The snob could give us *The Unquotable Chesterton,* and it would be lighter than this volume; but it would not be Chesterton. As Chesterton says in ways general and particular, a problem with snobbery is its way of cherishing right things for wrong reasons. " . . . the uneducated are, by their nature, the real conservers of the past; because they are the people who are really not interested in beauty, but interested in interest. The poor have this advantage over the cultivated class, that the poor (like a few of the best of the very rich) are not affected by the fashions: they keep things because they are quaint or out of the current line of thought. They keep Old Masters because they are old, not because they have recently been 'discovered'. They preserve old fashions until the time when they shall become new fashions. For the man who is ten years behind his time is always ten years nearer to the return of that time" (December 16, 1905).

Many of the lines in his *London Illustrated News* essays reply to the very readers whom the above mentioned critic would not suffer to put thoughts into print: "the old, unaltered, fighting, beer-drinking, creed-making, child-loving, affectionate, selfish, unreasonable, respectable man". His subject was the soul and body; every declaration he could muster doomed the idealist dogma of man as mind and mind alone. That conceit to him was vulgar; and it was the definitive vulgarity. But nothing could be farther from his vision of the true man than a crusade to protect the Chesterton literature from what is more vulgarly called vulgarization. You might as well object to the Vulgate. With close to moral certainty we may say that Chesterton esteemed the Vulgate as the book of great common speech with the same passion he would have hurled against the *haut vulgarization* of The New American Bible. His feet were firmly planted against the condescending snob whose commitments to flat impressions overwhelmed commitments to the romance of creation. "Of two bad things it is better to be the barbarian who destroys something which for some reason he dislikes or does not understand rather than to be the vulgarian who erects something exactly expressive of what he likes. . . . "

The following book displays the kinetic imagination of Chesterton as it continues to escape the attempt of collectors and critics to catch it and pin it down. It is not a display case, but it is the display itself alive in a natural habitat. As he often wrote on the run, he can often best be read on the run. To do a thing seriously does not always mean doing it slowly. A previous volume has gathered quotations from his books; this volume is possibly more important because for the most part it uses previously uncited newspaper essays which are more discursive and fragmentary than the books and better served by excerpting. For thirty-one years, beginning in 1905, Chesterton wrote a weekly column of about two thousand words which were read widely in the English-speaking world, possibly to the dismay of literate men in the farthest underparts of the planet. Against the background of nearly a hundred books and plays and collections of poetry, he continued this outpouring of 1,535 columns for the *Illustrated London News* which required him to announce early on: "I am not allowed in these columns to discuss politics or religion, which is inconvenient as they are the only two subjects which seem to me to have the slightest element of interest for a sane man" (April 7, 1906). He remained sane, and flaunted mental balance by writing about the great euphemism for politics and religion: that is, he wrote about the world. The columns in fact support some of the century's most astute political and theological discourse.

Journalism today, like the world of which it renders an account, is bereft of so wide a scope of reference. It was expected in his day. Chesterton was patient with the obtuseness of hired intelligence as it was beginning to make universities the monopoly of polemicists both idealist and materialist; but when he considered creative thought, as Coleridge described the domain of integral imagination, he anticipated its present tendency to nest everywhere but in the academic nest, and he did not underestimate the infinite capacity of professors to sit on eggs not their own. The formal study of English writing was a novelty in the university curriculum; previously it had been the domain of those who wrote English. The journalist of Chesterton's vintage was still a man of letters, though he was possibly the last and brightest of the breed: E. V. Lucas spun out the definitive life of Charles Lamb, and J. L. Hammond wrote his economic history, as newspaper men. Today it would be like Walter Cronkite editing the monographs of Montesquieu. We do not expect our journalists to be noble writers; and as for television commentators, we are content when they show an ability to read. As Dr. Johnson said in another volatile context, the fact that it was not done well would be overwhelmed by a general astonishment at it being done at all.

The quality of Chestertonian discourse is more than "wide" in scope, and he is more than a Renaissance man; his reference is positively deep, and deep enough to dig beneath a mere renaissance until he strikes the radical birth of order and truth. It is a gift for making obvious the obvious through parallelism, what Belloc called "the illustration of some unperceived truth by its exact consonance with the reflection of a truth already known and perceived". This was his gift for imagination, miles distant from fancy and illusion, and decidedly susceptible to insensible reality in the manner of the Greek *poietes*. The prose is unprosaicly pregnant with meter; many of the paragraphs can be written in verse form. He replies to a man who wanted shorter paragraphs: "My trouble is that I never can really feel that there is such a thing as a different subject. There is no such thing as an irrelevant thing in the universe; for all things in the universe are at least relevant to the universe" (February 17, 1906). The combination of introspection and extroversion had to conclude, as it always has, in delusion or Catholicism; as he put it in the *Life of Blake* a dozen years before his conversion, " . . . if every human being lived a thousand years, every human being would end up either in utter pessimistic skepticism or in the Catholic creed." The columns are paving blocks in his road to Rome which finally received him in 1922. If they seem to speak of everything but religion, it is because he decided from the start that there could be nothing but religion. He concocts his own *Summa* in his book on St. Francis: "Men will not believe because they will not broaden their minds. As a matter of individual belief, I should of course express it by saying that they are not sufficiently catholic to be Catholic." The hidden dogmas and high apologetic jut in and out with casualness born of a long tradition, for Christ was his own peripatetic school, tossing chunks of heaven to those who followed the broadlit Galilean paths. By a derivative equation, Chesterton wrote wherever he could, in trains and taverns, often dictating in a rush as the infernal deadline neared.

> But I, whose copy is extremely late
> And ought to have been sent an hour before
> I still sit here and trifle with my fate
> And idly write another ballad more.
> I know it is too late; all is o'er,
> And all my writings they will now refuse
> I shall be sacked next Monday. So be sure
> And read the *London Illustrated News.*

And the procrastination continued, but as the ruminations of an unseen labor; to the contradiction of Horace's epigram, when this mountain finally gave birth another mountain was born.

The columns are streams of consciousness, normally a pejorative but not so here; these were real streams, and not reflecting pools, and Chesterton plunged the readers into the cold current with him, giving them the shock of seeing the obvious for the first time. Reactions from more dormant minds were available to his analysis: "It is an almost invariable rule that the man with whom I don't agree thinks I am making a fool of myself, and the man with whom I do agree thinks I am making a fool of him" (June 9, 1906). The diction is loud, as befits one who hymned to: "the great lights burning on through darkness to dawn and the roar of the printing wheels". The Ciceronianisms of a certain Victorian were attributed to his habit of playing a violin before composition; Chesterton seems to have tuned up on a bugle. On a bugle, that is, and a set of chimes; for there is a crystalline cut in every declaration such as intimidates the modern essayist accustomed to muddy sentences flaccid with subjunctives. The situation cannot improve soon when today's minds are not adept at either fiddle or horn, and modernity's single instrument is the stereo amplifier.

Journalism in Decline

Chesterton watched the transformation of journalism from literate analysis to ideology. The record of the degeneration, with which he toys in his March 2, 1907 column, was summarized in the story of his own life when he read the Cadbury press's description of a feckless and droning speech in a liberal club: "Lord Spencer Unfurls Banner". The contrast between the fact and a version of the fact "was so huge a hiatus and disproportion that I do not think I ever quite got over it". The seared memory offered itself as a warning to a wider social apparatus; and one monument to heedlessness of the warning is the current state of journalism which grows in pomposity and monopoly of information as it shrinks in intelligence and comprehension of events. It has gone beyond the polemicism Chesterton knew. On the occasion of a recent plane crash a reporter asked a ten-year old girl what she thought about the death of her mother. The moral atrophy is different only in transparency, but not in degree, from the general ineptness of commentators in evaluating the facts of culture. Society is burdened by social critics who boast little awareness of the artifacts of civilization, whose word processors are bloodless and who do not feel the pulse of whole ages. These are the vulgarians whose defacements are worse than the depredations of mere barbarians. The tendency of contemporary editorialization is toward a morally bankrupt secularism which is a way of being of the world but hardly in it; it may be so because journalists of limited prudence are susceptible to the fatuousness of intellectual trends in whose derivative light they would bask. The commentary is commonly devoid of reference to the life of the virtues, even in a noble pagan sense.

As Chesterton saw in his own generation, as he saw it having its greatest crisis in metropolitan centers of a Christian culture which had lost sound moral vision, the worldly critics of culture are scornful of propositions based on objective truth and they are timid in the face of evil. The Fabian Socialists tweaked by Chesterton were playfully gamboling creatures compared to the lumbering dinosaurs of progressivism who now bellow on the edge of their own extinction. The occluded visionaries of theological modernism promised to soar through the Edwardian sky; at the end of the century they are plummeting with twisted talons already half-fossilized. Chesterton spent his life affirming what the modernizer denied, the axiom on which all the modern axes have been blunted: "The meanest man is immortal, but the mightiest movement is temporal."

If the bywords and asides of Chesterton's little essays expose one deceit more than any other, it is the modern refusal to acknowledge its surrender to the tyranny of the cliché. He did not live to see the pusillanimity of the academic establishment in the face of campus radicalism in the 1960s and 70s, but he studied its germ in the meeting halls of the vegetarian Socialists. In the early twentieth century, the statist utopians tried to eliminate illiteracy by means of philosophical commitment which, by undermining any confidence in objective truth, has quite effectively dismantled literacy by now. This was not by neglect or default, nor was it unravelled by unwieldy forces. It was crusaded and campaigned for as staunchly as the former literate reforms. The banalities of modern progressivism abound, and if their causes are ignored their consequences are inescapable. New York City for example, has consecutively legalized sodomy and criminalized smoking in public places; at the end of the twentieth century, unnatural carnal union is an indictable offense only if done while smoking a cigar. This would have been a parable in the *Illustrated London News* of 1907; it is a current event in the newspapers of 1987. By the 1920s, one already hears a booming prophecy from the man in Beaconsfield: "The next great heresy is going to be simply an attack on morality, and especially on sexual morality. The madness of tomorrow is not in Moscow, but much more in Manhattan."

17

In the lush Edwardian spectacle of life one would not have expected that the chief moral question at the end of the century would involve infanticide and the definition of motherhood, or that theological faculties would include self-proclaimed witches, or that the chief social fear would be about plague. But week by week, on trams or in his minute study, a conspicuous character with furrowed brow and shocks of trembling hair was diagramming how it all could happen. The intellectually honest response now is to re-examine what he wrote; in the universities he still is avoided and those of intellectual pretensions who ignore him continue their limp surrender to mediocrity, awarding each other meaningless degrees and wondering why the world has not gone their way. The only ones left who read Chesterton are the meanest men who keep being immortal. And, in a curious way, the one who points this out will find himself dismissed as an obscurantist and an elitist; in fact, such a one only has a democratic appetite for excellence, and that appetite is not highly developed by modern trendiness.

Truth and Tolerance

Chesterton's columns are on the whole happy essays; each goes up like a flare and for a moment signs of life are visible in the night. But only for a moment. Our new system of education has produced a servile mentality which is not habituated to acute perceptions, and the flares from Chesterton's pen may appear as sparks and not beacons. Chesterton expected more of the public than is expected now. A university president at a recent commencement benignly raised his robed arms over the graduates in a Mosaic gesture and, to my surprise, dismissed them with a decidedly un-Mosaic sort of burp: "May you find satisfaction." No longer would the end of human endeavor be happiness, the Scholastic mark of freedom and the true trophy after a length of Socratic discontent; now it would be satiety, and I would see row upon row of young upwardly mobile professionals marching out into the world to stuff themselves. It is probably a formula for unhappiness; it is certainly a formula for slavery. The placid nihilism of our generation is the deadliest laid by the departing modernist.

I would hope, not in a spirit of recrimination but as a scientific kind of historical duty, that a future generation will label the various ruins of our ages with the names of the movements and movers who wrecked them: that each denuded church sanctuary resembling a cocktail lounge would bear the name of the renovator who whitewashed the florid faces of the saints, that each ugly building would advertise the architect who relocated human life to fester in it, that the epitaph of each victim of vice might name the sirens who sang a sexual revolution, that each asylum be named for each psychoanalyst who said there is no sin. I propose it only as an act of that charity which does not exist without justice; I want it only as a guide away from the intolerable cruelty of unreality. Chesterton proposed something like it himself in an encounter with the lady who announced that the craving to do a thing shows you ought to do it. As the train in which they were traveling rolled on and the insanity flitted away, he saw the moral carnage of such flippancy on the passing of England and the world: "Madam, you will not, I am sure be anything but delighted to learn that you have convinced me. A man should always do a thing as long as he has a genuine craving to do it. How true that is! How illuminating! And yet how simple! My present genuine craving, which is to strike you suddenly and sharply on the bridge of the nose, is one which as it is far less destructive than meat-eating, will certainly command your theoretical acquiescence, and which also has this advantage, that it will give some sort of glimmering notion of what sort of world you are living in. As you say, I may survive the craving. After beating you on the nose for a day or two the desire itself may leave me. Then, no doubt, I shall pass to a higher plane" (April 28, 1906).

So Chesterton held before the public a truth, and he flaunted it with a glee which is still before us, perhaps more poignant now than then: the enemy of ideas is not dogma but ideology. Ideology is the secular equivalent of liberalism in religion, imputing authenticity to a thought just because the self has thought it. That philosophical father of communication theory, Marshall McLuhan, converted to Catholicism after reading Chesterton's *What's Wrong with the World;* it is right, I think, to locate the many faults of contemporary communication in the refusal to associate what is wrong with the world with evil. The secular notion of disorder, of which religious modernism is just a cultic expression, is essentially tragic, prescinding from systematic thought, estimating moral disintegration to be an inescapable consequence of absurdity. Gilson held, in words which were nearly verbatim Chesterton, that there is "no necessary connection between philosophical dogmatism and political tyranny, no more than between philosophical scepticism and political liberty". And why? Because "only those who hold something as true are in a position to be tolerant; sceptics cannot be tolerant, only permissive". The believing Chesterton spoke of sin and of forgivable sinners; his permissive opponents denied sin and gave no quarter to anyone who sinned nonetheless. In a recent political scandal, a public figure caught in adultery scandalized the press which had romanticized promiscuity; he had to quit the public scene because the modernist who denies that adultery is a sin refused to forgive him for doing it. It is the opposite of the Christian method. The secular mind is incapable of judgement because it is full of scandal; and apparently no one is more easily scandalized than the libertine. The libertine is obliged to humanize his social default by affecting the forms of civilization, but this only renders dignity pompous and morality legalistic; it needs its own shrines and ceremonies but, like those of Pharisees, they stand empty and faintly ridiculous. The rationalists were serious when they placed the heart of Voltaire in the Pantheon; there are sentimentalists today who would as reverently enshrine the brain of Jane Fonda. Chesterton represents the rare soul capable of enjoying the spectacle. By cultivating a sense of inferiority instead of superiority he avoided condescension in his indulgence of the human comedy, suffering fools gladly, even deliciously, because his only target was the cant which makes the grand comedy a farce.

The author measured disorder and order alike according to a scale which involved God and Satan. In *Orthodoxy* he says reform means "we see a certain thing out of shape and we mean to put it into shape. And we know what shape."

The procedure was according to high dogma, blushing through the pallor of civil events which are the incidental subject of the columns, making each essay a flickering votive to the creeds of orthodoxy. I cannot imagine Schopenhauer getting his ideas across through elegies to noses, snails, local cheeses, and The Mikado; it was done weekly in the *London News*. Chesterton was a foremost example of Quintillian's *vir bonus docendi peritus:* the good man who speaks from practical knowledge. And he was not content to pass on interesting bits of practical knowledge as isolated things; as surely as the whole Mediterranean washed well within the circumference of Virgil's fine skill and the Brooklyn Bridge spanned the lobes of Roebling's brain, the whole experience of Christian humanism cavorted in the head of Chesterton at his weekly dictation.

The Flight of the Ideologue

Chesterton's burden was the inclusive activity of creation dignified by its Creator, the "ethics of a good, sound, Christian sort, full of punching people's heads and love-making" (November 23, 1907). This was the idea behind the realistic psychology of the essays, the discernment and exposition of phenomenal truth. Secularism gets the world wrong because it commits the unnatural act of measuring nature apart from the immanent scale of God. And in this lies a secret of his towering humility: what he wrote about nature was not his own, but rather his own way of putting it. The "it" was the original shape of reality. It seemed novel only because the people encountering the oldest thing in the world were new. Chesterton plagiarized, but his was an inspired plagiarism which forsakes incidental sources for the Source. Such heavenly theft marks the genius from the hack.

While the excerpts in the following text cover various periods in his social and spiritual formation, the original obedience is constant: his tribute to the authenticity of Testaments Old and New which makes the columns themselves a running testament of the day. The perspective is an unsettling revelation to the media governors of the present age who fancy themselves a sort of shadow government. His insistence is as pertinent as it ever was, and now with wider social importance: when social commentary is not theologically sound, when it is not offered in reference to God who orders lesser predelictions, when it is a detour around the Cross, it turns in on itself and cannibalizes its own claim. Journalists and broadcast commentators who by every survey are overwhelmingly atheistic and libertine, are caught in a web of contradictions each time they volunteer moral judgments or propose moral solutions. They continue to speak of social experiments when experiment is the last thing they want; what they do want is public acquiescence to a private sentimental project of autonomous ethics and gratuitous comfort. It is hard to imagine, for example, tones more censorious than the journalist's as he condemns censorship; nor are there many more overly paid people than the news broadcasters who denounce economic inequities. The whole cranky blather was unknown in the modest parts of Beaconsfield or Fleet Street occupied by Chesterton.

Journalistic humbug is the substance of ideology which tries to function in place of theology, perceiving its end in influence rather than truth. The ideologue imposes a monopoly on mental industry. For all his arrogation of the prophetic mantle, he will not jeopardize his social perquisites for the sake of the social good. A symbolic case, and perhaps not a minor one, is that of the writer who thinks of himself as a bold humanitarian yet who does not dare to criticize the conspicuously malignant effects of rock music because its popularity has enormous financial and political power. With less cause, though with courage, Chesterton said of jazz what anyone with a fully developed brain stem should say of hard rock: that it is the "very reverse of an expression of liberty", for it is "the expression of the pessimistic idea that nature never gets beyond nature", and so "it is the song of the treadmill" (*Avowals and Denials*).

The ideologue's commentary occupies the airwaves and newspapers with a bias he would not permit in anyone else; indeed, the ideologue insists that the most informed and helpful prejudices of the wise are contemptible biases, while his own rampant biases are valiant convictions. The ideologue is incapable of friendly debate; as there is no truth but convenience to him, opposite opinion is nothing other than opposition. In his autobiography, Chesterton already lamented the intellectual friendships of the Victorian Age when "a glow of convivial courtesy covered everything; and the wine of friendship could never moult a feather". A photograph of him at adult play along with Bernard Shaw and H. G. Wells all dressed in cowboy suits is a fading image of that wild amity. It is not so today. He could speak of friends "who never differed except in opinion". He could not speak so freely now. And he would be sadly perplexed to meet the sort of people who no longer engage in debate, who do not volunteer forthright answers to forthright questions, who fall silent when asked their opinion and grumble later among the like-minded. This lack of simple nobility is the most defaming characteristic of false charity, the pretense to honest reserve by which mediocrity conducts itself when it substitutes ambition for ability. Once it was confined to the Trollopian world of careerist clerics and minor politicians; it has become the genre of the age. And when proved wrong by the facts of life and the tide of events, the creature of the age is not deterred; to be wrong is not to the ideologue what it is to the sage. The ideologue takes wrong to mean weak, and if he can place himself in a more advantageous position he will think himself vindicated, though every prophet and commandment points against him. If his argument is false he grabs it more tightly in a suffocating attempt to strengthen it.

As Chesterton's writings are recovered from the attics where ideologues stored him from sight, new ideologues continue to shun him; and when that fails, they patronize his "clever" style and change the subject. "Those who detest the harmless writer of this column are generally reduced (in their final ecstasy of anger) to calling him brilliant; which has long ago in our journalism become a mere expression of contempt" (September 28, 1907). But that can only be done with impunity, for Chesterton is not the subject; the subject is the Changeless, and how we are changed by Him whenever the soul catches a flash of His light. Like children he described (May 5, 1906), Chesterton resembled the Thomist God living "in an almost timeless world". Precisely because of that, his words have the impact of immediacy when nearly every other newspaper column ever written is devoured by anachronisms. It can only be because the first evangelists were journalists, and any great journalist must likewise be evangelistic if he is not to be an ideologue; loving to write, but also knowing the content of the love which impels the writing. And it will be so, not by reporting the great creeds and dogmas of life, for that is not the proper enterprise of the journalist, but by chronicling the daily life lived by peddlers and prime ministers as part of a spherical music, more mysterious than the chants of the great marine creatures and radio waves bounced off a far mercurial planet, the harmony Lorenzo rhymed of in *The Merchant of Venice* "still quiring to the young-eyed cherubins". Chesterton flung out words as lyrics to the universal song, and they remain to be sung even when the world seems close to forgetting the tune. The slapdash columns can seem so byzantine in their complexity to us in "this muddy vesture of decay" that they may best be understood by that most arcane of intelligences, whose laureate he hoped to attain after a lifetime of newspaper deadlines: the rare and dread species of thinker known as the amateur.

George William Rutler

A-B-C

Acts

It has been the boast of religion that all religious acts are irrevocable; the rite of baptism, the vow of celibacy, the vow of marriage. But, indeed, all acts are irrevocable; hence all acts are in their nature more religious than words.

—December 15, 1906

Advertisement

... advertisement in its nature... concerns the names of things and not the things themselves. But what is popularised in this fashion is simply a name, and even the popularity is of a very peculiar and definite kind, and not of a very dignified kind.

—April 15, 1922

Age

... every age is an abyss; every period of the past is an unfathomable infinity of human sensations that we shall never share, human secrets that we shall never know, and, above all, human virtues that we shall never be able properly to praise. None of us is good enough to appreciate the goodness of Mankind.

—August 15, 1925

Agnostic

... the agnostic should know what agnosticism is, as Huxley did; and that he should not be ignorant of the very nature of his own ignorance.

—March 15, 1919

Agnosticism

Mr. Aldous Huxley said that the universe is so queer that it may contain spirits, or almost anything else. That is a piece of sound agnosticism—a rare thing nowadays, and worthy of the name he bears.

—January 12, 1929

Alphabet

An alphabet is a set of symbols, like heraldry.

—November 20, 1915

America

... much that strikes an Englishman in America, like much that strikes him in Ireland, as being mere anarchy is only a different manifestation of mere courage.

—April 14, 1917

Now it is a common charge against the American republic that it is unhistoric and has no past; but the charge is singularly false. It has a past which is not only historic, but heroic. . . . We feel there was a heroic age of the republic; and a legend of its founding, like the legend of Rome. Its founders built on affirmations so wide and (as they themselves truly said) so self-evident that there was something about them beyond place and time. There really is something about the Declaration of Independence that is almost like the stone tables of the Ten Commandments.

—March 23, 1918

The American innovation was that aristocracy must no longer be absolute.

—March 23, 1918

America is alone in having begun her national career with a definite explanation of what she intended to be. And this is an experiment of the highest historical and philosophical interest. It allows of a sort of logical test from which the other nations are free, and may possibly, in some cases, think themselves lucky to be free. Some may judge the American experiments in the light of the American ideal. Others may judge the American ideal in the light of the American experience.

—January 8, 1921

The historic glory of America lies in the fact that it is the one nation that was founded like a church. That is, it was founded on a faith that was not merely summed up after it had existed; it was defined before it existed.

—January 8, 1921

I really did feel as if I were on another planet when I was in the United States.

—February 2, 1924

I pointed out a long time ago in these columns that what was the matter with America and Americans was not that they were bad or good, or wise or foolish, or corrupt or public-spirited, but simply that they were almost incredibly backward and behind the times. I pointed out that this involved virtues as well as vices. It is sometimes just as well to be behind the times, when they are such bad times as modern progress is apparently in for. But, for good or evil, America is a generation behind.

—August 1, 1925

Above all, we are especially taught to hail as the best thing in America what is certainly the worst thing in America. It is the horrible and repulsive thing called optimism.

—November 1, 1930

We are only called upon to admire the Americans for their hustle, their publicity, their commercial amalgamations. Nothing is ever said of the real republican virtues which still survive, in spite of the confused and corrupt politics of the republic.

—November 1, 1930

I believe a vast amount of what is really free and healthy in American life is due simply to the absence of the game laws. There is a space and atmosphere of adventure round boyhood, because there are no enclosures and the whole country-side is still largely treated as something with the promise of a wilderness. The poor as well as the rich have had "sport" with gun and fishing-rod, more freely in the old days than now, but still more freely in America than England.

—November 1, 1930

America may be a country of strange sects, but it is also a country of almost continuous satire on strange sects.

—November 22, 1930

It is when the stranger has absorbed all the strangeness that he begins to understand a goodness that is not a mere imitation of the goodness of Europe or of England; something that an American writer has lately and very truly called "the folks ideal," expressed in an astonishing acceptance of the most incongruous people as "folks," a toleration of human beings in their shirtsleeves, which is infinitely more distant and difficult than any pagan ranting about mere nakedness; an acceptance of humanity in obtuse angles and awkward attitudes, a thing altogether indescribable in English.

—December 6, 1930

Nobody had ever thought what would be the posture, what the pride, what the dignity of an impoverished America. Its citizens have grown so used to excusing themselves as a successful people that they have never learned how to defend themselves as a defeated people.

—December 19, 1931

America (Progressive)

It would commonly be said that America proved its progressive character by the dexterity of its inventions and the rapidity of its communications. But civilisation is to be tested not so much by the dexterity of inventions as by the worth of what is invented. Many of the instruments of torture in the Tower of London display great dexterity of invention. Civilisation is not to be judged by the rapidity of communication, but by the value of what is communicated. I can send to my next-door neighbour the message—"You are an ass." I have not greatly advanced in civilisation merely because I can send the same intelligent message to a man in Australia.

—February 16, 1907

America and Barbarism

... whether barbarism be good or bad, whether barbarism be near or distant, at least it will be admitted that it is the United States of America that are especially and primarily leading us towards this beautiful but doubtful goal. Almost every trait which is specially and solely characteristic of America is a savage trait. America was the last of the great Christian nations to keep slaves. America is almost the only one of the great Christian nations in which one can still find primitive private war, shootings and stabbings not under the rules of military service, and not even under the dignity and etiquette of the duel; mere private killing as it might have been among the cave-men. America is the one place in the modern world which has returned to the hearty old human custom of burning a man alive in public.

—February 16, 1907

American Culture and Smoking

The culture that is concerned here derives indirectly rather from New England than from old America. It really does not seem to understand what is meant by a standard of right and wrong.... The man who is silly enough to say, when offered a cigarette: "I have no vices," may not always deserve the rapier-thrust of the reply given by the Italian cardinal: "It is not a vice, or doubtless you would have it." But at least a cardinal knows it is not a vice; which assists the clarity of his mind. But the lack of clear standards among those who vaguely think of it as a vice may yet be the beginning of much peril and oppression.

—February 5, 1927

American Revolution

The American colonists had caught sight of an ideal which the English rulers did not understand, even as an ideal. It was not something that England would not give, but something that England could not give. It was something that England had not got. It was the idea of equality; that democratic level which some call a dead level. The colonists were not fighting because George III had this and kept it to himself; but because he had never heard of it. The English king had not locked up all the English equality in his cellar; there was no English equality to lock up.

—August 14, 1924

American Short Story

I find men writing as realists, indeed almost writing as reporters, who report (as if it were the most ordinary thing in the world) that a great criminal lawyer is the leader of a disciplined army of criminals, and systematically saves his clients by blackmailing judges and packing juries. The writers talk quite casually about whole cities which some corrupt mayor or chief of police holds in a silence of terror. I do not take it literally; my point is the calm way in which the writers take it. My point is that there seems to be an astonishing evaporation of all that virile idea of public virtue that surrounded the foundations of the republic; and that, if we were to go by these stories, we should say that the old and noble conception of the citizen was dead.

—March 1, 1930

Americana

. . . H. L. Mencken is not content with alluding scornfully to the most widespread customs and conceptions of his countrymen, whenever he happens to come across them. He has the almost malignant industry to collect a huge scrap-book of all the silly things that Americans say and do, and to call it *Americana*. I, for one, have never believed that America was identical with *Americana*.

—April 21, 1928

Americans

There are no men less prone than Americans to a mere materialism; indeed, their fault is quite the other way. In so far as America has really worshipped money, it has not been because money is tangible. Rather it has been because money is intangible; and Americans cultivate it always in its least tangible form—in the form of shares, trusts, promises, implicit understandings, and illegal powers.

—September 17, 1910

Anybody who ever supposed that Americans as such were "too proud to fight," in the ironical sense of being too timid to fight, was a fool whose impudence was simply ignorance, and especially ignorance of history. Within living memory America was full of fighting, in a literal sense even yet unknown to England. . . .

—April 14, 1917

In their own lighter moments, they do seek to imply that Benjamin Franklin must have been as much of a bore and a nuisance as Socrates. But men only deal thus lightly with things that they feel as ancient and fundamental; and there is this feeling about the American fundamentals.

—March 23, 1918

I like the Americans for a great many reasons. I like them because even the modern thing called industrialism has not entirely destroyed in them the very ancient thing called democracy. I like them because they have a respect for work which really curbs the human tendency to snobbishness. I like them because they do not think that stupidity is a superiority in business and practical life; and because they do not think that ideas are always insanities. I like what is rather unphilosophically expressed by saying that they are all optimists; at any rate, very few of them are pessimists. I like them because they are never guilty of the ghastly blasphemy of supposing that there is something fine about being bored, any more than about being blinded or lamed, or paralysed.

—January 21, 1922

... Americans not only like their national ideals expressed, but they like them expressed in that sort of snappy electioneering phrase. They also like every-thing measured in that sort of mathematical fashion. They talk in percentages as they talk in dollars. They talk in figures almost as much as in words.

—November 17, 1923

... Americans are a backward people, with all the very real virtues of a backward people; the patriarchal simplicity and human dignity of a democracy, and a respect for labour uncorrupted by cynicism.

—April 26, 1924

I prefer the American who wrote on a piece of plain paper or parchment with a quill pen, "We hold these truths to be self-evident; that all men were created equal," to the other American who prints simultaneously, in ten thousand syndi-cated Sunday papers, one silly question like: "What do you consider the greatest proof of the progress of the world in recent times?" If I have to choose between these two Americans, I vastly prefer the first American.... He states something fundamental as being to him self-evident; but he does state it and does not merely assume it; and it happens to be something that strikes me as true. The other man assumes that I assume something that I do not think in the least true, and then forgets all about what it is he has himself assumed.

—December 19, 1925

Americans and Prohibition

America has been the playground of every lunatic who wanted to make a legal experiment. Prohibition is only one of a hundred prohibitions. Whole districts are discussing the desirability of regulating love and marriage by force, according to the guesswork of some quack science they call eugenics. Whole sects and societies would treat tobacco not merely as a poison, but as a sort of infernal drug invented by demons. They are prone to this sort of inverted idolatry.

—November 17, 1923

30

Amusement

I must once more express my astonishment that, in an age which will have ten professors of psychology to tea, or strew the world with pamphlets and books about subconsciousness and psycho-analysis, nobody seems to notice the most normal and elementary facts of practical psychology. Otherwise, it would not be left to an irresponsible and ignorant journalist to point out the elementary fact . . . to anyone acquainted with our lighter entertainments . . . amusement can be a narcotic.

—May 3, 1930

Anarchism

The anarchist says that no man should work unless he wishes to. At that rate no healthy man would ever work at all; for I hope every healthy man can think of occupations much more entertaining. The anarchic philosophy fails utterly because it ignores this psychological fact of the initial reluctance to do even desirable things.

—January 8, 1910

Anarchists

One thing I cannot understand about Anarchists is the fact that they are so astonishingly behind the times. They profess to be a new movement, although, of course, no form of philosophic folly is really new. When they write they write nonsense indeed, but generally modern nonsense—full of phrases about Sociology and Capitalism and the means of production. . . . But when they come to murder they step back into the sixteenth century. They become a sort of inverted Royalists. They kill Kings, or try to kill them; they appeal to the sentiment of Divine Right. Dynamiters are, indeed, almost the only people in the modern world who treat Kings with an entire respect: they are the only people who take Monarchy seriously.

—June 23, 1906

Anarchy

Anarchy is defensible as the only atmosphere in which a new Government can be created; but anarchy will be very dreary as the permanent and continuous atmosphere in which an old Government shall live.

—November 21, 1908

Anarchy versus Order

. . . even anarchy on the right side is better than order on the wrong side.

—July 21, 1917

Anger

Human anger is a higher thing than what is called divine discontent. For you must be angry with something; but you can be discontented with everything.

—May 24, 1919

Anglo-Irish Dispute

It was this reality that convinced me a long time ago that the Anglo-Irish quarrel was not an internal but an international quarrel; and for the same reason. The Irish were not asking for equality with the English. They were not asking for something that we could give them and would not; but for something we could not give if we would. It was a state in another style of architecture; a community with a different picture of happiness.

—August 14, 1924

It is often said that the English do not understand the Irish; but that is really only another way of saying that Ireland is a nation. It is unreasonable to expect the ordinary Englishman to know Ireland—or, for that matter, the ordinary Irishman to know England. But there is a sense in which we can ask the ordinary Englishman to know what he is doing to Ireland. And the great trouble with the ordinary Englishman was that he did not know what he was doing.

—August 23, 1924

Anglo-Saxon

We made up a mythological person called the Anglo-Saxon—presumably a hyphenated alien vacillating between England and Saxony. Why, if there was a link between England and Saxony, it should also be the chief link between England and San Francisco, I never could understand.

—January 5, 1918

Anthropologists

If a modern man was buried like a primitive man the centuries would destroy his shirt and leave his shirt-studs. And I suppose that the scientific wiseacres of the future would prove beyond question that the Englishman of the twentieth century wore nothing but a collar-stud.

—November 9, 1907

. . . the bigotry of the missionary has been replaced by the greater bigotry of the man of science. And at least the missionary was right in thinking that, if he was right, anything that contradicted him on that point was wrong. But science is not supposed to be teaching people what to believe, but to be finding out what they do believe. Its disdain is not ennobled by indignation. It is not supported by the sense of bringing a superior faith, but simply by a faith in being superior. The materialistic investigator has really no right to his cold and contemptuous tone towards mythology. In scorning the savages, he is merely scorning the subject.

—January 26, 1926

What the earlier anthropologists did was to create a mythology about mythology.

—August 23, 1930

They invented, not only a mass of theories, but a mass of stories . . . catchwords and figures of speech, all implying that man at his simplest must be a sort of blundering black Sambo, merely chattering like a monkey rather than a child. This image of the anthropoid looks very odd beside some of the actual answers made by "savages" to more serious and sympathetic enquirers. A missionary asked what a Maori meant by saying that everything had a soul. To which the Maori answered, "if anything were not possessed by the shadow of a god, that thing could not have form." There is a good deal for metaphysicians and philosophers, let alone scientists, to think about in that; and it is a good deal more like Plato than Sambo.

—August 23, 1930

Anthropology (Modern)

. . . it is obvious enough that we cannot appeal to anything beyond the actual evidence of the cave. Plato traced his philosophy to shadows in a cave, and it is clear that the caveman has left nothing behind him but these coloured or painted shadows. It is not surprising if the theories dependent on them often seem a little shadowy.

—August 23, 1930

Apathy (Political)

The difference is while it was once the rank and file that cheered with all the partisan passions at their height, to-day it is the party leaders who are cheering themselves; and cheering all by themselves. The mob that is their audience is in one vast universal trance of abstraction; thinking about something else.

—October 24, 1925

Apology

If a man is arrogant when he apologises, what will he be when he demands an apology?

—June 22, 1918

Appeasement

The abhorrence of everything military is as abnormal as militarism. War-weariness is at least as deceptive as war-fever; both are delusions, and distort the reality of things. And that distortion just now is so mortally dangerous to England and Europe that, even in these idle jottings, I cannot refrain from setting it down as a thing as serious as it really is.

—May 6, 1922

Architecture

. . . strangely enough, while this art presents its symbols on a vast scale, and staring at the sun, they remain in many ways more elusive and delicate than a drawing in silver-paint or a light tracery in lace. The hieroglyphs are as huge as Assyrian bulls;

34

but they are not hieroglyphs that everybody can read. Strangely enough, they are not only things that few can read, they are sometimes things that few can see.

—July 19, 1924

Architecture is the alphabet of giants; it is the largest system of symbols ever made to meet the eyes of men. A tower stands up like a sort of simplified statue, of much more than "heroic size".

—July 19, 1924

Architecture is the most solid and striking assertion of man's sublime ambition of finality. . . .

—February 14, 1925

Argument

So long as learned men use their authority, I submit to it with the most exquisite meekness. But when learned men begin to use their reason, then I generally discover that they haven't got any. If a biologist contradicts me, I respectfully submit; he undoubtedly knows more than I do. But if a biologist condescends so far as to argue with me, I generally find that I have the best of the argument.

—October 31, 1908

People do not seem to understand even the first principle of all argument: that people must agree in order to disagree. Still less do their imaginations stretch to anything so remote as the end or object of all argument: that they should disagree in order to agree.

—March 9, 1929

Aristocracy

The old aristocrat, being humble (or vain, for the two things are much the same), asserted aristocracy by means of every human attraction. The new aristocrat, being proud, asserts aristocracy against every human attraction. The old system asked us to respect a nobleman because he was a splendid man. The new system asks us to respect a shabby man because he is a nobleman.

—July 7, 1906

Christianity has permitted aristocracy, but it has never permitted aristocracy to be taken seriously. It is Brahmanism to take aristocracy seriously. And I do feel myself that it is a great merit in the English aristocracy that it cannot possibly be taken seriously.

—November 3, 1906

In England we have an aristocracy instead of a religion: the nobility are to the English poor what the saints and the fairies are to the Irish poor, what the large devil with a black face was to the Scotch poor—the poetry of life.

—November 10, 1906

If the hordes of average human beings work in ugly factories, serve in ugly shops, drive ugly vehicles, or use ugly tools, it is not they that have invented and distributed these ugly things: it is the people who have riches and refinement; it is the very people who have the noble horses and the splendid parks. The grocer's assistant sells ugly tins of gum or jam, or what not; but the man who originally sold them is possibly a lord and almost certainly a landlord. In this sense it is quite true that our mercantile aristocracy has "made our England what she is"—and a very nasty sight it has made of it.

—June 18, 1910

The manners of this top class are extremely frank and cynical, and what the main body of England would call vulgar. Its women are often charming, but are exactly like charming actresses. Its men are blasé and contemptuous about the party politics which they conduct, but they are full of a strange curiosity and mental thirst about everybody's business but their own. . . .

—December 10, 1910

The governing class governed by the perfectly simple principle of keeping all the important things to themselves; and giving the papers and the public unimportant things to discuss. When Earl Balfour (one of the last great survivors of the governing class) said languidly that he never read the newspapers, everybody laughed, as if he had said that he could not read the alphabet. In fact, of course, he never read the newspapers because he had read the state papers. Why should he read all the nonsense that was served out to the public, when he knew all the real secrets which were kept as secrets of state?

—March 15, 1930

I know it was the fashion in the Victorian times to say that England was represented by its great middle class and not by its aristocracy. That was the artfulness of its aristocracy. Never did a governing class govern so completely, by saying it did not govern at all. The middle-class Englishman was always pushed into the foreground; while the rulers remained in the background.

—March 15, 1930

Aristocracy (English)

... the English political aristocracy will probably continue to reign. If they were regarded as a living aristocracy their energy and arrogance might irritate people into unrest or destruction. But as they are presented to us as a dying aristocracy, we do not mind how long they take to die.

—February 9, 1907

Aristocracy versus Democracy

The virtue of a democracy is that it is more impersonal. It is too large to be bribed or intrigued into sympathy with a family or a club. The democrat only hears that the flag or the cause has been insulted by somebody; and passes on that somebody a sentence which is indignant, but none the less impersonal, and even impartial. The aristocrat suffers from knowing that that somebody is really a somebody. He remembers that the man wrote a book, that he was eccentrically educated, and not infrequently that he is his own second cousin.

—June 7, 1919

Aristocracy versus Doctrines

Divine right and democracy are both doctrines; they can be denied, but we know when they are being denied. Aristocracy is an atmosphere; it is sometimes a healthy atmosphere; but it is very hard to say exactly when it becomes an unhealthy atmosphere. You can prove that a man is not the son of a king, or that he is not the delegate of a definite number of people. But you cannot prove that a man is not a gentleman, when he professes to be a gentleman. You can only feel perfectly sure of it.

—January 8, 1921

Aristocrat

The aristocrat is very seldom a man who objects to novelties. The aristocrat is generally a man who longs for novelties, and runs after novelties, and dies of inanition, so to speak, if he cannot get enough novelties. We should not expect to find a cubist picture in a cottage, or some new kind of vorticist dancing on a village green. A novelty is a luxury, and is found with all the other examples of the latest luxuries. Hence a profession of faith in progress is almost universal in plutocracy.

—June 26, 1920

Armchair

Many an armchair have I mellowed in my time; leaning backwards in it until the obstinate back gives way, with a comfortable crash. . . .

—July 9, 1910

Arms

Arms, like every other adventure or art of man, have two sides according as they are invoked for the infliction or the defiance of wrong. They have also an element of real poetry and an element of realistic and therefore repulsive prose. The child's symbolic sword and bow are simply the poetry without the prose; the good without the evil. The toy sword is the abstraction and emanation of the heroic, apart from all its horrible accidents. It is the soul of the sword, that will never be stained with blood.

—January 7, 1922

Arms Race

Now, the average citizen is not an expert either upon lances or battle-ships. He cannot know much about the subject; but he can (I think) know a good deal about the expert. The good citizen possesses a sense of smell, given to him by God, like that of the dog; he has, in a mystical way, a nose for nonsense. And he smells something wrong when people go on talking blindly about bigger and bigger ships, though he may know nothing about naval war; just as he would smell something wrong if people went on talking about longer and longer lances, though he might know nothing about the technique of tilting. Common-sense tells a man that indefinite development in one direction must in practice over-reach itself: that wearing ninety overcoats cannot be the way to cure a cold, that drinking ninety pots of beer is by no means a protection against thirst.

—April 10, 1909

Art

Art is a mirror not because it is the same as the object, but because it is different. A mirror selects as much as art selects; it gives the light of flames, but not their heat; the colour of flowers, but not their fragrance; the faces of women, but not their voices; the proportions of stockbrokers, but not their solidity. A mirror is a vision of things, not a working model of them.

—September 24, 1910

Art is born when the temporary touches the eternal; the shock of beauty is when the irresistible force hits the immovable post.

—July 15, 1922

Arts die of a false emphasis, which is generally the effect of fatigue. The Byzantines hammered away at their hard and orthodox symbols, because they could not be in a mood to believe that men could take a hint. The moderns drag out into lengths and reels of extravagance their new orthodoxy of being unorthodox, because they also cannot give a hint—or take a hint. Yet all perfect and well-poised art is really a hint.

—March 10, 1923

... art is often exaggeration because it is reaction. It may not be in the mood of the mob at the moment; but it is the mood of the artist at the moment. The mood of the artist is sometimes a reaction against the mood of the mob.

—*June 6, 1925*

... the moment of creation is the moment of communication. It is when the work has passed from mind to mind that it becomes a work of art.

—*November 27, 1926*

Art, like morality, consists of drawing the line somewhere.

—*May 5, 1928*

... art, which is the essence of human nature ... is almost the nature of man.

—*January 10, 1931*

... traditional art is the truly creative art ... it is truly more creative than the negative abstractions which tend, of their nature, not merely to anarchy, but to nothingness. And that is why a glimpse of these things encouraged me in my own life-long belief in particularism and the rules and traditions of a people. Where there are traditions there are tests; where there are traditions there are tasks and practical problems; but they are always stimulants to the spirit and cunning and imagination of man.

—*November 7, 1931*

Art Dealer

... this is a wild world, and I think the part inhabited by merchants and dealers is the wildest part of it. Not in the maddest religion that ever raved can there be anything quite so crazy as this business of the sale of pictures. There are two painted canvases, an original and a copy, which are so exquisitely alike that about two men in the world can tell the difference with a microscope; and they are often wrong. And yet stout, bald-headed men with watchchains, who would not like to be called poets, pay the worth of a townful of houses for one of them, and will hardly give a bottle of champagne for the other.

—*June 26, 1909*

Artist

I suppose Gauguin would not approve of his own imitators, for he said, "In art one is a revolutionary or a plagiarist." Remembering the old schools and traditions, we might answer that the great artists have been the plagiarists.

—*January 26, 1924*

That an artist might have more fun if he were lawless is obvious; so might anybody else.

—*October 17, 1925*

... the artist gets a great deal of concentrated pleasure out of all sorts of things that nobody else notices....

—*October 17, 1925*

Artists and Communication

... the artist is a person who communicates something. He may communicate it more or less easily and quickly; he may communicate it to a larger or smaller number of people. But it is a question of communication and not merely of what some people call expression. Or rather, strictly speaking, unless it is communication it is not expression.... The word "expression" implies that something appears as what it really is; and that the thing that is recognised outside is the same that has been realised inside.

—*November 27, 1926*

... there is still a vast amount of talk about the isolated and incommunicable spirit of the man of genius; about how he has in him things too deep for expression and too subtle to be subject to general criticism. I say that that is exactly what is *not* true of the artist. That is exactly what is true of the ordinary man who is not an artist. That is exactly what is true of the man who is called a Philistine. *He* has subtleties in his soul which he cannot describe; *He* has secrets of emotion which he can never show to the public. It is the haberdasher who weeps he knows not why. It is the chartered accountant who dies with all his music in him. But it should obviously be the aim of the musician to die with all his music out of him; even if this ideal state of things can seldom be achieved.

—*November 27, 1926*

41

The expression of a unique point of view, so that somebody else shall share it, is a very difficult and delicate matter. It will probably take the artist some time, and a number of experiments, to make his meaning clear. And it seems to me that the moment when he returns to a more normal style is very often simply the moment when he has managed to make it clear. The time when he is wild and revolutionary and unfathomable and ferociously original is the time when he is trying to do it. The time when he is called ordinary is the time when he has done it.

—*November 27, 1926*

Artists and Style

All we are doing, when we pick our words or try our experiments, is resisting the general trend of all style towards staleness. In other words, all artists are dedicated to an eternal struggle against the downward tendency of their own method and medium. For this reason they must sometimes be fresh; but there is no reason why they should not also be modest. There is nothing to brag about in the mere fact that your only mode of expression is perpetually going to the dogs. The dignity of the artist lies in his duty of keeping awake the sense of wonder in the world.

—*May 21, 1927*

Aryan as Superman

Never once would it flash across the Aryan mind on the heights of Hampstead that all such race theories are rubbish; that political, religious, and commercial groups of men come together because they agree about politics, religion, or commerce; and that there is no group which does not contain, within the range of local possibility, all shapes of skull and all shades of complexion.

—*May 14, 1910*

Aryanism

... a Teuton who cannot see that he is one white man among many, among the white Latins or the white Slavs, is almost literally a man who believes that white is not white. A man who tries to treat the other national types of Christendom as if they were brown or black is in an almost physical sense colour-blind.

—April 7, 1917

Asquith, Herbert Henry

It may be very comfortable to forget all the luminous legal distinction of Asquith, and agree that that statesman never said anything in his life except "Wait and see."

—October 11, 1930

Assassination, Political

I do not in the least approve of or defend political assassination. If I did approve of political assassination, the present state of English politics would offer to me, so to speak, an *embarras de richesses,* calculated to bewilder the most rapid and industrious bravo.

—April 13, 1907

Associations (Voluntary)

Several journalists lately burst out into denunciations of a clergyman because he would not marry an unbaptised person in his church. The journalists were so irrational, and so innocently irrational, that they actually supposed it was the clergyman who was guilty of irrationality. It never seemed to strike them that the man who could not bear to be christened in a church, and could not bear to be married outside a church, was guilty of some irrationality. If it is right to be unbaptised, why is it wrong to be married at a registrar's? Whether the Church of England is Catholic or Protestant, divine or human, dependent or independent, it obviously has the same rights as are possessed by a twopenny club.

—November 21, 1925

Atheism (Forced)

It is not natural to the normal agnostic, it is not natural to the normal pagan, it is not natural to the normal blind and ignorant child of this mysterious world, to jump up suddenly and shout at a child that there is no god. There are a hundred instincts of our own unexplored psychology crying out against it. . . . And the fact that the atheists of Russia have gone beyond the ordinary agnostics of Europe, and shown a black impatience to hammer their negation like a nail into the baby's head, is itself a proof that they are in a strained and unnatural and unhuman condition of mind; that they are in very truth waging a war not only against God, but against human nature.

—February 22, 1930

Atheist (Traditional)

His was a simple faith: that science is always right so long as it confines itself to proving that religion is wrong.

—May 9, 1931

Atmosphere

The truth is, of course, that every man, in dealing with his own affairs and in the enjoyment of his own wits, knows that atmosphere is the most practical thing in the world—perhaps the only practical thing in the world. The difference between heaven and hell is only a difference of atmosphere. Only a moral sense of smell enables one to guess whether young Smith in the Lancers will go with great heroes to glory or go with dog-fanciers to the dogs. Those principles of idealism and moral sensibility which sound so vague and pompous in a public speech or a leading article are, nevertheless, the only principles on which anyone ever chooses a butler, or a boarding house, or a schoolmaster, or a cook, or a clerk, or even a favourite horse.

—October 17, 1908

No art critic, however artistic, has ever succeeded in describing an atmosphere. The only way to approach it is to compare it with another atmosphere.

—December 26, 1931

Atrocities

No man has any notion of the end of which torture and infanticide are but the beginnings.

—June 22, 1918

Attack (Political)

We are familiar to-day with the general principle of decency which limits political attacks, and especially attacks upon leading politicians. That principle is simple enough: it is that a man may say anything whatever against a politician, however wild, so long as it is not true. Truth is regarded as treachery and a foul blow, as outside the ropes, as stabbing in the back or hitting below the belt.

—July 11, 1925

Attire (Modern)

Mediaeval costume and heraldry had been meant as the very manifestation of courage and publicity and a decent pride. . . . A man's dress was that of his family or his trade or his religion; and these are exactly the three things which we now think it bad taste to discuss. Imagine a modern man being dressed in green and orange because he was a Robinson. Or imagine him dressed in blue and gold because he was an auctioneer. Or imagine him dressed in purple and silver because he was an agnostic. He is now dressed only in the ridiculous disguise of a gentleman; which tells one nothing at all, not even whether he is one.

—July 3, 1909

Authority

. . . authority . . . is not a thing to be obeyed when it is strong; but, on the contrary, a thing to be obeyed when it is weak.

—September 18, 1915

I suggest this explanation here in general terms, because several critics have recently started up here and there to taunt me with some notion of theirs that authority is only a form of slavery. As a matter of fact, of course, it is the only alternative to slavery. Authority is the other name of right; and unless there is somewhere a right to call us free, any casual free-thinker may choose to call us slaves. And, as I have pointed out, nearly every casual free-thinker does call us slaves. The process of thinking without any reference to authority has left us without any claim to liberty.

—September 15, 1923

In short, the case for a sort of general guidance from the start is to be found in the fact that the road is beset with traps and temptations to the loss of liberty. There are not only pitfalls, but bottomless pits; there are not only mazes, but mazes without a centre. That is why I, for one, believe in the philosophy of providing a map of the road, with all the blind alleys and broken roads marked on it from the first. But that is not in order that men should not be free to walk the roads, but rather that they should walk the roads on which they will remain free. And until this distinction is understood the modern debate about authority and liberty will not have ended, for it will not even have begun.

—September 15, 1923

Authority (Right)

The other name of Authority is Right. To hit back when you are lawlessly hit is not to add a wrong, but, on the contrary, to add a right to the situation. This abstract claim of rectitude remains the same whether the claim is successful or unsuccessful.

—September 18, 1915

Aviator

We have heard of the boy who runs away to sea, but we have now a new sort of boy, who may be said to run away to sky.

—November 24, 1917

Baptist

The old ceremonial gestures of the human body are necessary to the health of the human soul: the gesture that pledged the guest in the goblet; that strewed the flowers upon the grave; that drew the sword for the salute or set up the candle before the shrine. . . . All religion that is without that gesture, all puritan or purely intellectualist religion that rages at ritual, is raging at human nature. If an ancient

46

pagan came from the city of Plato and the Temple of Pallas, and found himself in a certain type of town of the middle west, I admit that he would probably prefer to be a behaviorist rather than a Baptist.

—July 5, 1930

Barbarian

The barbarian is very little affected by the flag under which he marches to slay and spoil. For practical purposes the barbarian is the man who does not believe in chivalry in war or charity in peace; and, above all, who does not believe in modesty in anything.

—July 31, 1920

Barbarism

Civilisation in the best sense merely means the full authority of the human spirit over all externals. Barbarism means the worship of those externals in their crude and unconquered state. Barbarism means the worship of Nature; and in recent poetry, science, and philosophy there has been too much of the worship of Nature. Whenever men begin to talk much and with great solemnity about the forces outside man, the note of it is barbaric. When men talk much about heredity and environment they are almost barbarians. The modern men of science are many of them almost barbarians.

—August 18, 1906

Beatific Vision

The beatific vision is described by Dante about as well as it could be described by anybody—that is, chiefly by saying that it cannot be described at all.

—March 22, 1930

Beatrice

Beatrice is to be loved because she is beautiful; but she is beautiful because there is behind her a many-sided mystery of beauty, to be seen also in the grass and the sea, and even in the dead gods. There is a promise in and yet beyond all such pictures;

and the poet can see grass or the great sea or the great ship going over it, hearing a sort of whisper: "Thine eyes shall see the king in his beauty."

—March 22, 1930

The Beautiful and the Interesting

The cultivated classes go in for what is beautiful; but the uncultivated for what is interesting. For example, the more refined people concern themselves with literature— that is, with beautiful statements. But simple people concern themselves with scandal—that is, with interesting statements. Interest often exists apart from beauty; and interest is immeasurably better and more important than beauty. I myself know a man who is beautiful and remarkably uninteresting. The distinction is one that affects religion and morals and the practical philosophy of living. Existence often ceases to be beautiful; but if we are men at all it never ceases to be interesting. This divine creation in the midst of which we live does commonly, in the words of the good books, combine amusement with instruction. But dark hours will come when the wisest man can hardly get instruction out of it; but a brave man can always get amusement out of it. When we have given up valuing life for every other reason, we can still value it, like the glass stick, as a curiosity. For the universe is like the glass stick in this, at any rate: it is unique.

—December 16, 1905

Behaviorists

All that the behaviorist does is, in every sense, to dash out the brains of the old materialist. There is no question of his touching the soul, even the soul of an old materialist, for that escapes him as completely as it does every other kind of material analysis, including that of the old materialist himself. What he abolishes is not the soul, but the cells on which his predecessor depended for the denial of the soul.

—July 5, 1930

The Best and the Brightest

You and I, it is to be hoped, do not hold the theory that the highest and most prominent figures in Society are the highest and best specimens of the human race. We are not such desolate pessimists as all that. For certainly if the people who rule

England are the best people in England, England is going to the dogs, or, rather, has already gone there.

—November 16, 1907

Bigot

I have always found it best to understand by the word "bigot" a man who cannot imagine how other men can go wrong, granted that they do go wrong.... The bigot is not the man who thinks his opponent mistaken. The bigot is the man who will *not* think him mistaken.

—March 7, 1925

Bigotry

But the modern world has invented an entirely new kind of bigotry. The old bigot said, "I will argue with you because I know you are wrong; I will even kill you because I know you disagree with me." The new bigot says, "I will not argue with you, because I know you agree with me." The old bigot could not tolerate disbelief. The new bigot cannot even believe in disbelief. The old would extirpate the existence of heretics; the new would deny that existence. He would destroy his enemies before they are born.

—April 28, 1906

If you ask me why ghosts and devils are denied, while bats and shooting stars are reluctantly conceded, I can only answer that it is the not interesting and by no means undignified thing which we have to call Bigotry. Every time I have met a bat (I have never seen one) he has simply flapped me in the face and fled, which, perhaps, is considered humorous in bat circles. It would not be difficult for a sceptic to argue that the flap might have been a leaf blown in my face or a corner of my own cloak flapping, or one of my enormous and luxuriant whiskers fluttering on the midnight breeze. The more brilliant scientists would not stop at that. They would be capable of saying that I had hit myself in the face. They would appeal to the well-known physio-psychic fact that an absent-minded journalist, when walking along a lane at evening, will often (by a nervous trick) hit himself in the left eye with the right foot.

—October 30, 1909

Billboard

... the person who wants the street defaced by an advertisement of the sauce is the person who owns the sauce, or the person who owns most shares in the sauce. The person who owns most shares in the sauce is very probably in the House of Peers. He is, perhaps, voting in that Chamber that the Embankment shall not be defaced by electric-cars (which are often comparatively beautiful) at the very moment when hundreds of his vassals are making half the walls of London hideous with shrieking proclamations of his wares.

—June 18, 1910

Biographers

It never occurs to them that even Napoleon never said he was a god, or professed to be able to behave like a super-man towering over all mankind. For this reason I think the modern fashion of detailed depreciation in biography is generally very questionable, and often quite false. In this I think the legend is far truer than the literature. The legend represents the general impact and impression made by Napoleon on mankind. The literature of the hypercritical sort often consists of little notes made by one man from a motive of malice covered by a mask of impartiality.

—July 25, 1925

Birthday

A birthday does not come merely to remind a man that he has been born. It comes that he may be born again.

—November 28, 1908

Birth Control

The name of birth-control, for instance, is sheer nonsense. Everybody has always exercised birth-control, even when they were so paradoxical as to permit the process to end in a birth. Everybody has always known about birth-control, even if it took the wild and unthinkable form of self-control.

—June 30, 1928

I might inform those humanitarians who have a nightmare of new and needless babies (for some humanitarians have that sort of horror of humanity) that if the recent decline in the birth-rate were continued for a certain time, it might end in there being no babies at all; which would console them very much.

—May 24, 1930

Blatchford, Robert

Mr. Blatchford and I are both, I should imagine, merely random readers; but I suspect that his random reading is rather wider than mine. His view is not that of an uneducated man, but of most educated men; and that is just the trouble.

—March 22, 1919

Blue Laws

Prohibition is only one of a whole crop of crazy experiments which American rulers have enforced in various places and in various degrees. There are states in the union where it is a crime to smoke a cigarette in public. It is absurd to say of such societies that they are particularly careful of the legal liberties of the individual.

—November 17, 1923

All the American virtues and vices mingle in this national instinct for persecution. It has the democratic spirit, in the spontaneous movement of the masses. It has the optimistic spirit, in the facile faith in the result of a new law or regulation. It has the savage spirit, in the ease with which it can call up hatred and a horror of harmless things. But to say that it has the spirit of individual liberty is rank cant and claptrap. Men in Connecticut were talking lately of reviving the blue laws, which might more properly be called the blue devils. Americans scarcely think of liberty when they are making such laws. They have a considerable taste in lawlessness *after* they have made the laws.

—November 17, 1923

Boast

. . . the new fashion [is] to boast of boasting.

—June 21, 1930

Body and Soul

A reasonable man will begin by asking himself what is the right theory of the body and the soul. And if he is sensible as well as reasonable, he will soon see that the soul can best keep its right superiority to the body by not being bothered perpetually by debate about bodily conventions.

—June 21, 1930

Bolivar, Simon

Most Englishmen, as I say, know little of Bolivar; except those who know that he is a cigar.

—March 28, 1931

Bolshevism

Bolshevism may be made to mean a great many things, including an honest human hatred of the poor more remote from Berlin than from Babylon.

—December 21, 1918

. . . [it] ought not to be called Bolshevism, but crime.

—January 25, 1919

. . . we find that the word Bolshevism really covers three distinct and contrary things—in the country a quite human hunger for land; in the towns a rather inhuman theory of collectivism, and a still more inhuman practice of crime.

—January 25, 1919

It is not easy to discover what part, if any, was played by the old nihilistic notions of Bakunin in the movement that led to Lenin; or whether men thought they were leading Russia to nihilism when they were certainly reducing Russia to nothing.

—January 25, 1919

... which should be abbreviated into the equally mystical word bosh.

—March 8, 1919

... it puts the worst government at the top and the best government at the bottom. The small local soviet seems to be ... something like a small guild government ... But, though it would seem to be in theory the best thing in the world, it also seems to be in practice the weakest thing in the system. For the higher we rise in the hierarchy to the dominant powers in the constitution, the more we find it loaded with a type of oligarchic oppression which is actually the flat contrary of democracy. The Bolshevists ... have had all the higher councils elected by the lower ones, making a sort of ladder—the sort of ladder it must certainly be unlucky to walk under. In other words, the lesser parliaments elect the higher parliaments, up to the highest power in the state—which is thus representative at about ten removes. If this is really true, it is not surprising if the highest power in the state is an appalling tyranny. When we consider how hard it is to get any representatives to represent, we can imagine how much control there can be over the representative of a representative of a representative.

—October II, 1919

Bolshevism, I suppose in the sense of the action of the red guards, might truly be described as painting the town red. ... In other words, it is possible for revolution to paint the town red, as it has already been possible for smoke and soot to paint it black. But it is only possible because the process is not really a revolution, or even an anarchy, but rather an ugly uniformity. It is only possible because a society is ruled by only one group possessed of only one idea. A free people would prefer to paint their town all the colours of the rainbow.

—October 30, 1920

Everything that the very worst capitalists are accused of trying to do the Bolshevists are now avowedly doing. The more vulgar sort of plutocrat can be heard spluttering in a smoking-room, "Make the brutes work"; but the ... socialist does make the

53

brutes work. The more mentally deficient type of employer may be heard snorting at his dinner table, "Shoot 'em down, sir"; but the . . . socialist does shoot 'em down, sir. Many capitalists have tried to impose compulsory arbitration; and many [English] socialists have retorted, very rightly as I think, that compulsory arbitration would be slavery. But the . . . socialists do not even impose the compulsory arbitration; they simply impose the compulsory labour.

—November 12, 1921

The truth is that so long as Bolshevism looked like anarchy it was possible to mistake it for liberty. As soon as it became something like order it became certainly and obviously slavery. It was exactly when the Soviet system ceased to deserve the superficial slanging of the newspapers that it began to deserve the serious loathing and detestation of the free citizen.

—November 12, 1921

The Bolshevist formula is an amazing example of the power of words. But it is not, as some say, the power of words to incite and madden the mind. It is rather their terrible power to satisfy it, and send it to sleep.

—November 19, 1921

What is the matter with Bolshevism is that it swamps all such ideas of individual justice in a sea of impersonal materialism and fatalism. In other words, what is the matter with Bolshevism is that it is slavery. The soul of slavery consists in the fact that it will not treat a man as a moral end in himself, a soul intended to be happy and to glorify God; but will only treat him as a means to an end, whether to serve a machine or support a system or fulfil a "natural law."

—February 24, 1923

I think there is far *less* chance of Europe becoming socialist since Russia became socialist. There was much more socialism in the air when it was only in the air. Bolshevism has lost Europe because it has captured Moscow.

—September 27, 1924

The whole objection to socialism is in two words of the Roman poet: *"instans tyrannus."* For the workman those almost untranslatable words must be translated, perhaps roughly, thus: "Bolshevism is worse even than the present condition, because at present it is still possible that, if one man hates me and will not sell me bricks, another will; or somebody else may sell me timber and I will make a hut or a caravan. But if I have offended the officials, and they own all the bricks, all the timber, all the very ground, there is no liberty left but death."

—*October* 10, 1925

In all states there is some organisation, and in Bolshevist states there is rather too much organisation. And anybody who believes that the mere periodical collecting and counting of votes (to say nothing of the very undemocratic system of voting that Bolshevist states seem to favour) will of itself prevent a jack-in-office being a nuisance, while he is in office, must have an innocence about human nature almost superhuman.

—*October* 10, 1925

The precise peculiarity of this current argument against Bolshevism is that, whatever else it is, it is not an argument against Bolshevism. It ignores the Bolshevist's assumption, which is a wildly false assumption, but which must be faced by anybody who is arguing with him. That assumption is that there is nothing normal or necessary about property being in private hands at all.

—*October* 10, 1925

I have often expressed the wish that the papers would attack Bolshevism and not only Bolshevists. What we want is argument against the thing itself, not abuse of the people who may or may not be drifting towards it.

—*October* 10, 1925

The truth is that the Bolshevist movement has been an orgy of hero-worship. Lenin has been turned into a god. Karl Marx has been turned, if possible, into something greater than a god.

—*February* 12, 1927

. . . the doctrine of Bolshevism taught that it is really wicked to own an umbrella or still more wicked to wield a spear. . . . [One] might find, for almost the first time in human history, a people being systematically instructed in the theory that there is neither God nor gods.

—*April* 25, 1931

Bolshevism and Capitalism

. . . in the face of the resistance of the individual peasant, Bolshevism and big business are on the same side.

—*January* 17, 1925

Capitalism and communism are really not opposites at all. Capitalism and communism are very much alike. . . . They are alike, because they both imply an impersonal centralisation and the wielding of wealth in great masses and over large and vague areas. The thing that really contradicts communism is not capitalism, but small property as it exists for a small farmer or a small shop-keeper. It does not take very much to change a large store into a state department; it is almost a matter of official forms. It may take a civil war to change a small farm into a state farm: for that is to stamp out the independence and individualism of a peasantry.

—*January* 17, 1928

Bolshevists

It is tragic and comic to think what would have happened if the world had taken the Bolsheviks at their word, as many people wished it to do.

—*March* 2, 1918

. . . if they do use the senseless expression "Dictatorship of the Proletariat", I am sure it is chiefly for the pleasure of two long words.

—*July* 12, 1919

The most interesting thing about the Bolshevists is the way in which they have abandoned Bolshevism.

—December 20, 1919

Bolshevists and the Family

Now these dehumanised intellectuals do really want to do without the fire; in the practical sense of the fireside. They do want to amputate the arms of the woman; the arms that through all ages have held up the child. In other words, these moderns have some muddled idea that they can altogether get rid of the minimum of labour and responsibility required in daily life, and especially in family life. They talk perpetually about freeing woman entirely from the duties of the home; as Lenin did only the other day, with some qualifications about the painful difficulty of convincing the democracy of his doctrine. . . . The woman will cease to be a woman in her own house, in order to be a charwoman in somebody else's house. The issue is not that we shall all be equal citizens, but that we shall all be each other's servants.

—October 4, 1919

Bonaparte, Napoleon

For certainly if Napoleon, or some revolutionary soldier nearly as competent as Napoleon (there may have been one or two others who could have proved competent), had not appeared to save the French Revolution from the invading forces of the aristocracies and autocracies, reaction would have shut down on the first republican hope like a trap of iron, and all the democratic dreams that have since filled the intellect and imagination would have been utterly and perhaps finally destroyed. All that we call the modern world, with all its good and evil, was made by Napoleon; at any rate, was made possible by Napoleon.

—February 7, 1931

Book (Abridged)

It seems to me a very dangerous precedent in the reprinting of famous books, that the publisher should cut out what he chooses and never tell us that he has cut out anything. It seems intolerable that the reader should not only remain in ignorance of what he is losing, but remain in ignorance of having lost anything at all. There are people who read old books, and people who refuse to read old books. There are also people who have not read old books but say they have. But it will be worse if we add another class; of people who have not read old books but think they have.

—December 12, 1928

Book (Condensed)

People who want a sensational novel compressed into a novelette are perilously near the condition of wanting a Christmas pudding compressed into a tabloid.

—December 12, 1925

Book (Travel)

The most valuable book we can read, about countries we have visited, is that which recalls to us something that we did notice, but did not notice that we noticed.

—February 2, 1924

Book Cult

... but there is another very important characteristic about the cult of a book. It has marked the cult of very much better books, such as the Bible and the Roman law. Taken by itself, it always tends to inequality, even if its ideal was equality. It tends to inequality because the very act of reading may be more or less rare as a faculty, to say nothing of a taste. Since some read books more than others, some will read that book more than others. The book being the test, those who have read the book will always bully those who have not. And the book-readers, being bourgeois, will always refuse to read the things that are not to be read in books, the things that are to be read in birds and beasts, and crops and weather, and the very face of the world. The book-reader or bourgeois will always despise the peasant; but the bourgeois will never be so arrogant as when he calls himself the proletarian. Then he will be prouder than ever; for it is an even longer word.

—July 24, 1920

Book of Job

"The Book of Job" is better worth hearing than any modern philosophical conversation in the whole modern philosophical world. It is more philosophical. It is much more witty and humorous. It is, as that word is really meant, much more modern. From it the modern Agnostic may for the first time learn Agnosticism: a sane and a sacred and manly ignorance. From it the modern Christian may with astonishment learn Christianity; learn, that is, that mystery of suffering may be a strange honour and not a vulgar punishment: that the King may be conferring a decoration when he pins the man on the cross as much as when he pins the cross on the man.

—February 24, 1906

Bore

If there is one thing more dwarfish and pitiful than irreverence for the past, it is irreverence for the present, for the passionate and many-coloured procession of life.

—July 30, 1910

Bourgeois

His artistic dress seems so disreputable in the country that the finches might drop dead off the hedgerows and the cattle in the fields go mad at the sight of it. But while his appearance is thus disreputable, his soul is secretly respectable. He is all the more a Puritan for being an aesthete. He would never utter an impropriety, or even a cynicism; he takes himself with entire seriousness; his conscience never has a holiday; his eccentricities are not outbreaks of his temperament, but deductions from his principles; he is never so dull as when he is mad.

—July 23, 1910

He does not even see the whole of his own life. He does not know where the lines of his own life go to, or whence they come. Hence he has not half so much chance of being a philosopher as if he were a ploughman. His philosophy of life cannot be a philosophy of experience, but only of the reports of experience. He tends to depend more and more upon those printed reports—that is, to depend more and more upon being able to read. He cannot afford to be as illiterate as Homer or as indifferent to books as St. Francis. He has to depend on newspapers. . . .

—July 26, 1924

Bourgeois versus Peasant

... one great difference between the peasant and the bourgeois is this: that the peasant is proud of property, and the bourgeois is often half-ashamed of it. The business man is too prone to mutter, in mere cynicism, that after all business is business. But cynicism itself is only a rather restless kind of shame. A peasant's morality may be rude or narrow or superstitious, but it is always morality; he thinks he is right, and therefore he is not a cynic. What the conscience and common sense of a peasant, or any other simple person, tells him is that there is a fallacy in communism, considered merely as idealism. The fallacy consists in assuming that it is always unselfish to share, and always selfish to own.

—December 20, 1919

British

I am not fond of the word British, as applied to the sort of goods that are really good. For instance, there is such a thing as Scotch ale, and there is such a thing as English ale; and they are both very good. But there is no such thing as British ale. I am so painfully sensitive that I can hardly hear a man claiming boisterously to be British without expecting that he will next declare himself to be a Britisher and prove himself to be an American.

—November 7, 1931

Broadminded

For that is what is meant to-day by being broadminded: living on prejudices and never looking at them.

—May 5, 1928

Browning, Robert

He did believe in God; and, curiously enough, he is not entirely alone in that, and in some quarters the curious superstition is even spreading anew. But he did not believe that all was right with the world, in the sense that there is no wickedness, madness, or misery in it; and his works possibly contain a larger and more varied assortment of blackguards, miscreants, maniacs, and miserably deluded people than those of any writer of his time.

—November 22, 1930

Bryan, William Jennings

... the curious religious persecution now being conducted by Mr. Bryan and his fundamentalists ... seems to have the purpose of weeding out the unfortunate Darwinians—a very ironical form of natural selection and the elimination of the unfit.

—April 26, 1924

Brutality

Being brutal is quite a different thing from admiring brutality. The former may sometimes appear at the beginning of simple societies. The latter never appears until the end and final collapse of complex and over-civilised ones.

—March 20, 1926

Buddhism and Christianity

... when Buddha said, "I can only teach you two things: sorrow and the end of sorrow", he was not saying something trivial and personal, but something tremendous and profound. ... What he meant was that desire is one with despair, and the only way to be free from despair is to be free from desire. Over against this stands the great Christian conception; that the Creator will indeed give to the creature his heart's desire, since it is desire for the right thing; but that the creature is free to desire the wrong thing, though it be to desire despair.

—August 9, 1930

Buffoon

... I regret the new and solitary pre-eminence of the buffoon. ... I regret the fact [that] he must not receive from the state a serious tribute for revealing a serious truth. When, for the moment, the most intelligent art is the most flippant art, it will mean a certain abdication of the old claims of the artist. But it may mean much worse things than that. When people begin to ignore human dignity, it will not be long before they begin to ignore human rights. The pagan state, in which the artist is only a buffoon, will soon resemble the ancient pagan state in which he was only a slave.

—May 10, 1930

Businessman

He has never been taught to think, but only to count. He lives in a cold temple of abstract calculation, of which the pillars are columns of figures. But he has no basic sense of comparative religion (in the true sense of that tiresome phrase), by which he may discover whether he is in the right temple, or distinguish one temple from another.

—March 29, 1930

Businessmen and Ideas

. . . the man with only one hole in his head for one bullet of thought to penetrate his brain. He is often a very rich and successful and solidly important person, and I do not care a curse what happens to him. I do not mind the millionaire going down before the first stray shot or the first wandering germ. I do not mind the petrol king joining the Jehovist jumpers because he has never heard of anybody having a religion before. . . . I cannot help the man who is not used to ideas being bowled over by the first and silliest idea that comes his way.

—September 9, 1933

Byron, Lord

Byron himself, with all his parade of pessimism, had a sort of glamour of life about him that he could not get rid of, and a gusto that never left his language, even when he used it to deny its existence in his life.

—May 3, 1930

Byron, I think, divided men into the bore and the bored, presumably priding himself on being among the latter, and through that very pride occasionally figuring among the former.

—July 19, 1930

Caddishness

But for about fifty or sixty years nearly all our culture and controversial trend has been conducted on the assumption that, as long as we could get used to any sort of caddishness, we could be perfectly contented in being cads. I do not say that all the results of the process have been wrong. But I do say that the test of the process has been wrong from first to last; for it is not a case against the citizen that a man can grow *accustomed* to being either a savage or a slave.

—December 16, 1933

Calling One's Bluff

I can remember that in my ardent youth I carried about in my pocket a large but harmless revolver, and whenever anyone said, "Life is not worth living," I produced it, and always with the most satisfactory results.

—March 17, 1906

Calvinism

By the old Calvinism, a babe was predestined to perdition: by the new and more calamitous creed, a babe is predestined to be a Unionist or a Radical.

—December 17, 1910

Canada

Mr. Rudyard Kipling wrote a poem in praise of Canada, which very much annoyed the Canadians. Many of them stated with great sternness that, if he praised them any more, they would give him a good hard knock. The ground of the offence was that he had referred to the Dominion of Canada as "Our Lady of the Snows"; which was held to imply that Canada has no local industry except snow-balling; that her principal exports are icebergs; and that the typical Canadian culture is a sort of furry and inarticulate Eskimo. One Canadian poet haughtily replied that Canada contained glowing maple woods in which England might be lost.

—November 8, 1930

Cant

The cant of candour can be far more nauseous than the cant of concealment; for it is the former that really pretends to innocence and ignores evil.

—June 24, 1922

Capital Punishment

Personally, I am against hanging, though I admit that it would be enormously improved if it were public hanging. But none of the arguments on either side of that question ever give the main fact as it appears to the great masses of the people. The defenders of capital punishment talk as if every execution were an awful and separate act of justice. The opponents of capital punishment talk as if every execution were a special and fiendish violation of mercy. Both assume that the spirit of the thing will at least be dreadful and exact. . . . The poor, very rightly, regard hanging as the sort of thing that might happen to anybody—provided he is poor. . . . And the real case against Capital Punishment in our time is simply that—that the mass of men do not feel it as a law, but as an accident. I am sure we must be hanging on the wrong principle, at any rate, for mankind can discover no principle when we hang.

—July 10, 1909

I am never comfortable about capital punishment; but in any case I think it should be the punishment of certain kinds of treason and tyranny, rather than of all kinds of killing. But while I do not think homicide necessarily the worst of our crimes, neither do I think capital punishment the worst of abuses. And I wish to inform the newspapers that I, for one, am not so much troubled about whether a murderer ate a hearty breakfast, as I am about some thousands of other people who have had no breakfast, and yet have committed no murders.

—January 20, 1923

Capitalism

Anyhow, when I talk about capitalism I mean a perfectly distinct and definable thing; and I think most rational students of the problem now mean the same thing. I do not mean private property, or even private property in the means of production. I mean the condition in which there is such extreme inequality in private property, especially in the means of production, that great masses of people have practically no property at all. I call it capitalism when property is so unequal that the small man cannot live on his own property, but must hire himself out as a servant to work another man's property.

—March 31, 1923

Capitalism (Monopolistic)

Some think that there will now be a return to party politics, in the very old, and familiar form of a fight between free trade and protection—or rather (I hasten to add) a fight between free trade and empire free trade.

—June 7, 1930

Capitalism and Socialism

Modern capitalism is a curse—not because some men have capital, but because some men have not. A modern city can be a nightmare—not because its houses belong to those who own them, but because they do not belong to those who live in them. This is the real case against modern capitalism; and it is also the case against modern collectivism, or socialism, which is its child.

—March 1, 1919

Capitalist

So many a capitalist will now confess that he is at heart a communist. But he is also an idealist, patient, hopeful, and resigned; he will condescend to be a millionaire until the revolution comes; after which he hopes to be a commissar, though he is rather more likely to be a corpse.

—January 28, 1933

Carthage

Carthage was a complex and wealthy civilisation which happened to be founded on devil-worship. It was the culture of cruelty; the diabolist development of art for art's sake. This is not vengeance; it is nothing so good or Christian as vengeance. This is not even hatred, for it has nothing to hate. Hatred is human; to hate a general who has wasted your country is human; even to hate a general who has defeated your armies is human. But Carthage was inhuman; and inhumanity is something far beyond savagery, and even beyond cruelty.

—December 29, 1923

Casuistry

What impresses us is not a man's actions, but his avowed reasons for his actions. Words are sometimes more important than deeds. If a man in a crowd says to us, with polite expressions "Let me pass," we do not mind his passing. If he says, "Let me pass, because I am a fine handsome fellow of manifest high breeding, while you are clearly from your appearance a somewhat distasteful cad," then the practical action, which was in the first case harmless, becomes in the second case insupportable. The first request is one to be granted at the first flash; the second is one to be resisted to the last drop of the blood. Yet in both cases the ultimate external action is the same.

—February 2, 1907

Catch-Word

. . . inordinate love of long and lumbering words is alone enough to prove that a thing has not really a popular origin. . . . And I am quite sure that only a minority among the multitudes of poor men I have known and respected would bother their heads about anybody who could only talk in words of six syllables like proletarianism. So far as they go, these catch-words carry with them the evidence of belonging to minorities. They are not, and never could be, the cries of a revolution; they are rather the pass-words of a conspiracy.

—August 16, 1919

A Cause

A cause is one of the normal needs of a man, and a man feels not only much happier, but much more benevolent and universal when he has got one. The really bitter people are the people who have surrendered to compromise and who cannot henceforward believe in anything, even in their own courage.

—July 28, 1906

Causes (Great)

This tradition of great causes remained in art and letters, as well as in politics, in my own generation. . . . When Mr. H. G. Wells and Mr. Hilaire Belloc did have a controversy, everybody knew it was not only a controversy between two persons or even two philosophers, but also between two philosophies. But when there is a quarrel between two of the younger writers to-day, we feel that it is a quarrel of individuals, merely because everybody has become so intensely individualised. . . . It might even be maintained that big quarrels are better than little quarrels; and, anyhow, a million simultaneous private duels are a bad substitute for universal disarmament.

—September 26, 1931

Censorship

The Pope might object to an irreverent joke about him, but he would never dream of saying that all jokes about him must be irreverent. I must say that I regard with a very rigid dislike this new proposal of intellectual persecution; that we should not be repressed for certain statements, but restrained altogether from certain subjects. It is not enough that we may not call a millionaire a donkey. We must not even mention donkeys, for fear they should remind us of millionaires. It is not merely that the law will forbid us to say that the Cretans are liars; the law will forbid us to mention the island of Crete. We are not merely forbidden to say that the Scotch cannot understand a joke. We are forbidden even to make any joke for the Scotch to understand.

—March 20, 1909

The moral principle in such things, like most obvious moral principles nowadays, is one that nobody troubles himself to state clearly. But there is obviously a fundamental difference between the sort of secret that is really an open secret, but is covered or uncovered for fun, and the sort of secret that ought to be really a secret; some unrepresentative and repulsive accident, which should be entirely private because it is entirely peculiar.

—March 31, 1928

Central Heating

It is very like the journalism of the West; for it is hot air.

—January 9, 1926

Central heating is a form of pantheism. It is not so good a form as some that the philosophy of pantheism has taken in times of simpler and less scientific enthusiasm. ...It is part of the pagan worship of the unknown god, in a world where cosmology is more and more filled with unknown gods, as politics and economics are populated with unknown kings. For in modern bureaucracy and big business, our rulers are more and more masked or veiled, and we know not even the name of the ultimate bureaucrat or the invisible financier who is the real ruler of the affairs of men, just as we know not the source of this paralysing domestic climate.

—January 9, 1926

Ceremony and Symbols

All ceremony depends on symbol; and all symbols have been vulgarised and made stale by the commercial conditions of our time. This has been especially true since we have felt the commercial infection of America, and progress has turned London, not into a superior London, but into a very inferior New York.

—December 24, 1927

Cervantes, Miguel de

There is no more fantastic paradox in all history than the life and work of Cervantes. He is generally recognised as having written a book to show that romantic adventures are all rubbish and do not really happen in this world. As a matter of fact, the one man in this world to whom romantic adventures were incessantly happening was the author of "Don Quixote." As men go, he was really a pretty perfect pattern of the knight of chivalry; eventually he escaped and returned home to write a book showing that chivalry was impossible.

—October 18, 1924

Charlatan

The truth is there are two kinds of charlatan: the man who is called a charlatan, and the man who really is one. The first is the quack who cures you; the second is the highly qualified person who doesn't.

—February 15, 1908

Surely the humbug is not the noisy fellow who forces his wares upon you, but the decorous, dignified, really respectable gentleman who takes the money for them and decamps.

—February 15, 1908

Charles II

It has been the curse of our waxwork history that to each historical figure was attached some more or less legendary saying like a label, and even when the saying was partly true it always missed the point of the truth.... The label, or literary allusion, officially attached to Charles II is almost always that epigram by one of his intimates to the effect that he "never said a foolish thing and never did a wise one." But indeed it was the epigrammatist who said the foolish thing. It was, in reality, nearly the reverse of the truth.... Moreover, a man who must have made love to about forty women, must surely have gone to his grave having said a very large number of foolish things.

—November 21, 1931

Chair

The chair I sit on is really romantic—nay, it is heroic, for it is eternally in danger.

—July 31, 1909

Character

If we want character, in the old unique sense of being "a character," we are much more likely to find it in Christians who accepted the imitation of Christ than in all these millions of materialists who are taught to imitate each other.

—February 25, 1928

Chaucer, Geoffrey

... once or twice there appears in history the artist who is the extreme antithesis of the aesthete. An artist of this kind was Geoffrey Chaucer. He was a man who always made himself useful, and not only ornamental. People trusted him, not only in the moral, but in the more purely practical sense.... He performed job after job, of the most quaintly different kinds, to the increasing satisfaction of his employers. He was emphatically, as the vulgar phrase goes, a man of the world.

—December 26, 1931

Chaucerian Mood

... there was truly a special thing that may be called the Chaucerian mood, and it was essentially merry. There are any number of passages of pathos, and one or two passages of tragedy, but they never make us feel that the mood has really altered, and it seems as if the man speaking is always smiling as he speaks. In other words, the thing which is supremely Chaucerian is the Chaucerian atmosphere, an atmosphere which penetrates through all particular persons and problems; a sort of diffused light which lies on everything, whether tragic or comic, and prevents the tragedy from being hopeless or the comedy from being cruel.

—December 26, 1931

Chesterton, G. K.

I ... happen to have no ear for music, and if ever, by accident or compulsion, I find myself at an opera, I have the wholesome experience of feeling half-witted; it is disgraceful that all that deafening glory should break about my wooden head.

—January 16, 1909

It happens that most of my literary admirers live in asylums.

—November 27, 1909

We most of us suffer much from having learnt all our lessons in history from those little abridged history-books in use in most public and private schools. These lessons are insufficient—especially when you don't learn them. The latter was indeed my own case; and the little history I know I have picked up since by rambling about in authentic books and countrysides.

—*October* 8, 1910

My prejudices are of older date, and may possibly be of longer duration.

—*January* 26, 1918

. . . I am not a novelist, but a journalist.

—*February* 16, 1918

I am the reincarnation of the poet Virgil; but I don't make a fuss about it.

—*March* 29, 1919

Mr. Lynd expresses a scientific wish to cut me in two; a sentiment familiar to many of my fellow-citizens in tubes and trams. One half of him I should like to challenge to mortal combat as an enemy of the human race. . . . The other half of me will be only too delighted to remain in some remote tavern, writing unconvincing romances and nursery rhymes. . . .

—*July* 26, 1919

It might be expressed by saying that I may be a reactionary, but I am sure I am not a conservative. I am a reactionary, in the true sense that I would react against a great many things in the past as well as the present. I would test them not by a calendar which records whether they have happened, but by a creed which decides whether they ought to happen. Some of the things I desire have already happened, and I would therefore preserve them; others have not yet happened, and I would therefore join in any revolution to obtain them.

—*October* 30, 1920

I am a radical nationalist anti-imperialist anti-collectivist distributivist Christian social democrat. I am all that; and there are about three more of me. But my party, though of a wisdom and virtue vastly superior to all others, has not reached the stage which distracts it with the temptations of power and patronage. And my

71

revolutionary movement has at present no axe to grind, not even the axe of the guillotine.

—*July 16, 1921*

I am what most Bolshevists would call a jingo in foreign policy. I am what most jingoes would call a Bolshevist in domestic policy. I have never believed in internationalism or cosmopolitan pacificism, as do so many with whom I agree in supporting strong trades unions. I have never agreed with imperialism or capitalism, as do so many with whom I agree in supporting strong naval defences for England. I am sure that unless the country has sufficient ships we shall perish; and that unless the working class has sufficient wages we shall perish. I am by accident at the very angle of opinion from which to see these points simultaneously.

—*November 26, 1921*

I suppose that I am a spiritualist; if it means not having the necessary credulity to be a materialist.

—*February 7, 1925*

The other day I had to open a discussion about what will happen next. As a matter of fact, I never have the wildest notion of what will happen next; least of all when I am speaking in public. My prophetic powers over the future go no further than a desperate guess about the nature of the next sentence.

—*February 21, 1925*

I am myself so exceedingly Nordic, so far as physical constitution is concerned, that I can enjoy almost any weather except what is called glorious weather. At the end of a few days of that, I am left wondering how the men of the Mediterranean ever managed to do almost all the most active and astonishing things that have been done.

—*June 20, 1925*

Most of those who know me have been able to distinguish me at a glance from a haggard and emaciated genius, starving in a garret and spitting out curses against the critics and the human race.

—*October 31, 1925*

In short, the limitation of my literary experience is altogether on the side of the modern serious novel; especially that very serious novel which is all about the psychology of flirting and jilting and going to jazz dances. I have read hundreds of books bearing titles like, "Socialism: the Way Out"; or "Society: the Way In"; . . . or "Cannibalism: the Clue to Catholicism" . . . or "Must We Drink?"; or "Should We Eat?"; or "Do We Breathe?"; and all those grave and baffling questions.

—March 8, 1930

Looking back on a wild and wasted life, I realise that I have especially sinned in neglecting to read novels. I mean the really novel novels; for such old lumber as Dickens and Jane Austen I know fairly well. If instead of trifling away my time over pamphlets about collectivism or cooperation, plunging for mere pleasure into the unhealthy excitement of theological debates with dons . . . I had quietly sat at home doing my duty and reading every novel as it comes out, I might be a more serious and earnest man than I am to-day.

—March 8, 1930

Chesterton's "The Everlasting Man"

My thesis was roughly summed up in the statement: "The more we look at a man as an animal the less he will look like one." But it also suggested that when we look at him for the very first time, in the full and frank use of our common-sense before it is complicated with sophistry, we never *do* look at him as an animal. It is proved by the very fact that we say "animals" when we mean the other animals.

—October 31, 1925

The Child

There was recently reported in the papers the meeting of certain eminent ladies, of a political and philanthropic sort, who discussed the great modern problem of what is to be done with the child. I need not say that the child is always discussed as if he were a monster, of immense size, vast complexity, and strange and startling novelty. Nor need I remind the reader that the child is not a child; any child we comfortable people have ever seen. The child is not Jack or Joan or Peter; he is not cousin Ethel's child or one of Uncle William's children. He is a creature entirely solitary and *sui generis;* and he lives in the slums.

—March 5, 1932

Child Psychologist

I disagree with them when they treat the infantile imagination as a sort of dream; whereas I remember it rather as a man dreaming might remember the world where he was awake. And second, I deny that children have suffered under a tyranny of moral tales. For I remember the time when it would have seemed the most hideous tyranny to take my moral tales away from me.

—February 8, 1930

Children

The child does not fall into pessimism; he falls into the pond.

—May 30, 1908

Children have more life than we have; the only thing they lack is law. Children feel the whiteness of the lily with a graphic and passionate clearness which we cannot give them at all. The only thing we can give them is information—the information that if you break the lily in two it won't grow again. We need not teach them the good of admiring the lily; the only thing we can teach them is the evil of uprooting it.

—May 30, 1908

Children and Political Indoctrination

The attempts in the little school-histories to introduce older and subtler elements, to talk of the atmosphere of Puritanism or the evolution of our Constitution, is quite irrelevant and vain. It is impossible to convey to a barely breeched imp who does not yet know his own community, the exquisite divergence between it and some other community. What is the good of talking about the constitution carefully balanced on three estates to a creature only quite recently balanced on two legs? What is the sense of explaining the Puritan shade of morality to a creature who is still learning with difficulty that there is any morality at all? The general truth remains that we should teach, to the young, men's enduring truths, and let the learned amuse themselves with their passing errors.

—October 8, 1910

Children and Truth

What has a child to do with the search after truth? The most you can ask from a child is that he should tell the truth he does know: not that he should look for the truth he does not. But in these books and pamphlets, page after page, in a hundred elusive ways, is struck this same note: that the child must be progressive, that he must conceive morality as reform, that he must look for beautiful modern changes— in short that he must teach his grandmother how to suck eggs. Now, I am far from denying that, in the contact between the child and the grandmother, both have a great deal to learn. On the whole, I think the child has more to give the grand- mother. But it is the essence of a child that he should give what he has to give unconsciously. . . . It is the essence of a grandmother that she should give it con- sciously, out of the clear cunning of years. In other words, I do object to the child teaching his grandmother. I do not object to the grandmother learning from the child.

—May 30, 1908

A Child's Instinct

A child's instinct is almost perfect in the matter of fighting; a child always stands for the good militarism as against the bad. The child's hero is always the man or boy who defends himself suddenly and splendidly against aggression. The child's hero is never the man or boy who attempts by his mere personal force to extend his mere personal influence. In all boys' books, in all boys' conversation, the hero is one person and the bully the other. That combination of the hero and bully in one, which people now call the Strong Man or the Superman, would be simply unintelligible to any schoolboy.

—October 20, 1906

Chivalry

Chivalry really did succeed in doing the impracticable things, even when it failed to do the practical things. We may differ or feel doubtful about the ultimate success, or even the ultimate value, of various policies pursued in the past, but nobody can doubt the thrill and enthusiasm and courage of the pursuit. The only really reliable part of history is the romance of it.

—October 18, 1924

Christian

These are days when the Christian is expected to praise every creed except his own, and especially to lament that Christianity is not Christian, because it is not Buddhist.

—*August* II, 1928

Christianity never promised that it would impose universal peace. It had a great deal too much respect for personal liberty. The sceptical theorist is allowed to throw off Utopia after Utopia, and is never reproached when they are contradicted by the facts, or contradicted by each other. The unfortunate believer is alone always made responsible, and held to account for breaking a promise that he never made.

—*March* 2, 1929

It is the Christian Culture that is woven of many strands, of many fabrics and colours, and twisted into the single knot, the knot that holds the world together, but the knot that is of all knots the most difficult to trace out or untie. . . . Anyhow, it is the Christian who is the real cosmic mystery; the cross made by the cross-lights of the shafts of the sunrise and the sunset; the true cross of the world. But it is only just to say that this complexity, which produces the highest philosophy, does also produce humbug. It produces the worst kind; in which the humbug hardly knows he is a humbug.

—*June* 13, 1931

. . . a Christian is perpetually balanced between a Christian ideal of loving his enemies, a pagan ideal of punishing his enemies, and a chivalric ideal of only fighting his enemies fairly.

—*June* 13, 1931

Christian Creed

It was the intellectual value of the Creed that preserved it through any revolution of aesthetic values, just as it preserves it still amid the wildest changes in aesthetic taste to-day. Michael Angelo went on being a Christian then, just as Mr. Eric Gill goes on being a Christian now, because a man may be original without being separated from the origins; and because a man may be able to think, even if he can also draw.

—*January* 18, 1930

76

Christian Science

If a man brought me a cure which he called Jewish Science, and I found that it consisted entirely of pork and polytheism, I should, without throwing any doubts on the cure, express surprise that he had called it Jewish. If a thing called Moslem Science was based on denying the unity of God, or if a thing called Buddhist Science was based on the denial of Reincarnation, I should not denounce the medicines, but I should think they had very queer names. Now Christian Science is certainly based on the two ideas that there is no real flesh and no real pain. And Christianity is certainly based on the idea that the highest reality in the universe assumed flesh and endured pain.

—August 14, 1909

In short, the first and last blunder of Christian Science is that it is a religion claiming to be purely spiritual. Now, being purely spiritual is opposed to the very essence of religion. All religions, high and low, true and false, have always had one enemy, which is the purely spiritual. Faith-healing has existed from the beginning of the world; but faith-healing without a material act or sacrament—never. It may be the ancient priest, curing with holy water, or the modern doctor curing with coloured water. In either case you cannot do without the water.

—November 5, 1910

Some are surprised that the same American civilisation should produce Christian Science and commercial salesmanship. But in fact Christian Science is very like commercial salesmanship. Both rest on the idea that facts can be conjured away by moods and mesmerism.

—August 30, 1930

The primary principle of the cult obviously forbad them to run for a doctor if Mrs. Eddy broke her leg, since either the leg, or certainly the break, or possibly both, were illusions of mortal mind. Whether there really were people who would have let a man bleed to death, because the blood was a result of the mere flow of his thoughts, I have my doubts. . . .

—October 18, 1930

Christian Scientist

The friends of Christian Science say proudly that very good business men are Christian Scientists. The foes of Christian Science say, unkindly, that Christian Scientists are very good business men.

—October 18, 1930

Christian Spirit

The Christian Creed was not merely the Semitic spirit rushing west, because, when the Semitic spirit did undoubtedly and unmistakably rush west, all the Christians lived and longed and strove only to drive it back into the east. In other words, if the Church was only a vanguard of Eastern fanaticism, it was a vanguard that unaccountably waged war on its own rearguard without stopping for a thousand years. It seems only sane to suppose that there were not two forms of the Semitic spirit, but two very different spirits. I will not say that one of them was an anti-Semitic spirit, for the word has another and much sillier significance, and is a signal for all the fools on both sides.

—November 7, 1925

Christianity

The one really strong case for Christianity is that even those who condemn sins have to confess them.

—March 14, 1908

If I disbelieved in Christianity, I should be the loudest blasphemer in Hyde Park. Nothing ought to be too big for a brave man to attack; but there are some things too big for a man to patronise.

—March 28, 1908

Whatever else Christianity means or ever meant, it obviously means or meant an interference with the physical sorrows of humanity by the physical appearance of Divinity. If it does not mean that, I cannot conceive what it does mean. There seems to be no point in the story.

—February 21, 1914

Christianity is wronged, not by enemies who exaggerate its worldiness, but by those who exaggerate its unworldliness. Christianity is not Buddhism. If Christianity has failed ... it has failed by defiling itself with the world, but certainly not by feeling superior to it. The distinction is so clear that I do not care how you choose to put it. Say, if you like, that the temptation of the Buddhist is to be a prig. Say, if you like, that the temptation of the Christian is to be a snob. But do not say that a religion which really has no other point of difference from the other great religions, except that it maintains a material appearance of its highest divinity among men, is a religion that does not care about this world.

—February 21, 1914

... no other religion is like the Christian religion, I believe it to be supported not merely by faith but by facts.

—March 3, 1917

Christianity was always a domestic religion. It began with the Holy Family.

—July 5, 1919

Christianity (Failures of)

The cruel competition of classes went with an abandonment of charity—not merely of the primitive theory of charity, but of the Mediaeval practice of charity. The colossal evil of cosmopolitan finance came with a new toleration of usury. The Prussian superman, the supreme product of modern immoralism, arose through a denial not merely of the mystical humility of Christian saints, but of the ordinary modesty of Christian men. The wickedness that led up to the war may be called, if anyone likes to put it so, the failure of Christianity.

—July 5, 1919

Christianity and General Ludendorff

General Ludendorff, the eminent Prussian commander, was reported the other day as saying these words: "I repudiate Christianity as not appropriate to the German character." The remark set me thinking, especially about the general absence of thought, and a growing division in mankind upon that matter. To me it seems very much as if I were to say: "I deny the existence of the solar system as unsuited to the Chestertonian temperament." In other words, I cannot make any sense of it at all.

—September 23, 1933

Christianity and the Renaissance

... the truths were so true that they would have survived, in really thinking men, through ten renaissances and twenty revivals of learning. We see this vividly in the intensely intellectual character of the religious conviction in men like Michael Angelo and even Leonardo da Vinci. Nobody knew better than they that Christianity is really wiser, and even wider, than paganism; that Aquinas was not only better but broader than Aristotle. Not from such men came the clumsy denials of the deep dogmas of the faith. Michael Angelo was not the man to dispute that the truly Divine Humanity would be crucified; ... But if the whole thing had been a dirty asceticism of the desert, the mere monkey tricks of the Manichees, it would have fallen like filthy rags from men who had seen the grace of the Greek athletes.

—January 18, 1930

Christianity and War

Wars have resulted from every single secular and social ideal that was worth a button. Wars followed on the French revolution; wars followed on the Russian revolution; war was of the very essence of the American revolution, and needed another war to decide what the first war had decided. If wars are the horrid fruits of a thing called Christianity, they are also the horrid fruits of everything called citizenship and democracy and liberty and national independence. ...

—July 26, 1930

Christmas

One writer against Christmas went so far as to say that the shopkeepers for their own commercial purposes alone sustain Christmas Day. I am not sure whether he said that the shopkeepers invented Christmas Day. Perhaps he thought that the shopkeepers invented Christianity. It is a quaint picture, the secret conclave between the cheesemonger, the poulterer, and the toy-shop keeper, in order to draw up a theology that shall convert all Europe and sell some of their goods. Opponents of Christianity would believe anything except Christianity. That the shopkeepers make Christmas is about as conceivable as that the confectioners make children. It is about as sane as that milliners manufacture women.

—January 13, 1906

It is self-evident at first sight that Christmas is both conservative and liberal, so long as we have the sense to avoid capital letters for the two words. It would be nothing if it did not conserve the traditions of our fathers; it would be nothing if it did not give with liberality to our brethren.

—December 22, 1923

We hear a great deal of the Christmas vision of peace and reconciliation; and, like every other truth, it is not difficult to turn into cant. But here is a work of peace and unity that can really be done, and is not often attempted. We can clear out of our own minds the false antitheses and antagonisms which forbid us to take a truth where we can find it, because we have found a totally different truth somewhere else; which force us to spit out the truth with the falsehood of one party, and swallow the falsehood with the truth of another; which set our very thoughts to fight where they had no quarrel and to dispute where they do not disagree; which deny to us peace in the intellect and good-will among the ideals of the soul.

—December 22, 1923

The charity of Christmas can, in one sense, cover all men, but it cannot in any sense cover all principles, or it would cover the principle of uncharitableness.

—December 22, 1923

Christmas is, quite apart from all its really important elements, the central and supreme example of this idea of concentration and fixity; because it is not a moveable feast. Many excessive schools of lunatics have tried in vain to move it,

81

and even to move it away. In spite of all sorts of intellectual irritations and pedantic explaining away, human beings will almost certainly go on observing this winter feast in some fashion.

—January 3, 1925

Christmas (Abolition of)

Reformers in recent centuries, having very conspicuously refused to make all men equal, or even all citizens equal, have sometimes raised a rather dismal revolt in favour of making all days equal; as if they were three hundred and sixty-five citizens standing all in a row.

—January 3, 1925

A Christmas Carol (Modern)

Some of our more advanced ethical teachers might well write a new version of "The Christmas Carol"—a sort of Anti-Christmas carol. For the drama of Dickens might well appear to them not a comedy of conversion, but a tragedy of apostasy. The story would start with Scrooge as a lofty and idealistic vegetarian, partaking of a pure and hygienic diet of gruel. It would end with the same Scrooge, not degraded by superstition, and engaged in a cannibal conspiracy for the assassination of a turkey. It would exhibit that maniac as so morally depraved as to entrap even a small boy out of the streets and make him a tool in the consummation of the crime. . . . Eugenics, which often form a part of such ethics, might here suggest a thoughtful passage about the mistake made in the birth of Tiny Tim, and the desirability of correcting that mistake with all speed in some quiet and painless fashion. Anyhow, a large number of highly modern morals might be drawn from the new story.

—December 27, 1919

Christmas Magazines

The editors of the magazines bring out their Christmas numbers so long before the time that the reader is more likely to be still lamenting for the turkey of last year than to have seriously settled down to a solid anticipation of the turkey which is to come. Christmas numbers of magazines ought to be tied up in brown paper and kept for Christmas Day. On consideration, I should favour the editors being tied up in brown paper. Whether the leg or arm of an editor should ever be allowed to protrude I leave to individual choice.

—January 12, 1907

Christmas and Commercialism

Millions of perfectly healthy and worthy men and women still keep Christmas; and do in all sincerity keep it holy as well as happy. But there are some, profiting by such natural schemes of play and pleasure-seeking, who have used it for things far baser than either pleasure-seeking or play. They have betrayed Christmas. For them the substance of Christmas, like the substance of Christmas pudding, has become stale stuff in which their own treasure is buried; and they have only multiplied the sixpences into thirty pieces of silver.

—December 23, 1933

The Church

... as human institutions go, the Church was not peculiar in having evils, but peculiar in admitting them.

—March 14, 1908

People have tried to explain Christianity in various ways by saying it was not merely Christian. Some say it was Roman; as they put it. The Church is but the ghost of the empire sitting on the ruins of Rome. Others ... would have said that Hebraism prevailed over Hellenism, when Christianity prevailed over Paganism. The Christian Church proved itself independent of all these things because it was at war with all these things. Christianity was Christianity; it was not Hebraism, because it struggled to the death with Hebraism; it was not Manicheanism, because it fought like fury against the Manichees. The Church was the Church; it was not the empire, because it defied the empire—not only at the beginning, when the emperors were pagan, but also afterwards, when the emperors became Aryan.

—November 7, 1925

Church (Attendance)

Generally speaking, it is not true that the young knut who declines to go to church does so because he is already exhausted with his efforts to understand the *homoousion* or the definitions of the Council of Ephesus. I cannot bring myself to think that every young lady who prefers lawn-tennis to evening service is but relaxing herself after her rigid application, as a child, to the controversies of the Thomists and Scotists on the relation of the Incarnation to The Fall. I myself was brought up in the most modern and emancipated of all religious atmospheres, and I can generally manage to find motives of my own for not going to church.

— September 18, 1920

Church (Progressive)

People must be induced to "flock" to it, even if it has to be turned into an aquarium or an aerodrome.

— October 4, 1930

Church (Science and Weaponry)

I do not know whether Martin Luther invented mustard gas, or George Fox manufactured tearshells, or St. Thomas Aquinas devised a stink-bomb producing suffocation. But I should rather fancy, in my ignorant and artless way, that these things were invented by modern scientists, most of whom were probably modern materialists. There is no doubt at all that they were produced specially and solely in the one historical epoch given over to scientific materialism. What is perhaps even more important, it was the one and only historic epoch given over avowedly and systematically to secularism. I mean it was the only epoch in which public life was ever openly and officially purged of religion; the only period in which ideas like secular education or secular ethics were accepted as just.

— July 26, 1930

The Church and War

... the Great War was one enormous working model of the Church's moral theory about man. It showed that man has the mastery of all things except of himself. It showed that no amount of science in the preparation of things can

84

prevent there being sin in the use of them. It showed man doing things impossible to the animals, but not very far removed from the devils. And it showed that the spiritual issue of right and wrong remains in exactly the same proportions in a duel of battleships as in a duel of battle-axes, or a duel of stone hatchets. Anyone who knows what the Church did say will agree that the war was simply a huge illustration of what she had always said.

—January 19, 1924

People still go about gravely repeating that Christianity was refuted by the great war, which is rather like saying that Noah's ark was refuted by the flood. The ark was only built because men were likely to be drowned in a deluge; and the Church was only founded because men are liable to be swept away perpetually by a deluge of dark passions and destructive sins. But the Church certainly never said that there would be no sins and no wars; and some of the more mystical adumbrations about the last days seemed to suggest that there would be more sins and more wars.

—January 19, 1924

The Church and World War I

What does anybody or everybody mean—by saying that in the case of the recent war Christianity was a failure? What do they suppose that Christianity teaches about war? That it cannot happen? That it will never happen again? On the contrary, it was the opponents of Christianity—the people who thought themselves too progressive and enlightened for Christianity—who were perpetually telling us that war was an anachronism like the gladiatorial show.
The Church is first blamed for confessing itself a church militant, and then mocked because it turns out after all not to be a church triumphant. The truth is that there never was a historic event that so heavily endorsed the historic philosophy of Christendom as did the late war. The only part of it that concerns us here is this proposition—that no scientific changes have altered the soul, and that the business of the soul is with sin. Until the autumn of 1914, thousands of thinking people in this island really did not believe that men so scientific as the Germans could be so sinful as the Germans.

—April 12, 1919

85

Churchill, Winston

Mr. Winston Churchill, if he is in some sense a hereditary ruler, is at least a hereditary demagogue.

—November 20, 1909

Cigarette (Banning of)

If a policeman can take away my cigarette, there cannot be the slightest rational objection, on a warm day, to his taking away my overcoat. In wet weather he might change my boots for me violently in the street, or suddenly garrott me with a muffler. The thing is a typical mild human indulgence, enjoyed by most people and over-enjoyed by a few people, a thing like scent or sweetmeats. Realise that reality which we all know it to be, and then measure that mad abyss of disproportion, on the other side of which are the eight States holding up their streets with policemen and treating every man who is carrying a cigarette as if he were carrying a bomb. Thus all our cranks of culture are leading us back (or onward) into barbarism.

—September 11, 1909

Men must have wholly lost that instinct for individuality which is the crown of civilisation, that thing which we call freedom, if they can thus loosen all the tribal terrors against a thing like a cigarette. It is a mere wild taboo, imposed hypnotically by a few medicine-men. The physical danger of cigarette-smoking bears not the slightest proportion to such enormous and absurd spectacles of public panic. One might as well arrest people for walking about in the rain, a thing of which many a man has died. Possibly they will do that; perhaps we shall hear shortly that ten States of the Union have said through their Legislatures and their Governors that the rain must go.

—September 11, 1909

Cinema

. . . the only real objection to the cinema is one that nobody mentions. . . . It is the indictment against the whole of our modern mechanical and urban civilisation, and it is simply this—that people cannot enjoy themselves. That is, they cannot amuse themselves, and therefore they must be amused. They do not enjoy themselves, just as they do not govern themselves, because they are not free men and do not own themselves. They have to enjoy something that does not come from themselves, but from a class of men richer or more cunning or more scientific than themselves. So in the decline of Rome the semi-servile rabble cried to the emperor for circuses as well as for bread.

—*June 19, 1920*

Cinema and Automobiles

Cars on the film often go much too fast, not for the laws of New York or London, but for the laws of space and time. For nature has written a speed limit in the nerves of the eye and the cells of the brain; and exceeding it, or even trying to exceed it, does not mean going to a prison, but to a madhouse.

—*August 27, 1927*

The Citizen's Power

... it is like the power of the artist; it consists in drawing the line somewhere. The idea of the nation of kings is that every citizen respects every other citizen, as a king respects another king; not merely as a matter of equality but also of dignity. It is as if there were a flag on every roof and a frontier at the end of every front garden. The area of choice for the citizen is circumscribed by the city; but within that area of choice he does really choose. His home, his habits, his relation to the family he has founded and the friends he has made—these are really regarded in the true republic as invested with a certain dignity and even sanctity that descends from Rome.

—*June 5, 1920*

City Life and Nature

But for us who live in cities Nature is not natural. Nature is supernatural. Just as monks watched and strove to get a glimpse of heaven, so we watch and strive to get a glimpse of earth. This is unreasonable; it is even comic. It is as if men had cake and wine every day but were sometimes allowed common bread. That would not be more grotesque than our condition, that men should have great streets and tall buildings every day, but be sometimes allowed common grass.

—*August 31, 1907*

Civil Authority and the Citizen

A child of six months old owes some allegiance to human authority for the very simple reason that nothing except human authority would have taken the trouble to save him from being eaten up by wild beasts. The whole of the true theory of the State, as I pointed out in the passage to which I refer, is perfectly expressed in the epigram of St. Thomas Aquinas — "in auctore auctoritas." We owe some respect to existing civilisation only because without existing civilisation we should not even exist. Therefore, quite apart from the main problem, I take the liberty of dismissing the doctrine that anybody without a vote is a kind of unlimited outlaw or anarchist, who can do anything that he or she pleases.

—*March* 16, 1907

Civilisation

Civilisation itself is only one of the things that men choose to have. Convince them of its uselessness and they would fling away civilisation as they fling away a cigar.

—*October* 21, 1905

There is more hope for an old civilisation because it has much more varied memories from which to choose. It will be a stratification of many rich but variegated soils; and the innovator who has dug up one can dig down to another. When one historical revival is over, there are any number of other historical revivals to take its place.

—*October* 4, 1924

Civilisation (Chinese)

The great Chinese civilisation, one of the mightiest achievements of mankind, has been largely constructed on the principle that, if external customs can be settled, internal sanity will be safe. Chinese culture encased a man in custom, so that he could not go very far wrong or perhaps even very far right. The great agnostic Confucius really conceived the idea of giving men a church without a creed, but a highly ritualistic church; a church having all the more ritual for having hardly any religion. It was a secular ritual covering the whole of daily life, dress and manners and domestic habits. In short, it was a marvellous attempt to magnetise a man's soul through his own actions; and, as it were, to mesmerise him by the movement of his own arms and legs.

—December 10, 1921

Civilisation (Death of)

I have two reasons for doubting this doom: first, because Christendom has gone through such dark ages before, and always shown a power of recovery; and second, because I do not believe in doom at all. All this talk about optimism and pessimism is itself a dismal fall from the old talk about right and wrong. Our fathers said that a nation had sinned and suffered like a man. We say it has decayed, like a cheese.

—July 10, 1920

Civilisation and Culture

Civilisation is rather the limit or compromise laid upon this by the discovery that there are other peoples or other methods of production. In following culture, a man develops his arts; that is to say, his tastes. Consequently, true culture, like true charity, begins at home, and generally stays at home. With civilisation there appears something that is not only purely public, but a little homeless. Culture is growing such flowering trees as you prefer in your own front garden, and planting them where you like. Civilisation is having a law-suit with the next-door neighbour about whether your trees overshadow his garden, or calling the police-man to throw him out if he becomes violent upon the question.

—March 24, 1934

Civilisations (Comparing)

Those who praise mere civilisation (or the morbid modern form of it) are always pointing out the desolate state of various rude societies. They say, "The Zulus have no good eye-glasses." They do not remember that the Zulus have good eyes instead. They cry aloud, "The Ojibways fell on their knees with wonder and terror on first beholding a button-hook." They do not add that the Ojibways were thrown into agonies on first trying to wear buttoned boots.

—September 25, 1909

City

Paris is older than France and York is older than England; and Cologne is immeasurably older than Germany, let alone the German empire. These centres of civilisation have something in them more magnetic and immortal even than nationality, let alone mere vulgar imperialism. Ghosts haunt houses, they say, and the ghosts of whole peoples haunt whole cities, till half Europe is like a haunted house. It is only dull materialists who can wander away into any material environment. The spirit and all that is spiritual returns to its own environment. The world ebbs back again to its cities. . . .

—January 11, 1930

Claim (Abusive)

Most of the rebellions against oppression have been made, not at the moment when the oppressor first began to oppress, but only at the moment when the oppressor first declared himself as such. . . . Caesar was assassinated because he was trying to be a king, not because he had already become an autocrat. What smashed the Stuarts was their divine right, not any of their human wrong. It is always the *claim* that maddens men, much more than the acts. There is never any real revolt against any human abuse, until it has made its open and monstrous claim upon humanity.

—November 13, 1909

Class (Middle)

. . . I think that for good or evil this really genuine and isolated middle class is mainly disappearing. The old middle class may have been dull, but it was not vulgar, for dullness implies homogeneity, while vulgarity implies an incongruity, a contrast. The old middle class did not meet the aristocracy; perhaps they would not; it is possible that they could not. At any rate, they did not, and they did not talk of doing so or boast of doing so. But in the middle class of to-day the greatest difficulty is to find a middle-class man. The existing middle class can be broadly divided into the vulgar people who do not know the aristocracy and the yet more vulgar people who do know the aristocracy.

—August 11, 1906

In the old middle class tidy men were tidy, but, bless their hearts, they were never smart. In the old middle class untidy men were untidy, but, rest their souls, they were never artistic. The general ideal and exaction of the old class was that dress should be rather sombre and restrained; that it should not break out into fantasies either of fashion or anti-fashion. Then they did business in black clothes because it looked businesslike; now they do business in golfing knickers because it looks wealthy.

—August 11, 1906

Class Persecution

... public-houses and play-houses and picture theatres are no more specially perilous or poisonous than teashops and haberdashers' shops and hair-dressing saloons. And the habit of suspecting them and spying on them and picking particular holes in them is only a part of the worst hypocrisy of modern humanitarianism. It is part of the trick of attacking the pleasures of the poor before the problems of the poor. It is the fashionable amusement of dictating the hygienic arrangements of the home without knowing whether there is a home; of forcing the people to take physic when you do not know when they have taken food; and forbidding a man to have beer without allowing him to have bread.

—June 19, 1920

Classics and the Common Man

A great classic means a man whom one can praise without having read. This is not in itself wholly unjust; it merely implies a certain respect for the realisation and fixed conclusions of the mass of mankind. And it is as reasonable for a man ... who has no ear for music to assume that Beethoven was a good musician. Because he himself has no ear for music, that is no reason why he should assume that the human race has no ear for music. Because I am ignorant (as I am), it does not follow that I ought to assume that I am deceived. The man who would not praise Pindar unless he had read him would be a low, distrustful fellow, the worst kind of sceptic, who doubts not only God, but man. He would be like a man who could not call Mount Everest high unless he had climbed it. He would be like a man who would not admit that the North Pole was cold until he had been there.

—May 11, 1907

Clemenceau, Georges

Clemenceau is not a peasant, and he knows a great deal too much about a peasant to expect to get much money out of him for the benefit of a politician.

—*November* 29, 1919

Clichés

Clichés are things that can be new and already old. They are things that can be new and already dead. They are the stillborn fruits of culture. A new catch-word that really means nothing is more dangerous than an old custom that always meant something; even if it meant the veiling or masking or mystification of something.

—*May* 14, 1932

Climate and History

The argument, as it used to be stated in my boyhood, was so very simple. The Italian sat in the sun under a vine that dropped grapes into his mouth; so he did not need to do anything. The Scotchman had to walk about to keep warm on a cold moorland where nothing grew but thistles; so he was forced to begin to plough the soil if only to restore his circulation. There were some little details that did not seem quite to fit in with the explanation—little things like the Roman Empire, the Discovery of America, the Wars of Napoleon, and so on.

—*June* 20, 1925

Clique

Many are complaining of the cliques in the literary world. . . . It is natural for men to belong to a club, as it is natural for other men who do not belong to a club to call it a clique. . . .

—*June* 6, 1931

. . . we rather tend to lose the old idea that it is the business of the author to explain himself. We tend to adopt the idea that it is the business of the clique to understand the author; and even to explain the author, when he refuses to explain himself.

—June 6, 1931

This is the paradox of the clique; that it consists of those who understand something and do not wish it to be understood; do not really wish it to be understandable. But such a group must in its nature be small, and its tendency is to make the range or realm of culture smaller.

—June 6, 1931

Clothes

A human being is not even completely human without clothes, because they have become a part of him as the symbol of purely human things; of dignity, of modesty, of self-ownership, of property, and privacy and honour. Even in the purely artistic sense humanity would never have become human without them, because the range of self-expression and symbolic decoration would have been hopelessly limited, and there would have been no outlet even for the most primary instinct about colour and form.

—January 10, 1931

Cobbet, William

Cobbett had a way of coming on great truths by way of small quarrels.

—July 4, 1925

Communism

It is really the opposite of the truth that communism is the popular thing. It is the opposite of the truth that property is privilege. The truth is that communism is for the few and property for the many. Certain minds have always perceived that life would be simplified without possessions, as it would be simplified without passions. But so to simplify the whole of human life would be rather to nullify it.

—October 25, 1919

93

Men in armies and monasteries can be practically communistic; because there, for abnormal reasons, the common cause is very vivid to the imagination. But for normal masses of people, in normal times of peace, sharing has none of the generous emotions of giving and receiving.

—December 20, 1919

Communism (Soviet)

. . . I have very great sympathy indeed with the property-loving peasants and their antipathy to compulsory communism. Communism seems to me not so much nonsensical as simply narrow. Making everything public property is exactly like making everything private property. It is sacrificing everything to one solitary sentiment. The sentiment of sharing is a healthy one, with its place in human life, as when men share a public monument—or, better still, a public-house. But it is not a substitute for the other sentiments of giving and receiving, as when a man offers hospitality in a private house. To turn all private houses into public-houses is not even an irrational sentimentalism, but rather an irrational asceticism.

—September 6, 1919

It is brutal, it is monstrous, it is as mad or bad as anyone can call it.

—October II, 1919

It is now both an ideal and a reality; and its name is slavery.

—November 12, 1921

Communism: Theory and Practise of

. . . in plain truth a communist tests his own elasticity in allowing property to peasants exactly as a teetotaler tests his own elasticity by drinking half a bottle of brandy. In other words, he does not test his elasticity, but simply swallows his principles, as he swallows the brandy. He is not modifying communism; he is denying communism, and refusing to translate it into practice. If the property-loving peasants have a right to their property, the communists have no right to their communism—or, at any rate, no right to their compulsory communism.

—September 6, 1919

Communist (Soviet)

He may have gone the length of murder, or massacre, or torture; but he has not gone the length of consistency. For all I know, the communists have reached the point of cannibalism. But the communists have not reached the point of communism.

—*December* 20, 1919

Communist Reforms

One of the first reforms of Lenin and Trotsky was, I believe, to abolish Christmas.

—*November* 12, 1921

Communication

There is no more deadly delusion, none more full of quite practical peril, than this notion that trains and wires have created a real understanding between the nations. Do you think that Chinamen will love you because you can write a Chinese telegram? Chinamen (and very right they are) will not love you until you can write a Chinese love-letter. The world has not shrunk at all. It is not one iota more easy at this moment to understand the Cannibal Islands. It is only more easy to look at them and misunderstand them. The misunderstanding has actually grown greater, because we ourselves have abandoned many healthy and instinctive things which would have helped us to sympathise with the savages. On the same page on which I read of these hopes from the coalescing and combining of the planet. I found a Moslem service called dirty or disgusting because it involved the idea of blood. A few hundred years ago we should have realized that our own religion involved the idea of blood. But we have got further away from understanding their religion by ceasing to understand our own.

—*May* 9, 1908

Communication (Modern)

It is, as I have often remarked, a highly ironical and pathetic circumstance that the world has discovered how to say everything everywhere at the very moment in all history when it has nothing to say.

—*April* 4, 1925

Community (Sense of)

There were times when the democratic masses did have a philosophy. It was called a religion. But some of the thin theoretic spiders, unrepresentative but ubiquitous, have contrived to destroy that; and there is no mental machinery for common sense. I use common sense in its true mediaeval meaning of the sense of the community. In modern times spontaneous mental discipline, like spontaneous military discipline, has been made very difficult for the mob. In neutral things, as in military things, the modern advantage is with the trained minority.

—*December* 20, 1919

Comparative Studies (and Reductionism)

... there is no cheaper and yet no more unchangeable type of intellectual pride than that which is proud of not seeing the difference between two different things. For some strange reason it is now always thought liberal to lump everything together; to say we can see no difference between a man and a woman, or between a Christian and a Jew, or between a peasant and a serf, or between a weapon and an instrument of torture. The universal theologian is he who says that all contradictory theologies are the same. ...

—*August* 18, 1917

Compromise

Our chief fault is precisely this lazy readiness to think a thing black and white at the same time. We call it a compromise.

—*September* 8, 1906

The curse of our nation is that it will not understand that consistency and intellectual sincerity are not only better, but very much quicker, than compromise. We will not understand that a straight line is the nearest distance between two points. We think it more practical to wander, and our dream of a business-like directness can be best expressed in the old formula of the man who went straight down the crooked lane and all round the square.

—*September* 8, 1906

Compromise (Political)

There is an atmosphere of compromise everywhere at the present instant, and of what always goes with compromise—secrecy.

—July 9, 1910

Compulsion, Age of

Compulsion is the highly modern mark of a great many modern things; compulsory education, compulsory insurance, compulsory temperance, and soon, perhaps, compulsory arbitration. What is not so often noted is that even where we may think it necessary, it is never vital, in the sense of dealing with the life and soul of the subject. Education does not discover why the poor are ignorant; insurance does not discover why they are ill. Indeed, the one story the schools will not teach the poor is how they became poor; and the one disease the hospitals cannot cure is their poverty.

—June 5, 1920

Computer

The wild possibility which haunts the dreams of such men is that notion of inventing a machine that will render needless the labour of thinking for a man. If men could only make some great iron engine to do their thinking for them, they would willingly do the hammering and the stoking of the engine. . . . Then we might be thoroughly scientific without having to stop to be intelligent. Then we might have the whole day of judgment over in an hour or so, with every spiritual problem settled without having been examined, and every spiritual question answered without being asked. And we could all go back to the office, and make as much money as possible, with the extra satisfaction of despising our fellow creatures, especially foreigners and poor people. But, alas! there is just one faint, lingering, and elusive difficulty about the creation of what is called a thinking machine. It is a contradiction in terms.

—December 3, 1927

Comradeship

Winter encourages that thing called comradeship which modern humanitarians so often seem unable to understand, but which Walt Whitman so wisely perceived to be the permanent foundation of democracy. There is another thing I know which can be called comradeship, and which humanitarians do understand; the thing they call communion with nature. Summer does encourage the illusion (for it is an illusion) that one thing in the cosmos is as good as another, that we are finally attached to nothing, that we can enjoy and forget all things. On a bright blue day a man is apt to feel that he is a comrade of the birds, of the trees and even of the stones, and that he is a comrade of man, no less and no more. But in winter he will discover that, however happy we may be, we are still an army marching in a hostile country, and that no trees and no stones and no stars can give any adequate symbol of the thing that binds us together.

—May 19, 1906

One of these truisms is that comradeship is a natural and noble thing; and along with this comradeship there goes a certain case for Communism, in the sense of certain things held in common. The young Bolshevist is a great bore when he says this for the thousandth time; but even at the thousandth repetition it is still a truism, and therefore a truth.

—February 25, 1922

Comte, Auguste

Comte. . . . divided all human history into three stages. It is a long time since I have read him, but I think they were something like the Mythological, the Metaphysical, and the Positive. According to him, that is, man began by saying the sun was a god; he went on to say that heat was a principle; he ended his career on this earth by having nothing at all to say except that he felt devilish hot. Well, that theory need not detain us. We are well past the Positive stage now, and are (please heaven!) rapidly returning to the Mythological.

—December 10, 1910

Conceit

Each one of us is ludicrously ignorant of something; most of us of most things. The whole difference between a conceited man and a modest one is concerned only with how far he is conscious of those hundred professions in which he would be a failure, of those hundred examinations which he could not pass. . . . It may be difficult to keep all these potential failures of oneself before one's imagination at once. But it is worth trying, being full of gigantesque humility.

—February 5, 1910

Condiments

Condiments, like cookery, are obviously blasted by the fact that they are mere luxuries. They only exist for fun—or, as some would call it, the art of life. In other words, they are merely marks of civilisation; which seems to be considered a sufficient condemnation by the new champions of progress.

—May 11, 1929

I cannot understand how it is that no moral movement . . . has appeared to start some people interfering with other people in the use of condiments. . . . Surely there ought to be a crusade against these things, since a crusade is now commonly held to mean an attack upon some habit of Christian civilisation. Very little would be needed to set the Puritans, who are above all Manicheans, denouncing these things exactly as they now denounce beer or tobacco, and are, indeed, already beginning to denounce coffee and tea. . . . We should see the town plastered with the words "join the no-mustard club." By a slight emendation of scripture (which is nothing to the devout Puritan) we should be told that the salt which has *not* lost its savour is fit only to be cast forth and trampled under foot of men.

—February 21, 1931

Confession

I protest against that arbitrary gesture of self-ablution and self-absolution with which some characters in modern stories conclude the confession of their crimes; like that weak tyrant who tried to combine the contraries of despotism and irresponsibility by washing his hands when he had delivered the innocent to death.

—March 10, 1934

Conquest versus Victory

. . . a boy feels an abysmal difference between conquest and victory. Conquest has the sound of something cold and heavy; the automatic operations of a powerful army. Victory has the sound of something sudden and valiant; victory is like a cry out of the living mouth. The child is excited with victory; he is bored with conquest. The child is not an Imperalist; the child is a Jingo—which is excellent. The child is not a militarist in the heavy, mechanical modern sense; the child is a fighter. Only very old and very wicked people can be militarists in the modern sense. Only very old and very wicked people can be peace-at-any-price men. The child's instincts are quite clean and chivalrous, though perhaps a little exaggerated.

—*October* 20, 1906

Conscience

Conscience does not suggest "asparagus," but it does suggest amiability, and it is thought by some to be an amiable act to accept asparagus when it is offered to you. Conscience does not respect fish and sherry; but it does respect any innocent ritual that will make men feel alike. Conscience does not tell you not to drink your hock after your port. But it does tell you not to commit suicide; and your mere naturalistic reason tells you that the first act may easily approximate to the second.

—*December* 12, 1908

Hyde is the innocence of evil. He stands for the truth (attested by a hundred tales of hypocrites and secret sins) that there is in evil, though not in good, this power of self-isolation, this hardening of the whole exterior, so that a man becomes blind to moral beauties or deaf to pathetic appeals. . . . Precisely because Jekyll, with all his faults, possesses goodness, he possesses also the consciousness of sin, humility. He knows all about Hyde, as angels know about devils. And . . . this contrast between the blind swiftness of evil and the almost bewildered omniscience of good is not a peculiarity of this strange case, but is true of the permanent problem of your conscience and mine. If I get drunk I shall forget dignity; but if I keep sober I may still desire drink. Virtue has the heavy burden of knowledge; sin has often something of the levity of sinlessness.

—*February* 26, 1910

The sanctity of conscience consisted in its being the voice of God, which must be universal, or at the least in a *communis sententia* or moral sense of mankind, of which the whole point is that it is universal. If a particular man's opinion is not the voice of God, is not what men call morality, then his conscience is no more necessarily sacred than his nightmares.

—*June* 2, 1917

One is tempted to say that a man who has not got a troubled conscience is in danger of having no conscience to be troubled.

—*February* 18, 1922

Conscientious Objector

There still lingers—or rather, lounges—about the world a special type of conscientious objector who is luckily in a minority, even in the small minority of conscientious objectors. He might more properly be described as an unconscientious objector—for he does not so much believe in his own conscience as disbelieve in the common conscience which is the soul of any possible society. His hatred of patriotism is very much plainer than his love for peace.

—*May* 11, 1918

Conservative

I have never, for the life of me, been able to understand the conservative. The conservative seems to me to be always clinging to the last thing which the last radical has forcibly tied him to.

—*April* 16, 1927

Conservatives and Revolutionists

... the literal and derivative sense of political words is often very misleading. An intelligent Conservative is not one who wishes to conserve things just as they are for if he is intelligent he knows that, in the medium of time, they never remain just as they are. An intelligent Conservative is one who believes our society is such that it can safely be left to evolve. An intelligent Revolutionist is not one who wishes to revolve; he is one who wishes to construct—and therefore to destroy.

—July 21, 1917

Controversialists

It may seem absurd, but I believe I am a fair controversialist. It may seem even more absurd, but I have generally found controversialists the fairest people in the world. The people who pretend to be impartial are always partial, whether they are judges or (worse still) historians. The other men, the men who make history, such as criminals or clear fanatics, are really impartial, because they stand apart from the problem. But their great danger is a double one. First, that their intelligence will be called wit; and second, that their wit will be called bluff.

—February 14, 1914

Controversy (Modern)

The queer thing about controversy to-day is that men make a point merely because it is part of a controversy; without worrying about whether it is a part of a philosophy. The advocate is always satisfied with clearing his client; rather than making the law clear. The doctor is satisfied to find any remedy that will cure the disease; it does not bother him that, in the long development of the philosophy of medicine, the remedy is worse than the disease. So long as his argument is immediately applicable, he does not care if it lays the world waste by being universally inapplicable.

—May 2, 1936

Constitution

The thing that was defended sophistically by Burke and cynically by Bagehot had no principle of permanence. It was only a compromise falsely described as a constitution.

—April 16, 1927

Consumerism

Almost all codes of morals or manners, from the Ten Commandments to the Declaration of Independence, had been conceived from the point of view of the consumer. There was not then a new set of codes or commandments intended to inspire the trader. The man who was commanded not to covet his neighbour's ass was the sort of man who was employed in youth in keeping his father's asses. But it was in keeping the asses, not in getting rid of the asses to any human being who was ass enough to buy them.

—February 13, 1932

Contradiction, Age of

This is an age of contradiction; that is why it cannot really be an age of controversy. For contradiction is complete absence of agreement. And controversy depends utterly and entirely upon the presence of agreement. If anybody will examine all the great controversies of the past, he will see that men always agreed before they disagreed. In other words, controversy always means a parting of the ways; but that always means that men have walked together along one road to the point where it turns into two roads. It simply cannot happen at all if they walk along two parallel roads a hundred miles apart; and is even less probable if they are walking on two different planes, according to the mystical mathematics of the moderns; and one is moving in the fourth dimension and the other in the fifth. It is not even an argument between two sages who contradict each other. It is an argument between two sophists, both of whom claim the right to contradict themselves.

—November 4, 1933

Convention

In applications like aircraft there is a real motive to learn the latest thing and use the quickest thing. But in the philosophy of science the public is content with a convention, and leaves the philosopher to walk on alone. Thus it accepts the Darwinian convention about the evolutionary chain, in spite of the "missing link" in that chain. If there were a missing link in a real chain, it would not be a chain at all.

—April 8, 1922

A convention is a form of freedom. That is the reality that the realists cannot get into their heads.

—March 29, 1924

... it has become a convention to say we must disregard conventions; and the demand for something new is already old enough to be in its dotage or (if we had luck) in its coffin.

—December 26, 1925

Conversion

Conquest may produce bitterness, but conversion produces no bitterness. It can produce nothing but gratitude, if it is conversion at all. It may seem a paradox that men should hate you for dethroning their King, but thank you for dethroning their God; but they will thank you—if he is really dethroned. If a man is truly and vitally converted, he has the peace of surrender without the shame of treason.

—March 17, 1917

Conviction (Religious versus Civic)

It is true to say of a religious conviction, of course, that it must primarily be private—that it must be held in the soul before it is applied to the society. It is equally true of a political conviction, or an economic conviction, or any conviction. If this is what he means by calling religion a private affair, there is no such thing as a public affair. But, if he means that the conviction held in the soul cannot be applied to the society, he means manifest and raving nonsense. In other words, if he means that a man's religion cannot have any effect on his citizenship, or on the commonwealth of which he is a citizen.... The cosmos, of which we conceive ourselves the creatures, must include the city of which we conceive ourselves the citizens. A man's notion of the world in which he walks must have an effect on the land in which he walks.

—August 16, 1919

Convictions

My opinions, as opinions, are all quite correct. Any thinking person will see that to say this is only saying that they are my opinions. A man has not got a conviction if he is not convinced of it.

—March 25, 1922

I fancy that a man grows less controversial as he grows more convinced. Perhaps the moment when he is most controversial is when he is convincing himself. I know that since my own views have grown much more settled and satisfied, I am less inclined than I was to go about incessantly contradicting everybody who contradicts them.

—July 24, 1926

The man with a solid conviction generally is quite conscious of all the people who contradict him. If he is of the best type, he will even be able to entertain their ideas, as hypotheses or alternatives, to be called up by the imagination. A man may have any number of ideas, and still have only one ideal. But if this type of man has only one ideal, it is merely because he has never heard of any other ideas.

—September 9, 1933

Cosmologists

... there was a tendency to suggest that man must have been created a long while ago, so perhaps he was never created at all. These philosophers said of the creation as the old woman said of the Crucifixion, "Well, it was such a long while ago; let's hope it never happened."

—June 27, 1925

Costume

It is a modern custom to despise modern costume.

—January 10, 1925

Colour and Creed

I rather fancy that "colour" and "creed" have come to be associated by mere alliteration and have no more rational relation than whiskers and wisdom.

—August 31, 1929

Creed

... We perpetually come back to that sharp and shining point which the modern world is perpetually trying to avoid. We must have a creed, even in order to be comprehensive. We must have a religion, even in order to respect other religions. Even if our whole desire is to admire the good in other worships, we must still worship something—or we shall not know what to admire.

—October 29, 1910

Ever since I began, almost ever since I was a baby, I have been familiar with the statement that the creeds are crumbling. And, having watched the world from my first to my second childhood, I have come to the conclusion that the statement is quite untrue. The creeds, when they really are creeds, seem to me much the hardest and most indestructible material made by man, if they were made by man. Huge crowds of people are still reciting word for word the creeds that were composed before a single existing kingdom had a king, before a single existing nation had a name....

—November 26, 1927

Creed and Deed

In many ethical societies and ethical discussions which I have attended it was asserted, or rather assumed, that deeds were important and words were not.... People talk as if reasons and explanations were not important; as a matter of fact they are the only thing that is important. From a man's deeds you can only discover what he does; you must listen to his words to discover what he means. When he acts you will only learn what he has succeeded in doing. But when he speaks you will have learnt what he was trying to do. If I have to make a selection between Creed and Deed (I should prefer them both) I should certainly select Creed.

—February 2, 1907

Crime and Punishment

Mr. Shaw maintained (quite truly) that having committed a murder does not make a man a murderer—that is, does not make him a prospective and perpetual assassin. This he put in his own lively and legitimate manner by saying that we should allow a murderer two or three murders, as we allow a dog one or two bites. After that (apparently) we should shoot him without trial, like a mad dog. . . . The Shaw argument seems to be that we should not punish because a healthy man may sin: But it is exactly because a healthy man may sin that we do punish. We use the argument of consequences precisely because a good man may stab—or may not stab. The obedient dog may bite—that is, he may refrain from biting. Punishment exists to influence his open mind. If he must bite, he must be shot. But the Shaw sociology can only be maintained by saying that our whole human pack consists of mad dogs. In that case we must all be shot—I am not sure by whom.

—March 26, 1910

. . . robbers who rob in a very impersonal way, on the large, bewildering scale of modern . . . companies, are not punished at all. In the old days, when people really wanted a thief in prison, they very particularly wanted that sort of thief in prison. And they put him there. But the consequence that concerns us here is that the intellectuals have for the present fallen back on the highly illogical compromise of never putting the big thief in prison, of always putting the small thief in prison; and then pretending that the prison is only a hospital.

—August 29, 1925

Crime and Reform

. . . between this stupid scorn of sympathy (which is itself a form of sentimentality) and this sham pretence of sympathy (which is really the reverse of sympathy because it is superiority)—between these two forms of swaggering self-satisfaction the prospects of a real reform in relation to crime are very unsatisfactory. What we want is not all this morbid brooding upon the motives of criminals, not even the more occult problem of the motives of lawyers, but the old historic or prehistoric problem of the motives of law-givers.

—August 22, 1925

Criminal

... the longest run of the most successful criminal comes to an end.

—April 6, 1918

We often hear of a man becoming a criminal through a love of low company. I believe it is much commoner for a man to become a criminal through a love of refined company. There is a kind of people who cannot endure poverty, because they cannot endure ugliness. These people might rob or even murder out of pure refinement. I always remember that the only man I ever met whose literary delicacy was really shocked by the fact that I wrote gory and sensational tales, of the type of the *roman policier,* was also the only man I ever knew who himself went to jail for a crime. I fancy there are many such criminals; I fancy inquiry would reveal many bandits and even assassins of similar sensibility. The man does a brutal thing to escape from brutal surroundings, not to get into brutal surroundings. I doubt if any man ever committed a murder in order to buy a murder story. But many a man, I fancy, may have falsified the books in an office, and so been able to have more exquisite books in a library.

—October 2, 1920

Criminologist

If there is a contemptible creature alive, it is the criminologist who explains away crime as the result of poverty, with the delicate implication that it is only from poverty that we need expect crime. The answer to that sort of criminology is simply history, especially the history of crime. The criminologist implies that nobody will sin who is educated at a school for the sons of gentlemen only; and he seems to forget that Borgia and Gilles de Rais and the Marquis de Sade were certainly gentlemen and the sons of gentlemen.

—September 20, 1924

Criminologist (Modern)

Of course they will hasten to explain (with characteristic clarity of mind) that the new criminology has nothing to do with crime; and that the people who are being punished are not being punished for anything.

—November 4, 1933

Criminology

... the science of criminology is still very vague, like most things that are merely practical, not to say pragmatist. . . . But there has gone along with the change a whole growth of new theories of preventive science and indeterminate detention, which may land the man stealing the leg of mutton in any sort of asylum for any sort of period. The leg of mutton assumes a sort of frightful and Freudian significance as a symbol. The desire for a leg of mutton may be held to connote all sorts of secret and hitherto suppressed crimes. . . . And when all citizens become merely patients under that psychological treatment, it will be sufficiently shown that not all the mutton-heads in the world are quadrupeds. . . .

—September 17, 1927

Critic

As a rule, there is no difference between the critic and ascetic except that the ascetic sorrows with a hope and the critic without a hope.

—June 5, 1909

Now the peculiar point about the critics is this—that they are not, as far as one can see, bad representatives, but literally not representatives at all.

—November 20, 1909

... the art critics and the dramatic critics seem to be a totally distinct race; I can trace in them no resemblance to the human outline.

—November 20, 1909

They are separated by a great chasm of "culture" and fastidiousness from the people for whom they write. They foresee the amusements of the public, not as wine-tasters oversee wine-drinking, or horse-doctors inspect horses—that is, by right of knowing more than most people about something which most people know. Rather they oversee them as teetotalers count the public-houses. . . . This division and disgust is a dangerous attitude, even when it is a right attitude; for there is in all arrogance the beginning of ignorance. If you merely oversee a thing you are very apt to overlook it.

—November 20, 1909

. . . they are not simple enough, and therefore not imaginative enough, to know what that enjoyment is.

—*October* 18, 1919

There are critics who so completely misunderstand that they actually think they understand. They translate words literally into their own language, where they mean something else.

—*February* 21, 1925

. . . such people pounce upon what one says, as compared with the slowness with which they appreciate what one means. That is really very like the jerk of nervous laughter that comes from the public meeting when the joke of some rather mild sort comes from the public platform. Just as the crowd is quicker to applaud the point than to see it, so the critic is quicker to attack the point than to see it.

—*April* 18, 1925

There is a way of being right, as a photographic negative is right; right by being consistently and calculably wrong. Such a critic sees the same facts that we do, but he sees them in contrasted colours. Most critics do not see the facts at all.

—*February* 9, 1929

. . . it is obvious that the ordinary modern critic is entirely ignorant of history as a whole.

—*May* 2, 1931

Most people who curse Rousseau have never read Rousseau, or have only read the "Confessions" and not the "Contrat Social." The critics read the "Confessions," if only to condemn them; because the critics themselves are modern romantics and sentimentalists; men who like confessions and dislike contracts.

—*May* 2, 1931

Of course, any critic can complain of any anthology that some of his own favourites have been left out. He may sometimes even claim that some that are not on the high level of the anthology have been put in. As the critic skims an ordinary anthology to find an item which he can condemn as a blemish, so here the critic may pounce upon something that is not sufficiently half-witted to satisfy his high standard, and sternly point to several passages that are not so bad as they should be.

—*July* 18, 1931

Critics describe how much they dislike things, rather than why they dislike them. It is still supposed by many to be old-fashioned to dogmatise about dogmatic things, such as dogmas; but the new fashion is to dogmatise about undogmatic things, about mere likes and dislikes, about things that cannot be stated as dogmas even by the dogmatists.

—*September* 26, 1931

Critic (Progressive)

They always talk as if there were a simple artistic progress in history; so that, if they see something in it, their sons and grandsons will see more. But it is already doubtful if there is any such simple progress in politics; it is certain that there is no such simple progress in art. What there is, is a series of revolutions and reactions. . . . It is very likely that it will seem much more of a monster to our grandsons than to our grandfathers. Our grandsons may regard it as the first Renaissance pedants of the classic style regarded as gargoyle.

—*June* 6, 1925

Criticism (New)

In some ways there may have been a growth of good taste, but its chief mark is a growth of accusations of bad taste. Everybody is fastidious about everybody else; but, though so many noses are turned up at everything, there seems to be no rule except that everybody is to follow his nose.

—*September* 26, 1931

Cromwell, Oliver

The best case for Cromwell is that he was a moderately sane man in a very insane age. His best work was done as a moderator and maker of compromises; not as an originator or inspirer of enthusiasms. He saved works of art which the wilder Puritans would have destroyed; but we cannot picture him as a great patron of art in the sense of a friend of artists. He insisted that there must be good pay for good soldiers; but he was not the sort of man to be a romance to his own soldiers, like Napoleon. He was a seventeenth-century English squire, whose family had grown rich in the great pillage; and morally he was no worse than most of his kind.

—*October* 18, 1924

He was a born soldier; that is, he was born a sensible man, in the rather special sense of using his senses. He was what modern people call objective. And, though his own religion might be almost morbidly subjective, he could not look at much of the religion round him as an object without seeing that it was a rather deplorable object. Thus he became, it seems to me, in some aspects almost as much the great anti-Puritan as the great Puritan.

—*January* 21, 1928

The Cross

In criticising Christian symbolism, they talk much of dead churches and decaying creeds; they talk of a creed as a cant. But their own talk is itself a cant. They do not dislike the Cross because it is a dead symbol; but because it is a live symbol.

—*September* 20, 1919

Crusade

Men have fallen into the habit of talking about a crusade for anything or against anything. I remember a paper called the *Crusader* that was in favour of prohibition; which would have puzzled Richard or Raymond not a little. Considering that the Moslems were prohibitionists and the crusaders were not, the title was a little odd. But, as I say, men can talk now of a crusade against anything. They are quite capable of talking about a crusade against the Cross.

—*December* 27, 1924

Crusades

So far from the world merely moving on doubtfully towards a world state, it has been for nearly a thousand years moving away from one. There was once some thing very like a world state consisting of most, if not all, of the then known world—in the Roman empire; and there was once a league of nations, consisting of most, if not all, of the states now called national—in the Crusades.

—April 20, 1918

Culture

It is a knowledge of the roots and real origins; it is what the Roman poet meant by saying that he who knows the causes of things is happy.

—April 16, 1927

The whole conception of culture is bound up with that first fact about man; that he is not himself until he has added to himself certain things which are, in a sense, outside himself. As he is more powerful than any other creature with those things, so he is more helpless than any other creature without those things.

—January 10, 1931

Culture (Cosmopolitan)

...too much of cosmopolitan culture is a mere praise of machinery. It turns ultimately upon the point that a telegram can be sent from one end of the earth to the other, irrespective of what is in the telegram; that a man can talk on the telephone from China to Peru, irrespective of whether he talks Chinese metaphysics or Chinese morals.

—December 7, 1918

Culture (European versus Asian)

Now, it is really in the matter of ideas that our own civilisation is superior. There are some who do not believe this, because they always assume that deep ideas must be depressing ideas. They cannot bring themselves to believe, what is the truth, that the deepest of all ideas are inspiring ideas. Of those courageous and invigorating conceptions, the conceptions that make life possible to live, Christendom has had infinitely more than any other culture; more of the idea of free-will; more of the idea of personal chivalry and charity; more of the clean wind of hope. The metaphysics and morals of these things have been worked out by our fathers fully as deeply and delicately as any of the dark and disenchanted metaphysics of Asia.

—April 23, 1927

Culture (Modern)

Under all its parade of novelty, the modern world really runs to monotony, partly because it runs to monopoly. There are, indeed, some signs of breaking away here and there, but the momentum of the immediate past, at least, is entirely monopolist and monotonous. The culture of the nineteenth century went in ruts, just as the traffic of the nineteenth century went on rails. . . . I fear that, in the country where he was first provided with a Ford car, he is less than anywhere provided with a free mind. There, certainly, the culture is as much standardised as the car.

—May 14, 1927

There are many modern things called culture which one would be glad to see destroyed by Goths and Vandals, let alone by mild modern Germans, who do whatever they are told. There are many modern books, advertised as masterpieces of literary art, which I should be glad to see destroyed by rats and worms, let alone Hitlerites. There are many idiotic experiments in nakedness, in the northern climate of Europe, which might well be exterminated by germs, let alone by Germans.

—August 5, 1933

Cure (Moral)

. . . the essence of medical cure is that a man is a patient. But the essence of moral cure is that the patient must be an *impatient*. Nothing can be done unless he hates his own sin more than he loves his own pleasure. The distinction can be put simply in one sentence. A man can be cured of appendicitis while he is insensible. Can he be cured of theft while he is insensible?

—July 11, 1908

114

Curfew

But the other process of Temperance Reform, the limitation of the hours, is, I think, not only useless, but eminently calculated to defeat its own object. And here, again, it is no good discussing the thing with practical politicians: for it is not a question of the desires of men. God knows what practical politicians drink—petrol, I should think. But men inclined for moderate drinking are definitely encouraged to immoderate drinking by the shortening of hours. Anyone can see this who will sit and think for a minute, not about statistics, but about souls. Do not think of human nature as if you were making a law: think of it as if you were writing a novel. Think how people really feel. If you do you will see that to limit by the clock the time for drinking alcohol is to make normal people think a great deal more about alcohol than they ought to. Remember, in heaven's name, that alcoholism is a nervous habit: and looking at the clock makes people nervous. A man who might have drunk one glass of beer without knowing it and gone away arguing with his friend, takes three glasses of beer because it is three hours before he can get another.

—June 6, 1908

Curiosity

Curiosity is always rebuked as one of the restless weaknesses of humanity, but I am inclined to think that most people are not inquisitive enough. They have not what I may call clean curiosity—a mere appetite for the truth. They cannot be interested and disinterested too. They are not really concerned about their neighbours, except when they are quarrelling with their neighbours, or making love to their neighbours, or house-visiting in search of votes, or house-breaking in search of spoons.

—July 25, 1914

Cynic

... the man talking nonsense, that ornament of society, will generally be most valuable when he is frivolous and least valuable when he is serious. Cynicism is healthy in proportion to its levity, like pastry. But a solemn cynic is a loathsome thing, lowering the whole level of life.

—July 6, 1929

Cynic (Modern)

People are positively nervous about mentioning duty or conscience or religion, because of the high-strung and delicately poised sanity of the new sort of cynic. It is not altogether as a joke that he tells you that, if you say such words, he will scream. . . . This is something more than a perversity . . . and an inversion which amounts to a sort of mental malformation. If our aunts ought to have been able to hear of immorality without fainting, surely our nephews might brace themselves to hear about morality without throwing an epileptic fit.

—March 4, 1933

D–E–F

Dancing

Why should dancing be the only thing that people will not take any trouble to do properly? The act of moving one's limbs to music is absolutely primary; everyone tries to do it when he hears a barrel-organ. Why should young men who would not dare to break a little bye-law of lawn-tennis or croquet think the laws of dancing only made to be broken? Is it only because dancing is (unlike croquet) really beautiful, and a part of all the old religions of mankind? Dancing has slowly turned from a serious thing into a flippant one.

—August 25, 1906

Notice all the most typical changes which society has made to suit its latest conceptions of ease and convenience, and you will see in almost every case that they consist, not in abolishing luxury, but in abolishing all the manly or generous things that happened to be connected with luxury. For instance, everyone will tell you that dancing is on the decline. Dancing is on the decline because it was the one wholesome and honourable thing in the fashionable world. Evening dress has not declined, except in the sense that with some ladies it has fallen considerably lower. Stupid breastplates of starch have not declined. Silly little waistcoats which begin at a man's waist have not declined. There is no modification of the mad luxury of the dresses or the refreshments. There is no simplification of things. The only thing that is being dropped is dancing—because it is simple. The only reform of aristocracy consists in abolishing the one hearty and human thing which is also done by a peasant and a peasant girl. The luxurious class is only abandoning one luxury. And that is the one luxury that is really a poem as well as a pleasure.

—May 23, 1908

Dark Ages

When ... a critic says, for instance, that faith kept the world in darkness until doubt led to enlightenment, he is himself taking things on faith, things that he has never been sufficiently enlightened to doubt. ... Certainly there were dark ages following on the decline of the old pagan civilisation; but it is quite the reverse of self-evident that it was through religion that the civilisation declined. It is quite the reverse of the truth that it was by religion that the ages were darkened. It was by religion alone that they were illuminated, as far as they were illuminated at all. It is as if a riot were to wreck all the lamp-posts because street-lamps brought on the fog. It is as if a man were to blow out all the candles with one blast of fury, on the ground that they had encouraged the sun to set.

—February 13, 1926

Darwinism

Darwinism was made the scientific excuse for a moral anarchy which Darwin never defended and Huxley splendidly denounced, but which was, for all that, the great practical popular effect of the work of Darwin and Huxley. Thousands of business men excused themselves for brutality and cynicism by a vague notion of a newly discovered law of life. Darwinism was a failure as a true philosophy; but it was a success as a false religion.

—May 29, 1920

... Darwinism became a fashion long before anybody really thought it was a fact.

—October 11, 1930

Darwinism and Freudism

It is obvious that there is an element of evolution in nature; and that there is an element of unconsciousness in human nature. But the actual effect of Darwinism, on the generation following Darwin, was only a vague fashionable feeling that everything was evolution and that evolution was everything. The same thing will probably happen in the case of the conjectures of Freud, and there will be the same tendency to let a hypothesis harden into a dogma. ... Fashionable Darwinism seemed to remember everything about the missing link except that he was missing.

118

Fashionable Freudism will remember everything about the unconscious mind except that it is unconscious.

— May 29, 1920

Death

Black is dark with absence of colour; violet is dark with density and combination of colour: it is at once as blue as midnight and as crimson as blood. And there is a similar distinction between the two views of death, between the two types of tragedy. There is the tragedy that is founded on the worthlessness of life; and there is the deeper tragedy that is founded on the worth of it. The one sort of sadness says that life is so short that it can hardly matter; the other that life is so short that it will matter for ever.

— June 4, 1910

There is nothing about which the snob has more often mocked the mob than about what he would call the morbid taste of the poor for funerals. But it is the snob who is morbid and the mob that is healthy. This idea of a decent familiarity with death is far more manly than the plutocratic optimism that hides a horrid secret of pessimism. To fear death is normal; but to have a horror of the subject of death is an unnatural growth of luxury; scorned by the mob as by the ritual of monarchy. Those processions of men silently saluting the end of a good man, who had come at last to peace, were not afraid of facing that peace to which they too would come.

— February 1, 1936

Debate

Let us remember, as our fathers did, that there is such a thing as argument, and it is not the same thing as advertisement. Let us recall that there was an art of public oratory that was not the art of publicity. A man like Sir Robert Peel, for instance . . . argued on both sides of a good many questions. But he argued: he did not merely tell people to "rally" to this or "roll up" for that. He did not think that a head-line was a substitute for a definition, or that an incomplete sentence was as good as a complete system. If we cannot have fundamental debates on primary questions, we can at least have rational debates on practical questions.

— June 7, 1930

Debates (Broadcasting)

The first impulse of an enlightened person on hearing the proposal to broadcast the debates of Parliament is merely that it is one of the typical triumphs of modern science. It is telling us that everybody can listen to what nobody wants to hear.

—April 4, 1925

Debs, Eugene

The only thing I ever heard about him, beyond his leadership of American socialism and his candidature for the American presidency, was a story so entertaining that I fear it must be quite untrue. It was stated, I believe, in some sketch of American strikes in the old *Review of Reviews,* that Mr. Debs was a religious mystic of a rather remarkable kind. He thought the Messiah was incarnate, not merely in himself, but conjointly in him and a socialist comrade of his. The best part of the story, considered merely as a story, was that the other socialist strongly objected to this arrangement. He presumably preferred being one whole human being to being half a superhuman being—in which he has my entire sympathy.

—June 7, 1919

Decadence

An American millionaire gave a freak-dinner, if I remember right, in which the guests had to eat and drink sitting on horses. It is not humorous, it is not exciting, it is not beautiful, it is not even fancifully suggestive; it is simply unusual that guests should eat their dinner sitting on horses. It would be still more unusual if they sat on camels. It would be yet more odd if they sat on whales. It would be odder still if the whales sat on them; and I think, upon the whole, that that would be the most satisfactory termination to the entertainment.

—March 24, 1906

Declaration of Independence

The Declaration of Independence was a philosophy drawn up for men who did not yet exist; but that philosophy was a religion, in the most real sense, for multitudes of men who really existed. It embodied itself in real saints and heroes as much as the Gospel or the Koran. For instance, in all the talk there has been lately about Abraham Lincoln, there has been very little appreciation of the fundamental fact that he did understand the Declaration and did believe in it. . . . The English often find it harder to understand great ideas, and easier to understand great men. But in this case the great man is really unintelligible without the great idea . . . and in nothing was he more distinct from an Englishman than in this fact that he felt his country to be founded on a theory. And it cannot be too clearly comprehended that this attitude which distinguished him is really a distinction.

—January 8, 1921

De-Constructionism

The notion that mere doubt, which is only timid and indefinite destruction, can be a positive pleasure and a substitute for all other pleasures, is crazy enough to anyone who knows what more creative or constructive pleasures can be. But, crazy as it is, it could not even be conveyed to the mind of the reader if there were not some "certitude" about the meaning of the word that he reads. All this special sort of scepticism is not merely engaged in destroying or devouring life; it is engaged in destroying and devouring itself. Its own method would exterminate its own mood; and it could not even continue its own unnatural intellectual life if it were conducted in the full light of intellect.

—January 31, 1931

Delusion

A man who mistakenly supposes himself a prophet is, after all, in the same world with a man who mistakenly supposes himself a poet.

—June 6, 1919

Demagogue and Mystagogue

The demagogue succeeds because he makes himself understood, even if he is not worth understanding. But the mystagogue succeeds because he gets himself misunderstood; although, as a rule, he is not even worth misunderstanding.

—January 25, 1908

Democracy

I am afraid it must be frankly confessed that representatives do not represent; that politicians do not resemble the respectable working-classes in anything—except their highly respectable objection to work.

—November 20, 1909

If you dig deep enough into any ancient ceremony, you will find the traces of that noble truism called democracy, which is not the latest but the earliest of human ideas.

—May 28, 1910

... Democracy is a very deep and a very ancient thing. Democracy can ultimately force its way through anything—even through representative government ... even elected Parliaments cannot keep it down.

—January 20, 1917

I do believe in democracy. Since I happen to believe in it, I happen to know what it is. I believe that, though all human governments are faulty, that is least faulty in which the commonest sort of men can ask most directly for what they want and get it; and where they are least at the mercy of a superior class, even though it really is mercy.

—May 5, 1917

... the real difficulty of democracy is not that the voters are unworthy, but that their vote is generally the least worthy thing about them. When they are not defending their country they are earning their living, or educating their children, or falling in love, or finding salvation, or doing some other thing more interesting than politics, so that the latter is left for politicians as the only people too dull to be bored by it. Hence we find everywhere very unpopular persons powerful in politics when they are quite impotent in every other department.

—June 30, 1917

... "democracy" happens to be a word used more lightly in journalese than in Greek—or English.

—*October 6*, 1917

I really think the time has come to make some protest against this unfortunate political term being repeated in so ceaseless and senseless a fashion. As it is, it is employed anywhere because it is employed to mean anything.

—*June 7*, 1919

If our government were really a representative government, it would certainly not be a meddlesome government. No man wants a merely meddlesome law applied to himself; and most men are sufficiently generous to apply the golden rule at least so far as it is concerned with leaving alone and being left alone. There does exist, but only in a minority, the meanest of all forms of morality. There does exist a kind of citizen, fortunately a rare kind of citizen, who will make an unjust law for his neighbours in the hope of evading it for himself.

—*November 15*, 1924

Democracy came to an end when everybody adopted it. It became something like the "true Christianity" which can include every sort of heathenry. When a word can be adopted by all parties, it means that it has ceased to be anything except a word.

—*December 20*, 1924

... there have been very few times in history when the idea of democracy, as distinct from the name of democracy, has been less understood or valued than it has been in our own time. People have lived under various forms of government which were in certain ways more arbitrary than our own. But in many ways even our own is quite exceptionally arbitrary. People in the past would have been astounded to be told that children could not stay in their own homes to help their own parents, but were driven by the policeman to go to a particular kind of school.

—*December 19*, 1925

A democracy can be distinguished, if its citizens are distinguishable; if each has an area of choice in which he really chooses. To keep that area of choice as large as possible is the real function of freedom.

—January 4, 1930

I read in any number of new leaders and labour weeklies, and all sorts of papers supposed to be both progressive and popular, that the working-classes will now take over the government of the country; that the majority of manual workers will have their proper proportional right to rule in all matters of education and humanitarian reform; that the poor will at least inherit the earth. But if I say that one workman is capable of deciding about the education of one child, that he has the right to select a certain school or resist a certain system, I shall have all those progressive papers roaring at me as a rotten reactionary.

—May 31, 1930

We all remember the tragedy and the triumph that will be always associated with the phrase about "making the world safe for democracy." Nothing so much threatens the safety of democracy as assuming that democracy is safe.

—August 22, 1931

... at the moment, democracy is not only being abused, but being very unfairly abused. Men are blaming universal suffrage, merely because they are not enlightened enough to blame original sin. There is one simple test for deciding whether popular political evils are due to original sin. And that is to do what none or very few of these modern malcontents are doing; to state any sort of moral claim for any other sort of political system.

—July 16, 1932

The essence of democracy is very simple and, as Jefferson said, self-evident. If ten men are wrecked together on a desert island, the community consists of those ten men, their welfare is the social object, and normally their will is the social law. If they have not a natural claim to rule themselves, which of them has a natural claim to rule the rest? To say that the cleverest or boldest will rule is to beg the moral question. If his talents are used for the community ... then he is the servant of the community; which is ... his sovereign. If his talents are used against the community, by stealing rum ... why should the community submit to him? And is it in the least likely that it will? In such a simple case as that, everybody can see the popular basis of the thing, and the advantage of government by consent. The trouble with democracy is that it has never, in modern times, had to do with such a simple case as that. In other words, the trouble with democracy is not democracy. It is certain artificial anti-democratic things that have, in fact, thrust themselves into the modern world to thwart and destroy democracy.

—July 16, 1932

It grows plainer, every day, that those of us who cling to crumbling creeds and slogans, and defend the dying traditions of the dark ages, will soon be left alone defending the most obviously decaying of all those ancient dogmas: the idea called democracy. It has taken not quite a lifetime, roughly my own lifetime, to bring it from the top of its success, or alleged success, to the bottom of its failure, or reputed failure. By the end of the nineteenth century, millions of men were accepting democracy without knowing why. By the end of the twentieth century, it looks as if millions of people would be rejecting democracy, also without knowing why. In such a straight, strictly logical and unwavering line does the mind of man advance along the great path of progress.

—July 16, 1932

Now, there is a primary principle of democracy, though most modern democrats do not know it. And it is a just one . . . justice. Its ultimate nature might be stated thus: that man corporate, like man individual, has an indestructible right of self-defence. If it is normal for men to live in a society, that society has a right to live, and may, acting as a society, ward off danger and death. In one sense a man has a right to himself; in another sense a nation has a right to itself. It is not bound to be infinitely oppressed or pillaged, by foes . . . without or by traitors . . . within. And there is a real and reasonable sense, if we think the thing out, in which it is the ultimate judge of whether it is being destroyed or no. The difficulty has always been in the finding of true self-expression for a whole people.

—December 3, 1932

The actual effect of what we call democracy has been the disappearance of the mob. We might say there were mobs at the beginning of the revolution and no mobs at the end of it.

—November 25, 1933

Democracy (American)

... an American politician to-day does not say: "I salute the awful authority of the people, which rules itself by the light of reason and justice." He only says: "If I can carry California, I'm practically safe for the whole of the southwest." He is talking about means and not ends, still less origins. The enormous mass of technical teaching and discussion that gathers round an American presidential election, the libraries of statistics, the labyrinths of strategy, show that in one sense democracy has become a fine art, but only in the sense of becoming a rather low craft. But next to nobody, speaking with simplicity and sincerity, goes back to the original reasons for democracy; it is simply taken for granted.

—December 3, 1932

Democracy (Contemporary)

... it is, we shall, perhaps, be wise if we call it the cant of the hour, and recognise that that there is a sort of fashion—*not* of being democratic, but of talking democratically.

—November 3, 1917

Democracy (English)

The English are no nearer than they were a hundred years ago to knowing what Jefferson really meant when he said that God had created all men equal.

—March 1, 1924

Demonstrators

I should advise modern agitators, therefore, to give up this particular method: the method of making very big efforts to get a very small punishment. It does not really go down at all; the punishment is too small, and the efforts are too obvious. It has not any of the effectiveness of the old savage martyrdom; because it does not leave the victim absolutely alone with his cause, so that his cause alone can support him. At the same time it has about it that element of the pantomimic and the absurd, which was the cruellest part of the slaying and the mocking of the real prophets. St. Peter was crucified upside down as a huge inhuman joke; but his human seriousness survived the inhuman joke, because, in whatever posture, he had died for his faith.

—February 8, 1908

Despotism

Where despotism really is successful is in very small matters. Everyone must have noticed how essential a despot is to arranging the things in which everyone is doubtful, because everyone is indifferent: the boats in a water picnic or the seats at a dinner-party. Here the man who knows his own mind is really wanted. . . . because no one cares where he goes. It is for trivialities that the great tyrant is meant. But when the depths are stirred in a society, and all men's souls grow taller in a transfiguring anger or desire, then I am by no means so certain that the great man has been a benefit even when he has appeared. . . . I am by no means sure that Napoleon gave a better turn to the whole French Revolution. I am by no means so sure that Cromwell has really improved the religion of England.

—October 8, 1910

Detective Stories

. . . detective stories, being fictitious, are much more purely rational than detective events in actual life. Sherlock Holmes could only exist in fiction; he is too logical for real life. In real life he would have *guessed* half his facts a long time before he had deduced them.

—November 4, 1905

The true object of an intelligent detective story is not to baffle the reader, but to enlighten the reader; but to enlighten him in such a manner that each successive portion of the truth comes as a surprise. In this, as in much nobler types of mystery, the object of the true mystic is not merely to mystify, but to illuminate. The object is not darkness, but light; but light in the form of lightning.

—August 28, 1920

The essence of a mystery tale is that we are suddenly confronted with a truth which we have never suspected and yet can see to be true.

—October 18, 1930

The detective story differs from every other story in this: that the reader is only happy if he feels a fool.

—*October* 25, 1930

Determinist (Economic)

I should rather like him to answer me a little question of mine; which is: "If the mind is manufactured by conditions and cannot correct itself, how can a Bolshevist be sure that his own Bolshevism is any more correct than anything else?"

—*March* 3, 1923

Dictator

A dictator has to be a demagogue; a man like Mussolini cannot be ashamed to shout. He cannot afford to be a mere gentleman. His whole power depends on convincing the populace that he knows what he wants, and wants it badly.

—*June* 1, 1929

Dictatorship of the Proletariat

The expression "dictatorship of the proletariat" is an entirely meaningless phrase. Most highly modern and advanced phrases are.... As a description of a form of society, it is simply a contradiction in terms. There is no sense in a utopia called "omnipotence of omnibus conductors" ... it is still safe to say that if the man were omnipotent he would not be an omnibus conductor. In short, the fact that a man is a proletarian is a proof that he is not yet a dictator; and the fact that a man is a dictator is a proof that he is no longer a proletarian.

—*July* 12, 1919

The dictatorship of the proletariat will never be the dictatorship of the proletariat, but it might be the dictatorship of a few proletarians. It is much more likely to be the dictatorship of a few prigs. But it must be a dictatorship, or it would have no chance of doing even the good that it claims to do.

—*October* 10, 1925

Dictionary

The Encyclopaedists were no more impartial than the Bolshevists. They were a band of fighters determined to uproot and renew. And though the making of a dictionary sounds to us a mild occupation, Dr. Johnson was by no means a mild person, and sometimes almost made it a slang dictionary, when he had a chance of slanging the Whigs.

—July 14, 1928

Digestion

There is all that queer inversion of values in talking about music as an aid not only to dinner, but even to the digestion of dinner.

—September 29, 1923

Dignity

... the two things that a healthy person hates most between heaven and hell are a woman who is not dignified and a man who is.

—March 21, 1908

Dignity versus Hypocrisy

There is more dignity in a man who surrenders to a brigand, or even to a blackmailer, than there is in a liar who covers the brigandage by calling it brotherhood; or in a hypocrite who pompously pretends that the blackmailer is a beggar, that he may be seen of men to give alms.

—September 1, 1917

Diplomacy

... if diplomacy ever is democratic, it will not be cosmopolitan; it will not be, in the sense intended by the intellectuals, even international. If it is in the least popular, it will be very national. Does anybody believe that when an agricultural labourer from Hampshire or Berkshire enlists and fights and dies, he does it for any political combination except England, or appeals to any international tribunal except God? . . . . I do not think he ever will be, or ever ought to be, taught to forget his county and his country in favour of some piece of world-politics worked by wire-pullers at the Hague.

—July 13, 1918

Diplomat

There are (I am told) honest diplomatists; and it is quite certain, after the perusal of some police news, that there are dishonest detectives. But the vital pride and dignity of a detective is that he reveals secrets; that of a diplomatist, that he keeps them.

—April 2, 1910

The old assumption of the approximate impossibility of war really rested on a similar assumption about the impossibility of evil—and especially of evil in high places. The criminal of the slums, with his heredity and environment, was the villain of realistic fiction. But the diplomatist of the melodrama, with his evening dress and his diamond ring, has been the villain of practical politics.

—September 22, 1917

Somebody made the signal for that slaughter; somebody has originated every step of that decline. As it happens, we know who it was; but, whoever it was, he is now talking the language of the loftiest and most compassionate philanthropy.

—October 6, 1917

Direction (Criminal)

Where there is a popular religion and a recognised law of life, the opposition to it will be merely lawless, and a great deal of it will be merely senseless. But we have passed through a time of transition when even a sensible man might well be a sceptic, and when a sceptic might well be an anarchist. For mind as much as machinery depends for its good or evil not on its force, but on its direction. But if really educated and enlightened men have more and more turned in a criminal direction, there will be a great augmentation of the criminal force; and it will not be altogether surprising if it is sometimes too much for the police force.

—April 1, 1922

Disadvantage

. . . it is not always a disadvantage to have disadvantages.

—June 20, 1925

Discipline

. . . to produce real discipline a man must have some of the virtues of demagogue.

—January 20, 1927

Discovery

We have all heard of discoveries made by chance, and many of them, I imagine, must have been made by men who had already approached near to them by design.

—September 19, 1925

Discussion (Modern)

Discussion in the old decisive and systematic sense seems to have disappeared from our bewildered politics and journalism.

—October 10, 1931

Divorce

. . . if you say that marriage is for common people, but divorce for free and noble spirits, all the weak and selfish people will dash for the divorce; while the few free and noble spirits you wish to help will very probably (because they are free and noble) go on wrestling with the marriage. For it is one of the marks of real dignity of character not to wish to separate oneself from the honour and tragedy of the whole tribe. All men are ordinary men; the extraordinary men are those who know it.

—June 25, 1910

Divorce is a thing which the newspapers now not only advertise, but advocate, almost as if it were a pleasure in itself.

— September 2, 1922

I have always felt it in the conventionalised laxity of fashionable divorce, where people want to change their partners as rapidly as at a dance, and yet want again and again to thrill at the heroic finality of the sacramental vow, which is like the sound of a trumpet. They want to eat their wedding-cake and have it.

—August 20, 1927

... the point of divorce is not that people are professing to be reckless, but that people are pretending to be respectable.

—October 5, 1929

Divorce (Age of)

It [the world] cannot understand that divine paradox whereby two things become one and yet remain two; or the notion of their increasing each other's effect by something that is much more subtle than simple addition. The world has become a sort of wild divorce court, not only for individuals, but also for ideas. And even those whose beliefs or unbeliefs make them indifferent to the idea that those whom God hath joined become one flesh may be willing to consider the thesis that the thoughts which man has joined can become one fact.

—August 25, 1928

Divorce and Murder

Divorce and murder are both desperate remedies; but it is quite in the spirit of the age that they should be treated as universal remedies.

—October 19, 1929

Doctrine versus Ideal

Our fathers understood a thing called a doctrine; that is, a thing in which they did or did not believe. Our fathers also understood a thing called a duty; that is, a thing which they did or did not do, but which they recognised the rightness of doing, and even of doing promptly and properly . . . the slimy, slippery, sneakish ideal gets past both these old arresting conceptions. An ideal is not a thing you are required to believe in, in the old sense of believing that it really exists. On the contrary, for many modern idealists, it is a thing that is only called an ideal because it does not exist. It is at best a possibility, or perhaps only a pattern or abstract method of measurement. The less it is a reality, the more it is an ideal. . . .

—January 28, 1933

Dogma

The word is generally used, I think, solely for the sake of its sound. It has a short, ugly sound, like a gruff bark. Indeed, "dogma" is probably confused unconsciously with "mad dog."

—March 14, 1925

Dogma (Modern)

The special mark of the modern world is not that it is sceptical, but that it is dogmatic without knowing it. It says, in mockery of old devotees, that they believed without knowing why they believed. But the moderns believe without knowing what they believe—and without even knowing that they do believe it. Their freedom consists in first freely assuming a creed, and then freely forgetting that they are assuming it. In short, they always have an unconscious dogma; and an unconscious dogma is the definition of a prejudice.

—March 15, 1919

What seems to me to infect the modern world is a sort of swollen pride in the possession of modern thought or free thought or higher thought, combined with a comparative neglect of thought. So long as certain atmospheric phrases are adopted, or avoided, it does not seem to matter so much what is the actual substance of the statement. Certain turns of diction are marked down as progressive or provocative or obstructive or complimentary or uncomplimentary, long

133

before anybody troubles to consider the smaller problem of whether they are true.

—August 16, 1930

Dogmas

The real question is not whether we can teach without being dogmatic. It is not whether we can be dogmatic without dogmas. These questions are really contradictions in terms. The real question is whether we have any right to teach at all.

—June 28, 1924

Doing Nothing

... the most precious, the most consoling, the most pure and holy, the noble habit of doing nothing at all—that is being neglected in a degree which seems to me to threaten the degeneration of the whole race. It is because artists do not practice, patrons do not patronise, crowds do not assemble to worship reverently the great work of doing nothing, that the world has lost its philosophy and even failed to invent a new religion.

—July 23, 1927

Doubt

... if it is a joy to doubt anything, and the joy is the only justification of anything, there seems no possible reason why we should not doubt that Anatole France doubted; or doubt that Renan and Montaigne doubted; or doubt that Renan and Montaigne ever lived. And if we are justified by the sheer joy of doubt in doubting everything; if (in other words) we cannot really have proof of anything, what in the world is the sense of calling something a "proof-positive"?

—January 31, 1931

Doyle, Sir Arthur Conan

When all is said and done, there have never been better detective stories than the old series of Sherlock Holmes; and though the name of that magnificent magician has been spread over the whole world, and is perhaps the one great popular legend

134

made in the modern world, I do not think that Sir Arthur Conan Doyle has ever been thanked enough for them. As one of many millions, I offer my own mite of homage.

—August 19, 1922

Dragon

The first essay I ever wrote was on the subject of dragons; and I was an object of hearty and healthy derision among my schoolfellows because it began with the somewhat pedantic sentence: "The dragon is the most cosmopolitan of impossibilities." I am not sure that I was justified in jumping to the conclusion that the monster was cosmopolitan, though certainly that would be a sufficient justification for killing him. I could still enjoy with enthusiasm an epic in which St. George should kill the dragon of cosmopolitanism. Dragons are found in the decorative and imaginative work of almost all nations and ages; and that is all I meant by the pompous and polysyllabic impertinence of calling him cosmopolitan. But I do profoundly repent and repudiate the childish superstition which led me into calling him impossible.

—September 18, 1926

Drama (Modern)

... the trapdoor has been left open for the demon and the skylight has been locked against the fairy. We have had plays opening abysses of insane scepticism and despair, but not, as in the old tragedies and epics, any voice speaking in judgment, or in the name of order and light.

—April 2, 1927

I noted recently that modern drama, coldly contemptuous of melodrama, had solemnly banished the old fiction of the soliloquy or the aside; and then, equally solemnly, brought them back again, pretending they are a new futuristic technique for permitting people's subconsciousness to talk out loud without being heard.

—April 8, 1933

Dream

When poor old Herbert Spencer still had influence, it was often suggested that dreams were the origin of religion. To such thinkers, it would be a mere trifle to amend it by saying that religion was the origin of dreams.

—April 4, 1931

Dreams (Interpretations of)

There are doubtless a great many valuable truths to be learned by the interpretation of dreams, if these people could only keep awake to interpret them. But the first necessity for studying the unconscious mind is to possess a mind of some sort, and preferably a conscious mind—especially a mind that is conscious, or at least dimly conscious, of a joke. Without that perception we shall merely plunge into another passing flood of pessimism and morbidity; and those who profess to be explaining dreams will only be experiencing nightmares.

—May 29, 1926

Drink

. . . the question of drink is an entirely sentimental question. The man who drinks wine or beer with his friends does it from a good sentiment. The man who drinks absinthe or whisky by himself does it from a detestable sentiment. But they are both sentimentalists: they both wish to achieve a certain state of the emotions. And the real mistake of the practical politician who treats this question is simply that he tries to treat it practically. You might as well try to treat sunsets practically.

—June 6, 1908

. . . all drink is divided into two inspirations, conviviality and morbidity.

—June 6, 1908

Duel

The duel is always a confession of equality, and especially the duel to the death. For, undesirable as death is, and as we all (for various reasons) feel it to be, there is no doubt about the equality. The one and only advantage of the duel in the countries where it is practised is that you or I, the most powerless and broken man, may walk up to the most powerful person in Europe and ask him, with the utmost politeness, to die.

—August 8, 1914

Dullness

. . . dullness can be a stimulant.

—May 3, 1930

Eastern Wisdom

Eastern wisdom has a natural attraction for astonishingly stupid people. It is also true that some sorts of Eastern wisdom actually make them stupider.

—June 4, 1927

Eating

Thinking men can no longer accept the ancient creeds and ecclesiastical dogmas which taught them that the virtues of an enemy whom they had eaten passed into their own bodies; the belief lingers in various forms in the common practice of eating beef and mutton, in the hope of thus absorbing the energy of the bull and the innocence of the sheep. And the modern Englishman, eating eggs and bacon at breakfast, hardly guesses that his real motive for doing so is a desire to partake mystically of the higher virtues of the pig or the bolder qualities of the chicken.

—April 4, 1931

Editor

. . . editors have no other purpose on this planet except to attack politicians. . . .

—November 12, 1910

Educated

It is the curse of our epoch that the educated are uneducated, especially in the study of history—which is only the study of humanity.

—*March 22*, 1919

A man who cannot read or write may be essentially educated. But a man who can only read and write is not educated at all. In some social conditions these things are artifices not necessary to a man's culture; in other conditions they are art required to complete his culture. But a boy who has learned these things, without much simpler things, is like a girl who has gone to a finishing school and not to any other school. He has been finished without having ever been begun.

—*November 6*, 1920

Why is it that for the last two or three centuries the educated have been generally wrong and the uneducated relatively right? It seems to me that the cultivated class has been actually more practically and pertinaciously mischievous than the ignorant whom they attempted to instruct. The ignorant would actually have been better off without them. What the educated man has generally done was to run down everybody's throat some premature and priggish theory which he himself afterwards discovered to be wrong; so wrong that he himself generally recoiled from it and went staggering to the opposite extreme. Meanwhile, the ignorant man reacted differently as soon as the theory had been rammed down his throat, by practically demonstrating that it made him sick.

—*August 9*, 1924

Education

But the business of education is to tell us of all the varying complications, of all the bewildering beauty of the past. Education commands us to know, as Arnold said, all the best literatures, all the best arts, all the best national philosophies. Education commands us to know them all that we may do without them all.

—*December 2*, 1905

Without education we are in a horrible and deadly danger of taking educated people seriously. The latest fads of culture, the latest sophistries of anarchism will carry us away if we are uneducated: we shall not know how very old are all new ideas. We shall think that Christian Science is really the whole of Christianity and the whole of Science. We shall think that art colours are really the only colours in art. The uneducated man will always care too much for complications, novelties, the fashion, the latest thing. The uneducated man will always be an intellectual dandy.

—December 2, 1905

Educational conferences are always interesting, for the simple reason that under the title of Education you can discuss anything whatever that comes into your head. This is the main fact which, in spite of all the talk on the subject of education, no one seems to notice in connection with it. The chief thing about the subject of education is that it is not a subject. There is no such thing as education. The thing is merely a loose phrase for the passing on to others of whatever truth or virtue we happen to have ourselves. It is typical of our time that the more doubtful we are about the value of philosophy the more certain we are about the value of education. That is to say, the more doubtful we are about whether we have any truth, the more certain we are (apparently) that we can teach it to children. The smaller our faith in doctrine, the larger is our faith in doctors.

—January 26, 1907

Education only means the first stage of some creed, some view of life.

—October 3, 1908

... what we require is the expansion of education, until it includes much older and wiser things. That is, we do not want to restrict the subjects of education to the teaching of writing or arithmetic; though we might well wish to restrict the powers of education, at least until it has something better to teach. But the upshot of it is that we need to have popular education in a sense at once more literal and more living; that of men who are ready to be taught by the populace, and not merely to teach it.

—November 6, 1920

In short, if education is really the larger matter, then certainly domestic life is the larger matter; and official or commercial life the lesser matter. . . . It is a mere matter of simple subtraction that the mother must have less time for the family if she has more time for the factory. If education, ethical and cultural, really were a trivial and mechanical matter, the mother might possibly rattle through it as a rapid routine, before going about her more serious business of serving a capitalist for hire. If education were merely instruction, she might briefly instruct her babies in the multiplication tables, before she mounted to higher and nobler spheres as the servant of a milk trust. . . . But the moderns are perpetually assuring us that education is not instruction . . . it is not a mechanical exercise, and must on no account be an abbreviated exercise. It must go on at every hour. It must cover every subject. But if it must go on at all hours, it must not be neglected in business hours.

—*August 5,* 1922

Education has any amount of new nonsense in her abundant store. But education is no substitute for a sane social philosophy; it may only mean teaching an insane one, and making a mad world.

—*July 5,* 1924

Education has become a word like abracadabra. It has become a magic word, a spell, a word of power. It is the sort of spell that was supposed to raise spirits, but it does not raise my spirits.

—*July 5,* 1924

What is education? Properly speaking, there is no such thing as education. Education is simply the soul of a society as it passes from one generation to another. Whatever the soul is like, it will have to be passed on somehow, consciously or unconsciously; and that transition may be called education. The culture, the colour and sentiment, the special knowledge and aptitude of a civilisation must not be lost, but must be left as a legacy. But all this tells us nothing about what the legacy is like.

—*July 5,* 1924

... We cannot settle education until we settle religion.

—September 20, 1924

To say that the moderns are half-educated may seem to be too complimentary by half. But in truth the trouble of the moment is concerned with something worse than half-education. It is a question of which half. It is a question of whether people get the right half or the wrong half of education. It is, above all, a question of whether they get the first half or the second.

—June 2, 1928

The moment men begin to care more for education than for religion, they begin to care more for ambition than for education. It is no longer a world in which the souls of all are equal before heaven, but a world in which the mind of each is bent on achieving unequal advantage over the other. There begins to be a mere vanity in being educated; whether it be self-educated or merely state-educated.

—April 26, 1930

Everybody ought to learn first such a general view of the history of man, of the nature of man, and (as I, for one, should add) of the nature of God, as to enable him to consider the rights and wrongs of slavery in a slave community, of cannibalism in a cannibal community, or of commerce in a commercial community. If he is immediately initiated into the mysteries of these institutions themselves, if he is sworn in infancy to take them as seriously as they take themselves ... even before he becomes a true citizen of his own town, he will never be able to denounce those institutions—or even to improve them. Such a state will never have the ideas or imagination to reform itself. ...

—March 29, 1930

I mean that to train a citizen is to train a critic. The whole point of education is that it should give a man abstract and eternal standards, by which he can judge material and fugitive conditions. If the citizen is to be a reformer, he must start with some ideal which he does not obtain merely by gazing reverently at the unreformed institutions.

—March 29, 1930

... fortunately, I had learned some truths in my childhood before I began to learn lies in my boyhood. And all my subsequent knowledge had led me to prefer the pictures which honestly professed to be picturesque to the plans and diagrams which dishonestly pretended to be accurate.

—February 14, 1931

... my schoolmasters did not tell me that the Puritan stood for religious loyalty, which is true. They told me that he stood for religious liberty, which is a lie of that mountainous and monstrous order which ignorant traditionalists call a whopper. They were not concerned, like the traditionalists, with gathering up, however lazily, the loose fragments of a truth. They were concerned with covering up most carefully the most accidental glimpses of the truth; with so picking their words and arranging their sentences that no suspicion of the main truth of the matter should really penetrate to the reader.

—February 14, 1931

The real world, that roars round the poor little gutter-boy as he goes to school, is an utterly anti-educational world. If the school is really giving any education, the world is certainly engaged day and night in ruining his education. For the world gives him things anyhow, in any order, with any result; the world gives him things without knowing that he gets them; the world gives him things meant for somebody else; the world throws things at him from morning till night, quite blindly, madly, and without meaning or aim; and this process, whatever else it is, is the exact opposite of the process of education. The gutter-boy spends about three-quarters of his time in getting uneducated. He is educated by the modern state school. He is uneducated by the modern state.

—May 28, 1932

Education (Business)

first ... training youth to earn a living is not education at all; second ... a specific training may keep the youngster from earning the best kind of living; and third ... it can't be done in school anyhow.

—March 29, 1930

Education (Compulsory)

... compulsory education. It is the great paradox of the modern world. It is the fact that at the very time when the world decided that people should not be coerced about their form of religion, it also decided that they should be coerced about their form of education.

—August 25, 1925

Education (Contemporary)

It is obviously most unjust that the old believer should be forbidden to teach his old beliefs, while the new believer is free to teach his new beliefs.

—August 8, 1925

Education (Liberal)

Every man ought to have read enough good literature to know when he is reading bad literature, and to go on reading it. He ought to have had what is rightly called a liberal education, that he may know the largest purposes to which human language has been put. But the object of a liberal education is to make him liberal, not merely to make him fastidious. He should be able to recognise the ideas that have been clarified and codified by the utterances of great men, when they appear in a more fragmentary fashion in the utterances of ordinary men. But if he has lost all interest in the utterances of ordinary men, he had far better not have been educated at all.

—October 9, 1920

... a man might possibly learn to appreciate machines from a book; whereas I gravely doubt whether the most patient pupil would ever learn to appreciate books from a machine.

—August 4, 1928

Education (Mediaeval)

If they only wished to keep the people in darkness, why did they not leave them in darkness? If they wished to rule them like children, why did they not confine them to childish things? Why was it necessary to their benighted schemes to teach their dupes to argue like Aristotle? Why, if they wished to restrict the world to the narrowest of Christian doctrines, did they elaborately spread before it the largest of heathen philosophies? Why did they, in short, in the most emphatic meaning of the words, invite it to participate? It seems to me more consonant to suppose that they felt something of the honourable pleasure that can enjoy reason and knowledge, and can impart them because it can enjoy them.

— September 25, 1920

Education (Modern)

Education is treated as a settlement; and yet, at the same time, education is treated as an experiment. It is imposed on everybody as a platitude; and yet it is free to take the most fantastic forms of paradox. First a politician tells us that all children must go to school; and then a professor tells us that all schools must be conducted in the tops of trees. At least, that is the sort of thing the professor tells us. And the situation becomes alarming when the professor is supported by the politicians and even by the policeman. Of course, there is no objection to the professor teaching his own family at the top of a tree; or even to his hopping back to them with a worm in his mouth. But when this is connected up with a compulsory system for the whole state it is very different.... A thing will be imposed on everybody before it has been explained to anybody.

— June 12, 1920

. . . modern education is in a peculiar sense compulsory education. It is enforced by fine and imprisonment on the whole populace. It does not only subjugate the mind; it also constrains the body. It does not only weed out from the schools the growth of actual heresy; it punishes all abstention from the schools where it teaches its orthodoxy. I am not going to discuss here the advantages or disadvantages of this modern system; but it is quite obvious that such a system takes the full responsibility of subjugating the mind.

— September 25, 1926

... because modern education begins with the modern man, instead of beginning with man, it begins of necessity at the wrong end. It brings out, of necessity, the wrong result; a ridiculous result.

—June 2, 1928

But I dislike it, not because I dislike education, but because, given the modern philosophy or absence of philosophy, education is turned against itself, destroying that very sense of variety and proportion which it is the object of education to give. No man who worships education has got the best out of education; no man who sacrifices everything to education is even educated. What is wrong is a neglect of principle; and the principle is that, without a gentle contempt for education, no gentleman's education is complete.

—April 26, 1930

In one sense, this is supremely the educational age. In another sense, it is supremely and specially the anti-educational age. It is the age in which the government's right to teach everybody's children is for the first time established. It is also the age in which the father's right to teach his own children is for the first time denied. It is the time in which experimentalists earnestly desire to teach a jolly little guttersnipe everything, even criminology and cosmic poise and the Maya system of decorative rhythm. But it is also the time in which earnest philosophers are really doubting whether it is right to teach anybody anything; even how to avoid taking poison or falling off precipices.

—May 28, 1932

Education (Non-sectarian)

In this country we have all grown heartily sick of the discussion about sectarian and unsectarian education.... As far as I can make out, the unsectarian schools do teach the religion of the sects, while the sectarian, or Church schools, don't teach the religion of the church.

—April 30, 1910

In short, the theory was that a Christian and a Mahometan might learn the same lessons in the same class, on ninety-nine subjects out of a hundred, so long as nobody mentioned Mahomet or mentioned Christ. It seems strange that nobody

145

noticed the limitations of such a view. Men do not, indeed, talk incessantly at every dance or dinner-party on the subject of Mahomet. But men do occasionally talk about wine. Men do even in their wilder moments talk about wives. And the Moslem and the Christian must either be taught separately about wine and wives; or they must be taught together at the expense of one religion or the other; or they must never be taught about wine or wives at all. The latter is what ought logically to follow from unsectarian education, though it seems a little defective as a detailed scheme of instruction about life.

—August 25, 1925

Education (Political)

... political education ... involves more than the three R's of robbery, rape, and ruins.

—May 12, 1917

Education (Secular)

... all education is religious education—and never more than when it is irreligious education. It either teaches a definite doctrine about the universe, which is theology; or else it takes one for granted, which is mysticism. If it does not do that it does nothing at all, and means nothing at all, for everything must depend upon some first principles and refer to some causes, expressed or unexpressed.

—July 26, 1924

It is obviously unfair and unreasonable that secular education should forbid one man to say a religion is true and allow another man to say it is untrue. It is obviously essential to justice that unsectarian education should cut both ways; and that if the orthodox must cut out the statement that man has a divine origin, the materialist must cut out the statement that he has a wholly and exclusively bestial origin. The difficulty arises from the combination of the widening of education with the exclusion of religious education. But if the fundamentalists say that some secularists abuse the right of secular education, they say what is exceedingly probable—and, if they say it is intolerable, they tell the truth.

—August 8, 1925

Education (Soviet)

... such a system of education is like a school in which all the children should be stunned with clubs at the start of the lesson, and laid out cold for the day.... There is more and more incompatibility and conflict between the two modern tendencies— the tendency to rigid and co-ordinated instruction and the tendency to subtle and sympathetic education. Thus, while all over Western Europe are dotted psychological educators luring on little minds with flowers and feathers and coloured ribbons, the barbarians in Eastern Europe, filled with a passion for discipline, are conducting infant instruction with loud bangs, discharges of artillery, and deafening assertions that there is no God.

—*February* 22, 1936

Education (Universal State)

England taught all her poor children by compulsion to sing songs about Empire Day, and to read an English History which was a very English History.... And it is a grisly glimpse of the blindness of nations to reflect that our own nation throughout the nineteenth century only argued about whether the state school ought to teach religion. It never noticed that the state school did teach politics; it did teach not only politics, but ethics; it did teach morality and philosophy and a view of life. I do not despise patriotism; I do not even entirely despise education. I only say that education led to war.

—*December* 5, 1931

Without that mighty modern engine or invention, it would have been quite impossible to drill whole huge populations for the instantaneous and unanimous acceptance of one view of national and international history. An ordinary casual Bavarian, left alone with his beer and his music and his Mediaevalism (which is the polite name for his religion), would never have evolved out of his own capacious but very contented inside the notion that he and a frozen prig from Pomerania were part of one great ethnic evolution of the superman, scientifically predestined to conquer common humanity. *Tantum educatio* (if there is such a word) *potuit suadere malorum!* Nothing but education could fix such an infernal fad in five million different minds at the same moment.

—*December* 5, 1931

Education and Dogma

...religious teaching must be dogmatic, simply because all teaching must be dogmatic. The teacher is allowed to say that twice two is four, not because it is less dogmatic, but because it is less disputed. In other words, education is easy when dogma is universal. It only becomes difficult when men are divided about dogmas. But men are divided very much indeed about these new dogmas; possibly more than they ever were about the old dogmas. There are quite as many different versions of citizenship as there ever were different versions of orthodoxy. Men hate each other, and even kill each other, for differences about citizenship quite as much as for differences about orthodoxy. There is at least as much fanaticism in Bolshevist Russia as there ever was in Holy Russia. In short (I may repeat), it is really unfair to use force to teach everybody everything, unless you can teach everybody every aspect of everything. One schoolmaster can teach twenty boys the alphabet; but it would require twenty schoolmasters to teach one boy the arguments of the twenty schools of thought on any disputed subject.

—June 12, 1920

Education and Scientism

It is impossible to use the old arguments of the self-evident character of the three R's when the three R's really stand for reason, religion, and rationalism.

—August 8, 1925

Education and Social Class

But the... truth to be added to any description of public ignorance is much more sharp and arresting. The truth is this—that this ignorance is not separately, nor even specially, characteristic of the poorer classes. On the contrary, it is rather curiously common and continuous in the educated classes.

—February 5, 1910

Educational Authorities

...our educational authorities have already made sure that the system is rigid without making sure that it is right. They have already achieved universality but not unity. They have arranged to teach history without considering what history

148

teaches; they have obtained powers of compulsion for teaching the truth to everybody; and then, looking into their own minds, have found that the truth is not in them.

—June 12, 1920

Educationalism

The only mistake . . . of almost all the enterprising educationalism of our day . . . is simply that all the people who think about education never seem to think about children.

—May 30, 1908

Educator (Progressive)

. . . the evolutionary educator, having never since his birth been in anything but the dark, naturally believes that he is in the daylight. His very notion of daylight is something which is so blank as to be merely blind. There are no depths in it, either of light or darkness. There are no dimensions in it; not only no fourth, but no third, no second, and hardly a first; certainly no dimensions in which the mind can move. Therefore the mind remains fixed, in a posture that is called progressive. It never looks back, even for remembrance; it never looks the other way, even for experiment; it never looks at the other side, even for an adventure; it never winks the other eye. It simply knows all there is; and there does not seem to be much to know.

—August 6, 1932

Efficiency

Efficiency consists of taking everything that is mentally slow, and making it mechanically fast.

—February 7, 1925

Egoist

Above all, the true egoist can generally be detected by this diabolic mark: that he is not only willing to talk on any subject, but on any side of any subject. He has no creed, no cause, no conception of truth which he thinks more important than himself. He is willing to talk like a Turk to show that he has travelled in Turkey; he is willing to talk like a Buddhist to show that he has studied Buddhism. But he will not forget himself in fighting for the Turks; he will not sacrifice himself to Buddhism like a Christian sacrificing himself to Christianity. In all his varied travels he has discovered all wonders except one most wonderful thing—something bigger than himself.

—*November* 3, 1928

The Eighteenth Century

The eighteenth century itself is not a century, as centuries go, that is specially attractive to me. There were not enough fairy-tales in it for my taste; certainly there were not anything like so many people believing in fairies then as there are now. It had no great understanding of children. The men of that time had forgotten the holy child of mediaeval legend, and had not yet heard of the happy child of modern literature. They could not imagine a Peter Pan, for they had lost the religious traditions both of Pan and of Peter. They had silenced all those subconscious voices which speak to simple people of the wonders hidden in this world. In short, they were ignorant of all the thousand things that only the ignorant ever know.

—*October* 23, 1926

Einstein, Albert

For most people Einstein is not yet a theory; he is not yet even a hypothesis; he has not got so far as to be called a hint. But he is already what is called a household word by people who have no households—the sort of people who live and talk in hotels.

—*April* 15, 1922

People did talk about Darwinism as well as about Darwin. Most of those who talk about Einstein talk about Einstein.

—*October* 11, 1930

Elder

It is an error to suppose that advancing years bring retrogressing opinions. In other words, it is not true that men growing old must be growing reactionary. Some of the difficulties of recent times have been due to the obstinate optimism of the old revolutionary. Magnificent old men like Kropotkin and Whitman and William Morris went to their grave expecting utopia if they did not expect heaven. But the falsehood, like so many falsehoods, is a false version of a half-truth. The truth, or half-truth, is not that men must learn by experience to be reactionaries, but that they must learn by experience to expect reactions.

—April 26, 1930

... even the most intelligent of innovators is often strangely mistaken about the nature of innovation and the things that are really new. And the oldest inhabitant will often indulge in a senile chuckle as he listens to the village orator proclaiming that the village church will soon be swept away and replaced by a factory for chemicals. For the oldest inhabitant knows very well that nobody went to church in the days of his childhood except out of snobbishness, and that it is in his old age that the church has begun once more to be thronged with believers.

—March 14, 1931

I would not say that old men grow wise, for men never grow wise; and many old men retain a very attractive childishness and cheerful innocence. Elderly people are often much more romantic than younger people, and sometimes even more adventurous, having begun to realise how many things they do not know.

—March 14, 1931

Elder versus Youth

... it is not the young people who realise the new world. The moderns do not realise modernity. They have never known anything else. They have stepped on to a moving platform which they hardly know to be moving, as a man cannot feel the daily movement of the earth. But he would feel it sharp enough if the earth suddenly moved the other way. The older generation consists of those who do remember a time when the world moved the other way. They do feel sharply and clearly the epoch which is beginning, for they were there before it began. It is one of the artistic advantages of the aged that they do see the new things relieved sharply against a background, their shape definite and distinct. To the young these new things are often themselves the background, and are hardly seen at all.

—March 14, 1931

Elections

Anybody's death is more important than any General Election.

—December 24, 1910

Every newspaper is bound to tell you that the Election is a heroic crisis and crusade; but every newspaper man will tell you in hearty terms, that it is a nuisance and a devastating bore.

—December 24, 1910

Electoral Analysis

If sixty rational and respectable citizens choose to vote Tory, it is called the Flowing Tide. If the sixty rational citizens decide to vote Radical, it is called the Swing of the Pendulum. One witty candidate, menaced with the flowing tide by his opponent, pasted up a notice: "Vote for Smith and Dam the Flowing Tide." Similarly, I should say with decision, "Vote for whom you choose and hang the pendulum."

—August 13, 1910

Electron

The electron, as now expounded, is much more of a mystery than the Trinity. It is even, as Mr. Joad might express it, much more of a contradiction than the Trinity.

—April 12, 1930

Eliot, T. S.

Indeed, when he does make an epigram (and a very good one) he is so ashamed of it that he hides it at the end of a minute footnote, for fear some critic or other should accuse him of brilliancy.

—May 30, 1931

Emancipation

The ordinary Abolitionist, the ordinary Northern idealist, preached generosity to the blacks, saying, "We will give the negro liberty; we will give the negro light; we will give the negro education." Chandler Harris in "Uncle Remus" gave an indirect, unexpected, yet strangely forcible answer. He did not say— "I will give the negro whips and chains if he is mutinous," or, "I will give him a better light and liberty if he is good." He said— "This is what the negro has *given me*. You talk of educating the slave; this is how the slave educated me. He taught me the primal culture of humanity, the ancient and elvish wisdom without which all other learning is priggishness, the tales which from the beginning our Mother Earth has told to all her children at night. The negro has given something to the South and I will give it to the North."

—August 1, 1908

Emancipator

... the emancipator generally means one who brings his own special type of emancipation. The man bringing light brings his own special patent electric-light, and puts out all the previous candles. When we set the poor man free, it nearly always means that we set him free to learn from us. It ought to mean sometimes that we set him free to teach us. But we should be rather startled if he tried it on.

—August 1, 1908

Empire

You cannot have a King or a Republic until you have a People; both are creative and collective things. A Monarchy turns a million men into one man who can be seen. A Republic turns a million men into one woman who cannot be seen. Both require faith and a power of fashioning a fixed thing and fighting for it. But an

Empire merely makes an authority from nowhere attempting to master an anarchy from everywhere.

—September 3, 1910

It *is* commonplace that empires pass away, because empires were never very important. Empires are frivolous things, the fringes of a sprawling culture that has sprawled too far. Cities do not pass away, or very seldom pass away, because the city is the cell of our organic formation; and even those living in the vast void of empire can find no phrase for social duty, save to tell men to be good citizens.

—January 11, 1930

Empiricism

. . . what we have suffered from in the modern world is not in any sense physical knowledge itself, but simply a stupid mistake about what physical knowledge is and what it can do. It is quite as obvious that physical knowledge may make a man comfortable as it is that it cannot make a man happy. It is as certain that there are such things as drugs as that there are no such things as love potions. Physical science is a thing on the outskirts of human life; adventurous, exciting, and essentially fanciful. It has nothing to do with the centre of human life at all.

—October 9, 1909

England

England is most easily understood as the country of amateurs. It is especially the country of amateur soldiers (that is, of Volunteers), of amateur statesmen (that is, of aristocrats), and it is not unreasonable or out of keeping that it should be rather specially the country of a careless and lounging view of literature.

—April 18, 1908

. . . these English defects, the sentimental worship of wealth and the sentimental confusion of thought, are due to England having had no popular theology.

—September 14, 1918

England is a queer place, and few try to understand it; least of all the English.

— September 6, 1924

England, left to itself, returns naturally to sport and laughter, and a genial individualism known as minding one's own business. It knows and cares very little about politics; that is why it puts up with politicians.

— September 6, 1924

I happen to be one of the few and rather unpopular persons who like the cool and troubled temper of the English climate. It was said that Germany wanted a place in the sun; I cannot sufficiently congratulate myself that England succeeded in finding a place in the shade.

— June 27, 1931

England (King of)

It has actually been proposed in an English paper that the King of England should consent to be called Emperor of the British. The primary answer is obvious. Why not Sultan of the British? Why not Kaiser of the British, or Pope of the British? Why not Tsar? Why not Shah? Why not Grand Lama of Great Britain?.... We do not call our ruler an Emperor for the same reason that we do not call him a Brother of the Sun and Moon: because it is our national tradition to call him something else... and if you want something grander still, I am sure I could invent it. Uncle of the Universe would be good, or Cousin of the Cosmos. These are greater titles than King of England—in mythology. But not in history.

— September 3, 1910

England (Merry)

... one quite intelligent contributor apparently identified "St. George" as somebody supposed to have lived in "Merry England," and explained that his period (whatever it was supposed to be) was not really merry, because there was a great deal of mud in the streets, or people lived in mud hovels. Apart from everything else, I call it narrow for a man to suppose that mud is the opposite of merriment.

Did he never make any mud-pies? Was he not much merrier making them than contributing to intellectual weeklies?

—June 18, 1932

England and Prussia

Some Englishmen were fond of saying that America was three years late in joining the struggle against Prussia. I wonder how many years late England was in joining the same just and necessary struggle.... If England and everybody else had protested against the partition of Poland, there would probably have been no Prussia. There would have been no Prussianism, no pessimism, no militarism, no crushing load of debt and conscription, no panic of increasing armaments.

—June 11, 1921

"English"

... the English nation has for decades, and perhaps for centuries, sadly neglected its national quality. It has not insisted that even English goods should be English.... Some seem to be named out of sheer perversity after neighbouring nations. I suppose there are hardly two things more peculiarly English than Welsh rarebit and Irish stew.

—November 7, 1931

English Eccentrics

... just as the English were eccentrics about their own laws, and eccentrics in their own life, so they largely tolerated the eccentric laws and eccentric lives in the other lands, even the lands they colonised or conquered. Since they began as travellers and traders, and did not begin as soldiers and statesmen, they retained a great deal of the travellers' acceptance and enjoyment of alien and fantastic things. It may be said that they valued the larger lands in which they travelled as a larger arena for travellers' tales.

—May 24, 1924

English versus French

The Frenchman differs from the Englishman in knowing where his own arguments will lead him. A Frenchman may think socialism is robbery; as he may think capitalism is robbery. But he is not comforted in either case by being a moderate robber, or a cautious robber, or a gradual and evolutionary robber.

—November 29, 1919

Englishmen

Perhaps it is a good thing that the English boast of the virtues they have not got. Perhaps it is good for their souls that they remain in a beautiful and radiant ignorance of the virtues they have got.

—March 28, 1925

I for one should love to have a real moat round my house, with a little drawbridge which could be let down when I really like the look of the visitor. I do not think I am a misanthrope. I am only an Englishman—that is, an islander—and one so very insular that he would like even his house to be an island. . . . Perhaps there is the very faintest . . . tinge of exaggeration in all this. But I do quite seriously prefer my castle, my moat and drawbridge to the modern notion that humanity becomes more human by herding in a homeless fashion like the beasts that perish, by drifting about in packs like wolves, or being driven like sheep.

—September 26, 1925

Enjoyment

Most men need institutions to make them distinguish themselves; and they also need institutions to make them enjoy themselves. For, paradoxical as it sounds, men shrink from enjoyment; they make one automatic step backwards from the brink of hilarity; because they know that it means the loss of dignity and a certain furious self-effacement. The truth at the back of almost every human institution, from a marriage to a tea-party, is the fact that people must be tied by the leg even to do justice to themselves. People must be tied together in order to talk; for twenty minutes at a dance or for forty years in a marriage; for an hour at a dinner or for three hours at a Christmas dinner. But if anything is to be got out of the relation, it must be a secure one, so far as it goes; and this is true of all pleasure and of all toil.

—January 8, 1910

... it is always wiser to consider not so much why a thing is not enjoyable, as why we ourselves do not enjoy it.

— February 28, 1931

The Enlightened

There is something awful and uncanny about the brilliant blindness of the enlightened. Telescopes have they and they see not: telephones have they and they hear not: some secret paralysis in the mind or the knot of the nerves prevents them from being conscious of anything that is palpable and present.

— August 29, 1914

The Enlightenment

It believed it was abolishing ruins, but in truth it was building ruins; and there is no ruin so antiquated or so picturesque as that broken classical column on which was inscribed: "Deo erexit Voltaire."

— January 31, 1925

The Enlightenment (Age of)

It is almost a mark of being behind the times to go on talking merely of traditional religion. What we have to deal with in the modern world is traditional irreligion. The period between Voltaire and Bernard Shaw is merely the period of the rise and decline of something that began as a joke and ended as a prejudice.

— February 7, 1931

... The Enlightenment is not pure light; the illumination of the broad-minded is not simply the broad daylight. There are a good many lights involved; the inner light of the Quakers; the superficial sunlight of the pagans; the light that leads astray, even when it is light from heaven; the light that shines only in the darkness; the light that never was on sea or land. There is a mystical element in these political ideals, and the old liberals were wrong in supposing that the mere enlightenment of the intellect would secure them. And to say that all enlightened intellects now desire to secure them is simply a flat contradiction of all the facts of the modern world.

—August 22, 1931

Entertainment

. . . the cinema prevails over Punch and Judy not as great art, but merely as big business. There was probably more fun got out of Punch and Judy, but there was less money got out of it. And many modern people have a sort of imaginative reverence for a thing not only because a lot of money is got out of it, but merely because a lot of money is put into it. The reason why all such puppet-shows have died out, I regret to say, is the same as that which has caused the guilds and the local liberties to die out. It is the same that has destroyed the free peasant and the small shop-keeper. It is the denial of dignity and poetry to the poor, and the concentration of worship as well as wealth upon a smaller and smaller ring of the rich.

—October 8, 1921

Epistemological Relativism

. . . is the chaos in which there cannot even be comparison. It is, for instance, the destruction of the very first and most fundamental of human discoveries. I mean the discovery of language, which grows out of the discovery of logic. All communication between man and man rests upon the opposite principle, upon the principle of reason and the recognition of external truth; so that men have a sun and moon in common, like the figures of a giant alphabet. It is precisely because we can agree that yes is yes and no is no, in a philosophy wider than all our varying temperaments, that we can express ourselves at all, even by writing wild, sceptical speculations in American magazines. Even the ideas of the critic in question, in all their unreason, could not reach us at all if it were true that an idea is only the countenance of a mood.

—January 31, 1931

Epoch and Bias

We all have a little weakness, which is very natural but rather misleading, for supposing that this epoch must be the end of the world because it will be the end of us. How future generations will get on without us is indeed, when we come to think of it, quite a puzzle. But I suppose they will get on somehow, and may

159

possibly venture to revise our judgments as we have revised earlier judgments. Anyhow, ours are hardly in the divine sense last judgments.

—August 15, 1925

Err

It is human to err; and the only final and deadly error, among all our errors, is denying that we have ever erred.

—July 8, 1922

Ethics

... we all know that thousands of good men accept these ethics of the journalist, just as thousands of others accept the equally disputed ethics of the barrister. To my mind both are dubious, but those of the barrister much the more defensible; because he puts on a fantastic costume and stands in a particular place, by way of warning the public that for a certain definite period he is not going to tell the truth. If all the insincere opinions in the press were invariably printed in red ink, we should have something like the same fair warning.

—May 27, 1922

Ethics and Public Schools

At no English public school is it even suggested, except by accident, that it is a man's duty to tell the truth. What is suggested is something entirely different: that it is a man's duty not to tell lies. So completely does this mistake soak through all civilisation that we hardly ever think even of the difference between the two things. When we say to a child, "You must tell the truth," we do merely mean that he must refrain from verbal inaccuracies. But the thing we never teach at all is the general duty of telling the truth, of giving a complete and fair picture of anything we are talking about, of not misrepresenting, not evading, not suppressing, not using plausible arguments that we know to be unfair, not selecting unscrupulously to prove an *ex parte* case, not telling all the nice stories about the Scotch, and all the nasty stories about the Irish. . . . The one thing that is never taught by any chance in the atmosphere of public schools is exactly that—that there is a whole truth of things, and that in knowing it and speaking it we are happy.

—August 18, 1906

Ethics versus Morality

I saw a magazine the other day in which Ethics had turned into Ethology. Now, the word Ethics is already a nuisance to God and man; but its permanent defence and its occasional necessity is that it stands for conduct considered statically as a science, whereas morality (or moralitude) stands for conduct considered actively as a choice. One can discuss ethics. One cannot discuss morality: one can only violate it. The reasonable difference between ethics and morality is like the difference between geology and throwing stones or between jurisprudence and outrunning the constable.

—June 12, 1909

Eternal Return

Every detail of every life will return with exactitude, and return again and again to eternity. And everybody knows how Nietszche uttered this revelation, with something almost like a howl, from the last high and crazy peak of his strange existence; about the time, indeed, when he collapsed into complete insanity. I do not know whether he went mad because he believed the theory, or only believed the theory because he went mad.

—August 2, 1930

Eugenics

There are things going on all around us in modern civilisation which are, lucidly considered, quite as revolting as cannibalism. It is the business of journalism to report them (within reason), but it is not the business of anybody to pretend that they are beautiful because they are true. For instance, the most serious sociologists, the most stately professors of eugenics, calmly propose that, "for the good of the race," people should be forcibly married to each other by the police. Eugenics seems to me quite as barbarous as cannibalism. If we have a right to mate and breed men and women like beasts, I cannot see why we should not cook and eat them like beasts. If a citizen may not settle what is to happen to his live body, why should he be allowed to be fastidious about what happens to his dead body? In short, eugenics is obviously an indecent thing.

—March 6, 1909

... the science of eugenics is a mere speculation; and a risky, not to say rotten, speculation it is.

—*November* 20, 1915

... eugenics is chiefly a denial of the Declaration of Independence. It urges that so far from all men being born equal, numbers of them ought not to be born at all. And so far from their being entitled to life, liberty, and the pursuit of happiness, they are to be forbidden a form of liberty and happiness so private that the maddest inquisitor never dreamed of meddling with it before.

—*November* 20, 1915

... many of the eugenists practically propose that all marriages should be overseen and controlled. They have elaborate plans, sometimes worked out in considerable detail, and containing everything except a list of the names of the men who are to oversee and control. In this matter they are very lucid about the way in which human beings should be directed. Where they are, perhaps, a little vaguer is about the superhuman beings who are to direct them. If they accept an aristocracy of inspired matchmakers, we shall naturally want to know who they are, and why. If they do not admit aristocracy, and make any pretence of democracy, then they have tied themselves in a most horrible knot. All men must be so stupid that they cannot manage their own affairs; and also so clever that they can manage each other's!

—*September* 27, 1919

Eugenics and Abortion

We are not so very far off from even the sacrifice of babies—if not to a crocodile, at least to a creed. I have seen versions of eugenics that come very near to infanticide. I had recently a discussion with so distinguished a cleric as the Dean of St. Paul's in which he expressed a general sympathy with the eugenists, probably in entire innocence of what some of the eugenists say. In the course of the same discussion Dean Inge denounced the interference with the capitalist, and said we were killing the goose that laid the golden eggs. What struck me as quaint about the figure of speech was this—it seemed to me that a man who expressed such horror of killing a goose, even in metaphor, might well feel a little horror of certain wild theorists who would come very near to killing a child in reality. If they do not propose to

162

kill children, some at least propose to prevent them being born; and that negation may surely be a tragedy.

—December 4, 1920

Eugenics and the Nazis

... we see statements in the newspapers about schemes for supporting all the fads that have recently attacked the family. We read of all the stale theories of eugenics; the talk of compulsory action to keep the breed in a certain state of bestial excellence; of nosing out every secret of sex or origin, so that nobody may survive who is not Nordic; of setting a hundred quack doctors to preserve an imaginary race in its imaginary purity. Now, eugenics of that sort is, always has been, and always must be, merely a violent assault on the family. It is, by definition, the taking away from the family of the decisions that ought to belong to the family. When those decisions are made in the domestic and individual way, in which they should be made, nobody in his senses ever dreams of describing the decision as eugenics. The private persons involved do not call the issue of their own private affairs eugenics; they call it love, or childbirth, or childlessness, or whatever they choose. The whole point of these pseudo-scientific theories always was that they were to be applied wholesale, by some more sweeping and generalising power than the individual husband or wife or household.

—June 17, 1933

Everything (Theory of)

If, instead of claiming that everything is covered by his explanation, he confined himself to pleading that there is something in his suggestion, he would look considerably less of a fool when the next man, with the new explanation, comes along in about thirty years.

—July 5, 1930

Evil

Unless a man becomes the enemy of ... an evil, he will not even become its slave, but rather its champion. ... God Himself will not help us to ignore evil, but only to defy and to defeat it.

—April 14, 1917

Evil (Pride in Being)

Whether or no there be such a thing as an utterly unredeemed villain, it is quite certain that there is a kind of man who wishes to be thought an unredeemed villain, and probably wishes to be an unredeemed villain. All the mixed characters of more moderate and modern fiction depend on the assumption that defects are merely defects. They assume that there is no such thing as a definite attraction of diabolism. In this they are certainly wrong, as any wide experience—and especially any warlike experience—was bound to prove.

—September 22, 1917

Evolution

It is not science that is dangerous. . . . It is the huge superstructure which the human fancy erects in an instant upon the smallest and most trifling hint. If we know nothing about a man except that he is a Presbyterian and once bought a green umbrella, we cannot help making an immediate picture in our minds, complete, artistic, and alarming. Whereas in truth those two things may be quite minor matters in the man's life: he may have early abandoned Presbyterianism and only bought a green umbrella during the one evening of intoxication with which he celebrated his deliverance from that creed. In the same way, when we see a skeleton and a stone axe-head, we instinctively think of a naked man with a stone axe. The man may, as a fact, have been slightly overdressed and may never have used a stone axe in his life. It may have been a ritual to put quite useless axes into graves. It may be that one might as well say that every man with flowers on his tomb is a florist or that any man in a wooden coffin was a carpenter.

—November 9, 1907

Evolution itself does not even affirm that it has been upon the whole an improvement. But even supposing that it did, what man in his senses would ever apply evolution so as to mean that any one thing that comes after another must be an improvement on it?

—October 31, 1908

Evolution means a general theory that the varieties which are so vivid in this world of ours were produced slowly under the pressure of some necessity without or some power within; that necks grow shorter or noses longer in accordance with

164

some need which could only operate gradually. In the history of this business (if it ever happened) there were, of course, many ups and downs; but it depends on your philosophy of things in general what you call an up and what you call a down.

—October 31, 1908

Evolution has become not a perception but a prejudice; because it is not an invention, which most people can touch and even tinker with, but an origin, which most people prefer to leave undisturbed.

—April 8, 1922

Tennyson talked about evolution working out the brute, and letting the ape and tiger die. But the man does not necessarily cease to worship an ape because he ceases to be an ape. On the contrary, even in order to worship an ape he must be a man. ... The merest glimpse of the darker side of psychology will tell us that such luxurious decadence is quite as likely to delight in the tiger's cruelty as in the tiger's beauty. Nero was not a prehistoric man. The Marquis de Sade was not a simple savage. I should say that there was no time when men were more likely to worship wolves and vipers and alligators than at the end of what some call evolution and some education.

—March 20, 1926

Evolution (Political)

Everybody knows that, morally speaking, all our modern struggle might be called the survival of the unfittest.

—December 3, 1910

Evolution (Theory of)

Indeed, the one great example of evolution is evolution. The transformist theory itself did go through a number of transformations rather of its own type. It did rise from a rude and wandering thing to a specialised and complex thing. There never was what Grant Allen called the evolution of the idea of God. But there really was the evolution of the idea of evolution. And now it has reached an extraordinary climax which is not without a potentiality of complete collapse.

—May 30, 1925

Evolution and Ethics

The truth is that the evolutionary theory, if true, is totally useless for human affairs. It is enormous, but irrelevant. Like the solar system, it is a colossal trifle. Though the earth is going round we must not be giddy. Similarly, even if we are beasts, we must not be beastly. All these attempts to apply the parallel of physical evolution to our ethical progress end in one of two things. They end in cutting ethics to fit evolution, which means immorality and madness; or they end in cutting evolution to fit ethics, which means unscientific balderdash. Many of our men of science prefer (I am glad to say) the balderdash to the immorality.

— September 18, 1909

Evolution . . . (at this word you will please bow your head twenty-seven times or go through some other sacerdotal rite) however fascinating or even inspiring as a picture of the facts of the past, is totally useless as a moral code. . . . A great scientific theory has a dignity of its own. There is no reason why it should also profess to be a piece of ethical or social advice. Nor, I think, do people try to make new moralities out of any of the other great scientific generalisations. I have never heard the Law of Gravity adduced as a reason for knocking people down. I have never known the Circulation of the Blood offered as an excuse for blood-shed. I never knew running away from your wife called Centrifugal Force; or tearing her hair out described as Capillary Attraction. . . . Huxley, the greatest of the Darwinians, told them long ago that Evolution and Ethics were two totally different things, and that the less evolutionary their ethics were the better.

— April 23, 1910

Evolution and Sunbathing

Why not say, that all this cult of sunbathing and seabathing and life on the Lido means that we are all slowly going back into the sea, out of which all organic life originally came: so at least I am informed by the "Outline of History," and other fairy-tales of science. That vast return of all the earth-creatures to the water would be a fine imaginative panorama. . . . The profiteers parading in pink and purple would turn slowly into sea-beasts; nothing extra seems needed except the sea. Film stars evolving into star-fish and sun-bathers into sun-fish would still be a hopeful evolution. There would be macabre prose-sketches of how our suits of clothes dangled and decayed like scarecrows in the deserted lands and towns, the hollow husks or shells of the men who were already mermen and would return no more.

—July 23, 1932

Evolutionists

If they do injustice, they excuse it as the evolutionary struggle for life. If they have animal amusement, evolution excuses it by their animal origin.

—February 14, 1925

He cannot tell whether he ought to evolve into the higher morality or into the larger morality, unless he has some principle of pity or of liberty that does not evolve at all.

—March 16, 1929

Exaggeration

Every age has been an age of exaggeration; which has ended at last in vulgarisation. And it is the peculiar peril of the present age that it is actually proud of its unique capacity to vulgarise.

—December 13, 1930

Executioner

I read two articles this morning in two very able and distinguished periodicals which were devoted to this general consideration: "How extraordinary it is that the hangman is regarded with horror, while the soldier and the judge are not regarded with horror." The schoolboy would burst his Eton collar in his eagerness to answer so obvious a difficulty. He would say at once that a hangman is not so fine as a soldier, because he is not so brave. A hangman is merely a destroyer; a soldier is not. A soldier, at the best, is a martyr; at the worst, he is a good gambler. If the public executioner were obliged to have a personal conflict on the scaffold with the criminal, upon the issue of which depended which of the two were hanged, then general public sentiment would admire the hangman, just as general public sentiment admires the soldier.

—February 6, 1909

Expansion

The end of the process of expansion would seem to be disappearance: the vanishing of these vast things from the restricted senses and calculations of man. It is the ultimate upshot of the skyscraper; and upshot seems to be an oddly appropriate term. It is the end that the edifice should tower so high that we cannot see its towers; that the sky-sign should sprawl so wide that we cannot read its lettering. . . . I do not say it is very probable that things will ever go as far as that; chiefly because I think it much more probable that, long before that happens, people will have developed a taste for something totally different; perhaps for things that are microscopically small.

— *October* 31, 1931

Expansionism (Prussian)

I may say I do not intend to expand my back garden; but I may add one or two comments which make a considerable difference. One is that what my neighbour imagines to be his garden is really a part of my garden, which is therefore a large and handsome property, and needs no expanding. Another is that I propose to sit on the garden wall with a gun, and shoot him unless he manages what is theoretically his garden precisely as if it were my garden. The former is exactly the attitude of Germany towards Alsace and Posen; the latter is precisely her attitude towards Belgium and Luxembourg.

— *September* 1, 1917

Experience

It will be remarked that experience, which was once claimed by the aged, is now claimed exclusively by the young.

— *March* 7, 1931

Experience (Philosophy of)

In other words, so long as education is valued for the sake of experience, and not for the sake of right choice and of the truth, any miserable little diseased monkey is entitled to say that one experience is as interesting as another, and his experience more interesting than most.

— *September* 20, 1924

Experience and Writing

There are certainly all sorts of experiences, some great and some small. But the small ones are those which the critic imagines to be great and the great ones are those that he contemptuously dismisses as small. There are no more universal affairs than those which he imagines to be little and local. There are no events more tremendous than those which he regards as trivial. There are no experiences more exciting than those which he dully imagines to be dull.... A literary man who cannot see that a baby is marvellous could not see that anything was marvellous.

—March 7, 1931

Extremism

... everybody calls everybody else an extremist; it is now the fashionable term of reproach in all earnest controversies; and a very feeble and unphilosophical term too.

—December 20, 1919

Fable

Nearly all the fundamental facts of mankind are to be found in its fables. And there is a singularly sane truth in all the old stories of the monsters—such as centaurs.... The human parts of the monsters are handsome, like heroes, or lovely, like nymphs; their bestial appendages do not affect the full perfection of their humanity— what there is of it. There is nothing humanly wrong with the centaur, except that he rides a horse without a head.... Those old wild images included a crucial truth. Man is a monster. And he is all the more a monster because one part of him is perfect. It is not true, as the evolutionists say, that man moves perpetually up a slope from imperfection to perfection, changing ceaselessly, so as to be suitable. The immortal part of a man and the deadly part are jarringly distinct and have always been.

July 2, 1910

Fable versus Legend

The real mistake has been mixing up a fable with a legend; or a fairy-tale with a tradition. They are two totally different things. A fable is a thing that men make up because it is not true; a legend is a thing that men vaguely cling to because it is true. A tradition is always vague and dim, because it is the truth; A fairy-tale is always exact and clear, because it is fictitious. There are hundreds of tales of King Arthur or of Robin Hood; and you may mix them up as wildly as you will, because the men probably did exist at some time, and lived vague and varied human lives. But if you tell the tale of Puss in Boots to a child, you will soon discover that there is only one tale that you are allowed to tell.

—September 4, 1909

Facts

Facts as facts do not always create a spirit of reality, because reality is a spirit. Facts by themselves can often feed the flame of madness, because sanity is a spirit.

—August 10, 1929

Facts and Newspapers

Modern man is staggering and losing his balance because he is being pelted with little pieces of alleged fact, which are left afterwards in a heap because they cannot be fitted into anything. . . . Now, of course, anybody can collect any number of "facts" illustrating popular poverty or business success. Facts of both kinds are native to the newspapers; and, if they turn out not to be facts, that is still more native to newspapers.

—April 7, 1923

Facts and Truth

It is impossible for the human intellect (which is divine) to hear a fact as a fact. It always hears a fact as a *truth,* which is an entirely different thing. A truth is a fact with a meaning. Many facts have no meaning at all, as far as we can really discover; but the human intellect (which is divine) always adds a meaning to the fact which it hears. If we hear that Robinson has bought a new fire-screen, we always *wish* to be able to say, "How like Robinson!" If we hear nothing else at all but this, that a man in Worthing has a cat, our souls make a dark, unconscious effort to find some connection between the spirit of Worthing and the love of domestic animals, between the night-songs of the feline and the sound of the sea at night.

—November 18, 1905

Fad

I do not need to sail to strange islands, for my own island is becoming quite strange enough for me.... Why break through jungles to find black men who eat their meat raw, when the doctors may be telling us next year that white men ought to eat it raw?.... And why search for the Missing Link, living on nuts and roots, when, by all accounts, the Superman (who is expected shortly) will do just the same.... By merely sitting in an arm-chair and watching one's fellow-creatures progress, one may have all the exact sensations of a man traveling among savages.

—September 11, 1909

Fad (Intellectual)

There was a burst and buzz of talk in all the drawing-rooms; and the drawing-rooms had adopted Darwinism before they had heard what it was. Darwin and Huxley were great men, but they were not boomed because they were great men, but because it was great fun. So psycho-analysis is boomed because it is great fun. Then suddenly appears the psychologist who says it is great foolery.

—May 30, 1925

This is how it happens that perverse and pedantic fancies so often harden into fanaticism among professors and professional historians. They will maintain any paradox rather than lose any point that supports their pet generalisation, even if they do not personally care very much about the point itself.

—October 3, 1931

Fairy-tales

Civilisation changes; but fairy-tales never change. Some of the details of the fairy-tale may seem odd to us; but its spirit is the spirit of folk-lore; and folk-lore is, in strict translation, the German for common-sense. . . . The fairy-tale means extraordinary things as seen by ordinary people. The fairy-tale is full of mental health. The fairy-tale can be more sane about a seven-headed dragon than the Duchess of Somerset can be about a Board School.

—December 2, 1905

They said that fables had their origin among the ignorant, which, put into plain words, means that if everybody in a village says that the Squire is drowned in the horsepond, he must be somewhere else. But if the nineteenth century was the time of the destruction of legends, the twentieth century bids fair to be the time of the return of legends. It will be much more exciting to find out that half fairy-tales are history even than to find out that history is half fairy-tales.

—September 4, 1909

Children must hear nothing but the vital truth, so far as we can give it them. I say the vital truth: it is found mostly in fairy-tales.

—December 31, 1910

Faith

. . . I have long believed that the only really happy and hopeful faith is a faith in the FALL OF MAN.

—May 21, 1927

Faith is a thing to be respected, especially when it has no apparent supports but in the soul.

—March 1, 1930

Faith and the Modernist

I was asked to contribute an article under the general title of "Have We Lost Faith?" I answered the question, as it seems to me quite seriously by saying that we have lost faith in the Darwinian theory, in the higher criticism, in the cruder conception of progress, and so on. Nearly all the correspondents flew into a passion against my flippancy. They had expected me to say, as they all said, that we were gradually losing faith in various parts of Christianity, and liked describing the sensation. Apparently it is not cheek to say you have lost faith in deity or immortality, but it is cheek to say you have lost faith in Darwin.

—February 13, 1926

Faith and Reason

The most orthodox doctors have always maintained that faith is something superior to reason but not contrary to it.

—January 15, 1910

Faith versus Fads

Unless that part of the mind is satisfied by a faith it will be satisfied by a fad: those who have destroyed a church have only created a sect.

—June 20, 1914

The Fall

... [In Eden] all evil is traced to that ultimate unreasoning insolence which will not accept even the kindest conditions; that profoundly inartistic anarchy that objects to a limit as such. It is not indicated that the fruit was of attractive hue or taste: its attraction was that it was forbidden. In Eden there was a maximum of liberty and a minimum of veto; but some veto is essential even to the enjoyment of liberty. The finest thing about a free meadow is the hedge at the end of it. The moment the hedge is abolished it is no longer a meadow, but a waste, as Eden was after its one limitation was lost.

—April 9, 1910

Fame versus Fortune

To desire money is much nobler than to desire success. Desiring money may mean desiring to return to your country, or marry the woman you love, or ransom your father from brigands. It may mean something human and respectable. But desiring success must mean something inhuman and detestable. It must mean that you take an abstract pleasure in the unbrotherly act of distancing and disgracing other men.

—*November 7,* 1908

The Family

The Family is much more of a fact even than the State.

—*February 20,* 1909

The narrowness and dullness of domesticity, as described in so many recent plays and novels, was due not to an old tradition but to a new fashion, and a fashion that was rather peculiar to the suburbs of modern industrial cities. It was not due to the ancient and normal conception of a man talking to his family. It was due to the new and nasty conception of a man not talking to his neighbours. It was due to quite modern types of snobbishness; to the exclusiveness of small social pretentions; to "keeping oneself to oneself"; to nomadic habits and new surroundings; to the loss of the old patriotism of the parish and paternal quality of the parish church. . . .

—*March 5,* 1927

. . . in a present and practical form, it is called antiquated. Its practical form is called marriage or the family. It really does demand that a man and a woman should live largely for the next generation. It does demand that they should, to some extent, defer their personal amusements, such as divorce and dissipation, for the benefit of the next generation. And whenever we suggest that, a wail goes up about the wickedness and cruelty of depriving the poor dear parents of the innocent gaieties of divorce.

—*May 31,* 1930

Humanity has been organised from the beginning in families, and then in work-shops and other kinds of shops, more or less modelled on the framework of families. It is one of the dullest delusions of modern talk . . . to suppose that this

174

necessarily means a narrow isolation, as of bedridden cripples living indoors. There is a curious idea that our fathers thought that one of the virtues of the family was this inhuman segregation. On the contrary, our fathers thought that one of the virtues of the family was hospitality. Only they thought that there ought to be a family to be hospitable; it is much more the moderns who think that we should be all patients, or passive recipients of something given by nobody and received by everybody; as if there were nothing else except the hospitality of a hospital. The home was the nucleus round which there always gathered a number of things not actually of itself; neighbours and near relations and the friends of the rising generation; lovers and rivals and the apprentice who married his master's daughter.

—*February 25, 1933*

Over all the world tremendous transformations are passing over the state, so that a man may go to bed in one state and get up in another. The very name of this nation, the very nature of his common law, the very definition of his citizenship, the uniform and meaning of the policeman at the corner of his street, may be totally transformed tomorrow, as in a fairy-tale. He cannot really refer the daily domestic problems of this life to a state that may be turned upside-down every twenty-four hours. He must, in, fact, fall back on that primal and prehistoric institution; the fact that he has a mate and they have a child; and the three must get on together somehow, under whatever law or lawlessness they are supposed to be living.

—*June 17, 1933*

Take a very influential and creative culture in which the family has always been fundamental; take China. Is there any earthly sense, at this moment, in telling a Chinaman that he must cease to belong to the family, and be content to belong to the state? He may not unnaturally ask, "What state?" The Japanese armies may advance to-day, over the land occupied by one of five rival Chinese generals yesterday. To-morrow, both of them may have disappeared from practical politics.... In the break-up of the modern world, the family will stand out stark and strong as it did before the beginning of history; the only thing that can really remain a loyalty, because it is also a liberty.

—*June 17, 1933*

Family Lineage

There may be a few people who are proud of long lineage, or even a few who have long lineage to be proud of; but they are mostly yeomen and small squires without the smallest influence in politics. But in the case of the great political families, or even the great county families, the very last thing that they ever dream of doing is to shut their doors against the nouveau riche. Very often they were quite recently *nouveau riche* themselves. Never by any chance do they fail to welcome those that are obviously riche, however obviously nouveau.

—*June 26, 1920*

The Family and the State

... in an industrial country like ours, the framework of the state did really look stronger than the framework of the family. The modern industrial mob was accustomed to the endless and tragic trail of broken families; of tenants failing to pay their rents; of slums being condemned and their inhabitants scattered; of husband or wife wandering in search of work or swept apart by separation or divorce. In those conditions, the family seemed the frailest thing in the world; and the state the strongest thing in the world. But it is not really so. It is not so, when we take the life of man over large areas of time or space. It is not so, when we pass from the static nineteenth century to the staggering twentieth century.

—*June 17, 1933*

The total control of human life will pass to the state; and it will be a very totalitarian state. I know there are some who maintain that paid officials will be more devoted than parents; but it is very hard to see on what this can be based, unless it is the pay. Yet there is the ... whole modern world, to attest that those who are well paid can be badly bored. Those who imagine that they could not be bored with babies do not know much about babies. We always come back to the unanswerable argument of nature; that there do happen to be one or two persons, who are less bored with one particular very boring baby than everyone else would be. That common sense is the concrete foundation of the family; and no negative reaction against it comes anywhere near to having a positive substitute for it. Those who have a vague idea that educationists could take it in turns or divide the baby between them, are simply people who suppose that there can be twenty officials to one citizen.

—*January 4, 1936*

Family versus Factory

Certainly there is no case more moonstruck than the modern tendency to pit the factory against the family. Nothing could be madder, in the treatment of women, than to take them from conditions that are natural to women, and then put them in conditions that are unnatural for anybody. Nothing could be madder, except calling it the emancipation of women. There is no old crazy tale to compare with the notion of making a free wife and mother dependent on a commercial monopoly and then calling it the economic independence of woman. . . . The same philosophers, when they imprisoned the cuckoo in a hedge to keep the spring, were wiser than their followers who imprison woman in a factory to free her soul.

—*May 3,* 1919

Fanatic

A fanatic is merely the hostile name for a martyr, as a martyr is the friendly name for a fanatic. Tentatively, I suggest that a fanatic means a man whose faith in something he thinks true makes him forget his general love of truth.

—*March 7,* 1925

He may fairly be described as a man whose sense of a particular truth is too strong for his sense of the universal truth, even in so far as the larger truth supports the smaller. He will invoke even cruelty to prevent cruelty to animals.

—*March 7,* 1925

Farmer versus Businessman

They say that the farmer always grumbles; and so he does, for he can afford to grumble. He thinks the weather is bad, but he knows that his grumbling will not make it worse. . . . He is dealing with absolute and unalterable realities, and . . . he is dealing with real facts. . . . The commercial man almost has to be a romanticist because he so often deals with unrealities. And that is what Americans mean when they talk about the romance of salesmanship.

—*October 18,* 1930

Fascism

I can quite understand people saying that Mussolini's experiment is a violence or a tyranny or an intolerable freak. I can quite believe that others have reason to think the Hitler movement the hope of North Germany.

—*June* 11, 1932

Fashion

Men seldom seem able to penetrate a disguise where it is a very modern dress. Nay, in a sense, they never know a thing is fashionable until it is old-fashioned. . . . And the fallacy also infects the world of more general ideas. . . . For instance, I should say there are at least ten prophets of new religions who are mere humbugs to one priest of the old religion who is a mere humbug; but in our satiric fiction the humbug is still generally made a clergyman, and especially a bishop, rather than the irresponsible founder of some professedly idealistic movement.

—*October* 6, 1917

We sometimes call it progress. But what we ought to call it, if we want to be strictly accurate, is not so much even fashion, but rather fatigue. It is the rapidity with which we get tired of things. Fashions are customs of which people can easily get tired. We congratulate ourselves on inventing new things; when in truth it is because we cannot invent old things—that is, we cannot invent things that will ever live to be old. We give the name of enlightenment to a lightning succession of illusions and disillusions. This dream and self-deception are nowhere more dominant than in the thing we call science. Scientific ideas, more even than social and political ideas, are valued because they are new rather than true. The seekers after truth talk of wishing for "more light"; and they are given more lime-light.

—*May* 29, 1920

The old customs were at least old enough to become second nature. But a fashion is always sufficiently new to be unnatural.

—*August* 18, 1923

If I were asked why I think our whole industrial society is cursed with sterility and stamped with the mark of the slave, I could give a great many answers, but one will serve for the moment: because it cannot create a custom. It can only create a fashion. Now a fashion is simply something that has failed to be a custom. It is changed as a fashion because it is a failure as a custom. The rich, who are the most restless of mankind, do one thing after another, and prove in the very process that they cannot create anything that is good enough to last. Their succession of fashions is in itself a succession of failures. For when men have made really dignified and humane things, they have always desired that they should remain; or, at least, that some relic of them should remain.

—June 26, 1926

... fashion is almost the opposite of distinction.

—January 4, 1930

Nobody knows what will be the fashion a hundred years hence, except that it will almost certainly not be anything that is considered the newest fashion to-day.

—September 12, 1931

Fat

Believe me (I speak as an expert), it is impossible to be fat in secret.

—November 7, 1908

... fatness itself is a valuable quality. While it creates admiration in the onlookers, it creates modesty in the possessor. If there is anything on which I differ from the monastic institutions of the past, it is that they sometimes sought to achieve humility by means of emaciation. It may be that the thin monks were holy, but I am sure it was the fat monks who were humble. Falstaff said that to be fat is not to be hated; but it certainly is to be laughed at, and that is a more wholesome experience for the soul of man.

—May 8, 1909

Fate

I do not believe in a fate that falls on men however they act; but I do believe in a fate that falls on them unless they act.

—April 29, 1922

Fate versus Will

... there is a chasm between the man who believes in the soul, in the sense of the will, and the man who only believes in what he calls law, and what I call fate. It is a difference of kind, like the difference between organic and inorganic matter; or, in other words, between dead things and living ones.

—February 21, 1925

Fathers

Some object to a father being addressed as a father, and insist that his sons must call him Tom. ... This may be in many cases a very amiable pretence, like any children's game of "pretending." The father may even like pretending to be a boy, just as the boy or child likes pretending to be father. But it is pretending; and, whatever it is, it is not the abolition of pretence. Fatherhood is a fact, and to call a man father is to assert a fact; to assert a most primary, practical, and even physical fact. To call him Tom is a fiction. ... But children are well aware of the difference between the fictions and the facts. Only the new educationists practically deny the facts, and then boast that they are abolishing the fictions. They ignore a practical fact like a father, and then have the cheek to pretend that they are abolishing pretences.

—January 21, 1933

Feminism

Perhaps the greatest danger of exaggerated feminism is that there may be a much worse reaction of anti-feminism, in which polygamy and all the other practical but barbaric ideas may come in again like a flood.

—November 4, 1922

When the politicians went over in a body to female suffrage, the political leader-writers also went over in a body to what is called feminism. Politicians and political leader-writers seldom suffer, indeed, from a bigoted fixity of conviction. But it is taken for granted, and to a great extent it is true, that the public now accepts the intellectual independence of women. Sometimes the intellectual independence is completed with what is called economic independence. What is called the economic independence of women is the same as what is called the economic wage-slavery of men.

—April 21, 1923

There is the obvious contradiction that feminism often means the refusal to be feminine. There is the paradox that the modern girl considers herself frank and free because she uncovers her elbows, and then proceeds in the most prudish manner to make a coloured mask to cover her face. Even the most venerable Victorian never shuddered as she does at the nudity of the nose.

—August 18, 1928

... so that we have the last logical crown and conclusion of the long process of woman condescending to be merely the ape of man. First she demands to have what he has, merely because he has it, and not because it is worth having. And then she takes it for granted because he takes it for granted; and does it thoughtlessly, in order to be as thoughtless as he is.

—May 25, 1929

Feminism (Anti-)

... why has nobody founded (merely for fun) an anti-feminist case on the ferocity of females? It is generally founded, quite absurdly, upon the feebleness of females. It is no wonder that, having that foundation, it failed. But even in this short section of human history, of which I happen to have been reading, the feudal period and its gradual transformation, a man might make an exceedingly strong case for "the female of the species" being more deadly than the male. Mediaeval people were divided by rank, but not specially by sex; and many women exercised sweeping political power.... Quite an interesting theory might be worked out about the necessity of restraining a wild force of nature like fire or the sea, and the suggestion that the political omnipotence of women has been a sort of watchful terror on the part of men.

—May 14, 1927

Feminism and Chivalry

Feminism is against chivalry; but chivalry will always be rather in favour of feminism.

—*June* 12, 1909

Feminist

To begin with, why do they talk as if a woman was something that hadn't yet arrived, like a Superman or a visitor from Mars? Why are they always speculating and prophesying about what Woman "will say" when she learns to talk.... These people talk as if every woman wore a gag until she could get a vote. They talk as if she must have a vote before she can even know what she wants to vote for. Or sometimes they talk as if *they* knew what women would say and do, though we don't; how women would put down gambling or establish Eugenics, as if all women agreed about this or that reform, any more than all women think that Bacon wrote Shakespeare. Surely it is not we, but the Feminists, who deny the individuality and freedom of the female, when they predict positively that she will trot tamely like a sheep after "social reform"—that is, the current convention in fashionable slumming.

—*June* 6, 1914

Feminists are, as their name implies, opposed to anything feminine.

—*June* 1, 1929

Feminist Movement

My views on Female Suffrage, such as they are, were expressed some time ago in these columns; ... I said that I did not admit for a moment the argument which maintains that the actual Suffragist leaders have an infinite right to violate the law, merely because they have no part in making it. That would give every young man of twenty years and eleven months an infinite right of breaking the law. The claim of the State in one respect, I said, does not rest merely on the fact that we are a part of it. It rests also on the fact that it is the whole of us.

—*March* 16, 1907

182

... let a sex be kept apart to preserve it. But in either case we can complain of the ... type, who demands political responsibility, but brings into it exactly that looseness and laughing secrecy which is fit only for social intrigue. She wishes to be a candidate, but not to be heckled. She wishes to be a Cabinet Minister without any Question Time. She wishes to employ at once the vulgar repartee of a demagogue and the stunning silence of a hostess. This is not equality, but privilege.

—*March 6, 1909*

Fiction (Modern)

Fiction gave up its universal scope to achieve a universal appeal. French novels were written for adults, and confined to adults. English novels were thrown open to schoolgirls—and cut down for them. In Paris the baby was forbidden to read the man's literature; in London the man was often compelled to read the baby's. Both conditions can be described as liberty.

—*June 11, 1910*

I am very glad that our fashionable fiction seems to be full of a return to paganism, for it may possibly be the first step of a return to Christianity. Neo-pagans have sometimes forgotten, when they set out to do everything that the old pagans did, that the final thing the old pagans did was to get Christened.

—*March 20, 1926*

Fidelity (Oath of)

It is not the fact that young lovers have no desire to swear on the Book. They are always at it. It is not the fact that every young love is born free of traditions about binding and promising.... They do the craziest things to make their love legal and irrevocable. They tattoo each other with promises; they cut into rocks and oaks with their names and vows; they bury ridiculous things in ridiculous places to be a witness against them; they bind each other with rings, and inscribe each other in Bibles ... they are mad solely on this idea of binding and on nothing else. It is quite true that the tradition of their fathers and mothers is in favour of fidelity; but it is emphatically not true that the lovers merely follow it; they invent it anew.

—*July 2, 1910*

Fighting

There is no mere animal that fights as man fights; for there is no mere animal who will fight foreseeing defeat; man is the only fighting animal. But fighting in a just cause is so essential to man that only in doing so does he find any of his satisfactions, even the quietest or most casual. It is not merely that man cannot be happy unless he is fighting, it is that man cannot even be comfortable unless he is fighting. The saddle is the only seat in which he can even rest.

—*July* 28, 1906

Fighting to Preserve

We thought a man could fight to *improve* things; and especially to improve his own position. We forgot that a man may fight not to improve things, but to rescue them. He may fight, not to improve his position, but to save his life. It is not fantastically quixotic to say that he may sometimes even fight to save somebody else's life. To save things implies that they are worth saving; and the point is that their very peril makes us feel that they are worth saving.

—*May* 5, 1923

First Principles (Back to)

This is what we call thought; and shallow people always call it retrogression.

—*May* 17, 1910

Flattery

No good ever came of merely flattering one's nation: a man flatters the land he fears, but not the land he loves.

—*September* 25, 1915

Food Rationing

But I think it well that it should be made clear to our allies, and still more to our enemies, that our population is not in a frenzy about famine because the papers largely consist of warnings and calculations—any more than our population consists exclusively of criminals because the police news consists mostly of crimes.

—February 9, 1918

Fool

It is a true proverb, no doubt, which says "there is no fool like an old fool." Perhaps there is no fool who is half so happy in his own fool's paradise.

—March 14, 1931

Ford, Henry (and Prohibition)

I hear that Mr. Henry Ford, famous for the Ford that can go everywhere and the peace ship that went nowhere, has been delivering himself of an opinion on prohibition. Apparently it was to the effect that prohibition is a pure benefit to mankind, and that the only problem for a patriot or practical humanitarian is how to enforce it with sufficient severity.... I hardly think the line of thought altogether worthy of so wonderful a business man; and I rather doubt whether he would apply it to his own business.

—May 22, 1926

Forgery

... there is a tiresome journalistic habit of fulsomely praising ourselves, and fatuously despising our fathers, because we no longer hang a man for forgery. But, as a fact, it was not an early primitive habit, but a late progressive habit, to hang a man for forgery. For forgery did not become frightfully important until finance and commercial contracts, and banking business of all sorts, had become important. I am very glad that men are no longer hanged for forgery. But I can quite imagine a simple and artless tribe of savages among whom the habit of imitating another man's handwriting would appear as gay and innocent as making faces in imitation of another man's face.

—September 6, 1930

Fourth of July

Independence Day is, in fact, the most fantastic of all feasts. The Americans celebrate it because they have forgotten what it meant. The English now celebrate it because they have never found out what it meant. It is comic enough ... that an empire should be called upon to jump for joy because it has lost its largest colonies, and dance with never-ending delight on receiving the repeated news of its own defeat. But it is funnier still that it should show a warm and generous agreement with the ideals of the victors; ideals which, rightly or wrongly, the English disbelieved in then, and most disbelieve in still.

—July 31, 1926

France

Other nations are at peace with France; but France is never at peace.... In other words, the psychology of Frenchmen is the psychology of civil war.

—October 15, 1910

She is the one nation that has never been duped by the barbarian.

—February 23, 1918

Saint Francis

St. Francis really was a fountain and an origin; one of the very few in history. He was the sort of man whose discoveries go on being discovered. All those things that nobody understood before Wordsworth were exceedingly well understood by St. Francis. In other words, he knew all about that childish solemnity of pleasure that sees natural things in a white light of wonder. All those things that were so dreadfully revolutionary when they were revealed by Tolstoy were fully revealed by St. Francis. In other words, he knew all about the clear vision that comes of poverty and common living, and the popular origin of the real appreciation of the arts. All the best of the modern feeling about the attractiveness of animals, all the best of the modern feeling about the pathos of criminals, all the best of the modern feeling about the happiness of being a child, was in the mind of this mediaeval reformer long before modern reformers were born or thought of.

—March 10, 1923

Frederick the Great

Even Frederick the Great was a bad poet as well as a bad man; and, like many bad poets, he could only produce a strong effect of poetry by means of profanity. His hideous metaphor about "partaking of the Eucharistic body of Poland" was, of course, meant for an affront. . . .

—June 1, 1918

There is one fact I have never seen noticed about Frederick the Great and the founding of Prussian militarism. It is that, while he was modelling himself on something that was strong, he was also modeling himself on something that was moribund. His model was the monarchy of military France—not when it was firmly founded in the Middle Ages, but just before it fell into the chasm of the French Revolution. It might well be argued that the barbarian begins copying too late.

—February 8, 1919

The worship of Frederick the Great can hardly be called hero-worship. It is rather devil-worship softened by a touch of monkey-worship. It is superstition and therefore heresy to say such things seriously, but we may say symbolically that, if a demon could enter the body of a monkey, the result might be something like Frederick II of Prussia. It is not only true that he had a large mind and a small soul. It might almost equally truly be said that he had a large brain and a small mind. Even his intellectual pride was petty. . . . He substituted a new impudence and malignity for the last trailing traditions of mediaeval chivalry and Roman Law.

—October 18, 1924

Free Speech

. . . unless a man is allowed to talk he might as well be a chimpanzee who is only able to chatter.

—July 30, 1921

Free Verse

Read through any collection of free verse published to-day, and count up the number of utterances that are concerned with some form of distaste or even disgust. On the lines of the old songs of the sea there might be called the songs of the sea-sick. There is nothing in which the new poet fancies himself so much as in saying, like a barmaid at a beanfeast, that he does not fancy anything.

—June 13, 1925

I have not mentioned the fact that what is called "free verse" has become more common, and is in a sense a progress to which Whitman played the pioneer. If having caused other people to write a vast amount of bad poetry, or of stuff too bad to be called poetry, be a triumph for a great poet, by all means let it be added to his triumphs.

—June 13, 1925

Freedom

Men will not be truly free so long as they depend even on the most magic machine for the emotion of seeing other people falling off precipices or rescuing brides from burning houses. Freedom will mean a citizen's interest in his own wife, in his own hearth, or his own house on fire; and a free man will fall off his own private precipice.

—June 19, 1920

A man no longer says: "I am free to dig this land; to grow this apple-tree; to brew this cider; to drink this toast." For the modern man is most definitely not free to do things of this sort; there are hundreds of rules and regulations that stop him at every stage of such a process.

—October 20, 1928

... it is quite as easy, by the methods of the rationalistic heckler, to suggest that freedom is nonsense as that faith is nonsense.

—January 4, 1930

Freedom and Prohibition

I could never see, for instance, why a man who is not free to open his mouth to drink should be free to open it to talk. Talking does far more direct harm to other people. The village suffers less directly from the village drunkard than it might from the village tale-bearer, or the village tub-thumper, or the village villain who seduces the village maiden. These and twenty other types of evil are done simply by talking; and it is certain that a vast amount of evil would be prevented if we all wore gags. . . . In other words, if a man loses the responsibility for these rudimentary functions and forms of freedom, he loses not only his citizenship, but his manhood.

—July 30, 1921

French

. . . the French use oratory with an object; they impose silence with an object; and when they have torn people in pieces, it has been with an object, if only the object of revenge.

—October 27, 1917

French Revolution

. . . if a historian says, "The French Revolution ended in the despotism of Napoleon, and the return of the Bourbons," he speaks quite truly; but he speaks quite unjustly. The order is correct; but the use of the word *ended* begs the question. It would be equally true to say "The French Revolution ended in the Reform Bill, the liberation of Italy, and the beginnings of justice to Ireland." Perhaps it would be even truer to say "The French Revolution did not end at all."

—April 30, 1910

A critic might put it in the paradox that it destroyed life but preserved property. It would be truer to say that it destroyed an aristocracy, but it created a peasantry—a thing perhaps as stately, and certainly more stable.

—February 1, 1919

It was science, it was the natural philosophy encouraged by the encyclopaedists,

189

which begat zeppelins and mustard gas. It was the French Revolution that produced the conscription of whole peoples; that produced first Napoleon and then Moltke and then Foch. I do not merely deplore this militant development in the sense that pacifists deplore it. But I do say that Voltaire and his school would deplore it. They would all the more deeply deplore it, if they realised that they had done a good deal to produce it. If the scientific satirists of the Inquisition had seen some scenes of the great war, they would have hesitated between the hell they had denounced and the hell they had created.

—January 31, 1925

Freudians

I fancy, it will be the worst and not the best part of psycho-analysis that will be turned from a fad into a fashion. Already some are professing to find in it a whole encyclopaedia of excuses. They declare that psycho-analysts have told them that it is always unwholesome to repress an impulse; in which case I conceive that there will be no objection to my kicking the next psycho-analyst I meet. They say that certain deeds are done by the subconscious self and not by the real self; and I will gladly promise to blame my subconscious self for anything of the sort that I may do. They seem to provide the criminal with the invaluable gift of a double, and even of a double who cannot be caught.

—May 29, 1920

Freudism

There will be a fashionable fatalism founded on Freud, as there was twenty years ago a fashionable fatalism founded on Haeckel—or for that matter, two hundred years ago a fashionable fatalism founded on Calvin. And then, when it has had a run for its money, it will be suddenly discovered that it has not a leg to stand on. Another German professor will find out that Freud is entirely wrong; and that discovery will be new and that discovery will be a nine days' wonder. That also will be a fashion; and that also will be called a revolution. When all its work is done the lie will rot, and there will be only some of the consolations of a sense of humour for those who could see from the first where it was rotten.

—May 29, 1920

Friendship

But because our expression is imperfect we need friendship to fill up the imperfections. A man of our own type or tastes will understand our meaning before it is expressed; certainly a long time before it is perfectly expressed.

—*June* 6, 1931

Friendships of Convenience

All Christian history began with that great social occasion when Pilate and Herod shook hands. Hitherto, as everybody knew in society circles, they had hardly been on speaking terms. Something led them to seek each other's support, a vague sense of social crisis, though very little was happening except the execution of an ordinary batch of criminals. The two rulers were reconciled on the very day when one of these convicts was crucified. That is what many people mean by peace, and the substitution of a reign of love for one of hatred. Whether or no there is honour among thieves, there is always a certain social interdependence and solidarity among murderers; and those sixteenth-century ruffians who conspired to assassinate Rizzio or Darnley were always very careful to put their names, and especially each other's names, to what they called a "band," so that at the worst they might all hang together. Many political friendships—nay, even broad democratic comradeships, are of this nature; and their representatives are really distressed when we decline to identify this form of love with the original mystical idea of charity.

—*November* 25, 1933

Fundamentalism

... most Fundamentalists are not Fundamentalists. For, whatever we think of the thing now called Fundamentalism, it is not fundamental. It is not particularly fundamental to throw a big Bible at people's heads (or rather, a particular translation of the Bible, with a lot of books left out as apocrypha) any more than to throw the Encyclopaedia Britannica or the Institutes of Calvin.

—*January* 24, 1931

191

Fundamentalist

The fundamentalists are funny enough, and the funniest thing about them is their name. For, whatever else the fundamentalist is, he is not fundamental. He is content with the bare letter of scripture—the translation of a translation, coming down to him by the tradition of a tradition—without venturing to ask for its original authority.

—*June* 14, 1930

Funeral

In ancient times a funeral had many of the elements of a feast. In ancient times a dance could have much of the gravity of a divine service. They used the word "banquet" about the tragic occasion. . . . Achilles, mourning over Patroclus, summons the heroes to take part in games, as on a school holiday devoted to sports . . . and though our civilisation has grown in some ways more complex, and cannot express these truths with quite the same unconscious sincerity and natural tact, it is well not to forget altogether that our fathers felt this comradeship in their grief and this religion in their merriment.

—*December* 5, 1925

To find expression in emblem and established ritual for feelings that are most difficult to express in words is not merely a salute to the departed; it is also a liberating gesture for the living. It is even especially an expression of the life of the living. The practical alternative to it is not speech but silence; not simplicity, but merely embarrassment.

—*December* 5, 1925

Future

The future is always inhuman, as the futurist art is always dehumanised, because there is as yet no human footprint on those slimy sands of time.

—*February* 2, 1924

We cannot fling ourselves into the blank future; we can only call up images from the past. This being so, the important principle follows, that how many images we have largely depends on how much past we have. Even new ideas will depend on whether we have enough history to forget.

—October 4, 1924

Futurism

The Futurist does not really invade the future like a conqueror; he only flies to the future as a fugitive flies to sanctuary. In the street of Bye-and-Bye, said Henley, stands the Hostelry of Never. And indeed this is truer than he meant. The love of the untried is truly the love of Nothing: Futurism is very near to Nihilism. . . . In every practical matter you and I have known, Futurism has been a learned name for failure.

—December 18, 1909

There is one quite simple objection to the Future as an ideal. The objection is that the Future does not exist. . . . The Past is existent, and therefore the Past is alive. He who lives in past affairs lives in vivid and varied affairs, in turbulent, disputatious, and democratic affairs. He who lives in the future lives in a featureless blank; he lives in impersonality; he lives in Nirvana. The past is democratic, because it is a people. The future is despotic, because it is a caprice. Each man is alone in his prediction, just as each man is alone in a dream.

—December 18, 1909

I have no faith in the future of . . . Futurism.

—November 3, 1917

A good and happy humanity is, humanly speaking, the idea by which we test political and social ideas; it is the test; it is in that sense the ideal. This futurist religion will not accept it as normal, and goes forth hunting for a new normal that it can never find.

—March 8, 1924

Futurists

... Futurists ... commit this primary moral error of turning from the present and past, which are full of facts, to the future, which is void even of abstract truth. The real moral of the matter is this: that decadence, in its fullest sense of failure and impotence, is now to be found among those who live in the future, not in those who live in the past.

—December 18, 1909

G-H-I-J-K-L

Gaugin, Paul

Gaugin and other experimental artists have devoted themselves not merely to the study of savage subjects, but to some extent to the imitation of savage art. Some of them, or some of their imitators, have deliberately set out not merely to paint Hottentots, but to paint as badly as Hottentots would paint.

—January 26, 1924

Generation (the Now)

A generation is now growing old, which never had anything to say for itself except that it was young. It was . . . the first generation that believed in progress and nothing else. It covered a period roughly corresponding to the life of Mr. Bernard Shaw. . . . Whatever Mr. Shaw taught, there can be little doubt about what most of the admirers learnt. It was simply that the new thing is always better than the old thing; that the young man is always right and the old man wrong. And now that they are old men themselves, they have naturally nothing whatever to say or do. Their only business in life was to be the rising generation knocking at the door. Now that they have got into the house, and have been accorded the seat of honour by the hearth, they have completely forgotten why they wanted to come in. The aged younger generation never knew why it knocked at the door; and the truth is that it only knocked at the door because it was shut. It had nothing to say; it had no message; it had no convictions to impart to anybody. Now that it has grown old in its turn, it cannot influence its children . . . simply because it has nothing to tell them.

—July 9, 1921

Genetics and Psychological Determinism

A man kills because he is black-mailed, or because he is jilted, or because he is a political fanatic, and so on. But how do you inherit a blackmailer, or an unreliable girl, or a political theory? There certainly is inheritance, as of physical type, perhaps of physical temperament; of being indolent or restless and so on. But the number of lazy men who will murder a valet for waking them up is about as large as the number of impatient men who will murder him for keeping them waiting. That is to say, it is very small. The mysterious moral inhibition, or its absence, by which men do or do not murder, is in the individual soul; and I defy anybody to show that it is hereditary.

—February 15, 1930

If what is inherited is anything so vague as a lack of vigilance and self-control against pleasure itself, I cannot see why the drunkard should not have one son who was a jewel-thief and another who was always flirting with barmaids or bolting with ballet-girls. Of course, many children of drunken families are drunken; not because there is heredity, but because there are a great many other things besides heredity. . . . The next thing we heard was the cheerful news that assassination was a regular family feature, like a family nose.

—February 15, 1930

Genius

The genius who never replies to critics is an even more offensive person than the genius who is always replying to critics.

—October 31, 1925

Genius (Finding a)

The real tip for finding the genius, so far as there is any way of finding him . . . would be to advertise for a fool, and hope for a genius with a sense of humour.

—October 17, 1925

It would be dangerous enough in any case to call publicly on such people to call public attention to themselves. Anybody advertising for an original artist . . . would have the streets round his house blocked for miles with all the fools in the world, ranging from raving lunatics to the very dullest sort of dunces.

—*October* 17, 1925

Genius Loci

If there is one thing that men have proved again and again it is that, even when they furiously burn down a temple, they like to put another on top of it. They do not, generally speaking, want to worship St. George except on the very spot where they once worshipped the dragon. And, even when they have altered the universe, they do not alter the situation. What is the reason for this, and whether it is some hitherto nameless need of human nature, or whether there be indeed something behind those ancient legends of the *genius loci* or spirit of the place, need not now be discussed.

—*January* 11, 1930

Gentleman

In short, the old-fashioned gentleman felt in his heart that he was an ordinary man, and dressed like an extraordinary man in the symbols and totems of his house. The new gentleman feels himself to be an extraordinary man, and dresses like an ordinary man out of the unfathomable insolence of his pride.

—*July* 7, 1906

St. George

If the real original St. George did find himself interviewed by a modern newspaper man, he would think that hardly anything in the newspaper was new. He would not think primarily that he had come into a strange world, far away from dragons and princesses and mediaeval armour. He would think he had got back into the old bewildered and decaying world of the last phase of paganism, loud with denials of religion and louder with the howlings of superstition.

—*June* 18, 1932

German Atrocities

Germany is now doing things which she did not dare to do even in 1914; exactly as she did things in 1914 that she not dare to do in 1870. There are, of course, some shameless and shocking things which the Germans have not done even yet. There are not many; but there are some. They have killed prisoners; but they have not yet, so far as I know, eaten prisoners. But if anything can be calculated from any human tendencies at all, they would probably do it at a later stage, or in another war—if we go out of our way to give them the chance.

—September 15, 1917

German Culture

. . . imitation has been, first and last, the sincerest form of German culture.

—May 4, 1918

German Logic

. . . the Germans are now maintaining, that murder of peaceable men, women, and children, by a submarine which is as impartial as a shark, is really the height of humanitarianism, because it will "shorten the war."

—February 17, 1917

Germans

. . . the Germans do not believe in anything except organisation.

—August 17, 1918

Germany

. . . it is a far more practical problem for the future whether we can trust what is now the German Republic. . . .

—July 19, 1919

Germany and War

Every nation has been moved by unworthy motives or waged unjust wars; but in most cases this was done in one of two ways; either for a merely mean or material object; or else for a fixed and perhaps fanatical theory, which could be defined because it was fixed or fanatical. But there is something about this particular Nordic mood, or whatever you call it, that defies definition. . . . Both the pure fanatics and the mere materialists are objective; and have an object. . . . But the German in this mood fights for self-expression; and therefore there is nothing to limit his self-assertion. The spirit flows outwards from within; it is not a plan or a creed in which he believes; it is not merely a prize that he covets. The very form which the idea takes in his mind, in so far as there is a form, reveals that it is formless in the sense of limitless. For he nearly always bases his view, not on the idea of a nation, which has frontiers that are objective facts; but on the idea of a race, which overflows all frontiers, and has a sort of infinite destiny.

—*May* 20, 1933

Ghandi, Mahatma

In some respects he stands not merely for ancient Asiatic ideas, but also for ancient European ideas, and even for ancient English ideas. He said the other day, for instance, that, in spite of all the specious casuistry of "the economic independence of women," the normal thing was to preserve the unity of the family and the male as the external breadwinner of the family. There is nothing particularly Hindu, or even anything specially Indian, about that. Many of his remarks in that connection would remind the reader much more of Cobbett than of Buddha.

—*October* 10, 1931

Glory

Glory is only a good thing when it is a good joke.

—*June* 19, 1915

God (Modern Critique of)

A man looks at the sun and moon and stars and seasons of an obviously ordered world, and concludes that it has a design and therefore a designer. . . . But the old evolutionists of the Grant Allen sort could not bring themselves to admit anything so simple as that men affirmed the existence of a deity because they thought that a deity existed. They said it was because a primitive man had a curious dream which frightened him. He was apparently very easily frightened, which was why he perpetually passed his time in wars and raids and the hunting of huge prehistoric monsters. Or it was because he could not make out where his great-great-grandfather had got to, and could not take in the fact that the old gentleman was dead. Or he was thinking about the sun, or about the sex question, or about the seed and harvest; but, anyhow, not about the subject in hand.

—February 27, 1926

Good Old Times

It is always implied that the good old times are only praised by the bad old men. I do not know whether my years and crimes yet entitle me to be considered a bad old man, but I am quite sure that I have never at any time, or in any fashion, been fool enough to talk in mere praise of the good old times. I have praised particular times for particular things, and given particular and perfectly reasonable reasons. But even in my own lifetime I have been able to see that things cannot be judged in so simple and sweeping a fashion; that there were not two things definitely to be classed as a new time and an old time.

—June 13, 1925

Gossip

Private gossip is so much more serious than the Press. Private gossip is so much more responsible than the Press. A man does not wear a mask when he tells you a story in a club; but a man does wear a mask when he tells you a story in the columns of the *Daily Post* or the *Morning Telegraph*.

—February 1, 1908

... gossip is another name for democracy.

—*February* 1, 1908

Gourmet

Gluttony is a great fault; but we do not necessarily dislike a glutton. We only dislike the glutton when he becomes the *gourmet* — that is, we only dislike him when he not only wants the best for himself, but knows what is best for other people.

—*August* 22, 1914

Government

Our duty to human government is either to make it work swiftly or to stop it working.

—*November* 21, 1908

... government always becomes less popular in proportion as it becomes less local. The perfect democracy is a parish democracy; and though there are doubtless, defects in this type of community, there are far greater dangers in departing from it too far.

—*December* 7, 1918

Government (Mediaeval)

... the lively local government of mediaeval times gave men a particular kind of liberty which they have now almost entirely lost. It was the right to manage their own affairs, in the vivid and vulgar sense of a right to mind their own business.

—*October* 11, 1919

Grammar and Sophistry

Some of the most enormous and idiotic developments of our modern thought and speech arise simply from not knowing the parts of speech and principles of language, which we once knew when we were children. . . . For most fundamental falsehoods are errors in language as well as in philosophy. Most statements that are unreasonable are really ungrammatical.

−*October* 16, 1909

Grotesque

We may love the grotesque as humorous, or loathe the grotesque as ignominious, but it is immoral to love it as ignominious. It is immoral to regard its ugliness as seriously better than beauty.

−*September* 9, 1922

Growing Older

. . . one pleasure attached to growing older is that many things seem to be growing younger; growing fresher and more lively than we once supposed them to be. We begin to see significance, or (in other words) to see life, in a large number of traditions, institutions, maxims, and codes of manners that seem in our first days to be dead.

−*March* 14, 1931

Grumbling

Grumbling is anger in solution, as sentimentalism is love in solution. . . .

−*May* 24, 1919

Guessing

. . . the detective expresses his scorn of the mental operation known as "guessing," and says that it "destroys the logical faculty." It may destroy the logical faculty, but it makes the practical world. It cannot be too constantly or too emphatically stated that the whole of practical human life, the whole of business, in its most sharp and severe sense, is run on spiritual atmospheres and nameless, impalpable emotions. Practical men *always* act on imagination: they have no time to act on worldly wisdom. When a man receives a clerk who comes for employment, what does he do? Does he measure his skull? Does he look up his heredity? No; he guesses.

—November 4, 1905

Guild

The difference between mediaeval guilds and modern capitalism is not a difference of details that can be disputed, but of a design that nobody disputes. It is not a question of idealising the guilds, but of realising what were their ideals. The only superiority I here claim for them is one that nobody can deny to them. It is a hard historical fact that the guilds were an attempt to organise trade upon a Christian theory of fellowship and mutual help. It is an equally hard historical fact that modern industrial capitalism was nothing of the sort. It was and is exactly the opposite; I do not mean in practice but in purpose. It was and is founded on a non-Christian theory of the advantages of selfishness and materialism.

—October 25, 1924

Gun Control

It would be easy to imagine an Arabian romance about a sultan whose grand vizier had his throat cut by his barber; and who immediately forbade razors throughout the length and breadth of his empire.... But he would hardly be attacking the deepest causes of the discontent of that empire.... Then when he has carefully excluded all razors, he will be very much surprised when the next grand vizier is killed with a red-hot poker. He will be still more surprised to find that an increasing number of his critics have passed from razors to red-hot pokers, as an increasing number of Americans are passing from drink to drugs. Thus slowly will that sultan ... begin to have a glimmering of the great first principle of practical politics; that the sin is in a man's soul and not in his tools or his toys; and that in so far as his soul is affected by them, it is affected by all of them, and not by one in unique ... isolation.

—June 5, 1920

Haeckel, Ernst Heinrich

Personally I think Haeckel ... an extravagantly ignorant man; to anybody who knows Christian history, his remarks about Christian history are enough to make an ox laugh.

—February 5, 1910

It may be only a practical joke to pull away a chair; but it is gratifying that it should be Professor Haeckel's chair, at the University of Jena.

—March 29, 1919

Twenty years ago, it would have been atrociously antiquated to say that Haeckel was not really a scientist, though it is now much less clear that he was a scientist than that he was a monist. He was, anyhow, a propagandist, and a pretty unscrupulous propagandist; but we were all supposed to swallow what he said at once, because he was science.

—June 14, 1930

Hair (Curly)

This is why the Negro should wish to make his curly hair straight, especially as so many White people take the trouble to make their straight hair curly. It is said that the Negroes regard it as a sign of a servile status; but I cannot imagine why. It would seem more natural to regard straight, limp hair as drooping in captivity, or hair that lies flat on the head as lying prostrate before the conqueror. It would seem more reasonable for them to regard their own strong, erect, tenacious hair as constituting a sort of cap of liberty.

—June 21, 1919

Half-Truth

That a heresy is a half-truth is a very old and familiar example of a whole truth, but a truth that is not often realised as a whole. . . . If we look back on history we shall see it largely encumbered and crushed with half-truths; we shall wonder how it happened so often that a whole age or generation was content with a half-truth, without making the faintest effort to find the other half. . . . It may be that we shall never fully understand why our fathers did it, for we certainly do not in the least understand why we do it ourselves.

—*April 25, 1931*

Hamlet

The whole point of Hamlet is that he is really saner than anybody else in the play; though I admit that being sane is not identical with what some call being sensible. Being outside in the world, he sees all round it; where everybody else sees his own side of the world, his own worldly ambition, or hatred or love. But, after all, Hamlet pretended to be mad in order to deceive fools. We cannot complain if he has succeeded.

—*September 14, 1927*

Hansom Cab

No, if you wish to impress the foreigner, cling convulsively to your hansom cab. Never let him see you except in this vehicle. Drive round your back-garden in it; drive it up the centre aisle when you go to church. When the British Army advances into battle, let each private soldier be inside a hansom cab, and its enemies will flee before it.

—*October 14, 1905*

Happiness

Happy is he who not only knows the causes of things, but who has not lost touch with their beginnings. Happy is he who still loves something that he loved in the nursery: he has not been broken in two by time; he is not two men, but one, and has saved not only his soul but his life.

—*September 26, 1908*

Hardy, Thomas

Mr. Hardy is wholly of our own generation, which is a very unpleasant thing to be. He is shrill and not mellow. He does not worship the unknown God: he knows the God (or thinks he knows the God), and dislikes him. He is not a pantheist: he is a pandiabolist. The great agnostics of the Victorian age said there was no purpose in Nature. Mr. Hardy is a mystic; he says there is an evil purpose. All this is as far as possible from the plentitude and rational optimism of Meredith. And when we have disposed of Mr. Hardy, what other name is there that can even pretend to recall the heroic Victorian age? The Roman curse lies upon Meredith like a blessing: "Ultimus suorum moriatur"—he has died the last of his own.

—June 5, 1909

Mr. Hardy has been not only a pessimist, but a propagandist. It never would have occurred to me that anybody could consider him a non-combatant. We have as much right to attack the pessimism of Mr. Thomas Hardy as the socialism of Mr. Bernard Shaw or the pacifism of Mr. Bertrand Russell.

—July 18, 1925

Hatred (Higher)

... the purpose of the higher hatred, or whatever you choose to call it, is to ensure a violent reaction as a result of what is wrong that shall drastically distinguish it from the results of what is right.

—March 16, 1918

Headline

There is much more interest in the papers than anybody could guess from the posters. A newspaper column is never quite so dull as one would infer from the headlines that are meant to make it attractive. It is by this time a convention of journalism that the most trivial things should be printed in the largest letters, while anything at all significant or suggestive should be printed in very small letters, or, by a more frequent accident, not printed at all.

—November 6, 1920

... there is something a little amusing about the claims of publicity and business requiring us to reverse all that we mean, in order to get anybody to listen to what we say. There is something comic about sacrificing everything to the head-line, and letting it insist that the article should stand on its head.

—January 25, 1930

What I lament is the importance of head-lines and the unimportance of headwork; the eagerness to state a man's views, compared with the carelessness about whether his views are really stated, let alone whether they are really sound.

—May 24, 1930

Heart (Broken)

There are some things that are irrelevant to the subject of Smith having a broken leg. But there are no subjects that are irrelevant to Smith having a broken heart. Anyone can discover if his leg is mended or not. No one will discover, until the end of all time, whether his heart is mended or not. That question will have to wait until that great day when the world shall be ended—or mended.

—July 11, 1908

Henry VIII

We forget that Henry VIII was intellectual, but we remember that he was fat.

—July 14, 1906

Hen-pecked

Most men have it on their conscience that they give a good deal too much trouble to their female surroundings—or rather, they ought to have it on their conscience that it is so seldom in their consciousness.

—July 18, 1925

Hero (Modern)

First, he must be a teetotaler; or, as I should say, he must be a Moslem rather than a Christian on the moral problem of wine. Second, he must take very seriously the business of getting on in this world, prospering in his profession and obtaining the solid rewards this world has to give. Third, he must worship progress or the spirit of the age; which can only mean (so far as I can make any sense of it) that he must allow his own conscience and conviction to be twisted into any shapes that the pressure of the present state of politics and society may tend to produce.

—February 23, 1929

Historian

Such a story as that of William Tell could literally be told of any epoch; . . . The point of it is . . . as eternal as tyranny and fatherhood. Now, wherever there is this function of the fine story in history we tell it to children only because it is a fine story. . . . But the historians have quite a different business. It is their affair, not merely to remember that humanity has been wise and great, but to understand the special ways in which it has been weak and foolish. Historians have to explain the horrible mystery of how fashions were ever fashionable. They have to explain, as best they can, how anyone ever came to have a top hat, how anyone ever endured an asbestos stove.

—October 8, 1910

The difficulty of history is that historians seldom see the simple things, or even the obvious things, because they are too simple and obvious.

—January 18, 1930

It is all the difference between the chronicler and the historian. And the difference is that the chronicler sometimes told fables; whereas the historian never tells fables, but only falsehoods.

—February 14, 1931

Historian (Humility of)

... before the historian goes on to show that the heroes of history were lacking in this or that, he will do well to admit that not only heroes, but even historians, are human beings, and may possibly be lacking in something.

—August 15, 1925

Historian (Progressive)

... to hear these people talk, one would suppose that, but for what they call superstition, there would always have been progress. The truth is that, but for what they call superstition, there would simply have been savagery.... They assume that if the Huns had not been Christians ... there would have been no theological squabbles to divert them from scientific culture and social reform. In short, if the Huns had been heathens, they would have been humanitarians.... It is suggested that border chieftains would all have been arguing in debating clubs about evolution and ethics, but for the blighting influence of theology.... It is suggested that the cloud which darkened these dark ages was superstition or religion. But the truth is that the clouds that rolled up over the end of the Roman Empire came from all quarters of the sky and all causes in the nature of things: from Asia, from Africa, from the hungry north, from the economic breakdown and the failure of communications, from half-a-hundred other historical causes; and that the clouds were so dark that religion, even if it had really been superstition, would still by comparison have been enlightenment. One may like or dislike that candle, but it is quite certain that it was the only light in that gloom.

—February 13, 1926

Historians and Newspapers

We have all heard it said that the historians of the future will be under no such disadvantage as the historians of the past in the matter of scarcity of material; that they will have before them thousands of newspapers with the most minute exposition of events. I do not believe this. I think that the future historians if they go by the newspapers, will know far less about this age than we know about simpler ages, touching which we collect our evidence from the most various human sources—popular rumours, private diaries, angry allusions, cries in the street, anonymous and scurrilous pamphlets.... But I have a suspicion that the future historian will largely throw the newspapers on one side, as we throw aside some merely florid and servile State proclamation in which the King is called the fountain of art and learning and the conqueror of the world.

—*March* 2, 1907

Historical Bias

... a man ought not merely to say, "I will now narrate the history of such-and-such a Greek or mediaeval city, where the people were so narrow and primitive as to believe that certain gods or saints guarded the citadel against its enemies." Rather, the writer ought to say, "I have the misfortune to be writing these words in Ealing, where I can find no trace of any gods being worshipped, or even of any saints being invoked. My capacity for dealing with the question is therefore considerably limited. ... "

—*August* 15, 1925

... the historian ought to be made to understand that his day is only a day. He is apt to treat it as if it were a day of judgment.

—*August* 25, 1925

History

History will be wholly false unless it is helped by legend.

—*September* 12, 1908

... that there are two quite distinct purposes of history; the superior purpose, which is its use for children; and the secondary or inferior purpose, which is its use for historians. The highest and noblest thing that history can be is a good story. Then it appeals to the heroic heart of all generations, the eternal infancy of mankind.

—*October* 8, 1910

As it is in politics with the specially potent man, so it is in history with the specially learned. We do not need the learned man to teach us the important things. We all know the important things, though we all violate and neglect them. Gigantic industry, abysmal knowledge, are needed for the discovery of the tiny things—the things that seem hardly worth the trouble. Generally speaking, the ordinary man should be content with the terrible secret that men are men—which is another way of saying that they are brothers. For every man knows the inmost core of every other man. It is the trappings and externals erected for an age and a fashion that are forgotten and unknown. It is all the curtains that are curtained, all the masks that are masked, all the disguises that are now disguised in dust and featureless decay. But though we cannot reach the outside of history, we all start from the inside.

—October 8, 1910

. . . there is no intelligible history without a religion.

—November 19, 1910

. . . history far back to its first beginnings is, and was, made of men like ourselves; that landscape over the better part of this earth is made almost as much by man as by Nature; that the most interesting things about a people are not the things it makes and exports, but the things it makes and consumes; and, above all, that the true bond of nations is neither in commerce nor diplomacy but in a common facing of the facts of our being, a common love of life, a common pride of death: "Comrades and soldiers in the land of the living."

—October 30, 1915

Fortunately, history never does repeat itself. If it did, all our own blunders and brutalities would ceaselessly repeat themselves. The one element of truth in the rather priggish notion commonly called progress is that we have at least a chance of not making exactly the same mistake twice over. History does not repeat itself; in that sense it is truer to say that history reforms itself. At the best, it may justly be said that history repents of itself. When it will not do so, it does not merely repeat its mistake; but rather rushes on the ruin that is the result of its mistake.

—August 23, 1919

The whole object of history is to enlarge experience by imagination . . . the whole object of history is to make us realise that humanity could be great and glorious, under conditions quite different and even contrary to our own. It is to teach us that men could achieve most profitable labour without our own division of labour. It is to teach us that men could be industrious without being industrial. It is to make us understand that there might be a world in which there was far less improvement in the transport for visiting various places, and there might still be a very great improvement in the places visited.

— February 4, 1922

I believe what really happens in history is this: the old man is always wrong; and the young people are always wrong about what is wrong with him. The practical form it takes is this: that, while the old man may stand by some stupid custom, the young man always attacks it with some theory that turns out to be equally stupid.

— June 3, 1922

The excavations of the past are not half so fatal to the faiths of the past as they are to the pretensions of the present; and many a novelty has only remained new until it was superannuated by something much older. In that sense many of our discoveries have destroyed many of our inventions. In fact, the difference has become one of detail and degree, and is no longer a decisive difference of kind. History is no longer a complacent contemplation of how far we have left these people behind. It is a doubtful speculation about how far they had gone along a path parallel to us, or even got ahead of us. The past has ceased to be merely a foil and become a rival.

— July 22, 1922

History, especially contemporary history, could no longer be the object-lesson of politics. As it is, even a revolution is a tradition; and riot itself is a part of the established past. A mob remains to be judged like a monument; and the rebel as much as the reactionary awaits the criticism of posterity. But in a universal system innovation must be a universal novelty. It cannot be tried by anybody until it is tried by everybody. It must always mean experiment, and never experience.

— September 27, 1924

. . . a man without history is almost in the literal sense half-witted. He is only in command of a part even of his own mind. He does not know what half his own words mean, or what half his own actions signify.

— December 5, 1925

History is not a science; certainly not an exact science. History is not merely a progress; nor is it merely a degeneration. But at least history is a joke; and it never fails in that eternal freshness that can surprise us like a practical joke.

—*April* 17, 1926

... the happiest moment of history is something that is not so much a goal as a turning-point. Men are sometimes at their sanest and merriest at the moment when some new good thing has begun, but some old good thing not quite departed.

—*September* 11, 1926

I do not care much about dates, but they are occasionally useful.

—*January* 3, 1931

... there is no historical truth without historical imagination.

—*September* 5, 1931

The disadvantage of men not knowing the past is that they do not know the present. History is a hill or high point of vantage from which alone men see the town in which they live or the age in which they are living. Without some such contrast or comparison, without some such shifting of the point of view, we should see nothing whatever of our own social surroundings. We should take them for granted, as the only possible social surroundings. We should be as unconscious of them as we are, for the most part, of the hair growing on our heads. ... It is the variety of the human story that brings out sharply the last turn that the road had taken, and it is the view under the arch of the gateway which tells us that we are entering a town.

—*June* 18, 1932

In short, human history will remain utterly unintelligible to us, in art and in everything else, so long as we try to interpret it merely in terms of progress, or, worse still, of evolution. But man is not merely a creature who evolves. On the contrary, man is man because he is a creature who does not evolve. All his great inspirations have been great recollections. There never was a revolution that was not a renaissance. The artists of what we call the renaissance partly conceal the very meaning of their own name by their realistic method and their accidental appeal to certain modern elements. We have before us a more stark and startling example, in the resemblance between the very harshness and crudity of the very first and the very last of artists.

—December 10, 1932

There are some of us who do hold that the metaphor of inheritance from human history is a true metaphor, and that any man who is cut off from the past, and content with the future, is a man most unjustly disinherited; and all the more unjustly if he is happy in his lot, and is not permitted even to know what he has lost. And I, for one, believe that the mind of man is at its largest, and especially at its broadest, when it feels the brotherhood of humanity linking it up with remote and primitive and even barbaric things.

—January 7, 1933

It is natural enough that history should be mixed with myth, to make it interesting to the populace. But it is utterly unnatural that history or myth should not be interesting to the populace. And the mystery of the modern mob, in this matter, is not so much that a history-book is not so popular as a horse, as that it is not popular at all.

—February 8, 1936

History (Scientific)

The scientific sort of history is much too easy to write. It is also much too easy to criticise when it is written; and though I have never written a scientific history, thank God, I have very often criticised those of others, and found it, so far as that is concerned, a pleasant and facile way of earning one's living.

—June 20, 1925

Hitler, Adolph

President Wilson eventually entered into the Great War, remarking that it was a war to make the world safe for democracy. Herr Hitler is undoubtedly ready to wage another great war to make the world safe from democracy.

—December 3, 1932

... thousands of us think he is perfectly right in regarding books that have been boomed of late as "realistic" and "ruthless" as being largely a heap of dirt to be taken away in a muck-cart. But when this is combined with saying that the mathematical speculations of poor old Einstein must be poisonous because he is a Jew, or that it is un-German to express the ordinary hope for peace for which all Christians pray, we know he is encouraging the sceptics to prove that the ideal of pure literature is pure bosh. He is making even decency itself indecent.

—June 3, 1933

Holiday

This solemn character in holidays is, of course, implied in their very name: the day that is made a holiday is the day that is made holy. And in practice it will generally be found that holidays are opportunities for the emergence of the more serious side of a man. He has been kept during the rest of the year at trifling and passing matters—the writing of articles or the canvassing of soap. Now he rushes away to the things that are most eternal, sports in the simple country, hunting on the great hills. He is a clerk spending all the rest of his time in the newest and most changeable of all things—the suburbs. What does he do for his holiday? He rushes away to the oldest and most unchangeable of all things—the sea.

—October 14, 1905

... normal people enjoy special occasions without knowing why, just as the learned, lofty, cultivated, enlightened people despise them without knowing why.

—January 3, 1925

Holocaust

America is the one place in the modern world in which there is a mere race-war, a war uncomplicated by any question of religion, undignified by any principle of patriotism, a mere brutal war of breed against breed, of black against white. The point is not merely that a negro is killed savagely in America. A Protestant was killed savagely in Spain and a Catholic in England. But in these religious persecutions the principle of division was a philosophical principle, and was at least the result of thought and laborious mental distinctions. But the negro is not only killed in a savage way: he is killed for a savage reason. His holocaust is a mere orgie of taste, or, rather, of distaste. Men burnt a heretic as they burnt a book: because

215

they disagreed with him. But men burn a negro as they burn an old hat; because they dislike the physical notion of his having anything to do with them. Doubtless this primitive action of the nerves is a very human and real thing; but it is not civilisation, it is nature. Dislike is, perhaps, a stronger thing even than hatred.

—February 16, 1907

Home

I do not know whether I despise drifting more when it is done by plutocrats who lounge about in large hotels or by socialists who yearn after communal kitchens. . . . I do know I am most indignant of all when rich people, who cannot appreciate their own homes, drive poor people out of the homes that they do appreciate.

—September 26, 1925

The Home and Bolshevism

The only truly and legitimately communist institution is the home. "With all my worldly goods I thee endow" is the only satisfactory Bolshevist proclamation that has ever been made about property. It is, therefore, of course, the one proclamation which Bolshevists would be the first to attack. The twisted and unnatural posture of the modern controversy, like that of a serpent with its tail in its mouth, biting and tearing at itself, is excellently illustrated in this queer revolt of communism in the wrong place against communism in the right place. We no longer make the normal attempt to break up society into homes. We only make an attempt to break up homes, and even that by a principle of division which we dare not apply to anything else in society.

—November 28, 1931

Hoover, Herbert

Mr. Hoover is neither better nor worse than all modern statesmen, who are apparently obliged to state ambiguously what everybody else is stating plainly.

—December 20, 1930

House of Lords

The men who get to the top are not "picked men." They are not picked by God, which is merit. They are not picked by man, which is democracy. As every rational man of the world knows, they are picked by vanity and vainglory—by one vulgar fellow helping another vulgar fellow to a peerage, in the hope that he may get one himself.

—December 3, 1910

Any of these dull men might, perhaps, have been respectable enough to be summoned on a jury; none of them, perhaps, would have been so ambitious or wicked as to be elected for the House of Commons. If I defended the Peers, it would always be the Peers who do not attend. The stupid Peers are a genuine English gentry: I would trust them with many things. The clever Peers are mostly mere adventurers: I would not trust them with a postage-stamp.

—December 3, 1910

Hubris

Whenever a man puts on spectacles to see a statue, he is making himself unbeautiful in order to see beauty. And whenever a man assumes "culture" in order to admire antiquity, he is becoming all that is crude and vulgar in order to study what is ancient and sublime.

—October 9, 1909

The same blunder is made in the field of politics as in the field of philosophy or theology. There is a very unwise habit of assuming not merely that certain liberal ideals are right, but that all really educated people think they are right.

—August 22, 1931

Huckleberry Finn

What makes "Huckleberry Finn" one of the most glorious of all epics of boyhood is the indescribable sense that Huck really does potentially own the earth, that the world is all before him where to choose, and that America is itself one vast adventure story.

— November 1, 1930

Human Body

All that talk about the divinity and dignity of the human body is stolen from theology, and is quite meaningless without theology. It dates from the Garden of Eden, and the idea (which I happen to hold firmly) that God created man in his own image. But, if you remove that religious idea, there is no more sense in saying that every human being is lovely than in saying that every hippopotamus is lovely. It is a matter of taste; and many of us, after watching a sufficient number of human beings at Brighton, might prefer the hippopotamus.

— September 13, 1930

Human Dignity and War

There are some things more important than peace, and one of them is the dignity of human nature. It is a humiliation of humanity that humanity should ever give up war solely through fear, especially through fear of the mere machines that humanity itself has made. We all see the absurdity of modern armaments. It is a grotesque end for the great European story that each of us should keep on stuffing pistols into his pockets until he falls down with the weight of them. But it is still worse that we should only be friends because we are too nervous to stand the noise of a pistol. Let the man stop the pistol by all means. But do not let the pistol stop the man. Civilised man has created a cruel machinery which he now, it may be, finds bad for his soul. Then let civilised man save his soul and abandon his machinery. It hangs the machinery *in terrorem* over the head of all humanity to frighten them from going to war for any cause, just or unjust. Man is cowed into submission by his own clockwork. I would sooner be ruled by cats and dogs. They, at any rate, are our fellow-creatures, not merely our creatures. I would have any war, however long and horrible, sooner than such a horrible peace. I would run any risk rather than submit to such a spiritual indignity as that man dare not, for the most crying justice or the most urgent chivalry, turn one of his own handles. Then let man silence his guns; but, in the name of human honour, do not let his guns silence him.

— May 9, 1908

Human Equality

If we are not to have human equality, based on all being human, then the next best thing is a leisured and liberal class with some chance of growing up humane. It is better than being governed despotically by alternate gutter-boys who never grow up at all.... It is better than being ruled by money marked with all the curses of where it comes from, and never cleansed with any of the cultural environments of where it goes to. I myself should prefer to meet the onslaught of Bolshevism in that square formation which I know is the strongest: the formation of the peasants and the guildsmen. But it would be better to be led by knights and nobles than by much wealthier camp-followers, whose own highest boast is that they have long been laden with loot.

— September 10, 1932

Human Life

I obstinately maintained... that human life is not only dramatic, but melodramatic.... The view was regarded with contempt by the culture of that time, which specialised in the semitones and small touches of the scientific or psychological novel... human souls are much wilder, whiter, and blacker than the realistic school ever managed to realise; and that grey souls, like grey cats, are the exception rather than the rule. I have since spent much of my life in looking for the dull, colourless, commonplace man who constitutes (according to the realists) the great mass of mankind and I have never been able to discover him.

— September 22, 1917

Humanitarians

The humanitarians, in their gross, animal way, think that a flogging and a prize-fight are very much the same because they bruise a man's body. You might as well say that taking off your hat to a lady was the same as having your hat knocked off by a gentleman. The physical effect is the same; you are for some brief period without a hat. But I have been told by psychological experts, who have tried both, that the emotions are remarkably different.

— March 31, 1906

It is impossible to make a list of the things that humanitarians do not know about humanity. On thousands of things the men who talk most of the common bond are ignorant of what is really common.

—January 11, 1930

Humble

It is the small soul that is sure it is an exception; the large soul is only too proud to be the rule.

—July 2, 1910

Humour

Nature is inferior to man in many things, but most of all in respect of the human speciality of humour.

—January 10, 1931

Hurry

. . . People complain that journalism must be frivolous or unreliable because it is done in a hurry. But all the very serious things are done in a hurry. All the really reliable things are done in a hurry. A commercial decision involving millions is always made in a hurry. I have never been in a battle; but my military friends tell me that a battle often takes place in a hurry. Very serious things generally are done quickly; getting married for instance, or getting hanged. Some evolutionist philosophers do not believe this, I know. They think that a man gets slowly hanged and gradually married. But the practical world, as it is, could not be run at all without these definite lines and decisive convictions.

—October 13, 1906

Huxley and Spencer

I think Huxley was a great man, and Herbert Spencer a very small man. Many of their contemporaries worshipped both of them; and I do not very greatly agree with either of them. But Huxley held the very ancient agnostic philosophy; and it is a large though a negative philosophy. And Huxley could write; that is, he could write that large philosophy on a small scale. Herbert Spencer could only write a small philosophy on a large scale. He spread out all the prejudices of one very priggish type of dissenter, in one industrial type of society, so as to cover thousands of pages.

—February 26, 1927

Hypocrite

Really to be a hypocrite must require a horrible strength of character. An ordinary man such as you or I generally fails at last because he has not enough energy to be a man. But the hypocrite must have enough energy to be two men. It is said that a liar should have a good memory. But a hypocrite must not only have a good memory of the past, but a consistent and creative vision of the future; his unreal self must be so far real to him. The perfect hypocrite should be a trinity of artistic talent. He must be a novelist like Dickens to create a false character. He must be an actor like Garrick to act it. And he must be a business man like Carnegie to profit by it. Such a genius would not be easy to find in any country; but I think it can fairly be said that it would be exceptionally difficult to find him in England.

—July 17, 1909

The divine punishment of hypocrisy is fatigue. Those, in Shakespeare's fine simile, whose hearts are all as false as stairs of sand, must really have much of that exhausted sensation that comes of walking through sand when it is loose and deep. The hypocrite is that unluckiest of actors who is never out of a job. . . . Threescore years and ten is too long a run for the most successful play or the most energetic cast. And whenever there is this unreality in the lives and business of human beings, sooner or later the note of fatigue is heard. The man is tired of the mask, and still more of the task—the task of "humbugging all the people all the time."

—June 13, 1914

. . . instead of calling things dogmas when he accepts them as dogmas, he only calls them dogmas when he does not accept them. Other people's dogmas are dogmas but his dogmas only truths.

—March 21, 1925

I. Q. Tests

Most of us are aware of any number of actual cases in which there has been a complete collapse of these tests when they were tested. Obvious fools have come out first and recognised geniuses last. For that matter, there are almost as many different kinds of fools as there are different kinds of geniuses. It is folly thus to generalise about folly, let alone genius. The subtlest brain may be stumped by the stupidest problem; and somebody may be just sufficiently silly to ask a question which somebody else will be much too wise to answer.

—December 3, 1927

Idea versus Force

... ideas cannot expel force from its own realm except by entering that realm. The limitations of force are that it cannot prevent an idea from being an idea, but it can prevent it from being a fact.

—July 6, 1918

Ideal

... the more definite is our ideal the more indefinite, in the sense of infinite, must be our patience. You can define how long you will work, if you will be content with anything you can get in that time. You cannot define how long you will work if you have defined what you are working for.

—July 6, 1918

Let a man have what ideal of human costume or custom he likes. That ideal must still consist of elements in a certain proportion; and if that proportion is disturbed that ideal is destroyed. Let him once be clear in his own mind about what he wants, and then, whatever it is that he wants, he will not want the tide of evolution to wash it away. His ideal may be as revolutionary as he likes or as reactionary as he likes, but it must remain as he likes it. To make it more revolutionary or more reactionary is distortion; to suggest its growing more and more reactionary or revolutionary for ever is demented nonsense. How can a man know what he wants, how can he even want what he wants, if it will not even remain the same while he wants it?

—January 28, 1922

222

Idealism

To dismiss idealism as impossibilism is not even practical. . . . To have an ideal is simply to have an aim; and there is nothing practical in being aimless.

—July 13, 1918

Idealism is an excuse for insurrection. . . .

—January 26, 1918

Ideals

Democracy loves—but it does not know. Aristocracy knows—but it does not care. If you want the facts, it is much better to go to the governing class. But if you want ideals, it is immeasurably better to go to the mob. The bulk of a people always has a fairly sane and honourable philosophy. It is its science, its accumulation of accurate phenomena, which is commonly in fault.

—August 22, 1908

If your ideals ignore reason, your instincts will ignore restraint.

—April 21, 1923

Ideals versus Ideas

. . . nowadays the insistence on ideals is almost in inverse ratio to the insistence on ideas. If ever we encounter a pompous politician on the platform, a pretentious and maudlin play at the playhouse or picture-house, a sentimental sensational report in the newspapers, a limp and patronising leading article, a broad-minded and empty-headed sermon, a mealy-mouthed and meaningless message to all the nations, probably about peace . . . in short, if we encounter any of the voices or organs of expression that chiefly rule civilised society to-day, we shall find them all at one in the possession of two characteristics: a lack of ideas and a lust for ideals. Ideals are the substitute for ideas among people whom the modern rule of enlightenment and compulsory education has left without so much as the idea of an idea.

—January 28, 1933

Ideas (Modern)

We hear a great deal about ideas being accepted without examination because they come by authority. It is my experience nowadays that any idea will be accepted without any examination so long as it does *not* come by authority.

—June 16, 1917

Ideas (Scientific)

. . . the history of them seems to follow a rather curious course. First we have a general idea, often very old and perhaps very vague; and afterwards, when it breaks up into suggestions, very varied. Then we have one particular suggestion identified with the whole idea. Then we have the particular suggestion disputed. Then we have the whole idea disputed. That is what has happened to evolution and Darwin; that is what seems to be happening to psycho-analysis and Freud.

—May 30, 1925

Idolatry

. . . the essence of barbarism is idolatry; that is the worship of something other than the best reason and justice of the Universe. Idolatry is committed, not merely by setting up false gods, but also by setting up false devils; by making men afraid of war or alcohol, or economic law, when they should be afraid of spiritual corruption and cowardice. The Moslems say, "There is no God but God." The English Moslems, the abstainers, have to learn and remember also that there is no Satan but Satan.

— September 11, 1909

Ignorant

. . . the ideals of co-ordination and comradeship and organised interdependence, had begun long ago among the ignorant. These were things that the ignorant taught and the learned had to learn—or more often refused to learn. In these things it was the uneducated who educated the world. In defiance of all the instructed who were preaching ruthless individualism, the uninstructed had already begun to establish trade unions. . . . It is one of the queerest and most ironic contrasts in history. All the polished professors were teaching that men are a pack of wolves. All the obscure ruffians were assuming that men are the citizens of the Republic of Plato or the *civitas dei* of Aquinas.

—August 9, 1924

Imagery

. . . the only real lion is the lion that a child can dream of. . . . This concerns artistic truth, of course, as distinct from scientific and historical truth, which have their own objective object. But, if we are talking of the effect of symbols on the soul, it is broadly true that they are best when they are most symbolic. For in man also is something of the divine, and the things that enter his world pass through a second creation.

—July 25, 1931

Imagination

Imagination is a thing of clear images, and the more a thing becomes vague the less imaginative it is. Similarly, the more a thing becomes wild and lawless the less imaginative it is. To cook a cutlet in a really new way would be an act of imagination. But there is nothing imaginative about eating a cutlet at the end of a string, or eating it at the top of a tree, or catching it in one's mouth, or consuming it while standing on one leg. Nonsense of this sort is not imaginative for the simple reason that it is infinite.

—March 24, 1906

I am just old enough to remember the world before telephones. And I remember that my father and my uncle fitted up the first telephone I ever saw . . . reaching from the top bed-room under the roof to the remote end of the garden. I was really impressed imaginatively by this; and I do not think I have ever been so much impressed since by an extension of it. The point is rather important in the whole theory of imagination. It did startle me that a voice should sound in the room when it was really as distant as the next street. It does not startle me any more if it is as distant as the next continent. The miracle is over. Thus I admired even the large scientific things most on a small scale.

—February 8, 1930

The ordinary poetic description of the first dreams of life is a description of mere longing for larger and larger horizons. The imagination is supposed to work towards the infinite; though in that sense the infinite is the opposite of the imagination. For the imagination deals with an image. And an image is in its nature a thing that has an outline and, therefore, a limit. Now I will maintain, paradoxical as it may seem, that the child does not desire merely to fall out of the window, or even to fly through the air or to be drowned in the sea. When he wishes to go to other places, they are still places, even if nobody has ever been there.

—February 8, 1930

...most normal persons are now taught to neglect far too much the sort of excitement which the mind itself manufactures out of unexciting things. And anybody who can feel the fine shades, in fiction or philosophy, will agree that what the old school called romantic, or even Byronic... had really about it a curious confidence in life, an unbroken hope in the heart....

—May 3, 1930

We hear a great deal of the huge inhuman impersonal powers of cosmos or chaos, and how inspiring they are to the imagination; but they are not really very inspiring until the imagination has worked on them for some time.

—July 25, 1931

Impartiality

There is a fallacy in the argument from impartiality. Impartiality means at best indifference to everything, and more often hostility to everybody.

—July 5, 1919

Impartiality is another name for impossibility; but I have found, for such purposes as my notes on this page, that there really is a way of talking politics without talking party politics. I have found that the one way to please all parties is to abuse all parties. I remember being asked to take part in a debate about votes for women, at the most heated crisis of that conflict before the war. Having to say something, I got up and said exactly what I thought. I pointed out that nearly all the arguments for female suffrage were bad, but that the arguments against female suffrage were, if possible, worse. The result was that I sat down amid a roar of unanimous applause, and people of all opinions came up to me afterwards with radiant faces to thank me for the truth and wisdom of my words.

—November 11, 1922

Impudence

. . . impudence is not an element of the freshness of youth, but of the hardening of old age.

—August 2, 1924

Incompatibility

If married people are to be divorced for incompatibility of temper, I cannot imagine why all married people are not divorced. Any man and any woman must have incompatible tempers; it is the definition of sex. It is the whole point of being married. Nay, it is the whole fun even of being engaged. You do not fall in love with a compatible person. You do not love somebody exactly like yourself.

—September 19, 1908

Independence

It is suggested . . . that every individual should be independent, and that this applies even to the very young individual. The schoolboy, the schoolgirl, the infant in the infant school, and almost the infant in arms, are all to be regarded as individuals. It is constantly repeated that they are all to be regarded as citizens. But it never seems to occur to anybody to make the next and most obvious inference. . . . Nobody suggests that they should assert their independence by being in-dependent. Nobody points out that, if the father and the child are only two citizens, there is no more reason for asking the father to support the child than the child to support the father. If the mother and the baby are both independent individuals, the other must be as independent of the baby as the baby of the mother; and the mother must be free to say, "I do not like this individual," and throw the baby out of the window.

—March 13, 1926

Indeterminate Sentence

. . . I think it doubtful if we are doing well in making a sentence indeterminate. For a sentence only means a thing that has been determined. Even to talk of an indeterminate sentence is like talking of an immeasurable measure. It is like talking of a shapeless shape or of an unlimited limitation. If a man tied up a horse in a field with an indeterminate rope it would mean that the horse might be drowned because it could reach the Pacific, or starved because it could not reach the grass.

—June 27, 1908

Individual

. . . all common sense tells us, till we begin to read books of sociology, that the individual does count for something, even where the tribal custom counts for too much. But nobody is ever content with this common sense, least of all the most brilliant and thoughtful men of the age.

—February 12, 1927

Individualism

Individualism kills individuality, precisely because individualism has to be an "ism" quite as much as Communism or Calvinism. The economic and ethical school which called itself individualist ended by threatening the world with the flattest and dullest spread of the commonplace. Men, instead of being themselves, set out to find a self to be: a sort of abstract economic self identified with self-interest. But while the self was that of a man, the self-interest was generally that of a class or a trade or even an empire. So far from really remaining a separate self, the man became part of a communal mass of selfishness.

—February 25, 1928

Industrial Revolution

The industrial revolution was really a revolution, in one sense that is very little realised. It was as destructive as any revolution; it was also as headlong as any revolution. The spinning-jenny cut things short quite as sharply as the guillotine.

—April 14, 1923

It was the radicals who made the industrial revolution, with its sweating and its slums, its millionaires and millions of wage-slaves. But as soon as the progressive has done this happy thing, it instantly becomes the duty of the conservative to prevent it from being undone. Capitalism is simply the chaos following on the failure of mere individualism.

—April 19, 1924

Democracy existed fully as an idea, and largely as a fact, before the industrial revolution came to destroy it.

—January 3, 1931

Industrialism and Anomy

It is quite true . . . that too many people were shut up in their homes. But the cure is not to shut up the homes altogether. The cure is to open them altogether; to re-establish the old natural relations with neighbours; to make a Christian house almost as human as a red Indian wigwam or an Arab tent. Hospitality, the most ancient of human virtues, may appear again in the last days to meet the most modern of social problems, and men once more remember that Zeus is the protector of the stranger, as they did in the morning of the world.

—March 5, 1927

Infant

It is almost a matter of religion that every infant is a terrible infant. Every child is, both in the most superficial and in the most solemn sense, a holy terror.

—August 2, 1924

Injustice

There is no bitterness in the heart of man like the bitterness that follows the denial of right. There is not so deep a fury in the thief when he is punished as there is in the innocent man when he is let out on the ticket-of-leave of a thief.

—February 3, 1917

Inquisition

I should like the professors to be moved almost to tears by the thought that they had no real intimate inside knowledge of the reign of terror or the Inquisition. I should like to know that historical scholars really felt the void in their experience, the deplorable gaps in their own personal knowledge, due to their having never come into close touch with assassination or torture. That sort of confession would be the preface to a true history; and all the better a history because it would be a history of the historians.

—August 15, 1925

Insignificant

It is a misfortune of modern language that the word "insignificant" is vaguely associated with the words "small" or "slight." But a thing is insignificant when we do not know what it signifies. An . . . elephant lying dead in Ludgate Circus would be insignificant. That is, one could not recognise it as the sign or message of anything. One could not regard it as an allegory or a love-token. One could not even call it a hint. In the same way the solar system is insignificant. Unless you have some special religious theory of what it means, it is merely big and silly, like the elephant in Ludgate Circus. And similarly, modern life, with its vastness, its energy, its elaboration, its wealth, is, in the exact sense, insignificant. Nobody knows what we mean; we do not know ourselves.

—July 3, 1909

Institutions

Really healthy institutions are always supposed to be dying—like nations. Thoroughly diseased institutions are always praised as being in a state of brutal and invincible health—like empires.

—January 11, 1908

English institutions serve all sorts of excellent purposes always excluding the purpose for which they were founded. The universities have real value, but they are not particularly universal. The public schools have their own virtues, but they are not by any means public. . . . The ministers of the Crown are anything else except the servants of the King, which is the plain English meaning of their name. Constitutionalists contend that they are the servants of the Parliament. Poets imagine that they are the servants of the people. Cynics have been heard to suggest that they are the servants of much worse things. The Parliament itself, which was originally meant to check the executive, now only exists to endorse the executive; and the same principle runs through all our politics.

—July 3, 1920

Intellect

. . . there is present something I for one have invariably found wherever there is the mere worship of the intellect—I mean the decay of the intellect.

—May 11, 1918

Intellectuals

That intellectuals almost always *are* wrong, will be evident everywhere to the wise and good at a glance. The only question is whether they are only wrong-headed, as were most Russian revolutionists, or also wrong-hearted, as were most Prussian professors. But the challenging feature of modern society, and the chief fact of modern history, is not the obvious, simple and self-evident fact that intellectuals are a little wrong in the head; or in that general sense that intellectuals are wrong. It is in this other more strange and startling catastrophe; that intellectuals can actually find out that they are wrong. Or rather, to speak with greater accuracy, they can find out that they were wrong. For however often they find out they are wrong, they always go on being right.

—February 15, 1936

Intellectuals (Modern)

. . . I think there is another real reason for the revolt against dons. It is that these particular dons really had dogmatism without dogmas. In other words, they were sceptics but not honest sceptics. The academic authorities of a certain type or kind

231

did continue to speak with authority when they no longer believed in anything, even in their own authority. . . . But the just rebellion against that sort of old humbug does not prove anything except that men dislike being humbugged. It does not prove that they dislike being taught, or that they dislike being taught with sincerity, or even that they dislike being taught with authority.

—June 28, 1924

Why do we find to-day this fast and vague mass of trivialities, which have nothing in common except that they are *tall* in reaction against the very best of human traditions: why has this cheap and really worthless sort of scepticism got into such universal circulation? In other words, I am not now thinking of the gold standard of the highest truth, or the bimetallism of the higher scepticism which discusses whether there can be a rivalry in truth; . . . I am puzzled by the circulation of all these millions of brass farthings, hardly more valuable than bad pennies; I am wondering where they all come from, and why they can be produced in such handfuls; and whether there is not something wrong with the mint of the mind. I am wondering what has debased the currency of current thought and speech, and why every normal ideal of man is now pelted with handfuls of such valueless pebbles, and assailed everywhere, not by free thought, but by frank thoughtlessness.

—October 22, 1932

International

It can hardly be too often repeated that a man commonly calls himself international only because he is insular.

—April 20, 1918

Internationalism

What is the matter with internationalism is that it is imperialism. It is the imposition of one ideal of one sect on the vital varieties of men. It is actually the imposition of indifference. If the internationalist were really the interpreter or reconciler of nations, he would find himself expounding and excusing the very things he is now denouncing and deriding, the militarism of France or the fanaticism of Ireland. To teach internationalism he must talk nationalism. He must throw himself into other people's enthusiasm; as it is, he is only saddling other people with his own indifference. Moreover, this philosophy always fails, because the peacemaker not only wishes that the special love and loyalty did not exist, but assumes that it does not exist. He ignores it, and his whole attitude becomes one of ignorance. His attitude can truly be called indifference, because he does not know the difference.

—June 17, 1922

Internationalist

Internationalists are never interpreters between nations. It is what their name almost implies; it is what we should logically expect them to be, or at any rate to try to be. And yet they do not do it, and I rather doubt whether they really try. What really happens is that the internationalist, while he is often mildly but sincerely horrified at the nationalism of his own nation, is almost always even more horrified at the nationalism of some other nation. And it so happens, as the history of humanity has in fact developed, that very often the nationalism *is* the nation.

— September 5, 1931

Interruption

The man who makes an interruption is generally regarded in the newspapers as a very dreadful and deplorable person; and anybody who makes a really sensible and constructive suggestion will almost certainly be out of order. But, after all, the man who makes the interruption is only a man who has the wisdom to make a very short speech. That he can say what he has to say in that space is itself evidence of some power of artistic compression and restraint. Any one of us, in his heart, would probably rather be the man who interrupts a speech than the man who makes the sort of speech we all want to interrupt.

—April 4, 1925

Irish Famine

The Irish famine was more than an earthquake; it was an explosion. As an explosion scatters the arms and legs of a single man, so this catastrophe scattered the separated parts of a single people; and that most tragically, before our own people had attempted any real justice to that people. For that reason, the ruin of

Ireland simply strewed the whole earth with the enemies of England. "What region in the world," cried the Trojan after the fall of Troy, "is not full of our ruin?" What region in the world is not now full of that wrong which we remedied so late?

—April 4, 1936

Irish Free State

I think the Irish Free State does already fulfil the three terms of its title, and that is the test for any man with any grasp of the problem. I think it is Irish, I think it is free, and I think it is a state—that is, a sane and stable and ordered and creative thing; and there are moods when I wish the immediate prospects of my own country were so confident, so continuous, or so clear.

—August 23, 1924

Issue versus Personality

When all is said that can be said—and I have said a great deal of it myself—against the badges and banners of party conflict, it is true that they draw something out of men which makes the issue larger and more imaginative than their private personalities. And when we have nothing left except their private personalities, it becomes in another sense a matter of personalities, and the critics become very personal.

—September 26, 1931

Italians

It is amusing to watch the successive stages of the attempt to prove that the Italians are not a vigorous people. It is like watching the successive attempts of speculative builders to prove that Vesuvius is not a volcano.

—December 6, 1919

Italy

It has always got civilisation. It cannot get rid of it, not even when it tries. There is in all that world a corporate, continuous and fairly clear memory of real history; it knows its own past for nearly three thousand years. Any number of people have learned all that history who have never learned to read. The capitol; the grave of Virgil; the chains of Peter; the shrine of St. Francis; the monument of Dante; these are things which were known in a different fashion from that of newspapers or elementary schools. They are distant, but distant in a clear horizon of indefinitely extending daylight; of daylight that is not even dawn. For, alone of all the European provinces, Italy never really endured the Dark Ages.

—June 11, 1932

Jailor

... there may be a cruel illogicality in the human tradition which says of tortures and punishments. "It is written indeed that these things come, but woe unto them by whom they come." It may be very unjust to order a man to be whipped, and then despise the man who whips him. I only say, with absolute confidence, that all mankind always has despised the man who whips him; and despised the man who imprisons him, who guards him, who spies upon him, or who (in short) for any purpose ties the hands of another man.

—June 27, 1908

James, William

What Mr. Bernard Shaw did for the discussion of economics and politics Professor James did for the discussion of psychology and metaphysics. He forced them to join the undignified dance of common-sense; he insisted that the philosopher should have modesty enough to make a fool of himself, like the rest of mankind.

— September 17, 1910

Like Bernard Shaw and others among the intelligences of our unrestful age, William James will probably be counted valuable rather for a revolution in the mode of teaching than for any of the actual things he taught. Of course, he himself cared more for his dogmas than for his art of exposition, because he was a capable and healthy man. One cannot teach a truth clearly if one is actually thinking about the teaching and not about the truth.

— September 17, 1910

Jargon

. . . the very phrases that seem most fresh and fashionable are often almost identical with those that seem most faded and out of date. . . . For instance . . . it became the modern fashion to claim for any theory or policy that was to be praised that it was above all things "constructive." The word "constructive" dominated all social debates; and constructive reform was commonly contrasted in the newspapers with destructive revolution. It was not really a very intelligent distinction. . . . It would be easy to ask them whether cutting up wood to make a fire was destructive or constructive. It might not unreasonably be called entirely destructive, since it first destroys the tree with a hatchet and then destroys the wood with a flame.

— August 28, 1926

Jargon (Scientific)

We call it mesmerism instead of magic, or hypnotism instead of sorcery, merely because we have learned the trick of soothing ourselves with a certain sort of long words that have scientific terminations. If a witch were found successfully sticking pins into the wax image of an enemy, it would be thought enough to call it something like punctuationism . . . though it would need a little more learning and ingenuity to find a word to express the fact that she had a broomstick. In . . . more important branches of spiritual speculation . . . the same process of elaborate evasion has been frequently applied. The ascension of various Saints into the air was regarded as a manifest miracle, and therefore as a manifest myth. Then it was discovered that some people certainly could and did ascend into the air. But the resources of science are never exhausted, and the supply of long words had not run short. It was agreed that what everybody else had called ascension must henceforth be called levitation. This had all sorts of obvious superiorities over the older term; for one thing, it was one syllable longer. . . . I have since seen signs among the learned of a disposition to admit the idea of resurrection, by calling it resuscitation.

— December 31, 1921

Jerusalem

At least five empires have successfully claimed suzerainty over little Jerusalem upon the hill; and they are all now mere names—Egypt and Babylon and Persia and Macedonia and Rome; and for those unaffected by names are unimportant. But Jerusalem is not unimportant; it is, at this very moment when I write, the scene of surging and threatening conflict that may bring the British empire in its turn into grave peril.

—January 11, 1930

Jesus Christ and Freethinkers

I was looking at a recent collection which contains the opinions of many famous freethinkers about Jesus Christ. It is amusing to note how all of them differ among themselves; how one of them contradicts another and the last is always repudiated by the next. And I was specially amused to note that the earlier sceptics, like Strauss, blamed Jesus of Nazareth for his contempt for commerce and capital (then the gods of the hour), while the later sceptics, like Shaw and Wells, praised the same Jesus of Nazareth for the same contempt for the same commerce, because in the interval the sceptic had turned from an earnest individualist to an earnest socialist. Anyhow, it was not Christ or the Christian idea that had changed; it was only all the criticisms of all their critics. And the later sceptic actually became more orthodox than the earlier sceptic, simply by going bolshevist. This is merely an example, for the moment, of how the whole tone of the world has changed about property in relation to privacy.

—May 28, 1932

Jews

I am no more of an Anti-Semite than any Zionist or detached and independent Jew who thinks that the solution of the Jewish problem would be the separation of the races. It is perhaps doubtful whether the Jewish problem can be solved thus. It is also doubtful whether the Jewish problem can be solved at all. But, in answer to the charge of fanatical anti-Semitism, I should like to add one word, and an even more emphatic one. If I were an enemy of the Jews; if I were anything that could be called Anti-Jew, I should wish to be called Anti-Jew. But under no circumstances whatever would I consent to be called Anti-Semite . . . and I trust that, whatever be the merit of my views in the matter, I myself am neither one nor the other.

—September 20, 1930

I have been accused of being an enemy of the Jews, though I do not admit that I am. But if I were anti-Jewish, I hope I should say in plain English that I was anti-Jewish. I should certainly not condescend to say I was anti-Semite. There are such things as Jews, whether you like or dislike them. But what sort of things are Semites?

—*June* 11, 1932

Joan of Arc

It is not for us to explain this flaming figure in terms of our tired and querulous culture. Rather we must try to explain ourselves by the blaze of such fixed stars. Those who called her a witch hot from hell were much more sensible than those who depict her as a silly sentimental maiden prompted by her parish priest. If I have to choose between the two schools of her scattered enemies, I could take my place with those subtle clerks who thought her divine mission devilish, rather than with those rustic aunts and uncles who thought it impossible.

—*March* 28, 1908

Jolly Time

. . . being happy is not so important as having a jolly time. Philosophers are happy, saints have a jolly time. The important thing in life is not to keep a steady system of pleasure and composure (which can be done quite well by hardening one's heart or thickening one's head), but to keep alive in oneself the immortal power of astonishment and laughter, and a kind of young reverence.

—*January* 11, 1908

Journalism

For my part, I feel snippets to be the one thoroughly honest and genuine and valuable and philosophic part of journalism. The part of journalism that I would feel attempted to suppress would be the serious part: the leading articles and the learned reviews and the authoritative and infallible communications from special foreign correspondents. Everyone seems to assume that the unscrupulous parts of newspaper-writing will be the frivolous or jocular parts. This is against all ethical experience. Jokes are generally honest. Complete solemnity is almost always dishonest. The writer of the snippet or cheap par, merely refers to a fugitive and frivolous fact in a fugitive and frivolous way. The writer of the leading article has to write about a fact that he has known for twenty minutes as if it were a fact that he has studied for twenty years.

—*January 6, 1906*

All that anybody ever really meant as the evil of gossip is much more characteristic of established journalism: the fact that gossip comes from nowhere in particular and from everywhere at once: that no name can be put to it as the name of an author, that you cannot run it to earth, but when you attempt to contradict it strange obstacles of entanglement and denial seem to cross your path. All this, which is so true of private scandal, is very much truer of public journalism. The frivolous chatter is now all in public journalism. The public responsibility is all in private conversation.

—*February 1, 1908*

. . . it is a criticism of life that must be always criticising. It is no matter for wonder if it sometimes criticises too much, or if (which is the much more real complaint) it criticises the wrong things. In a sense, the journalist aims at giving pointed and picturesque expression to the attitude of the average man; but there is one very important part of that attitude which journalism is by its nature forbidden to express. And that is its healthy, and indeed heroic, indifference. The journalist cannot treat things as the average man treats a vast number of them—with what is, properly considered, one of his worthiest and most philosophic gestures. He cannot pass them by.

—*February 9, 1918*

It is the convention of journalism at this moment to support what is feminist against what is feminine.

—*August 5, 1922*

. . . our current journalism is written in a dead language.

—*June 21, 1924*

It may be defined as the art of doing dull things in a hurry.

—February 7, 1925

Its syndications and distributions are all founded on the feeblest of all fallacies. It is the notion that you can make a stale thing fresh by repeating it.

—February 7, 1925

It is one of the misfortunes of journalism that its very name implies a criticism from day to day, which is too like a criticism from hand to mouth. It is the tragedy even of good journalists that they have to say something, and may even be driven to say anything before they have anything to say.

—April 6, 1929

Journalism (Nameless)

We are discussing whether in this wicked world a very powerful profession should be allowed to keep peculiarly to itself some of the advantages of a secret society, and especially whether it should be allowed to do so at a time of which the typical heresy and weakness is to quiet the individual conscience with a talk about the system and the social trend. We are talking about whether we will encourage anonymous writing in an existing society in which we know it must often mean anonymous combination, anonymous tyranny, or anonymous vengeance. In short, we will leave on one side the question of whether, in the perfect city, the man who makes a brick ought to write his name on it. But we will say decisively that the man who *throws* a brick ought to write his name on it; and (with complete respect for those who use the current custom) those who feel no echo at all of our emotions we shall venture to call persons somewhat unduly emancipated from the prejudice of honour.

—July 25, 1908

Journalism (The New)

It seems possible that popular journalism may become unpopular merely by pursuing popularity. A baby has a fine intellectual disdain for people who talk in baby language. A schoolboy feels a grave and dignified disapproval of those

240

speaking in what they suppose to be schoolboy slang. And I fancy the ordinary citizen will soon get tired of being talked down to with the same supercilious superficiality.

—September 3, 1921

Journalism and Fiction

Journalism only tells us what men are doing; it is fiction that tells us what they are thinking, and still more what they are feeling. If a new scientific theory finds the soul of a man in his dreams, at least it ought not to leave out his day-dreams. And all fiction is only a diary of day-dreams instead of days.

—April 21, 1923

Journalism and Sensationalism

... sensationalism has been confined to small things rather than large; that is, private things rather than public. A murder is, after all, a private affair; indeed, in most cases a purely domestic matter. A divorce also is a domestic matter even if it is a matter of escaping from domesticity. This sort of revelation of intimate and even trivial things we do indeed find in the press. But we hear very little of the sensations that concern big matters as distinct from small ones.

—April 4, 1925

Journalists

Very often, while the journalist is doing his best to imitate the tone of the paper, the editor (torn with despair) is trying in vain to find someone who will alter the tone of the paper.

—August 21, 1909

I could give many further instances of this in the case of living English politicians. They would let me repeat freely all the frantic lies that are told about them. But if I began, however faintly, to say what I thought true about [journalists] ... they would all bring libel actions in a body. There is only one articulate English person

I can think of who will not bring a libel action against me however much I provoke him, and that is myself.

—*December* 11, 1909

Their private life becomes in a sense public life: it is what is said in their inner chambers that is proclaimed on the housetops—and it is what is proclaimed on the housetops that is heard by the enemy in the gate.

—*February* 9, 1918

... to write on all sorts of subjects of which I know nothing. That, I imagine, is almost the definition of a journalist.

—*November* 7, 1925

He knows nothing whatever about his own opinions. You cannot find out the first principles from which he started, because he apparently never had any. You cannot prove the absurdity of really carrying out his suggestions, because he never does carry out even his own suggestions. You cannot say that he began with a false assumption, because he never began at all. You cannot say that he will end in an impossible conclusion, because he never ends. He is still going on.

—*November* 21, 1925

The journalists have got into a sort of rut or routine of revolt; a sort of tame rebellion and timid revolution. And all their revolt is directed against what they call organised religion. It is not directed against any of the hundred other things which are highly organised in our highly organised modern society. It is not directed against organised government, still less against organised misgovernment. It is not directed against organised political corruption or elaborately organised secret societies.... The only sort of organisation that is attacked is religious organisation; though it is nowadays entirely voluntary, entirely free, entirely moral in its mode of pressure; and though, under modern conditions, it is much more likely to be persecuted than to persecute.

—*May* 24, 1930

Exactly what Cobden did admirably was exactly what modern journalists never do at all. He stated a complete case. . . .

—June 7, 1930

Journalists (Advice for)

There is only one piece of advice that is generally given by all advisers on this subject: the advice to write with reference to the tone of the paper for which the contribution is meant. . . . That is the one piece of positive counsel which is always given to the young journalist. And even that is wrong. Many a man has succeeded simply because he wrote all the wrong articles for the wrong papers. If his remarks had appeared in the right place they would have appeared ordinary. But as they always appeared in the wrong place they seemed quite brilliant. My own effect, such as it is, is entirely due to this simple process.

—August 21, 1909

Journalists and Christianity

. . . if these journalistic philosophers really carried out their own conception, the result would be a torrent of tedium, a howling wilderness of boredom. What would be eliminated would be mysticism, in which men are really interested, if only as they are interested in mystery stories and mystery plays. What would be left would be moralising, which men find the dreariest experience on earth. What these men call true Christianity would consist entirely of priggish sermons telling Tommy to be a good boy. Everything that a grown man, of active intellect, can really find interesting would have disappeared with the disputes about dogmas and creeds. Our heretical clergy are boring enough even on the exciting subject of orthodoxy. What they would be like if they were told to talk nothing but morality, the imagination freezes in the attempt to fancy.

—November 5, 1927

Journalists and Newspapers

The talk in the newspapers is old-fashioned, tiresome, and materialistic; it is all concerned with saying that things are impossible which already exist, and that things are disappearing which have reappeared long ago. It is a veil of dull and quite unreal rationality; behind it the real people are full of rapturous experiment and uproarious superstition. Do not judge us by what we write. We are not so dull as our articles. . . . You go to a newspaper for fine old-fashioned assumptions, but not for news.

—October 13, 1906

Journalists versus Politicians

. . . you can say anything about a man so long as it is not true.

—December 11, 1909

Journalistic Statement

There are three ways in which a statement, especially a disputable statement, can be placed before mankind. The first is to assert it by avowed authority; this is done by deities, the priests of deities, oracles, minor poets, parents and guardians. . . . The second way is to prove it by reason; this was done by the mediaeval schoolmen. . . . The third method is this: when you have neither the courage to assert a thing nor the capacity to prove it, you allude to it in a light and airy style, as if somebody else had asserted and proved it already. . . . The third method, which is usually adopted, is to say, "Professor Gubbins belongs to the old school of scientific criticism, and cannot but strike us as limited in this age of wireless telegraphy and aerial swine". . . . In short, this third method consists in referring to the very thing that is in dispute as if it were now beyond dispute. This is known as the Restrained or Gentlemanly method; it is used by company promoters, by professors of hair-dressing and the other progressive arts, and especially by journalists like myself.

—August 7, 1909

Joy

. . . the modern world has had far too little understanding of the art of keeping young. Its notion of progress has been to pile one thing on top of another, without caring if each thing was crushed in turn. People forgot that the human soul can enjoy a thing most when there is time to think about it and be thankful for it. And by crowding things together they lost the sense of surprise; and surprise is the secret of joy.

—December 9, 1922

de Jure

To-day every government is a government *de facto*. People have forgotten the very notion of a government *de jure*. No longer having the idea of a religion, they no longer really have the idea of a right. Least of all do they realise what democrats used to call the rights of man. For in truth every right is a divine right. If it exists, the right to vote must be as mystical as the right to rule. . . .

—December 20, 1924

Justice

And the whole original object of law, of statutes, of assizes, of open courts, of definite verdicts, of the *Habeas Corpus,* of the rules of evidence, was simply the idea that we must have public justice and not private justice. Or, at the worst, we will have public injustice. Even a legal quibble is better than a mere caprice.

—June 27, 1908

Justice (Individual)

The question in debate, if it could be presented in any form fitted for debate, is whether modern ethics are called upon to consider the case of indignity and injustice to individuals. It is perfectly easy to construct an ethical system for the hive or the ant-hill, in which it is clear that they are not. Our answer to it is to drag in the zoological detail that we do not happen to be ants, or even bees; that we belong to a very queer race of animals marked by a certain peculiarity. It is this fact: that we do not suffer most when we are smashed or smoked out, or trampled with large boots, but when we are wronged. The wrong is felt by the individual more realistically than by the community; and that instinct about injustice is a much more solid and fundamental fact than any generalisations about the tribe.

—November 4, 1933

The Kaiser

He is a public man—the kind of man who has no inner life at all. God is neither his master nor his servant, but his favourite metaphor. And the deep and real irritation which people so different as the French, the Poles, and the Serbians feel against the

Germans is largely an irritation against this underbred cleverness. It is the anger of people who have had tragedies against a people that has never had anything but melodramas.

—August 28, 1915

The Kaiser is so exceedingly fond of small nationalities that he desires all other nationalities to be as small as possible.

—August 17, 1918

"Keeping the Party Together"

I have just read a remarkable and doubtless reliable interview between Lenin and Mr. Arthur Ransome, which is largely concerned with the way in which "The communist theories are being modified in the difficult process of their translation into practice." There is something that reminds us pleasantly of our own politicians, engaged in "keeping the party together," in this suggestion that communism may be slightly modified by the fact that people flatly refuse to be communists.

— September 6, 1919

Kite

Why do children like playing with kites? Why do adults like playing with kites, and falsely profess to be playing with children? It is because there is something that makes any healthy human being almost lightheaded in the notion of sending something human, something like a part of ourselves, to travel among the clouds and the clear spaces round the sun and moon.

—November 24, 1917

Ku Klux Klan

It is sufficient to say that one of its brightest ideas is to call a gentleman a kleagle, thereby (it will be noted) achieving the triumph of assimilating the word "eagle" to the alliterative diction of the klan. The thought of being terrorised by people on that intellectual level suggests a nightmare of falling into the hands of cheerful chimpanzees. There is something quite sub-human about such stupidity as that. It is enough to say that it is certainly worse than anything that the wilder element in America has yet produced.

—September 13, 1924

Labour and Leisure

If a man is practically compelled, by a sort of social pressure, to ride in the park in the morning, or play golf in the afternoon, or go out to grand dinners in the evening, or finish up at night clubs at night, we describe all those hours of his day as hours of leisure. But they are not hours of leisure at all, in the other sense—as, for instance, on the fanciful supposition that he would like a little time to himself, that he would like to pursue a quite solitary and even unsociable hobby, that he would like really to idle, or, on a more remote hypothesis, that he would like really to think. Now, when modern social philosophers are generalising about labour and leisure and the greater or less degree of liberty for men and women in the modern world, they necessarily lump all these different meanings of leisure together and bring out a result that is not really representative.

—July 23, 1927

Labour versus Liberal

Everyone argues and explains about the relations between the Liberal Party and the Labour Party. No one points out the evident truth that there can be no relations between a Liberal Party and a Labour Party; any more than there can be an argument between agnostics and auctioneers. There cannot be either antagonism or agreement between the fact that ten men have worked with their hands and the fact that ten other men have come to certain conclusions with their heads. They might actually be the same ten men. As a fact, most Labour men are Liberals; and many Liberals undergo labour. I am a Liberal, and I am undergoing labour of the most laborious description at this moment.

—October 22, 1910

Lamp-post

. . . lamp-posts are poetical; not merely from accidental, but from essential causes. It is not merely softening, sentimental associations that belong to lamp-posts, the beautiful fact that aristocrats were hanged from them, or that intoxicated old gentlemen embrace them: the lamp-post really has the whole poetry of man, for no other creature can lift a flame so high and guard it so well.

—July 31, 1909

Language

But language, in its written form, especially exists for the purpose of suggesting shades of thought and starting trains of association. For this entirely poetic and emotional purpose all language exists. For this purpose every word is important. For this purpose every letter in every word is important. The letters are important because they make up the recognisable colour and quantity of the word. It is not an accident that the very word "literature" has a meaning which connects it with the alphabet. It is not an accident that when we speak of a literary man we call him a man of letters.

— September 15, 1906

The truth is that language has been from the dawn of the world used for two purposes, which may be simplified into the two divisions of poetry and prose. It is not necessary in this sense that the poetry should be in verse; fairy-tales and country proverbs are full of it. But poetry simply consists of connotation. It is all in the atmosphere created by the terms, as an incantation calls up spirits. It is almost more made up of the echoes of words than the words themselves. It is not really even the images, but the haloes round the images. "Of perilous seas in faery lands forlorn" does not owe its effect to the assertion, as on an admiralty chart, that certain seas are dangerous for navigators. It owes it to the suggestion of all sorts of other dangers not . . . covered by the definition of a dangerous sea. Wherever this element of pure poetry enters—and it enters into much that is commonly called prose—it is hopeless to expect that dictionary definition should be observed, even if dictionary definition were really reasonable. . . .

—January 8, 1927

In the matter of language, which is the main matter of literature, it is clear that words are perpetually falling below themselves. And, in this fall of man's chosen symbols, there may well be a symbol of his own fall.

—May 21, 1927

Language (French)

The best French speech is not only very much more than mere sound, but very much more than mere music. It is flexible, because it is not less but more articulate than what we commonly call articulate speech. It is significant that we use the word articulation in two senses; we talk of the articulation of a sentence and of the articulation of a skeleton. The French tongue is like a serpent, in that it has so many articulations as to produce the general impression of a curve. It has so many joints that it seems to have no joints at all.

—July 25, 1931

Language (Modern)

Modern language—scientific, political, and journalistic—is not given to man to conceal his thoughts. It is given him to conceal his thoughtlessness. Indeed, it makes him much more thoughtless than he would be by nature. Men are twisted out of the path of truth by the very terms they have to use.

—March 8, 1919

Language and Social Science

We all feel that the only entirely inferior thing is to be superior; and various forms of cheap superiority are the most irritating facts of our modern life. One impudent piece of pedantry I have noticed as very much on the increase—it is the habit of arbitrarily changing the ends of abstract words (which are bad enough already) so as to make them sound more learned. I heard a young man, with thin, pale hair, speak some time ago at some Ethical Society; and words cannot convey the degree to which he drooped his eyelids whenever he said "Christianism," instead of Christianity. I was tempted to get up and tell him that what was the matter with him was Tomfoolerism, called by some Tomfoolerity, and that I felt an impulsion to bash his physiognomics out of all semblity of humanitude.

—June 12, 1909

249

Last Word

To know the last word of a sentence, without knowing the first, is really to be too late to know anything.

—June 2, 1928

Laughter

I realised that a very large number of people never see a joke, but only see that there is a joke. They see that somebody is jesting about something, and they laugh indulgently or rage indignantly, according to their attitude towards recognised buffoons. It is a truth that explains a great deal of the "laughter and cheers" at public meetings.

—April 18, 1925

Law Enforcement

It is therefore the very opposite of the truth to say that the police fail through lack of organisation. It is much nearer the truth to say that they fail because society is being far too much organised. A scheme of official control which is too ambitious for human life has broken down, and broken down exactly where we need it most. Instead of law being a strong cord to bind what it is really possible to bind, it has become a thin net to cover what it is quite impossible to cover. It is the nature of a net so stretched to break everywhere; and the practical result of our bureaucracy is something very near to anarchy.

—April 1, 1922

Laws

There are laws of the mind, analogous to laws of the eye. And the laws of the eye are not altered by everybody putting on the same sort of horned spectacles, that each one of them may look separate and distinguished.

—May 18, 1929

When laws are passed forbidding a citizen to do something, like lighting a cigarette or eating a chocolate cream, bureaucracy must in its nature arrive at bankruptcy. Swindling or stabbing can be stopped, because the neighbours, who are not officials, will help the official pursuit. But if the official is the only person pursuing or condemning the criminal, we can never distribute the force on the principle of one criminal, one official. There never were and never will be, fortunately, enough officials to go round.

—August 24, 1929

Lawyers

In our legal method there is too much lawyer and too little law. For we must never forget one fact, which we tend to forget nevertheless: that a fixed rule is the only protection of ordinary humanity against clever men—who are the natural enemies of humanity. A dogma is the only safeguard of democracy. The law is our only barrier against lawyers. In the same way, the Prayer-Book is our only defence against clergymen.

—September 22, 1906

League of Nations

To say that a peace league must be founded on an equal treatment is simply to say that a court of arbitration must be founded on its own incapacity to arbitrate.

—February 3, 1917

Legal Weapons

... orthodoxy loses, every time it uses these legal and official weapons. For the weapons are not merely antiquated weapons; they are such very weak weapons. We cannot give our enemy a gag; we only give him a grievance! Cynically, these powers do us no good. Ideally, they do us harm. It is as if two duellists had to fight with sharp swords, but one was allowed to wear a shirt and not the other. The shirt would be a privilege: but yet not a protection. It would not be enough to give him the victory: but it would be just enough to make his victory unpopular.

—February 1, 1908

Legend

I myself was unfathomably ignorant. I therefore believed what they told me; I proceeded to believe, to believe blindly, credulously, and in hopeless intellectual servitude; to believe in the much more fabulous fable, in the legend of the learned.

—*February* 14, 1931

Leisure

It is very essential to realise that leisure is not in any way identical with liberty. If we do not realise it, we shall almost certainly all lose our liberty, for any reasonably intelligent tyrant may have the sense to give us a great deal of leisure.

—*July* 14, 1923

I think the name of leisure has come to cover three totally different things. The first is being allowed to do something. The second is being allowed to do anything. And the third (and perhaps most rare and precious) is being allowed to do nothing. Of the first we have undoubtedly a vast and very probably a most profitable increase in recent social arrangements. Undoubtedly there is much more elaborate equipment and opportunity for golfers to play golf, for bridge-players to play bridge, for jazzers to jazz, or for motorists to motor. But those who find themselves in the world where these recreations are provided will find that the modern world is not really a universal provider. He will find it made more and more easy to get some things and impossible to get others.

—*July* 23, 1927

The Leisure State

But there is another strong objection which I, one of the laziest of all the children of Adam, have against the leisure state. Those who think it could be done argue that a vast machinery using electricity, water-power, petrol, and so on, might reduce the work imposed on each of us to a minimum. It might, but it would also reduce our control to a minimum. The occasional adjunct to the intermittent machine would have no control whatever over the means of production. He might have more control over his own leisure, but less over his own life.

—*March* 25, 1925

Lenin, Vladimir Ilyich

He said in so many words that the "ignorant peasantry" of Russia—who are, of course, the great majority of Russia—have even now no comprehension of what has occurred. He said that the interval between now and the next sanguinary world-war may be happily and profitably whiled away by seeing that the new revolutionary ideas "ripen in the mind of the masses." Now it is surely obvious, on a revolutionary and not a conservative assumption, that revolutionary ideas ought to be tolerably ripe before they produce a revolution. It is absurd, upon any argument, to make the disturbance first and the discontent afterwards.

—March 30, 1918

Liberal

Most modern liberality consists of finding irreligious excuses for religious bigotry. The earlier type of bigot pretended to be more religious than he really was. The later type pretends to be less religious than he really is. He does not wear a mask of piety, but rather a mask of impiety—or, at any rate, of indifference.

—December 27, 1919

The liberal has got into a position in which he cannot plead for liberty. He has taken too much of the colour of the collectivism of labour and the coercionism of empire. By becoming half a socialist he has missed the chance of scoring as an individualist. The old yellow flag of individual radicalism might now be hailed as something really distinct from the red flag of communism, only it has been content to become a sort of pink flag of a cautious collectivism.

—August 11, 1923

As it is, I think they want to procure all possible pleasures and amusements for their own, including the mild amusement of prophesying some utopia that can only come long after they are dead. If their novels and newspapers were less filled with the sublime spiritual liberation of eloping with the chauffeur, and more filled with the duty and dignity of remaining with the baby, I might admit that their faces are set towards the future and their souls full of the song of a good time coming. As it is, it seems to be an impatient and even pessimistic lyric about a good time now.

—May 31, 1930

253

Liberty

Democratic liberty consists in trusting the common people to do the common things. Nor does this merely concern democratic liberty; but concerns also democratic order.

—October 4, 1919

I am very much afraid, as things are going at present, that the next generation will have quite as little idea of what their fathers meant by dying for liberty, as the last generation had of what their fathers meant by dying for religion or sound theology or the true faith. There is already a large number of modern writers who talk as if the old notion of independence, national or personal, were something simply inconceivable as well as impossible; exactly as the champions of liberty, a hundred years ago, spoke of the mysterious dogmas of the Church.

—January 4, 1930

It is easy to show that liberties are local; it is much less easy to prove that liberty is universal.

—January 4, 1930

I have felt that the world is conceiving liberty as something that merely works outwards. And I have always conceived it as something that works inwards. . . . It is plain on the face of the facts that the child is positively in love with limits. He uses his imagination to invent imaginary limits. The nurse and the governess have never told him that it is his moral duty to step on alternate paving-stones. He deliberately deprives this world of half its paving-stones, in order to exult in a challenge that he has offered to himself. . . . In that sense I have constantly tried to cut down the actual space at my disposal; to divide and subdivide, into these happy prisons, the house in which I was quite free to run wild.

—February 8, 1930

Liberty and Order

. . . the ordinary talk is now in favour of liberty rather than order, whereas the ordinary talk used to be in favour of order rather than liberty. But this does not mean that we are all agreed, any more than our fathers were, about the proper limits of liberty and order. What it means is that, as it is the fashion to be liberal, it requires a little more originality to be traditional. Any fool can see the case for liberty; any fool has a natural instinct for profiting by the case for license; it is precisely the very intelligent who are left watching with some suspicion the general indifference to authority.

—July 30, 1927

Liberty and Property

The simplest sense of the sentiment of property is that indicated in any common object of possession—let us say a walking-stick.... A man ... would hardly be able to say exactly when he would want it, and this doubt could be most substantially summarised by saying that he would always want it. He desires to have it ready to hand—that is, he desires to be the complete and unconditional owner of it. Now this is perhaps the first, or at least the most practical, fact about the psychology of property. Any limitation on property is here a limitation of liberty—that is, of a thousand things that are too light and loose to be analysed. Any alternative to property is the codification of conditions under which he may or may not obtain the object from the hands of others. He might have to leave the walking-stick in an official and universal umbrella-stand.

—October 25, 1919

Liberty versus Centralisation

I do not by any manner of means take naturally to the notion of dictatorship. All my instincts, as well as all my traditions, are in favour of the old liberal conceptions of a free press or a free parliament. It is native to my nationality, and ... to my personality, to prefer local liberties and the refusal of centralised power. I also profoundly distrust most of our own modes of reaction. I would much rather have even the Victorian compromise of constitutional freedom.

—February 20, 1926

Life (Primitive)

... we were all left to suppose, in the age of Huxley and Herbert Spencer, that all primitive life was cruel and crushed the weak without pity. The actual scientific evidence is in many cases quite to the contrary.... Wissler, an authority on the

255

Red Indians, says that the whole control was once exercised "by admonition and mild ridicule." Of course, it was never really so simple as that. There is complexity; and, what is more important, there is sin.

—August 23, 1930

Life (The Riddle of)

For the riddle is simply this: For some mad reason in this mad world of ours the things about which men differ most are exactly the things about which they must be got to agree. Men can agree on the fact that the earth goes round the sun. But then it does not matter a dump whether the earth goes round the sun or the Pleiades. But men cannot agree about morals; sex, property, individual rights, fixity and contracts, patriotism, suicide, public habits of health—these are exactly the things that men tend to fight about. And these are exactly the things that they must not fight about. These are exactly the things that must be settled somehow, and settled on strict principles. Study each of them, and you will find each of them works back certainly to a philosophy, probably to a religion. Every Society has to act upon dogmas, and dogmas are exactly those things that are most disputable. It puts a man in prison for the dogma of the sanctity of property; it hangs a man for the dogma of the sanctity of human life. All punishment is religious persecution.

—March 16, 1907

Life (Simple)

For my part, I believe that the Fall of Man was due to the introduction of the simple life. In a state of innocence our first ancestors (I suppose) ate beef and drank beer like Christians. Then came the Tempter, the spirit of intellectual pride and intellectual perversity; he took the form of a Serpent because that form is full of an evil simplicity. And he said, with the elaborate lucidity of modern hygiene, "All these meals are unnecessary to health. Take one raw apple, Madam, in the early morning; another at noon. The apple best suited for our purpose is of particular chemical properties, at once nutritious and light; it grows on a tree which I will show you in a moment. This simpler regimen will expand the moral powers, clear the intellect, purify and exalt the feelings: it will lead you up the endless spiral of Science and Moral Evolution. You will become as gods, knowing good and evil." But the divine justice smote that liar and put him also upon a regimen. "On thy belly shalt thou go and the dust shalt thou eat." That is something like a Simple Life for you.

—July 7, 1906

256

Life (Unity of)

If all life is a unity, there still remains the question of what sort of life and what sort of unification. In one sense the wolf and the sheep are one, and the cannibal and missionary are one. But the missionary has never been quite satisfied with the scriptural fulfilment when the lamb lies down inside the lion. If man is merely to regard himself as one with the whole life of nature, we may doubt whether that ideal of humanity will be purely humanitarian. It is at least as good an argument for being as fierce as the wolf as it is for being kind to the dog. The truth is, obviously, that the man ought to be kind to the dog, not because he is entirely unified and absorbed and melted into the dog, but precisely because he has himself a dignity and a duty that cannot be expected of the dog, far less of the wolf.

—June 18, 1927

Limitation

I am not allowed in these columns to discuss politics or religion, which is inconvenient; as they are the only two subjects which seem to me to have the slightest element of interest for a sane man.

—April 7, 1906

The short hair of the modern girl is, by its very nature, a limitation. It may be a wise or sensible limitation, as compared with complicated masses of coiled hair, but it is the disappearance of a feature. It is subtraction and not addition. It is making a girl look like a boy; like making an elephant look like a hippopotamus.

—October 20, 1928

Lincoln, Abraham

Almost alone among politicians, he was an opportunist who was not twisted by his own opportunities. Most politicians have no politics. They are entirely made by the circumstances and even accidents of their career. Lincoln kept clear in his mind from first to last his pure theory of politics. He never compromised by an inch in the statement of his principles, even when he had to compromise in the application of them. And those principles, for which he had an intellectual passion, were the principles of pure equality. . . . And the chief thing for Englishmen to learn from Lincoln is not hazy rhetoric about ruggedness and righteousness, but that more virile form of idealism that consists of having a clear head.

—December 17, 1921

Lincoln was most certainly not a man bound to succeed. For the greater part of his life, he looked much more like a man bound to fail. Indeed, for that matter, a great many of his cold and uncomprehending colleagues, right up to the very end of the Civil War, thought he really was a man bound to fail. The truth is that he was a very clear and even beautiful example of the operation of the opposite principle — that God has chosen the failures of the world to confound the successes; and the true moral of his life is that of the poets and the saints. He was one of a very rare and very valuable race, whose representatives appear from time to time in history. He was one of the failures who happen to succeed.

—November 17, 1928

The great glory of Lincoln is that, almost alone among politicians, he really knew what he thought about politics. He really thought slavery was bad, but he really thought the disruption of America was worse. It is perfectly possible for an intelligent person to disagree with him on either or both of these points. But he was an intelligent person when he stated them in that way, and put them in that order.

—November 17, 1928

He was not always right; but he always tried to be reasonable, and that in exactly the sense which his special admirers have never understood from that day to this. He tried to be reasonable. It is not surprising that his life was a martyrdom and that he died murdered.

—November 17, 1928

Lincoln and the Union

Lincoln may have been right in thinking that he was bound to preserve the Union. But it was not the Union that was preserved. A union implies that two different things are united; and it should have been the northern and southern cultures that were united. As a fact, it was the southern culture that was destroyed. And it was the northern that ultimately imposed not a unity but merely a uniformity. But that was not Lincoln's fault. He died before it happened; and it happened because he died.

—December 14, 1929

Lion (Legendary)

... the only kind of lion that is of any earthly practical importance is the legendary lion. He really is a useful thing to have about the place. He holds up the shield of England, which would otherwise fall down, despite the well-meant efforts of the Unicorn, whose hoofs are deficient in a prehensile quality. The African lion does not matter to anyone. But the British Lion, though he does not exist, does matter. He means something; it is the only true object of existence to mean something; and the real African lion has never succeeded in meaning anything at all. The legendary lion, the lion that was made by man and not by Nature, he is indeed the king of beasts.

—November 11, 1905

Literacy

The alphabet is very useful, but it is an error to identify the alphabet with that alpha and omega which is the beginning and the end.

—July 26, 1924

It has been the great tragedy of our time that people were taught to read and not taught to reason.

—November 21, 1925

Literary Character

... every novelist's characters talk a special language, sometimes amounting to a secret language.

—September 19, 1925

Literature

A Dickens novel represents intensity spread through three hundred pages. A modern short story represents infinite and everlasting vagueness concentrated into one page.

—December 21, 1907

The highest outcome of an interest in literature is a finer interest in life; and bad literature as well as good may throw a light on life, if we have learnt to know light from darkness. And there are a great many other reasons for reading books besides the fact that they happen to be good books.

—October 9, 1920

... as a mere matter of guess-work, given the tendencies of our time, I should think it would be extremely probable that literature will give up all this notion of experiment, and not only return to type, but even to the classical type.

—September 12, 1931

Literature (Modern)

... what is hailed as a new style or a new school in literature often consists of doing as a novelty what a Victorian did long ago as a joke. Thus we have, in Mr. James Joyce or Miss Gertrude Stein, the coining of new words by the confusion of old words; the running of words together so as to suggest some muddle in the subconsciousness. I do not recall the particular examples, but they would think nothing of saying that somebody was "drurgling," meaning "gurgling when drunk." ... I do not doubt that they really do this much more clearly than I can imitate it. In expressing confused ideas, the moderns have great subtlety and sympathy. It is in expressing clear ideas that they generally find their limitations.

—September 12, 1931

Literature (Trashy)

I for one have a great taste in trash, and I am proud to say that I have even considerably swelled the amount there is in the world. It may fairly be added that there is trash and trash; as, for that matter, there is truth and truth. One distinction in particular may be noted though it is often neglected. The worst sort of bad book is the book that not only bores the reader, but obviously bores the writer. And this often arises not so much from the writer's vulgarity as from his fastidiousness. He himself despises the work he is doing, and it is naturally at its worst when he is not even doing his best. This is generally the explanation of the almost unnaturally bad writing of much of the most popular fiction. The style is abominable—not so much because the writer is ignorant or incompetent as because he does not enjoy the process, but only the result, if that. He writes down any sort of jaded journalese that occurs to him; he never looks twice at a sentence or even a word, because the only word he really wishes to write is "finis" or "the end."

—*October 9*, 1920

Locution (Modern)

I remember an occasion when a leading socialist politician said there were several things in the Creed that he had no use for. I remember remarking at the time that there were probably a good many things in the "Encyclopaedia Brittanica" that he had no use for. But that does not exactly prove that they are useless; still less that they are untrue. Hazy language of this sort, whether it is hazy on the popular or on the pedantic side, prevents people from getting to grips with each other, as they did in the old days of strictly logical argument, whether among the Greek sophists or the Mediaeval schoolmen. . . . The sort of phraseology I mean is too unobtrusive to· be called jargon and too educated to be called journalese.

—*December* 12, 1931

If it were literally true that some ancient creed had "lost its meaning" for the modern mind, it would simply mean that the modern mind was incapable of criticising the ancient creed.

—*December* 12, 1931

Log Rolling

A great deal of what is called log-rolling is as easy as falling off a log. I have generally found that it was precisely because a man was generously and enthusiastically rolling the log of a friend that he complained so bitterly of the log-rolling among his enemies.

—*June 6*, 1931

Logic (Modern)

... the modern man who says "be logical"... cannot take his own advice, and therefore he cannot state his own first principles. But, though his logic is nonsense as he states it, it does refer to some first principles if he could only state them.

—*June* 27, 1931

Logic and Nihilism

There seems to be a sort of public holiday from logic just now, a saturnalia of escape from the slavery of the syllogism. There is nothing to choose between the sexes in this matter; nothing to choose between the social classes; not very much to choose even between the schools of science and philosophy. Even the rationalists are not much more irrational than their neighbours.

—*October* 22, 1927

Logicians (Modern)

If he is blind, he cannot see the proof of his own blindness, any more than he can see anything else. If he reasons that reason is unreasonable, he is simply contradicting himself. But then if reason is unreasonable, why should he not contradict himself? And then again, if reason is unreasonable, why should we not contradict him, and why should we not deny that he has a right to contradict himself? So there you are; and there you will stay; for you will not get much further along these lines.

—*December* 13, 1919

Logicians and Lunatics

A logician might legitimately say that clothes are the sign of our rise out of savagery, and grow more elaborate as we rise higher. A lunatic might logically say that, in consequence of this, the more clothes we wear the better; and he might hasten to put on ten hats and twelve overcoats. He also might rear a pagoda of hats and hide in a labyrinth of coats before he had arrived at finality.

—*December* 31, 1927

London Fog

... London fog is a product of modern science. It is full of carbon and chemicals and is produced by the efficiency of industrial factories and furnaces. Men lived in a much clearer world in the sixth century; in what has been finely called "that long evening by the Mediterranean."

—October 11, 1924

Lost Ten Tribes

If I went in for the problem of the Lost Ten Tribes, I should say that the Ten Tribes were England, France, Germany, Austria, Italy, Spain, Portugal, Russia, Greece, and Sweden. That is what one might call being lost on a large scale.

—July 31, 1909

Lost Way

The one thing that the modern English will not understand is that when you have lost your way quite hopelessly the quickest thing is to go back along the road you know to the place from which you started. You may call it reaction, you may call it repetition, you may call it a tiresome theory; but it is the quickest way out of a wood.

—July 28, 1906

Love (Free)

Free love is the direct enemy of freedom. It is the most obvious of all the bribes that can be offered by slavery.

—September 2, 1922

Love and Liberty

... one very simple thing was true both of love and liberty: the gods of the romantics and the republicans. They were both simply fragments of Christian mysticism, and even of Christian theology, torn out of their proper place, flung loosely about and finally hurled forward into an age of hard materialism which

263

instantly destroyed them. They were not really rational ideas, still less rationalistic ideas. At least, they were never rational ideas after they had left off being religious ideas. One of them was a hazy human exaggeration of the sacramental idea of marriage. The other was a hazy human exaggeration of the brotherhood of men in God.

—August 27, 1932

Love thy Neighbor

The Bible tells us to love our neighbours, and also to love our enemies; probably because they are generally the same people. And there is a real human reason for this. You think of a remote man merely as a man; that is, you think of him in the right way. . . . He also has been bewildered and broadened by youth; he also has been tortured and intoxicated by love; he also is sublimely doubtful about death. You can think about the soul of that nameless man. . . . But you do not think about the soul of your next-door neighbour. He is not a man; he is an environment. He is the barking of a dog; he is the noise of a pianola. . . . The remote man, therefore, may stand for manhood; for the glory of birth or the dignity of death. But it is difficult to get Mr. Brown next door . . . to stand for these things in any satisfactorily symbolic attitude.

—July 16, 1910

Loyalty

On the one side is the individual life and its passions and affections, which has its own reasonable claim and importance; on the other is something entirely different, which is the duty of human beings to hand on—the permanent possibilities of human culture and citizenship. For that purpose it is emphatically not true that love is enough; it is necessary to have something that is, if possible, even greater than love, and of which the name is loyalty.

—August 26, 1922

Luxury

We are chiefly concerned with the heresy of the Manichees, which has already expressed itself in the denunciation of wine and even tobacco, and might just as well express itself, I would suggest, in the denunciation of mustard or even salt.

For the essence of that idea is that every pleasure as such is suspect; or that, unless a thing can be specially shown to be morally good, it is almost probable that it is morally bad. There is no real defence of a luxury except to prove that it is a necessity. . . . There is a truth behind the joke of the man who said: "Give us the luxuries of life and we will dispense with the necessities"; and the truth can be more soberly stated by saying that, in one sense, human beings are not even completely human until they are civilised.

—February 21, 1931

M-N-O

Macbeth

For the play of "Macbeth" is, in the supreme and special sense, the Christian tragedy; to be set against the pagan tragedy of Oedipus. It is the whole point about Oedipus that he does not know what he is doing. And it is the whole point about Macbeth that he does know what he is doing.

— *September* 14, 1929

All men are always being influenced; or every incident is an influence. The question is, which incident shall we allow to be most influential. Macbeth was influenced; but he consented to be influenced. He was not, like a blind tragic pagan, obeying something he thought he ought to obey. He does not worship the three witches like the three fates. He is a good enlightened Christian, and sins against the light.

— *September* 14, 1929

Machinery

No scientific instrument has ever transformed society. It was always the soul of the society that transformed the scientific instrument. If it set the machinery to good work it is not because there is anything good in machinery, but because there was something good already in the community that happened to use it. If it set the machinery to bad work it is not because there is anything bad about machinery, but because there was something very bad about that portion of humanity. A machine is used mildly by a mild society; it is used wildly by a wild society; it is not used at all by a lazy or stagnant society.

—*February* 10, 1923

Machines

Sometimes there was something really to be called the madness of machinery; as where men no longer used their machines to produce their material, but rather used their material to feed their machines. I admit a certain grandeur in the modern American machine as in the ancient Assyrian sculpture; but the sculpture of Assyria is a wreck upon the desert sands.

—*April* 11, 1936

Machines and Employment

At the beginning of a month twenty men are working in a field and thus getting food and shelter. At the end of the month two men are working in the field, because it needs only two men to work a machine. The other eighteen men have no food and no shelter. And then this sociologist talks about an unreasoning fear of machines. He might as well talk about an unreasoning fear of tigers.

—*February* 22, 1936

Madness

The truth is, I fear, that madness has a great advantage over sanity. Sanity is always careless. Madness is always careful. A lunatic might count all the railings along the front of Hyde Park, he might know the exact number of them, because he thought they were something else. A healthy man would not know the number of the railings, or perhaps even the shape of the railings, he would know nothing about them except the supreme, sublime, Platonic, and transcendental truth, that they were railings.

—*March* 9, 1907

A man in a minority may think he is right; he may even turn out to be right; but if he really supposes that the majority thinks it is wrong then he is in a minority of one; he is mad.

—July 13, 1929

Magistrate

The only two successive reasons that should make anyone a magistrate or a member are, first, that he is a man; and, second, that he is a suitable man. But the principle accepted at present is something like this: that because an aristocracy of dentists have gained too much power in the State we must instantly balance them with a new aristocracy of hairdressers. Only a few faint voices would join mine in suggesting that we might balance it by a democracy of men.

—October 22, 1910

Malice and Spite

If a man says that I am a dwarf, I can invite him to measure me. If he says I am a cannibal, I can invite him to dinner. If he says I am a coward, I can hit him. If he says I am a miser, I can give him half-a-sovereign. But if he says I am fat and lazy (which is true), the best I can answer is that he speaks out of malice and spite. Whenever we see that phrase, we may be almost certain that somebody has told the truth about somebody else.

—November 13, 1909

Man

If Man is not a divinity, then Man is a disease. Either he is the image of God, or else he is the one animal which has gone mad.

—January 12, 1907

Man has stepped into a totally different world of imagination and invention; like a man turning into a god. If this startling and stupendous difference can co-exist with exactly the same material origins, the only possible deduction is that it does not come from the material origins. In other words, the only possible deduction is that by some special spiritual act, as in the ancient record, man became a living soul.

—October 15, 1927

Man, to whom alone is revealed the divine humility, has everywhere founded his superiorities on his inferiorities. Being an outcast without protection against the cold, he has made himself an artificial skin; and, while he was about it, he has made the purple robes of Tyre and the golden copes of Milan. Being unable to sleep under the stars like the stronger creatures, he has huddled ignominiously under a roof; and, incidentally, made the roof a thing like Glastonbury or the Taj Mahal. And having, for some strange reason, broken down in the rhythm by which all the other unconscious creatures live, he has made a rhythm of his own, with special crises and high moments of festival; because the deep mystery of his nature demands variety and the concentration of contentment into conviviality. Therefore he is no more ashamed that ale is artificial than that clothes or cookery are artificial; knowing that with that artificiality would perish all the arts.

—January 7, 1928

Man (The Best)

The good man is welcome whether at the moment he is sad or glad; but what is utterly intolerable is the Best Man—the man who is consciously better than others. Perhaps that is why the young man at weddings is called "the Best Man," because he is secure, supercilious, and solitary like Satan. The bridegroom, on the other hand, is the Good Man, because he is divinely distracted, and full of holy fear. I do not vouch for the historical truth of this derivation. I have heard others. Some people will tell you that the best man is so called because he was the best warrior of the tribe in the times when women were married by capture. But you will pay no attention to that sort of bosh, I hope. Women never were married by capture. They always pretended they were; as they do now.

—July 31, 1909

Man (Categories of)

Everyone knows that men have been divided into Platonists and Aristotelians. . . . Sir William Gilbert uttered his dark Calvinistic dogma that every child is born a liberal or a conservative; an American wit offered us the alternative of being a bromide or something equally chemical and unpleasant; a Scottish metaphysician said that all men were either anabolic or catabolic; and I say that all men are either fond of sweets or fond of savouries, and that this is a far more profound moral distinction than all the rest.

—July 19, 1930

Man (Common)

The snag is that when one of these people begins to "improve himself," it is exactly at that moment that I begin to doubt whether it is an improvement. He seems to me to collect with remarkable rapidity a number of superstitions. Of which the most blind and benighted is what may be called the superstition of school. He regards school, not as a normal social institution to be fitted in to other social institutions, like home and church and state, but as some sort of entirely super-normal and miraculous moral factory in which perfect men and women are made by magic.

—April 26, 1930

When I said that I wanted the popular feeling to find political expression, I meant the actual and autochthonous popular feeling as it can be found in third-class carriages and bean-feasts and bank-holiday crowds; and especially, of course (for the earnest social seeker after truth), in public-houses. I thought, and I still think, that these people are right on a vast number of things on which the fashionable leaders are wrong.

—April 26, 1930

Now, if there is one thing of which I have been certain since my boyhood, and grow more certain as I advance in age, it is that nothing is poetical if plain daylight is not poetical; and no monster should amaze us if the normal man does not amaze.

—March 7, 1931

Man (Dignity of)

Man is no more overshadowed and outdone by the tail of a comet than by the tail of a peacock or the tail of a monkey. All three tails may be called superiorities; but can hardly without a stretch of language be called moral superiorities. Comparatively early in his historical career man realised, and faced with some stoicism, the melancholy fact that he was without a tail. . . . But he retains an inward conviction that there is in his very defect a certain indefinable dignity; and that (as a flippant man would say) it was when his tail ended that his story began.

—*February* 19, 1910

Man (Eminent)

Let us clear ourselves of this suffocating modern superstition about eminent individuals. Great names do not necessarily mean great intellects; and certainly great intellects do not mean great souls.

—*December* 24, 1910

Man (Equality of)

If any man really fails to understand the mystical dogma of the equality of man, he can immediately test it by thinking of two men, of totally different types and fortunes, falling on the same field at some terrible crisis in the war which saved our country. One might be, and often was, a gentleman of the fine tradition, fortunate in his friends, in his tastes, in his culture as well as his character. Another might be some stunted serf of our servile industrial slums, a man whom all modern life conspired to crush and to deform. In the hour when the flag of England was saved, there was no man who dared to say, or would have dreamed of saying, that one death was less glorious than the other.

—*November* 20, 1920

It was the highly mystical idea expressed in the Declaration of Independence: "that all men were created equal." . . . The equality of men is an idea not only mystical, but theological. Anyhow, nine men out of ten would tell you they did not believe in it because some men are taller than others, some talk more amusingly than others, some play the trombone more loudly and arrestingly than others, and so on, through a somewhat lengthy list of examples. The very use of such examples shows that the old understanding of the doctrine of equality has largely disappeared.

—*December* 19, 1925

Man (Genius of)

Briefly, it is always assumed that the poem that somebody made is vastly superior to the ballad that everybody made. For my part I take the other view. I prefer the gossip of the many to the scandal of the few. I distrust the narrow individualism of the artist, trusting rather the natural communism of the craftsmen. I think there is one thing more important than the man of genius—and that is the genius of man.

—April 2, 1910

Man (Great)

[This] is the mark of the truly great man: that he sees the common man afar off, and worships him. The great man tries to be ordinary, and becomes extraordinary in the process. But the small man tries to be mysterious, and becomes lucid in an awful sense—for we can all see through him.

—June 5, 1909

As with all really great men, the legends are more appropriate than the facts.

—August 27, 1910

Man (Honest)

I would suggest that the main object of any honest man in this present epoch ought to be that of going about asking the proper philosophical question. In order to cheer you along the path, I may remark that one of the few men I ever heard of who went about asking the proper philosophical question was immediately poisoned by the very enlightened community of Athens.

—January 5, 1907

Man (Literary)

The last and most important lesson of humility that we literary men of Western Europe have to learn is that the race will go on being healthy even if we go on being morbid. It used to be our first pride that our wisdom would save the world. It is now our last pride that at least our madness will ruin the world. It will do nothing of the kind. Humanity will be so occupied for ever and ever in pulling crackers after supper that it will not even know whether we have taken our medicine after breakfast.

—February 17, 1906

Man (Modern)

The man calls himself Agnostic who would naturally have called himself ignorant; but ignorance is higher. The average man, even the modern man, has a great deal to teach us. But the nuisance is that he won't teach it; he will only repeat what he has been taught. We have almost to torture him till he says what he does think, just as men once tortured a heretic till he said what he didn't think. We have to dig up the modern man as if he were Palaeolithic man.

—March 6, 1909

Moderns have not the moral courage, as a rule, to avow the sincere spiritual bias behind their fads; they become insincere even about their sincerity.

—December 27, 1919

... the modern man is in favour of introducing order into everything except his own ideas.

—April 1, 1922

... there are some modern people who are a great deal too modern; who are quite certainly devouring and destroying themselves with the nonsense of novelty, and trying always to hear of something later than the very latest. They are visibly growing old in order to keep up with their youth. They are wasting away to nothing, for want of a little nothing to do. If only some of their friends would persuade them to go away for a few centuries of superstition and ignorance, like the people of the Dark Ages, they might come back and astonish the world by something that the world had never seen before, like Gothic architecture or the portraits in the Canterbury Tales.

—September 6, 1930

Man (Practical)

Practical men have been responsible for practically all our practical disasters. The perpetual demand for a practical man is a demand for something that would make those disasters more disastrous.

—February 28, 1925

...he admits that he cares little for reasons; he constantly affirms that he cares only for results. And this is an incompetent proceeding to start with, for to look for results without looking for causes is not to understand the results as results, even when you have got them. This is the perpetual and pitiful tragedy of the practical man in practical affairs.

—February 28, 1925

Man and Brute

Our treatment of animals at the worst restrains their wildness; our treatment of human beings makes them wild. Caging a canary, at the worst, can only tame it; caging a man may madden him.

—March 7, 1914

Man and Children

A man saying that he will treat other people's children as his own is exactly like a man saying that he will treat other people's wives as his own. He may get a certain amount of poetic or sentimental pleasure out of the children, but so he may out of the wives.

—March 5, 1932

Man and Cosmos

...that argument about man looking trivial in the face of the physical universe has never terrified me at all, because it is a merely sentimental argument, and not a rational one in any sense. I might be physically terrified of a man fifty feet high if I saw him walking about my garden, but even in my terror I should have no reason for supposing that he was vitally more important than I am, or higher in the scale of being, or nearer to God, or nearer to whatever is the truth. The sentiment of the overpowering cosmos is a babyish and hysterical sentiment, though a very human and natural one. But if we are seriously debating whether man is the moral centre of this world, then he is no more morally dwarfed by the fact that his is not the largest star than by the fact that he is not the largest mammal. . . . "The vertigo of the infinite" has no more spiritual value than the vertigo of a ladder or the vertigo of a balloon.

—July 19, 1910

Man and Theology

Man, and especially newspaper men, are excited about the problem of determining whether the dean of St. Paul's is a Christian or a Platonist or a Pyrrho-Buddhist. They are not specially interested in whether the gloomy dean is a good man in relation to his grocer or green-grocer. People are *not* merely interested in morality, or even merely in religion. They are intensely interested in theology—if possible even more than in religion.

—November 5, 1927

Man at the Wheel

I refrain from speaking to the man at the wheel not because he is wiser than anybody, or even wiser than I, but because it is the paradox of steering that one man, who may not be wiser than anybody individually, must be wiser than everybody put together. There must be a man at the wheel simply because there cannot be a mob at the wheel—or even a crew at the wheel.

—November 27, 1915

Man in the Universe

It is unavoidable that such debates about the position of man in the universe should shade away by degrees from anthropology to philosophy, exactly as evolution is supposed to shade away from anthropoids to men. None of the parties in this great discussion about apes and primitive men is free from the colour of its own conceptions of cosmic life. The materialists are moralists, every bit as much as any mystics are moralists. Every professor who finds a skull really philosophises over it like Hamlet.

—September 10, 1927

275

Man versus Beast

Now, the difference between the human and the non-human mind infinitely exceeds the difference between flying and not flying, because it covers a thousand things of that sort and not one. . . . The truth is that men make houses and a thousand other things, including hives. The whole position and poise and gesture of the man in turning from one thing to another is different in kind from that of the monomaniac and mechanical insect. . . . It is not merely a question of man doing more or less things; he might do less, and he would still at any moment be capable of doing more. It is a quality and not a quantity in the way in which he does anything at all; or even, in his most divine moments, does nothing at all.

— September 10, 1927

Mr. Wells claims the moral right to sacrifice all the other animals to man; and yet he would say that man is only a more or less accidental variety of the other animals. He assumes the very distinction that he denies. Mr. Shaw demands of man a moral magnanimity utterly unknown in all the rest of nature; and yet he would say that man is only a passing product of nature. He assumes the very distinction that he denies. For it seems strangely forgotten that the unique authority of man is as much asserted in insisting on his mercy as in insisting on his mastery. If he is merely at one with nature, as all the other creatures are at one with nature, there is no more obligation for him than for them; and they certainly are not entirely at one with each other. . . . We are, in fact, treating him exactly as he was treated in the old theological dogma which both Mr. Wells and Mr. Shaw would reject, and not in the least as he is treated by the new scientific dogma which both Mr. Wells and Mr. Shaw would accept.

— October 15, 1927

Man's Folly

. . . the wisdom of man alters with every age; his prudence has to fit perpetually shifting shapes of inconvenience or dilemma. But his folly is immortal: a fire stolen from heaven.

— October 8, 1910

Man's Purpose

A little while ago an intellectual weekly started an argument among the intellectuals about whether man has improved the earth he lives on; whether nature as a whole was better for the presence of man. Nobody seemed to notice that this is assuming that the end of man is to grow more grass or improve the breed of rattlesnakes, apart from any theory about the origin or object of these things. A man may serve God and be good to mankind for that reason; or a man may serve mankind and be good to other things to preserve the standard of mankind; but it is very hard to prove exactly how far he is bound to make the jungle thicker or encourage very tall giraffes.

—December 11, 1926

Maniacs

As a point not of virtue but of vanity, I should be less insulted by the title of a murderer than by the title of a homicidal maniac. The murderer might be said, not unfairly, to have lost the first fragrance of his innocence, and all that keeps the child near to the cherubim. But the maniac has lost more than innocence; he has lost essence; the complete personality that makes him a man.

—September 14, 1929

Mankind

I am so far merely on the side of the men, of the great mass of reverent and reasonable human beings, who would much rather admit that they are blind in the dark than be burdened in the dark with old-fashioned scientific spectacles, and told by a quack that they can see.

—August 21, 1926

Manners (Bad)

Unconscious carelessness may sometimes mean genius; conscious carelessness never means anything but bad manners.

—March 7, 1908

Marriage

Life is a real thing; it really matters whether you marry a good husband or a bad husband. And just as it is certainly to a woman's advantage to have a kind husband, it is certainly to a man's advantage to have a clever wife. What man ever does keep his wife in darkness and inferiority? Why should he? It is much jollier to have an intelligent wife than a stupid wife, considering the great amount of time that one has to pass in her company. I have met wives who were kept stupid because their husbands were stupid. But I have never met a wife who was kept stupid because her husband was clever.

—August 29, 1908

Marriage (Re-)

It is a very good thing, by the way, to be frequently married again—always, of course, to the same person.

—October 9, 1909

Marriage and the Comics

An intelligent man from Mars turning over some stacks or volumes (poor devil!) of our English comic papers, would in the same manner form one firm and clear opinion. He would believe that the whole English people were on the point of rising against the institution of marriage and of destroying it for ever. He would find every paper covered with jeers and sneers at the man who was contemptible enough to tie himself to a wife and a perambulator. He would find the married man invariably represented as a man of improbably small stature and manifest mental deficiency. He would find that these million jokes were all variations of two jokes: the glee of the married man when he escapes from his married life, and the woe of the married man while he is tied to it. And, finding our popular humour one long scream against the married state, the man from Mars would naturally, in his intellectual innocence, suppose that the country was really raging with this revolutionary passion. He would suppose that mobs were battering upon the doors of the Divorce Court, demanding, *en masse,* to be admitted and divorced. He would imagine that wedding-rings were being melted down publicly in a great pot in Trafalgar Square. He would suppose that any couple daring to get married would be assaulted at the church-door by the infuriated populace and pelted with bricks instead of confetti.

—October 28, 1905

Martyrdom

The Secularists laboriously explain that martyrdoms do not prove a faith to be true, as if anybody was ever such a fool as to suppose that they did. What they did prove, or, rather, strongly suggest, was that something had entered human psychology which was stronger than strong pain.

—February 8, 1908

Martyrdom (Modern)

The incident of the Suffragettes who chained themselves with iron chains to the railings of Downing Street is a good ironical allegory of most modern martyrdom. It generally consists of a man chaining himself up and then complaining that he is not free.

—February 8, 1908

Martyrdom (Pseudo)

The modern notion of impressing the public by a mere demonstration of unpopularity, by being thrown out of meetings or thrown into jail, is largely a mistake. It rests on a fallacy touching the true popular value of martyrdom. People look at human history and see that it has often happened that persecutions have not only advertised but even advanced a persecuted creed, and given to its validity the public and dreadful witness of dying men. The paradox was pictorially expressed in Christian art, in which saints were shown brandishing as weapons the very tools that had slain them. And because his martyrdom is thus a power to the martyr, modern people think that anyone who makes himself slightly uncomfortable in public will immediately be uproariously popular. This element of inadequate martyrdom is not true only of the Suffragettes; it is true of many movements.

—February 8, 1908

Marx, Karl

The professor may claim humanity for the work of the most inhuman of professors, Karl Marx.

—December 21, 1918

Marx's Communist Manifesto

The manifesto guards itself against the charge of destroying every small property, but it avows its general aim "further to centralise the forces of production and to subject all of production to a systematic plan." We know that systematic plan. Things centralised are managed by the few; they cannot possibly be managed by all the proletarians, let alone all the peasants. They will be managed like our own coal control or beer control. . . . And some prigs really ask us to believe that the people are shouting "Less beer! More state control!"

—August 16, 1919

Marxism

Briefly, I may call it the trick of giving parallels without proportions. In the most obvious case, the Marxian appeals to the proletarians of all lands, because there are proletarians in all lands. He seems to think that this means that all lands are proletarian. As a matter of fact, of course, it might just as well say that, because there are hills in all lands, all lands are equally hilly. Most internationalist philosophy depends simply on two fallacies—first, calling every generalisation about a nation narrow; and then applying that same narrow generalisation to all the nations of the earth.

—February 23, 1918

The system of Marx is as logical as that of Calvin, and as limited as that of Calvin. In a generation or so it will have gone into the limbo of most heresies, along with the heresy of Calvin. But meanwhile it will have poisoned the Russian Revolution, just as the other poisoned the English Revolution.

—July 12, 1919

Like most bourgeois religions, it is especially the religion of a book. As with most bourgeois religions, there is something narrow, specialist, or sectarian about the book, or the interpretation of the book. The book of Karl Marx has not even the large and loose human applicability of the Koran. It is, on the face of it, the sort of book that is only read in the first instance by middle-class intellectuals, familiar with certain polysyllabic political and social terms. Such books are often effective; they are always ephemeral. They represent the truth to which Joubert referred, when he said that books do more harm than good when they go beyond the

280

general purpose of giving a pleasure superior to monetary and carnal pleasure; that they "only bring fresh sects and crotchets into the world."

—July 24, 1920

It amounts to saying that only economic desires exist in the mind of man; which is manifest bosh.... Vanity is not an economic motive; and curiosity is not an economic motive. And as it is obvious that people do not act only for economics, why on earth should they fight only for economics? And, as a matter of fact, of course, they do not fight only for economics. There have been wars of religion, there have been wars of revenge, there have been wars of mere prejudice against the rites or customs of aliens. But, though the maxim is such that it would be easy to destroy, its supporters scarcely seem to think it necessary to defend it.

—November 19, 1921

Marxism and World War I

It was the Marxian materialists who did positively promise that the international proletariat would prevent a war in Europe. I never heard of any priest who thus promised that the Church would do it.

—January 19, 1924

Marxist Maxims

... that the whole world is divided into "workers" and employers or capitalists. It can be answered immediately by taking the plain figure of a peasant—plain in every sense; for his problem is a simple one, and his figure is a conspicuous one all over Europe, and for that matter, all over Asia. He owns his own field, and works in his own field. Is he a worker or a capitalist, an employer or an employee? He is certainly a worker, because he works; and he is certainly a capitalist in the sense that he owns capital. But if he is an employer, it is because he employs himself; and if he is an employee, it is because he is employed by himself. Against all these obvious facts stands the fixed and formal answer; the answer that does not answer them.

—November 19, 1921

Materialism (Age of)

... it is pretty clear that both the age of mere industrialism and the age of mere scientific materialism have only been interludes, and that older things are near enough to us to appear again as new. The materialistic system has broken down in theory, and one of the greatest of modern physicists has written, "the world seems to be rather like a great thought than a great machine."

—January 3, 1931

Materialist

... suppose a certain event in our daily life is alleged to be magical or miraculous. My faith does not forbid me to attribute it to a natural cause. But his philosophy does forbid him to attribute it to a preternatural cause. A materialist or a monist cannot believe in miracles and remain a materialist or a monist. I have the happiness of believing that I live in a rather larger world.

—December 8, 1923

In one sense, to do him justice, this melancholy materialist is the most disinterested of men. The mystic is one who will serve something invisible for his own reasons. The materialist is one who will serve anything visible for no reason.

—October 4, 1930

Materialists

The materialists of the nineteenth century believed that the terror and tragedy hanging over men would be the rise of population and the scarcity of food. In many places the real tragedy is the decline of population; in most places the real tragedy is the abundance of food. And it is all the more a real tragedy because it is also a comedy, and almost a farce.

—April 11, 1936

Matrimonial Agencies and Séance

Spiritualism is to religion exactly what a Matrimonial Agency is to love. . . . Spiritualists do not worship gods; they advertise for gods. We all know what does happen only too often to such silly women as advertise in matrimonial papers for a single gentleman. They get someone who is hardly ever a gentleman and is often not even single.

—October 30, 1909

May the Best Man Win

The most gloomy of all possible theories is the theory that the best man wins. We know the man who wins, and if he is the best man we can only express our feelings in the words of a vulgar music-hall song about a wedding, which ran (if I remember right)—"I was the best man, the best man, the best man; Oh! Jerusalem, you ought to have seen the worst!" If Mr. Rockefeller really rose by superior merit, America must be a kind of hell. But I am an optimist, and I believe that evil is frequently victorious; a thought full of peace, comfort, and possibilities of human affection. We can all love mankind if we remember not to judge them by their leaders.

—November 16, 1907

Means before the End

One very common form of the blunder is to make modern conditions an absolute end, and then try to fit human necessities to that end, as if they were only a means. Thus people say, "Home life is not suited to the business life of to-day." Which is as if they said, "Heads are not suited to the sort of hats now in fashion." Then they might go round cutting off people's heads to meet the shortage of shrinkage of hats, and calling it the hat problem.

—December 11, 1926

Mediaeval

The word mediaeval is generally used as a term of abuse, to be applied especially to things that did not exist in mediaeval times, such as capitalism, militarism, conscript armies, jingo patriotism, the act of union, the Kaiser, or the censorship of plays. Sometimes it is used as a term of abuse where it is really one of respect. Thus Trotsky . . . said that at least capitalism was better than mediaevalism. By this he meant that the monstrous modern accumulations of property were at least better than a decent and democratic distribution of property.

—November 18, 1922

Mediaevalism

There were serfs in the Middle Ages; but the serfdom was merely the remains of the servile state of pagan antiquity. The peculiar achievement of Mediaevalism was not serfdom, but the dissolution of serfdom. But the co-operative craftsmen were not serfs in any sense or by any argument. They were trades unionists whose trades unions were richer, more responsible, more recognised by the state, and more respected as contribuors to culture, than are our own trades unions to-day. They demanded good pay from the purchaser, as ours do; they also demanded good work from the craftsman, which ours cannot do.

—November I, 1919

... note the queer, automatic assumption that it must always mean throwing mud at a thing to call it a relic of Mediaevalism. The modern world contains a good many relics of Mediaevalism, and most of us would be surprised if the argument were logically enforced even against the things that are commonly called mediaeval. We should express some regret if somebody blew up Westminster Abbey, because it is a relic of Mediaevalism. Doubts would trouble us if the government burned all existing copies of Dante's *Divine Comedy* and Chaucer's *Canterbury Tales,* because they are quite certainly relics of Mediaevalism. . . .

—March 12, 1932

Mediaevalists

Mediaevalists do not maintain that Mediaevalism was morally perfect, but only that it was moral. What they complain of is that their opponents find out that it was moral, and then deny that it was mediaeval.

—June 2, 1923

Mencken, H. L.

I have so warm an admiration for Mr. Mencken as the critic of puritan pride and stupidity that I regret that he should thus try to make himself out a back number out of mere irreligious irritation. He has been the hammer of those false idealists who call themselves moral because they demand the prohibition of a few hard drinks, and dare not say a word of the prohibition of hard dealings, of hard bargains that break the poor, and the brutal ethics tolerated in business. I sympathise

284

so much with this that I do not mind the hammer being flourished sometimes a little cheaply and ostentatiously, like an auctioneer's hammer. . . .

—*June* 14, 1930

Menu (French)

The principle of a French menu is rational enough. I always know what the names on a French menu mean, because they mean nothing.

—*May* 16, 1908

Metaphor

Men tell more truth by their metaphors than by their statements.

—*December* 17, 1910

Metaphysics

Even the physical conditions of the world bear witness to something in man that is strictly to be called metaphysical, that is unique and detached and raised above the obvious physical order.

—*January* 10, 1931

Method

It is odd to notice in this age of machines how often the machines fail and the old methods succeed.

—*September* 25, 1909

Middle Ages

The man of the Middle Ages certainly did not think there was anything specially sacred about the Middle Ages, merely because he was in the middle of them. That confusion of thought is rather characteristic of the modern ages, which might well be called the muddle ages. The mediaeval man thought that men would be tempted to sin in all times and places while the earth endured. And if the modern man had thought the same thing he would have been readier for the war of 1914, not to mention such a trifle as the peace of 1919.

—April 23, 1919

Millennium

It has often been said that signs and portents will accompany the advent of the millennium, or the coming of the heavenly kingdom upon earth. Oliver Wendell Holmes demanded that certain miracles should precede that Apocalypse; as that raspberries and strawberries should grow bigger downwards through the box; or that lawyers should take what they would give and doctors give what they would take.

—September 5, 1931

Millionaire

They worship the invisible strength of money; they adore it as a sort of airy magic; no men on the earth think less of the actual pleasures that it stands for. The Yankee millionaire likes adding more noughts on to a figure in his private books; it is a spiritual pride with him. Nothing can make him see that, in adding noughts, he is truly and indeed adding nothings.

—September 17, 1910

It is possible that many good Presidents have been shamefully shot in South American Republics. But it is equally obvious that many eminent financiers have been shamefully and indefensibly left unshot in the North American Republic.

—November 19, 1910

We may admit that there may be too much mistrust in Nicaragua. But few will deny that there is too much Trust in New York. According to the ordinary human, healthy, heathen, common sense of things, the case of North America is infinitely more awful: streets full of men dead is not so frightful a vision as one of the millionaires mildly alive. Doubtless the South Americans must be asked in judgment for the lives of the men they have slaughtered; and even the North Americans will have a good many black and red men to answer for. But when the

North Americans are asked about the men they have not slaughtered, I wonder what excuse they will have to offer.

—November 26, 1910

Millionaires and Misers

The modern rich began to be hunted by the modern hatred when they had abandoned the wise precautions of the misers. The misers hid their wealth. The millionaires display it. In both cases the common-sense of the public pierces through the pretence. But in the old case it found only a harmless eccentricity; in the new case it discovers a harmful concentration. When all is said and done, however, the difference between the two types of money-getting is not difficult to state. The fact is that a man was ashamed of being a miser; a man is not ashamed of being a millionaire. This amazing truth can only be explained as the insolence of the profligate has been explained. The usurer, the man-killer, can, like the lady-killer, stun and strengthen himself with the small drug of pride. The moment he can sincerely admire himself, all other men will admire him.

—August 22, 1914

Milton, Age of

All generations are fairly ignorant of the remote past. The peculiarity of this generation was that it was forcibly made ignorant of the immediate past.

—December 13, 1924

Milton versus Shakspere

Milton is possessed with what is, I suppose, the first and finest idea of Protestantism— the idea of the individual soul actually testing and tasting all the truth there is, and calling that truth which it has not tested or tasted truth of a less valuable and vivid kind. But Shakspere is possessed through and through with the feeling which is the first and finest idea of Catholicism—that truth exists whether we like it or not, and that it is for us to accommodate ourselves to it.

—June 8, 1907

Milton's Paradise Lost

Everybody knows the first three lines of *Paradise Lost:*

> Of man's first disobedience and the fruit
> Of that forbidden tree, whose mortal taste
> Brought death into the world and all our woe

... and Milton may himself have paused at that point, and heaved a sigh of relief, to think that he had got the whole story packed pretty thoroughly into the three lines, even if all his readers refused to read him any more. He had successfully informed the public of the incident called the Fall of Man, had explained its connection with the fruit of the Tree of Knowledge, and attached to it all the results of the doctrine of Original Sin.

—August 2, 1930

The Mind

Let us never mention anything as a mere inconceivability—as something that literally cannot be entertained by the human mind. The mind is an infinity, even if it is an infinity of nonsense. The mind of man is divine, even in the unfathomable nature of its darkness. Men can think of anything seriously, however absurd it is. Men can believe anything, even the truth.

—September 22, 1906

I must trust my mind as a mind, or become a bottomless sceptic, or give myself up to the keepers of a lunatic asylum. But in so far as I trust it as a modern mind, I am not trusting to its liberty, but to its limitation. I am trusting it merely because it is conditioned and constrained by the accidental prejudices of the twentieth century....

—March 26, 1932

Mind (Mediaeval versus Modern)

The mediaeval reasoners knew better than most men that reason is not everything. What I complain of is that, while the mediaevals invoked something that is above reason, which they called faith, the moderns often invoke something which is below reason, which they call subconsciousness or herd instinct or libido or will to live.

—March 26, 1932

288

Mind (Modern)

Go into a crowded drawing-room and say, "I have had a revelation from heaven that it is dangerous to wear galoshes," and your friends will see, even if they do not say, that it is a silly idea. They will think it a silly idea *because* you give what is, after all, a reason for it. But if you simply say, without any reason or authority whatever, "Don't you know it's very dangerous to wear galoshes?" all their faces will instantly alter with intelligence and alarm, and they will discuss every aspect of this important piece of news except the question of where it came from. It is, after all, even in the rational sense, *something* in favour of any formula that any public authority has made itself responsible for endorsing it. But in practice, if your remark has some authority, people will resist and criticise it. If it has no authority, they will surrender and swallow it. Such is the detached and daring freedom of the modern mind.

—June 16, 1917

Mind (Open)

I remember once arguing with an honest young atheist, who was very much shocked at my disputing some of the assumptions which were absolute sanctities to him (such as the quite unproved proposition of the independence of matter and the quite improbable proposition of its power to originate mind), and he at length fell back upon this question, which he delivered with an honourable heat of defiance and indignation: "Well, can you tell me any man of intellect, great in science or philosophy, who accepted the miraculous?" I said, "With pleasure. Descartes, Dr. Johnson, Newton, Faraday, Newman, Gladstone, Pasteur, Browning, Brunetière—as many more as you please." To which that quite admirable and idealistic young man made this astonishing reply—"Oh, but of course they *had* to say that; they were Christians." First he challenged me to find a black swan, and then he ruled out all my swans because they were black. The fact that all these great intellects had come to the Christian view was somehow or other a proof either that they were not great intellects or that they had not really come to that view. The argument thus stood in a charmingly convenient form: "All men that count have come to my conclusion; for if they come to your conclusion they do not count."

—May 4, 1907

An open mind is really a mark of foolishness, like an open mouth. Mouths and minds were made to shut; they were made to open only in order to shut.

—*October* 10, 1908

...the modern man fancies he has reached supreme culture because he opens his intellect. But the supreme culture (in the forcible modern phrase) is to know when to shut your head. There is one odd aspect of the man with this sort of open mind—a man whom one imagines with an open mouth. It is that being thus gaping and helpless, he is really brutal and oppressive. He tyrannises; he forces on all other men his own insolent indecision. He forbids his followers to come to any conclusion till he has done so. He will allow no one else to find the truth, as Peary will allow no one else to find the Pole. He is the worst tyrant that the world has seen; he is the persecuting sceptic.

—*October* 16, 1909

The truth is that if a man wishes to remain in perfect mental breadth and freedom, he had better not think at all. Thinking is a narrowing process. It leads to what people call dogma. A man who thinks hard about any subject for several years is in horrible danger of discovering the truth about it. This process is called becoming "sectarian," also "hardening in later life"; it can also be described as "giving up to party what was meant for mankind." It is a terrible thing when a man really finds that his mind was given him to use, and not to play with; or, in other words, that the gods gave him a great ugly mouth with which to answer questions, and not merely to ask them.

—*October* 16, 1909

...the open mind is a little too like the open mouth. Sometimes it is a little too much akin to the empty soul. But in a very large number of cases, it is something that corresponds to an honest workman out of work; it is simply unemployed.

—*October* 24, 1925

I do not call any man imaginative unless he can imagine something different from his own favourite sort of imagery. I do not call any man free unless he can walk backwards as well as forwards. I do not call any man broadminded unless he can include minds that are different from his own normal mind, let alone moods that are different from his own momentary mood. And I do not call any man bold or strong or possessed of stabbing realism or startling actuality unless he is strong enough to resist the merely neurotic effects of his own fatigue, and still see things more or less as they are; big mountains as big, and great poets as great, and remarkable acts and achievements as remarkable, even if other people are bored with them, or even if he is bored with them himself. The preservation of proportion in the mind is the only thing that keeps a man from narrowmindedness.

—*November* 12, 1932

Minority

...I can never accept the mere case of the minority against the majority, because of the simple fact that at least there is only one majority, while there are any number of minorities.

—*June* 7, 1924

Most moderns believe in minorities, each having a pet minority of his own.

—*December* 20, 1924

Minority and Propaganda

This is the age in which thin and theoretic minorities can cover and conquer unconscious and untheoretic majorities, being spread over them like spiders' webs. A small group that has a philosophy, even if it is a heresy or merely a fallacy, has now an abnormal advantage over the masses that have no philosophy, but only a sort of broad bewilderment produced by the reading of newspapers.

—*December* 20, 1919

Miracle

The greatest miracle is the fact that politicians are tolerated.

—*December* 22, 1906

Miracles

The element of the supernatural in practical affairs has always been regarded (even by those who most strongly believed in it) as exceptional. If a miracle is not exceptional, it is not even miraculous. Nobody was ever taught by any sane creed to count upon or expect anything but the natural. To put the point briefly, we are commanded to put our faith in miracles, but not to put our trust in them.

—November 7, 1908

... nobody can begin to understand the theoretic defence of the miraculous who does not understand the idea of a positive fight against positive evil. We should be right in thinking it silly for the good angels to interfere, if none of us believed in bad angels. A miracle, if you like, proclaims martial law in the universe. But it is not unreasonable; for it may be the only way of reconciling reason with liberty.

—March 21, 1914

Missing Link

... modern people did try to make a law out of the Missing Link. They made him a law-giver, though they were hunting for him like a criminal. They built on the foundation of him before he was found. They made this unknown monster, the mixture of the man and ape, the founder of society and the accepted father of mankind. The ancients had a fancy that there was a mongrel of horse and man, a mongrel of fish and man. But they did not make it the father of anything; they did not ask the mad mongrel to breed. The ancients did not draw up a system of ethics based upon the centaur, showing how man in a civilised society must take care of his hands, but must not wholly forget his hooves. They never reminded woman that, although she had the golden hair of a goddess, she had the tail of a fish. But the moderns did talk to man as if he were the Missing Link; they did remind him that he must allow for apish imbecility and bestial tricks. The moderns did tell the woman that she was half a brute, for all her beauty; you can find the thing said again and again in Schopenhauer and other prophets of the modern spirit. That is the real difference between the two monsters. The Missing Link is still missing and so is the merman.

—September 5, 1908

The idea of the Missing Link was not at all new with Darwin. . . . Men had always played about with the idea of a possible link between human and bestial life, and the very existence—or, if you will, the very nonexistence—of the centaur or the mermaid prove it. All the mythologies had dreamed of a half-human monster. The only objection to the centaur and the mermaid was that they could not be found. . . . So it is with the Darwinian ideal of a link between man and the brutes. There is no objection to it except that there is no evidence for it. The only objection to the Missing Link is that he is apparently fabulous, like the centaur. . . . In short, the only objection to the Missing Link is that he is missing.

—*September 5,* 1908

"Missionary"

. . . the European travelling in Asia does not seem to know that he represents [Christian Culture]. . . . He is still under the innocent delusion that he only represents some firm for selling hair-grease or golf-clubs. And when he comes back from the East he is quite as likely as not to be talking Eastern pessimism in the intervals of boasting of Western commercialism. Having never learnt his own religion, he is very likely to learn somebody else's and that one which is really inferior to his own. If we consider these things, we may possibly begin to see a new meaning in the much-abused word "missionary."

—*April 23,* 1927

Misunderstand

The state of being ignorant, which is comparatively innocent, goes with a confession of ignorance, even if it is also a confession of indifference. But the man who misunderstands is the man who is mistaken in supposing that he understands. . . . The point is that the narrow-minded bureaucrat who understood nothing may well have been wiser than the broadminded and progressive prig who can misunderstand anything.

—*October 10,* 1931

There is a very important difference between not understanding a thing and misunderstanding it. And it is misunderstanding that always does harm, where merely not understanding may be relatively harmless. I do not understand harmony or the higher laws of music; but I am not so dangerous as a gentleman who should wander about the world with the conviction that "contrapuntal" means getting angry with people in pants.

— October 10, 1931

Mob

A mob may, indeed, be immoral; but a mob is hardly ever anti-moral. A mob is hardly ever morbid; for secrecy is the chief part of morbidity. The mob is like a child, not like a lunatic. Its moral ideas are few, but as far as they go they are innocent; killing tyrants, abolishing hunger. It is very rare, it is almost unknown, for any large mob to have ideas in themselves hysterical, fads, heresies, cranks, and ethical side-issues.

— January 18, 1908

I believe that some ancient writers did maintain that the populace was always right. I know that most modern writers (especially revolutionary writers) maintain that the populace is always wrong. Yet the real and reasonable limits of popular wisdom and popular folly are not particularly hard to state. The mob generally has justice, but the mob generally has not got truth. The mob will generally be right in its view of the facts—if they are facts. Unfortunately, they are frequently not facts, but news from the newspapers.

— August 22, 1908

A real mob is sadly rare in modern politics.

— September 26, 1925

Moderation

... when a great nation is defending itself against a powerful and oppressive enemy in a great war, it is not in the least unnatural that mere moderation has all the effects of treason. It may never be anything like an act of mutiny; but it can still be an act of desertion.

— February 20, 1926

Modern Age

The modern age . . . is the age of conscription. It is, indeed, generally speaking, the age of compulsion. No period before our own ever dreamed of the sort of universal persecution that is called compulsory education. No period before our own ever dreamed of such a persecution as prohibition. In military matters, it follows the minute or scientific method of getting every ounce or grain of fighting energy out of the whole population; just as it follows the same scientific method of getting every ounce or grain of gas. . . .

—*May* 16, 1931

. . . in dealing with men, as in dealing with materials, it uses up all its by-products, and a good many which can only be used by being misused. It puts poison in the bullet and poltroons in the battle-line.

—*May* 16, 1931

Perhaps there never was a moment, in which so many men of high culture and keen intelligence were in reaction against what is called liberty or the Enlightenment.

—*August* 22, 1931

We might make more permanent records of our opinions. But we have not got more permanent opinions to record.

—*October* 31, 1931

Modernism (Saints of)

They start out to live by the Spirit of Christianity, and proceed to fling themselves with frenzy into preventing poor people from getting any beer, preventing oppressed nations from defending themselves against tyrants (because it might lead to war), tearing backward children away from their heart-broken parents and locking them up in some sort of materialistic madhouse, and so on. . . . In point of fact, they have kept some of the words and terminology, words like peace and righteousness and love; but they make these words stand for an atmosphere utterly alien to Christendom; they keep the letter and lose the spirit.

—*December* 26, 1925

295

Modernists

Men are actually denouncing the fact of degeneration, while they are still dogmatically affirming the faith in progress; and while they themselves clamorously declare that we have come to the wrong place, they still obstinately insist that we have come by the right road. . . . Now, I not only deny that we have come by the right road, but I deny that we have come by a road at all. At any rate, we have come by a road that had so zigzag a direction that it would be truer to say it had no direction. . . . This may be a change, or even a lark; but it cannot possibly be a progress, or even an evolution. The same is true, of course, of the more modern morals which are concerned rather with ethics and economics than with religion and theology.

—*September* 4, 1920

They have seen all there is to be seen of the last stages of beliefs; but they do not seem even able to imagine what the beginning of a belief would be like. They seem to think there is something archaic and antediluvian about those first acts of the mind, by which it opens the open question of the world. It seems a mere mad negation to start from scratch. It seems a barbaric fantasy to begin at the beginning. They no more employ first principles than flint arrows, and regard the first proposition of Euclid as a palaeolithic drawing on a rock.

—*April* 3, 1926

Modernity and Democracy

Modernity is not democracy; machinery is not democracy; the surrender of everything to trade and commerce is not democracy. Capitalism is not democracy; and is admittedly, by trend and savour, rather against democracy. Plutocracy by definition is not democracy. But all these modern things forced themselves into the world at about the time, or shortly after the time, when great idealists like Rousseau and Jefferson happened to have been thinking about the democratic ideal of democracy. It is tenable that the ideal was too idealistic to succeed. . . . Democracy has had everything against it in practice, and that very fact may be something against it in theory. It may be argued that it has human life against it. But, at any rate, it is quite certain that it has modern life against it. The industrial and scientific world of the last hundred years has been much *more* unsuitable a setting for the experiment of self-government than would have been found in old conditions of agrarian or even nomadic life.

—*July* 16, 1932

Modernity as Dystopia

I once very nearly wrote a fairy tale on the old theme of a country where all wishes come true; and where, as a matter of fact, everybody maintained a terrified silence, being afraid to mention anything for fear it should happen. Not only their fancies, but their figures of speech would instantly materialise; so that, if a man inadvertently observed "I must have lost my head," his head instantly rolled away like a cannon-ball. . . . I rather fancy we must be living in a fairyland of this kind. The world is growing so wild and experimental that almost everything that can be suggested as a fancy is found to be already a fact.

—September 12, 1925

Moderns and Myth

It is not only true . . . that the whole legend about Santa Claus coming down the chimney and the child hanging up the stocking raises the whole question which moderns least understand. It is that which Matthew Arnold called by a rather clumsy German word for "extra-belief"—all that fringe of mere fancy that is attached to faith, and yet is detachable from it. . . . For it is not only to the stocking itself, but to almost everything in the stocking, that the priggish and progressive person might raise an objection. Suppose, for instance, that the child has received as a Christmas present a box of tin soldiers or a toy cannon. Many modern intellectuals would instantly tear it away from the screaming infant, on the ground that it was an incitement to militarism. I do not know whether they would or would not be careful to replace it by a box of little tin figures representing conscientious objectors.

—December 27, 1919

Modesty (False)

. . . there is a milder form of the truth that it is a very bad thing to be proud of being humble. And that is that it is a very silly thing to be vain of being modest.

—March 28, 1925

Monarchy

Monarchy is a social ritual; and if the Monarchy begins to abolish social rituals it will end by committing suicide. The whole point of a modern King is that if he is no longer master of the State he is still master of the revels. In other words, he will on due and proper occasion consent to bore and to be bored.

—*May* 23, 1908

Monocle

...the new business man always tries to look as like as possible to a slightly dissipated Major. He even wears a single eyeglass; a thing in its nature altogether monstrous and devilish. The man who can put a glittering decoration in one eye and not in the other is blaspheming the balance and decency of the human form. He is capable of wearing a trouser on one leg, or his moustache on one side of his face. If I did not know so many nice people who do wear single eyeglasses (an irritating difficulty in all these generalisations) I should say that the wearing of a single eyeglass was inconsistent with any possibility of sincerity and simplicity in the soul. I should say that a man could not have a single eyeglass and have also a single eye.

—*August* 11, 1906

Monopoly

If the collective economic power is not strong enough to tyrannise, it is not strong enough to do anything that a socialist wants it to do. If it has not power enough to commit injustice, it has not power enough to prevent injustice.

—*October* 10, 1925

But it is the very definition of monopoly that the other fellow will not be content with his own job. It is the very definition of it that your own job will not remain really your own. If he buys up your business, it will be quite useless for you to do your job better; first, because you will be doing it for his benefit; and second, because you will have to do it according to his notions of what is better. Optimism of this sort is certainly good for trade, in the sense that it is good for trusts. But I do not see how extinguishing a hundred individual businesses helps each individual to mind his own business.

—*February* 9, 1929

Moral Code

...a lady writer has been ...good enough to say that morality may be all very well for common and conventional people, but that artists of this original type must be permitted a more original code. ....Anybody of common-sense can surely see that it is sheer madness to announce that anyone may become an anarchist by becoming an artist, or pretending to become an artist. To announce that you have a soft job for a genius will not suddenly produce a race of geniuses. It will only produce a rush of people who are quacks enough to say they are geniuses, or fools enough to think they are.

—October 17, 1925

The Moral Imagination

Now, the little histories that we learnt as children were partly meant simply as inspiring stories. They largely consisted of tales like Alfred and the cakes or Eleanor and the poisoned wound. They ought to have entirely consisted of them. Little children ought to learn nothing but legends; they are the beginnings of all sound morals and manners. I would not be severe on the point: I would not exclude a story solely because it was true. But the essential on which I should insist would be, not that the tale must be true, but that the tale must be fine.

—October 8, 1910

Moral Relations

The definition of the moral relations of men and animals may present many difficulties; but the moral relation in practice does not depend on any conceivable theory about cosmic unity. To suggest that it does is to weaken the case in an attempt to strengthen the case. It is to appeal to a minority of advanced thinkers when we could appeal to a majority of average men. It is as if we were to say, in order to stop a man beating his wife: "Some advanced evolutionists have held that the female of the species will recover the superiority found in the south American spider, who eats a hundred husbands a day." It is as if we discouraged the efforts of a young forger by saying: "Some advanced sociologists believe that the art of writing will be entirely superseded by wireless telegraphy and the cinema."

—June 18, 1927

Moral Relativism

This notion that "there's nothing either bad or good but thinking makes it so" is enormously widespread in the world just now, and has many modes of expression much less normal and much more nonsensical. . . . The essential heresy involved is the idea that the world is not real; that the lamp-post outside a man's door is not really there. . . . To the mass of poor people who pass the lamp-post every day, to the tramp and the typist and the errand-boy, and charwoman and the city clerk . . . and all who rise to their daily work and worry, it will never be any consolation in the battle of life to tell them that life is not a battle. It will be no good to tell them that evil does not exist, or that pain is only mortal mind.

—November 14, 1925

Moral Types

. . . there run and caper and collide only four characters, who seem to sum up the four ultimate types of our existence. These four figures are: St. George and the Dragon, and the Princess offered to the Dragon, and the Princess's father. . . . You have everything in those figures: active virtue destroying evil; passive virtue enduring evil; ignorance or convention permitting evil; and Evil. In these four figures also can be found the real and sane limits of toleration. I admire St. George for being sincere in his wish to save the Princess's life. . . . I am ready to admire the Princess's wish to be eaten by the Dragon as part of her religious duties . . . if a little perverse. I am even ready to admire the sincerity of the silly old potentate . . . who gave up his daughter to a dragon because it had always been done in his set. But there is a limit . . . and I refuse to admire the dragon because he regarded the Princess with a sincere enthusiasm.

—October 29, 1910

Morality

That is why I can never agree with Mr. H. G. Wells, that admirable man, when he or others suggest that all morality is a matter of hypothesis and convenient assumptions rather than of fixed lines. I say that a man must be certain of his morality for the simple reason that he has to suffer for it.

—August 4, 1906

It seems to me that the mass of men do agree on the mass of morality, but differ disastrously about the proportions of it. In other words, all men admit the Ten Commandments, but they differ horribly about which is the first Commandment and which is the tenth. The difference between men is not in what merits they confess, but in what merits they emphasise. . . . The spoilt son of some Chicago millionaire who puffs smoke in his father's face for fun will not, in so many words, deny the rightness of the commandment, "Honour thy father and thy mother." He will only think it a small and somewhat laughable matter; while he will be quite solemn about the command "Thou shalt do no murder"—all the more because he must feel that he is the kind of person whom one murders.

—October 23, 1909

Morality (Modern)

Unluckily, it is not true, it is quite the reverse of the truth, that as our science grows more accurate our morality grows more defined. It is not true (as it ought to be) that as our method grows more unfailing our creed grows more infallible. It is, in fact, exactly the other way.

—August 20, 1910

Morality (Positive)

The freedom of true morality is finely expressed in the Eden story, which shows how Man was free to eat all the fruits in the garden except one. But if the Book of Genesis had been written by modern idealists, there would have been only one exquisite, artistic, hygienic fruit that Adam was allowed to eat.

—January 29, 1910

. . . the "advanced" people are always trying to introduce what they call positive morality, which really means positive slavery. Instead of saying that I must not think of So-and-So, but may think of anything else, they say that I may think of the sublime and daring So-and-So, and must not think of anything else. They destroy the large liberality of the old negative code. They make a new and dreadful narrowness—the narrowness of taste. It is not now enough that I do not do what my neighbour dislikes: I must like what my neighbour likes.

—January 29, 1910

Morality (Positive versus Negative)

A little while ago, all liberal and cultured persons were expected to agree that negative morality was nothing as compared with positive morality. Enlightened clergymen took a pride in removing the Ten Commandments from . . . their sermons, and substituting those two great mystical commands concerning the positive duties of the love of God and man. Famous and fashionable writers, like Stevenson, spoke for their generation in saying: "Christ would not hear of negative morality; 'thou shalt' was ever his word." Some enthusiasts carried the distinction to rather fantastic lengths, elaborately framing sentences from which negatives were excluded. . . . Rushing into the nursery, just in time to prevent the new toy chisel from the little tool-card being driven into the little sister's eye, they yet had time hastily to rearrange their words and sentences, to avoid saying, "Don't do that," and say instead, "Occupy yourself in some other fashion," or "Employ your tools in the delightful craft of carpentry."

—October 1, 1932

Morals (Bad)

Tolstoy was a good man who taught thoroughly bad morals. Human history has been full of these men; in fact, they are responsible for a great bulk of the calamities of human history.

—December 24, 1910

More's Utopia

It was he who invented the very word Utopia; and then, finding the changes he saw so different from the changes he desired, would not have the book translated into English. Utopia is not at the beginning of the world or the end of the world. Utopia has been something always near and never discovered.

—April 27, 1929

There have been endless problems and controversies and hypothetical theories thrown out about St. Thomas More's book called "Utopia." The critics and controversialists have stiffened and studied almost every word in "Utopia." The only word they seem to have neglected is the word "Utopia." For, as St. Thomas More would have written it in Greek, it simply means "nowhere."

—June 13, 1936

Mormon

And anybody who knows anything of Americans can feel quite certain that most of the Mormons were sincere. They were sincere as only serious Americans can be sincere. And though, of course, only a tiny minority of Americans would ever have dreamed of being Mormons, it is none the less true that there was something very American in the Mormon crimes and not less in the Mormon virtues.

—February 2, 1924

Mother

We cannot insist that every trick of nerves or train of thought is important enough to be searched for in libraries and laboratories, and not important enough for anybody to watch by simply staying at home. We cannot insist that the first years of infancy are of supreme importance, and that mothers are not of supreme importance; or that motherhood is a topic of sufficient interest for men, but not of sufficient interest for mothers. Every word that is said about the tremendous importance of trivial nursery habits goes to prove that being a nurse is not trivial. All tends to the return of the simple truth that the private work is the great one and the public work the small. The human house is a paradox, for it is larger inside than out.

—August 5, 1922

Mothers-in-law

... it is not in the least true that mothers-in-law are as a class oppressive and intolerable; most of them are both devoted and useful.... Yet the legend of the comic papers is profoundly true. It draws attention to the fact that it is much harder to be a nice mother-in-law than to be nice in any other conceivable relation of life. The caricatures have drawn the worst mother-in-law a monster, by way of expressing the fact that the best mother-in-law is a problem.

—March 21, 1908

Motive

What people do is often not the supreme question, even if they blow up cities or lay waste continents. What people do is often of far less importance than why they do it.

—August 29, 1908

Motives

... people seem to forget that there can be corrupt motives leading to the simple life as well as to the Scriptures or the sacraments; and that there are socialists who betray Socialism as well as Christians who betray Christianity. It is certainly not by becoming Puritans that we can make certain of not being Pharisees. For that matter, it is not even by being early Christians that we can make certain of not being Simon Magus or Judas Iscariot. No creed or philosophy, simple or complex, ancient or modern, can be altogether free from the peril of being employed for ends of venality or vanity.

—February 18, 1922

Mourning

... let us think not only of the virtues of the dead, but of the living; and above all of that universal human virtue of veneration for the dead. Grief is a thing really popular; that fact, if we consider it, will appear very notable and impressive; and when we have understood it we may understand why the great voice that said of old upon the mountain: "Blessed are the poor," added but a moment afterwards: "Blessed are ye that mourn."

—December 5, 1925

Murder

... murder always is partly accidental. It is exceedingly accidental for the man who is murdered, in the sense that he has not generally participated to any great extent in the design.

—*February 24, 1917*

Murder Stories

As for the people who say that murder stories incite to murder, one is tempted merely to the reckless reply that their criticisms of murder stories really might.

—*June 19, 1926*

Museum

With the establishment of that entirely modern thing, the museum, we have a new conception, which, like so many modern conceptions, is based on a blunder in psychology and a blindness to the true interests of culture. The museum is not meant either for the wanderer to see by accident or for the pilgrim to see with awe. It is meant for the mere slave of a routine of self-education to stuff himself with every sort of incongruous intellectual food in one indigestible meal. It is meant for the mere sight-seer, the man who must see all the sights.

—*February 28, 1931*

Musicians

... it is not enough that the musician should get his music out of him. It is also his business to get his music into somebody else. We should all be reasonable enough to recognise that the somebody else will depend to some extent on the sort of music. But if all he can say is that he has a secret of sealed-up power and passion, that his imagination is visited by visions of which the world knows nothing, that he is conscious of a point of view which is wholly his own and is not expressed in anything common or comprehensible—then he is simply saying that he is *not* an artist, and there is an end of it. He is simply saying what his stockbroker or his dentist or his dustman have probably got a perfect right to say.

—*November 27, 1926*

"My Country, Right or Wrong"

. . . the objection to the phrase, which was then very popular, "My country, right or wrong," is not only an objection of mere logic, but of mere grammar. It is not a bold and militant statement defying the world; on the contrary, it is so very timid and weak a statement that it could not even be completely stated. The man who said it thus was not a hero fighting for his own country. He was a coward who dared not even finish his own sentence. Anybody who will try to finish that sentence will find that he has to think; a painful process. For the sentence must either end, "My country, right or wrong, retains some rights," which is so true as to be merely a truism; or else the sentence must end, "My country, right or wrong, must be treated as if she were right," which, being obvious nonsense, was generally what the jingo journalists did mean, so far as they meant anything.

—February 20, 1932

Mysticism

I think there is a mystical minimum in human history and experience, which is at once too obscure to be explained and too obvious to be explained away. It may be admitted that a miracle is rarer than a murder; but they are made obscure by somewhat similar causes. A medium is criticised for not submitting to a sufficient number of scientific and impartial judges; and a murderer seldom collects any considerable number of impartial witnesses to testify to his performance. Many supernatural stories rest on the evidence of rough unlettered men, like fishermen and peasants; and most criminal trials depend on the detailed testimony of quite uneducated people. It may be remarked that we never throw a doubt on the value of ignorant evidence when it is a question of a judge hanging a man, but only when it is a question of a saint healing him.

—August 30, 1919

There is undoubtedly a deeper element in man than the superficially rational; all men realise that, except the superficial. There is an inner power that alters the values of the outer world. . . . There is something that may make him see a special providence in a falling star, or an intense imaginative significance in some sign in heaven, even when the best scientific education has taught him that the earth is the most insignificant of stars, or man the most insignificant of monsters. That is a need never neglected safely, and indeed never neglected for long. To make a culture entirely without that mystical element is like trying to build a dry civilisation in the desert, and forgetting the very existence of water.

—May 24, 1930

Myth

In a number of solid historical cases, I myself began rather early to disbelieve them, and have come eventually to believe them. I seriously think that the popular sentiment that created those characters was often a tradition of truth, where the pedantic cynicism which destroyed them was often a much more deliberate perversion of truth. The tradition may have come down rather loosely and vaguely, through a long line of nurses and grandmothers. But the nurses and grandmothers were not paid to tell lies, and they did therefore, to a considerable and very valuable extent, tell the truth. The critics and historians were paid to tell lies. . . .

—February 14, 1931

Myth versus History

However this may be, I have known a curious number of cases in which mere sentimental gossip surrounded my childhood and serious historical scholarship surrounded my manhood; and the sentimental gossip was right.

—February 14, 1931

What I complain of in the schoolmaster is that he always taught only one side of the story. So, it may be said, did the merely nurse story-teller. But her story was a story in the literary sense of a legend. His story was a story in the nursery sense of a lie. It was a lie in the very real sense that he was not merely reporting what he had heard, but very carefully selecting from what he had read.

—February 14, 1931

Mythology

. . . any mythology is saner than materialism, and immeasurably less difficult to believe.

—January 26, 1924

Name-dropping

We should not be interfering with the freedom of debate by eliminating it, for the men who only deal in such unknown qualities are not debating. They are simply showing off. The distinguished name is stuck into the sentence as the diamond tie-pin is stuck into the tie, for the sake of swagger or snobbishness. . . . Of course, the argument does not only apply to science; there are any number of cases of the same sort of pedantry in literature. There are certain quotations from poetry which are always dragged in as if they were texts of scripture, professedly to prove something that obviously proves itself, but really to prove that the writer is well acquainted with the hundred best authors.

—May 25, 1931

Narrowness

. . . those who would broaden history with human brotherhood too often suffer from a limitation. . . . They exchange the narrowness of a nation for the narrowness of a theory, or even a fad. They think they have a world-wide philosophy because they extend their own narrowness to the whole world.

—February 4, 1922

It is something that fixes its mind on a fashion, until it forgets that it is a fashion. Novelty of this sort narrows the mind, not only by forgetting the past, but also by forgetting the future. There is a certain natural relief and refreshment in altering things, but a wise man will remember that the things that can be altered will be altered again. There is a certain type of modernist who manages to accept a thing at the same time as fashionable and as final.

—November 12, 1932

Nation

Nations never rebel against injury: they only rebel against insult.

—November 14, 1908

... every nation is a new nation, with every new generation. And every nation is an old nation, since the very word generation takes us back to the word genealogy— and, indeed, takes us back to Genesis.

—*March* 23, 1918

Any nation is in its nature a unique thing. That is where it differs decisively from any mere official division made within any independent state at present, or within any united states of the future. A nation, like a man or a dog or any other living thing, is large or small, like us or unlike us; but it is like itself.

—*January* 4, 1919

National Self-criticism

The right and proper thing, of course, is that every good patriot should stop at home and curse his own country. So long as that is being done everywhere, we may be sure that things are fairly happy, and being kept up to a reasonably high standard.... So long as good Americans go on railing at their anarchy and graft, so long as good Englishmen curse our snobbery and squirearchy, so long as there are Germans to murmur at officialism and Scotchmen to make game of theology, so long as Irishmen insist that they are conquered, and Frenchmen are quite sure they are betrayed—so long as this genial and encouraging groan goes up from all Europe, so long we may feel certain that Christendom is going forward with her mighty cohorts triumphant on her eternal way.

—*October* 1, 1910

National Types

... when a man says that there is a general character in the United States, or in the Jewish nation, or the English nation, he does not in the least necessarily mean that all of them "are approximately alike." He means it no more than he means that all sea-creatures are alike when he collectively connects them with the sea. He means, not that all the items are identical, but that the common and containing atmosphere is a real thing. There is an air, an assumption, a primary condition common to all the varieties of a certain thing; though they may be very various indeed.

—*March* 15, 1924

National Unity

It is natural to ask for national unity in war. . . . It is impossible to have national unity in that sense in politics . . . because it is obviously a matter of opinion whether people are trying to hurt us or not. A politician will not boast of having lowered the people's wages, as a popular sailor might boast of having sunk the enemy's ships. A candidate will not eagerly claim that he has ruined a countryside, as a captain might claim that he had raided a country. In internal political disputes the question must always be not merely what the enemy has done, but who is the enemy.

—December 14, 1918

Nationalism

. . . what really makes the Irish angry with the English attitude is not that we hate the Irish, nor even that we try to absorb them: it is that we try to do the two things at the same time. We try to include them because they are English and also to despise them because they are Irish. When the Ogre had eaten the Princess, he no longer disliked her, since she became part of himself. It would be a very unreasonable Ogre who should expect the Princess to remain intact in his inside solely in order to be hated. The Irish people might conceivably have come into our civilisation if we had simply told them to be British and to boast of Shakespeare. But no people can consent to remain separate solely in order to be the foil to the self-flattery of another people. But there are other instances of this attempt to have it both ways. For instance, some excellent Jews suffer from a sad fallacy: they think it glorious to be a Jew, and yet they think it insulting to be called one. But of all these floundering examples of falling between two stools, there is none more absurd than the present notion of a nobleman. He is superior to us: he is not to think so; we are not to say so; and yet the superiority must remain as an institution of the State.

—November 28, 1908

Nationalism versus Patriotism

By nationalism I meant, and mean, a general recognition of the right of all nations to be national; the right of other nations, and especially of small nations. I find it more confusing to call this patriotism, because patriotism, when it was rammed down my throat in the old jingo days, always meant that the

British empire had a right to do everything and nobody else had a right to do anything.

—April 18, 1931

Nationalities

I do not blame the Englishman for feeling himself distinct from the Irishman. I only blame him for having fancied that England could be distinct from Ireland without Ireland being distinct from England—or, in other words, for imagining that he could have another man tied to him, without being tied to the other man.

—August 30, 1924

Nations and Law

... it is true that the genuine German has a positive pleasure in obeying the law; while the true Irishman enjoys resisting the law, and the true Englishman enjoys evading it.

—July 17, 1909

Natural Selection

Natural selection began as something that explained everything; it went on as something that had to be explained; it has ended as something that has to be explained away.

—July 8, 1922

Nature Worship

Nothing has encouraged so many crimes against nature as that sort of Hellenism and hedonism which is founded on nature-worship. The truth is, of course, that it is not natural to worship nature. It is not even human to worship human nature. Man is not fully man unless he feels he is something more.

—October 20, 1928

Nazi Myths

The special Nazi story of the truth about the great war: with its colossal paradox of a completely victorious Germany disarmed in the hour of victory by the cunning of two or three Jews—that is really the very newest thing in myths; and the use of the word "myth" almost suggests that its authors not only admit that it is new, but come very near to admitting that it is mythical. Anyhow, they seem more interested in what it will produce in the future than in how it was produced in the past.

—*May* 16, 1936

Nazis

The Germans, not being realistic, have already forgotten that they were defeated ten years ago; but they still remember vividly that they were victorious fifty years ago. That is the advantage of being a sentimentalist. You only remember what you like to remember. It is also the advantage of being a barbarian.

—*August* 5, 1933

Nazism

Mythology has returned; the clouds are rolling over the landscape, shutting out the broad daylight of fact; and Germans are wandering about saying they will dethrone Christ and set up Odin and Thor. But we cannot understand it by looking only at the last ten years of peace, or even at the original five years of war. The meaning of it, like the meaning of the insular placidity even of the most bewildered Englishman, is hidden in those previous years which are often forgotten, between the end of history and the beginning of journalism. We must realise how strongly the German believed, as in Luther's hymn, that he was an impregnable fortress; just as the Englishman once believed that he was an unbreakable bank.

—*April* 29, 1933

I need not describe at length the things in which I think the Hitlerite boom is essentially idiotic. The nonsense about a Nordic race, which no reputable ethnologist now alive could call anything but nonsense, is a thing that would be as unworkable in practice as it is unsupported in theory. . . . Pride is always a poison; but pride in false history instead of true history and pride in bad morality instead

312

of good morality, is an alien and quite deadly poison, not to be used even in small quantities as a medicine. Or again, I have pointed out here that the whole heathen business of the swastika is utterly tenth-rate, and only makes one guess vaguely whether Mr. Hitler (or one of his inspirers) has been some sort of medium or fortune-teller, or the sort of man who deals in tarot-cards and talismans and shabby occultism. I do not suppose he did, but that is what the swastika *really* symbolises.

—June 3, 1933

That evil of egomania, or making the self the centre of the universe, is a purely spiritual evil. It is, and always was, utterly futile to trace it to an animal origin. It is not in the least like the unconscious and contented self-satisfaction of the animals. Nor are the extravagances it exhibits possible to the animal. A wolf does not persuade thousands of other wolves in the tribe all to wear the same military muzzle; and that is what has happened to political liberty in Germany. He does not find certain scratchings on the rock, which are found in China and North America, and then declare that they are strictly peculiar to Aryan wolves. All the wolves in the world are not made to lift the right paw and bark out the name of one particular and not very important wolf. Animals are not such asses — or asses are more sensible animals.

—December 2, 1933

Nazism and Legend

The new myth is generally a part of a new theory; not a confused remembrance, but a conscious reconstruction. It may be part of the propaganda and programme of a government; or an outline of history taught by the professors in a university; but anyhow, it comes from the professors or politicians to the people and not from the people to the professors or politicians. . . . I should call it a legend that the Germans are a sleepy, kindly, fair-haired folk, in love with the eternal flowing of the Rhine and equally eternal flowing of the lager, in large beer-gardens and beer-halls, surrounded by forests full of fairy-tales, and crags and castles bristling with romances. To a great extent it was true, to some extent it is still true; and it is a healthy and happy and humanising sort of truth. I should call it a myth that the Germans are primarily Aryan, that they have some curious cult or corner or proprietary right in the swastika; or that they have a mission to restore the now meaningless mythology of Thor and Odin.

—May 16, 1936

313

New

. . . it is only too easy to admire anything as new.

—March 29, 1924

News

. . . while fact is necessarily private, fiction is normally public.

—April 25, 1925

Newspapers

The real way of reading the newspapers is to read nothing but the posters and head-lines. If we read nothing but these, we can keep, like a perpetual childhood, the belief that wonderful things are really happening on every side of us. If we are unwise enough to read the journalistic text itself, we discover that nothing has happened at all.

—June 2, 1906

It may or may not be true that man's great use for language is to conceal his thoughts; but I suppose that we should all agree to the somewhat analogous proposition that the one great use of newspapers is to suppress news. It is quite arguable that suppressing news is sometimes a good thing; and it is quite unquestionable that, whether it is good or bad, newspapers do it. Before newspapers were invented, it was quite impossible to suppress news; the news broke out all over the town like an epidemic.

—March 2, 1907

. . . the newspaper has invented a new kind of superior or authentic statement, the statement in print, and this can be now used to overawe and silence the other natural expression. Two lines of print can silence the tongues of twelve hundred truthful witnesses. Suppose (for the sake of argument) that Dr. Clifford and I got drunk at the Holborn Restaurant and tried to kill each other with champagne bottles: the tale would be told all down the street and by every man when he went home to his wife; and in the age before newspapers it would become as much a piece of solid history as the battle of Blenheim. But nowadays

314

the newspaper would immediately be set in motion to suppress and deny the scandal.

—March 2, 1907

It is by this time practically quite impossible to get the truth out of any newspapers, even the honest newspapers. I mean the kind of truth that a man can feel an intelligent curiosity about—moral truth, truth that is disputed, truth that is in action and really affecting things. Doubtless, the daily paper reports certain events in their simple actuality; but those events will generally be found to be the events that end an affair, not the events that produce it. One can find the fact that a man is hanged, but not the truth about his trial; one can believe the journalist when he says that war has broken out, but not when he says that war was inevitable.

—January 23, 1909

We must first of all establish the principle that we do not want a newspaper to give us a vision of the world made perfect; we want a church for that. We do not want a newspaper to give us good news; we want a gospel for that. We want a newspaper to give us true news, not elevating news or improving news. And whichever ideal is the higher, mine is the harder. Ask any ordinary editor to elevate and ennoble his readers, and he will tell you, with a heat of sincerity, that he is trying to do it all the time. Ask him to tell the exact truth, and he will have you thrown out of the office.

—March 6, 1909

The idea of difference of opinion has managed to destroy itself.... First people argued with other people and made newspapers to print their arguments; then they hid behind their own newspapers and read only their own arguments. The result has been that true controversy has become almost impossible, because the judge who hears the counsel for the prosecution is not the same as he who hears the counsel for the defence.

—February 12, 1910

The ancient cynic said that speaking exists to conceal the thoughts. That was a suggestive paradox. But there is no paradox in saying that printing exists to conceal the facts.

—November 26, 1910

315

The plain truth is that, from official journalism, we cannot get the plain truth. The daily paper is really a rich and suggestive document: personally, I love reading the day before yesterday's daily paper. Some of the finest fun and wisdom in the world can be found buried in the files of old newspapers. But the daily paper is never daily. The daily paper is never up to date.

—*May* 16, 1914

The ordinary newspaper-reader is utterly bewildered by his newspaper. The headlines hit him on the head, and the columns fall on him and crush him. He receives shock after shock, from the abrupt presentation of problems of the most diverse and difficult sort, problems to which he has not the remotest notion of a real answer. For a problem can only be solved by a principle. He is first asked to consider national policy without knowing what a nation is, then to consider religious unity without knowing what a religion is, then to decide the fate of some murderer without knowing the meaning of murder, then to consider the merits of some divorce without knowing the meaning of marriage. To most of these questions he really returns no answer at all. His self-government is merely negative; and democracy is something that goes by default.

—*April* 7, 1923

. . . the newspapers never give us the news.

—*April* 26, 1924

I notice all the newspapers and most novelettes read by typists are now arranged upon the fixed principle that there cannot be any climax at all. Everything that the journalist has to say he must say in large letters and short words, in the head-line at the top of the column.

—*September* 5, 1925

I notice nowadays that even the weekly papers, which might be supposed to sum up the last seven days at least, have grown more fond of speculating on what the Prime Minister or the President of the United States will decide to do, than commenting (with anything like the good old violence or enthusiasm) on what they have just done. Soon, I suppose, the daily paper will profess to print to-morrow's event instead of yesterday's; and the weekly paper will be entirely precipitated into the middle of next week. Unfortunately, no engine has yet been found of sufficient power to precipitate me into the middle of next week.

—May 10, 1930

It is needless to say that newspapers are not specially opposed to organised commercial combines; for they are so often organised commercial combines themselves.

—May 24, 1930

The mark of the newspaper . . . is, the mark of ignorance about everything except news; of the limitation of the mind to novel and very recent things.

—May 16, 1931

There is so much that is nonsensical in the daily news-sheet, and so little that is new in the daily life, that there may be a dangerous breach between the unreal and the real. It is not the most commonly discussed of the problems of the press; but it is one of the most vital, or deadly.

—January 14, 1933

Newspapers (Disciple of)

It had never crossed his mind, you see, even for one wild moment, that a man might read his papers and not implicitly believe them. No suspicion had ever dawned on his mind that there was a slight party bias delicately discernible in the *Evening News* or the *Star,* that there was a slight note of eagerness, almost amounting to exaggeration, in the *Daily Mail.* For him every printed word was not only a solemn fact, but was the supreme form of truth, beyond which there was no appeal. And he could only suppose that some defect in my eyesight, or in my education, prevented me from learning the great truths which the posters of the *Daily Mail* had to tell . . . and so I was shut out from those feasts of infallible information of which the gates stood so wide for him.

—January 22, 1910

Newspapers (Faith in)

I am distressed by this spread of simple faith. I am sure that no yokel ever believed in the ghost as . . . yokels believe in the newspaper. I am sure no peasants in the Middle Ages gave such smooth and swift and automatic credence to any tales of fairies or legends of saints as these honest lads do to the vast cosmopolitan crazes and partisan travesties of the halfpenny Press. There was always a dim element of irony and doubt mixed with popular poetry and popular religion. But journalism demands blind and prostrate faith. And journalism seems to get it.

—January 22, 1910

Newspapers (Modern)

. . . a well-equipped modern newspaper is not much behind a barbaric chronicle or saga of the dark ages. They . . . delighted to record that a child had been born with the head of an elephant, as we to record that a prize eugenic child is destined to grow up as a superman.

—January 14, 1933

Newspeak (Soviet)

A paragraph in the newspapers reports, I know not with how much truth, that the minister controlling education in the present Russian regime has ordered the elimination of references to angels, devils, and even fairies. The paragraph states that "Angels are to be supplanted by scientists and technicians who have served humanity." I do not know whether this substitution is to be literal in every case where such things are mentioned. In that case the condition of the great literature of the past would be rather curious. Perhaps Titania, instead of saying, "What angel," will say, "What technician wakes me from my flowery bed?"

—August 20, 1921

Newspeak and Oppression

But by calling the thing a health ministry instead of a disease ministry, we let in the false principle with all its possibilities. Only a few people have diseases that must be isolated, but thousands of people have health that could be improved. By the change the state passes from its right to restrain the few to a power to oppress the thousands.

—March 17, 1923

Nihilism

Mere questions unanswered, or even unanswerable, end in a vacuum, in which the intellect cannot act at all. The intellect exercises itself in discovering principles of design or pattern or proportion of some sort, and can find nothing to work on in the only really logical atheist cosmos—the fortuitous concourse of atoms of Lucretius. . . . But suppose all such things established, and man an animal, an automaton, without vision, without free will, without any reason to believe even in the authority of reason, and there would really be nothing to think about and no particular motive for thinking—certainly no assurance of the value of any thought.

—February 22, 1930

Nineteenth Century

It was a great century, in producing great men and great works, but it suffered from one great folly: that of forgetting its own follies. It committed one great crime: it denied its crimes.

—October 23, 1920

Noah's Ark

About the fantastic animals of the ark there was no deception. They were facts, as all avowed fables are facts.

—July 25, 1931

Nonsense

Learn to be nonsensical, and then to be sensible again; to create strange things and still to be independent of them. Learn to suggest a thing, to urge it, to prove it, and

319

still to disbelieve it. For the very few things that are really worth believing are not worth proving.

—May 22, 1909

Nominalism

... that the common type does not exist because the variations exist, is a very old one. At the very beginning of the Middle Ages, it was called nominalism; it was also called nonsense.

—March 15, 1924

Novelette

It is the custom of these writers to scoff at the old sentimental novel or novelette, in which the story always ended happily to the sound of church bells. But, judged by the highest standards of heroic or great literature, like the Greek tragedies or the great epics, the novelette was really far superior to the novel. It set itself to reach a certain goal—the marriage of two persons, with all its really vital culmination in the founding of a family and a vow to God; and all other incidents were interesting because they pointed to a consummation which was, by legitimate hypothesis, a grand consummation.

—March 8, 1930

Novelist

Everybody who has any real experience knows that good writing would not necessarily come from people with many experiences. Some of the art which is closest to life has been produced under marked limitations of living. Its prestige has generally lasted longer than the splash made by sensational social figures. Jane Austen has already survived Georges Sand.

—March 7, 1931

Novelist (Intellectual)

The sensational story-teller does indeed create uninteresting characters, and then try to make them interesting by killing them. But the intellectual novelist yet more sadly wastes his talents, for he creates interesting characters, and then does not kill them. What I complain of in the advanced and analytical artist in fiction is that he describes some subtle character, full of modern moods and doubts; that he expends all his imagination on realising every fine shade of the sentiment and philosophy of the sceptic or the free lover. And then, when the hero in question is at last alive and ready to be murdered, when he is in every detail of his character demanding and requiring, and, as it were crying aloud to be murdered, the novelist does not murder him after all. This is a serious waste of a fine opportunity, and I hope in future to see the error rectified.

—August 28, 1920

Novelist (Modern)

I do not think that the most brilliant novelists of to-day shine at the exposition of a philosophy, let alone a religion. It is amazing to note how brilliantly they interpret other people's feelings, and how badly they interpret their own thoughts. They seem to know far more about the secret emotions of a Hungarian waiter in an American hotel than they know about their own reasons for holding their own opinions. I say opinions; for in this case it is very difficult to say religions.

—October 2, 1925

Novelist (Victorian)

. . . the old Victorians had a way with them about that sort of furniture. The padding of their stories was like the padding of their arm-chairs. It may not have been artistic; but they knew how to pad.

—December 12, 1925

Novelists and History

One of the mysteries of the modern world is why those who are so very subtle in giving an account of men are so very simple in giving an account of mankind. The novelist, who sees the finest shades for the purpose of fiction, seems to see everything in the crudest colours when he comes to consider history. He would be ashamed to leave one of the seven sisters in the tooting villa (which is the scene of his new passionate and pulsating novel) undistinguished by her own tint of temperament or shade of religious doubt. But if he talks at large about things

321

being "mediaeval," and you tell him that there was a good deal of difference between the beginning of the thirteenth century and the end of the fifteenth, he imagines you are splitting hairs and making Jesuitical excuses.

—August 6, 1927

Novelists and Life

But if they *do* argue it out, they will find it implies certain dogmas; as that there is a design; that it is a benevolent design, but that it does allow of free will, and makes the good a matter of choice. Those who thought they could hold that healthy romance for ever, merely by being healthy and without holding any of the dogmas that justify it, are more and more finding out their mistake. Hence, when they are asked to state what they really do believe about life, they become "desperately vague." And they have now reached the point where it is not only more and more difficult to state a creed, but even more and more difficult to tell a story.

—October 2, 1925

Novels

If instead of leading a riotous life, scrapping with Mr. Shaw about socialism, or Dean Inge about science, I had believed everything I was told about marriage by an unmarried young woman in an avowedly imaginary story, I might now have a more undisturbed faith and simplicity. Novels are the great monument of the amazing credulity of the modern mind; for people believe them quite seriously, even though they do not pretend to be true.

—March 8, 1930

Novels (Detective)

... veneration for logic, combined with a complete misunderstanding of it, is very common in those popular works of fiction which are the joy of my existence—the crime novels and the police romances and the rest. There is a queer notion that the detective, who is distinguished from all human beings by having the gift of reason, is bound in logic not to like anything or anybody. Even Sherlock Holmes (the friend of my childhood to whom I shall always pay a tribute of piety) is described somewhere, I think, as being incapable of falling in love because of his logical nature. You might as well say that he could

322

not be expected to have much appetite for lunch because of his proficiency in mathematics.

—June 27, 1931

Novels (Great)

... I find a very acute American lady writing like this: "After an American child has been told that *The House of the Seven Gables* and *David Copperfield*... are great novels, he naturally grows up with a strange conviction—the conviction that a great novel is necessarily a dull, long, solemn novel." This observation is funny enough as it stands; but the fun becomes fast and furious when we observe that elsewhere this symposium is largely devoted to the glorification of Mr. Theodore Dreiser, who generally tosses off a little story about as long as the *Encyclopaedia Britannica*.

—August 13, 1927

Novels (Modern)

... pastoral poems and prose romances in which they delighted are not, as many modern people suppose, merely artificial and affected. They are not half so artificial and affected as half a hundred modern realistic novels about absinthe or gin.

—January 24, 1925

All these novels and notes of the day are full of queer physical revulsion. People in this world want to be divorced, not even for incompatibility of temper, but for individuality of feature or costume. Existence becomes an agony because somebody's ears stick out at a particular angle, or somebody's brown boots are of a particular shade. There is an insult not only in the way they speak, but in the way they sneeze; and, especially, of course, in the way they snore. The novelists and the critics yearn with sympathy of the tenderest sort over these sensibilities. It seems to be admitted that nobody could be expected to endure such things from their fellow-creatures. It never seems to occur to anybody that people ought to be taught to endure their fellow-creatures. It never seems to strike them that the same culture and training of a citizen ought to strengthen him to resist the shock of a loud sneeze or a large ear. Culture seems to mean the cultivation of disgust.

—July 10, 1926

These grave and laborious and often carefully written books come out season after season; and somehow I have missed them. Sometimes they miss me, even when hurled at my head by publishers.

—March 8, 1930

... the modern serious novel seriously denies that there is any goal. They cannot point to the human happiness which the romantics associated with gaining the prize. They cannot point to the heavenly happiness which the religious associated with keeping the vow. They are driven back entirely on the microscopic description of these aimless appetites in themselves. And, microscopically studied in themselves, they are not very interesting to a middle-aged man with plenty of other things to think about.

—March 8, 1930

Novelties

... in most things the real democracy is traditional; and the novelties are aristocratic at best and plutocratic at worst.

—October 1, 1921

Novelty

It is necessary to have novelty; but the novelty is not necessarily improvement. It does not necessarily give the man for whom the old things are stale any right to scorn the man for whom the old things are fresh. And there always are men for whom the old things are fresh. Such men, so far from being behind the times, are altogether above the times. They are too individual and original to be affected by the trivial changes of time.

—October 6, 1928

Novelty versus Permanence

People read old books, but they do not read old newspapers. The quaint old volume about heraldry and the Howards is sometimes picked up on the bookstall; but the newspaper-flies ... have long ago been used to light the fire.

—November 12, 1927

Nudism

... man could not exist at all, in the ordinary sense, if he had not discovered the dreadful and astonishing thing that is called fire. It would be just as easy to elaborate a philosophy against fire as a philosophy against clothes. In fact, the two things often serve the same purpose, but fire is by far the more questionable and dangerous of the two. It is not very often that a man is actually killed by a hat or tortured by a pair of trousers.

—January 10, 1931

... in this illustrated paper, there is a continuous and by this time rather monotonous stream of articles and illustrations advertising the new gymnosophists of Germany. I mean the cult of cranks who insist in a crazy degree on certain notions connected with sun-cures; to me, more suggestive of sunstroke.

—January 10, 1931

Nudity

Man is not independent of artificial things, even in the most natural sense. Nakedness is not even practical, except on selected occasions that are entirely artificial.

—January 10, 1931

Nursery Rhymes

In spite of all the educationists, it is a kindness to children to teach them nursery rhymes. But a man ought to be imprisoned for cruelty to children, if he recites to them rhymes that do not rhyme.

—July 18, 1931

Occidental

The Occidental is always saying that he cannot understand the Oriental; but the truth is that he cannot understand himself.

—June 13, 1931

325

Officer: German versus British

That a British officer might conceivably be more of a fool than the Prussian officer; that he might be a stupider or a wickeder man; that he might even in his secret heart be a prouder man—all that is quite arguable. But that British officers do not draw their swords on waiters or spurn ladies into the gutter with their spurs is not arguable; it is certain. There is, as a hard historical fact, a different culture and code of manners in the two countries, whatever may be the spiritual and interior truth about any individual in either.

—September 23, 1933

Old

It is obvious that a thing can always be new if it is sufficiently old; that is, that it may seem to be fresh so long as it is stale enough to be forgotten.

—March 29, 1924

Old (Growing)

I have lived to see the dead proverbs come alive. This, like so many of the realisations of later life, is quite impossible to convey in words to anybody who has not reached it in this way. It is like a difference of dimension or plane, in which something which the young have long looked at, rather wearily, as a diagram has suddenly become a solid. It is like the indescribable transition from the inorganic to the organic; as if the stone snakes and birds of some ancient Egyptian inscription began to leap about like living things. The thing was a dead maxim when we were alive with youth. It becomes a living maxim when we are nearer to death. Even as we are dying, the whole world is coming to life.

—March 14, 1931

Old Age

It is something to come to live in a world of living and significant things instead of dead and unmeaning things. And it is youth in revolt, even in righteous revolt, which sees its surroundings as dead and unmeaning. It is old age, and even second childhood, that has come to see that everything means something, and that life itself has never died.

—March 14, 1931

Omen

Healthy humanity uses such signs and omens as a decoration of the tragedy after it has happened. Caesar was right to disregard Halley's Comet; it had no importance until Caesar had been killed. Rationalists, who merely deride such traditions, fail by not feeling the full mass of inarticulate human emotion behind them.

—May 28, 1910

Omnibus

The word "omnibus" is a very noble word with a very noble meaning and even tradition. It is derived from an ancient and adamantine tongue which has rolled it with very authoritative thunders: *quod ubique, quod semper, quod ab omnibus.* It is a word really more human and universal than republic or democracy. . . . It is true that the dignity of this description has really been somewhat diminished by the illogical habit of clipping the word down to the last and least important part of it. But that is only one of many modern examples in which real vulgarity is not in democracy, but rather in the loss of democracy. It is about as democratic to call an omnibus a bus as it would be to call a democrat a rat.

—January 13, 1917

Opinions

I should never dream of defending my books, well knowing them to be utterly indefensible. But I shall always take every opportunity of defending my opinions, well knowing them to be entirely correct; which is the only possible meaning of having any opinions.

—July 26, 1919

I believe a new and enormous number of people now have no opinions at all. Some have open minds; some have empty minds; but few have the positive and partisan opinions that prevailed in my boyhood. A few have convictions—indeed, there is some reasonable hope that the passing of opinions may be the coming of convictions. But most people have not yet got the convictions and have already lost the opinions.

—April 3, 1926

327

Optimism (New)

The new optimism, though it expresses itself in commerce and journalism, and especially in advertisement, probably has, like everything else, its roots in religion. Its essence, or at least its extreme expression, is to be found in what is called Christian Science. Anyhow, it does what Browning and the old optimists never dreamed of doing — it denies the actual reality of evil in experience.

—November 22, 1930

Optimist and Pessimist

The optimist and the pessimist are brothers, one might even say twins. Certainly they are not opposites; the real opposite to both of them is something so opposite that they never even think of it. However much they differ, they agree on one point, and it is much the most important point. They agree that man's course is marked out for him, and that man has very little to do with it. They both believe that man is a machine, being started uphill or being started downhill. They both believe, in that sense, that man is a motor-car. Or rather, to speak more strictly, they believe that man is the car but not the motor. In short, they may really believe very different things, but they disbelieve in the same thing. They disbelieve in the great dogma that "man is man and master of his fate."

—July 10, 1920

Orators

I have seen many meetings — political, religious, irreligious, festive, funereal, and even financial. And I can with a clear conscience lay it down, as the outcome of all human experience, that there are in this world of ours only two kinds of speakers. There are two public orators and no third. The first is the man who is making a good speech and won't finish. The second is the man who is making a bad speech and can't finish. The latter is the longer. It does not in the least follow that the speech which seems too long is unworthy of attention; the fault may be in the atmosphere.

—February 24, 1906

Orators and Sentences

Men in the eighteenth century were proud of ending a sentence, not only because they were orators, and it was therefore a rounded sentence, but also because they were wits, and the sting was in the tail of the sentence. Some of the wits in contemporary comedy seem almost too frigid and detached to start a sentence, let alone to finish it. They seem to welcome being interrupted; which is fortunate, as they always are interrupted. They seem almost as much relieved not to have to finish their sentence as if it were a sentence of ten years penal servitude.

—November 5, 1932

Oratory (Modern)

If a modern writer or speaker has to denounce Socialism, for instance, he says, "The raving Atheist with his red tie and his red flag will be repudiated by every moderately decent citizen." If he has to praise Socialism, he says, "Become a Socialist and a hero."

—December 24, 1910

Organisation

Organisation very often means merely turning men into machinery; and it is quite a mistake to suppose that machinery as such is efficient. Machinery can move slow as well as fast—indeed, machinery left to itself does not move at all.

—April 1, 1922

Originality

... originality only means the power of returning to origins. But there is still a difference between those who are in touch with origins through a living tradition, and those who only come back to them by a lonely journey among the dead. One difference is that tradition is always more full; that is, tradition is always more free. To find a thing by adventure is to find it in one aspect; it will remain fixed in one form in the mind. To receive it by legend and living popular story is to receive the whole of it, the lesser and lighter as well as the weightier and more solemn aspects.

—September 20, 1919

Orthodoxy, Criticism of

What is always crumbling is not the Creed but the criticism. Especially when it is of the sort which calls itself, with the well-known humility of science, the higher criticism. The person whose position is perpetually growing shaky, shifting, sliding, and breaking away from under him, is the advanced sceptic who is attacking the tradition of Orthodoxy. It is he who has to abandon position after position, in order to continue the battle or even to remain in the field.

—*November 26, 1927*

Orthodoxy, The New

It is the new orthodoxy that a man may be uncertain of everything; so long as he is not certain of anything.

—*August 19, 1933*

Ouija Board

When I was a boy I used to play with a planchette as carelessly as I played with a cricket-bat; I have never operated through a medium, but I suppose that the doubts and the certainties are much the same. If it had ever occurred to me to believe the things that the planchette wrote down I should be a raving maniac by this time. Gladstone pronouncing on the Budget would have been a very mild interlude in our old orgies of supernatural interviewing. Moses was perfectly ready to provide us with ten new commandments; Cromwell would be converted to Catholicism as soon as look at you. There was one story in particular about a secret marriage of one of my aunts to Cardinal Manning, which I am very glad did not find its way to the serious newspapers.

—*November 27, 1909*

"Out of the Frying Pan ... "

The old proverb about the frying-pan and the fire has a logical point not always noticed.... it is the whole point of the homelier phrase that the fire is worse than the frying-pan, because it is the cause of the frying-pan; because it is only the fire that makes it fry. The act of sitting in a frying-pan, if there were no fire, would be an eccentric, but not necessarily a painful habit.

—December 15, 1917

Overwork

Work is not necessarily good for people; overwork is very bad for people; and both often begin with a bad motive and come to a bad end. Many a modern industrialist has prided himself on being as industrious as he was industrial. And it meant little more than that he was ready to sweat himself, as well as his neighbours, when he wanted to swindle his neighbours.

—March 21, 1925

Oxford

Oxford is meant to be a place where people can talk nonsense. It has no other object . . .

—June 28, 1924

Matthew Arnold, for reasons best known to himself, described Oxford as the home of lost causes. It would be much truer to call it the home of found causes. I mean of very newly found causes; of the sort of causes that young people have just begun to hear about and are therefore delighted to shout about; and all the louder because it was supposed to shock the orthodoxy of aged dons who (as a matter of fact) are generally exceedingly unorthodox themselves. When I was young, my friends at Oxford consisted largely of Fabian socialists, and not a few of the dons were themselves socialists. To-day, of course, they would not call themselves Fabian socialists, but Marxian communists. You cannot expect young bloods to be thirty years behind the fashion; but I doubt if these ones are particularly ruddy.

—September 16, 1933

P

Pacifism

. . . the real point against the cause of pacifism is that it is not a cause at all, but only a weakening of all causes. It does not announce any aim; it only announces that it will never use certain means in pursuing any aim. It does not define its goal; it only defines a stopping-place, beyond which nobody must go in the search for any goal. Now you do not get the good out of any cause by saying from any motive, that you will never fight for it. A Buddhist is not a better Buddhist, but a worse Buddhist, if he refuses to draw the sword even to avert the extinction of Buddhism—or, if he is not so far the worse Buddhist, Buddhism is so far the worse religion.

—August 3, 1918

The Athenians ought, no doubt, to have thrown away their shields and spears, and trusted everything to that enlightenment and enthusiasm for international peace for which barbarians are everywhere renowned.

—April 3, 1918

A morality which makes it immoral to fight against any possible form of wrong strikes me as more monstrous than any mystical exaggeration of the idea of the image of God or the divine presence in the soul. It is more of a madness, because it alters objective and not merely subjective things. . . . But a man who thinks a tortured Belgian child a tolerable sight, when he could prevent it with a blow, is more like a man who thinks a lamp-post is a cow,

332

or a tree is an elephant. He has literally lost his senses, and not merely his sense.

—June 7, 1919

A man gets up and says that war is unthinkable at the very moment when everybody is thinking about war, and because everybody is thinking about war. . . . Let us say that war is unbearable, or that war is unjustifiable, or that war is invariably indefensible, if we think so. But to say that it is unthinkable is to say that we refuse to think.

—April 19, 1930

Pacificism (American)

Pacifism really was in America something which it never is anywhere else, though it always pretends to be. It was democratic. The people, or great tracts of the people, really wanted peace; and were not (as in Europe) merely told by horribly unpopular Socialists that they really wanted peace.

—April 14, 1917

Pacifists

The Pacifists are, even among modern men, the most ruled by phrases rather than ideas. It is notable that any one of their questions has to be put in a particular form of words. Translate the question into any other form of words, and it can no longer rationally be answered as they wish. Thus they will say, "Can war be the right way of settling differences?" Ask instead, "What shall prevent me from putting forth my whole strength to defend whatever makes life worth living?"—and they have no answer.

—July 24, 1915

In order to weaken what they call international hatred, the peacemongers are driven to palliate the Prussian habit of war. . . . Such is our human frailty that the notion of nailing up a live baby to bleed to death on a wooden door moves many of us to emotions of some warmth and impatience. The friends of peace wish to dilute these emotions, and they talk about "the necessities of military rule" until

333

they seem almost to have persuaded themselves that nailing up the baby was quite a normal style of mural decoration.

—*March* 24, 1917

... people who happen to think a Pacifist a mad dog, even if well-meaning in his madness, would still be entitled to regard the dog as capable of communicating rabies.

—*June* 23, 1917

They claim to be very advanced because they have not yet got far enough even to respect a common soldier, far less really to respect a common labourer.

—*April* 13, 1918

Mr. H. G. Wells has written a thousand pages in favour of peace, but not one page in favour of Poland. Lord Russell has said much, from his point of view, to deter men from fighting, but nothing that would deter Mussolini from fighting, and nothing certainly that could deter any communist from fighting Mussolini. To examine, prove, disprove, or reconcile the philosophies of Europe—that would be a task for a philosopher, but not for a philosopher like Bertrand Russell. That is the only way to peace; and few be they that find it.

—*March* 25, 1933

Pacifists and Militarists

It was actually and even earnestly said that this war-like world must be worse in order to be better. The more hateful war became, the sooner men would learn to love peace. Only when war had done its very worst, would humanity fully realise that peace is best. This argument was gravely advanced by many men of humane and intelligent spirit; by some of the followers of Mr. Wells, if not by Mr. Wells himself. And it always filled me with amazement that men should use such an argument, without seeing where such an argument would lead. It is surely an astounding thesis; that we should all be as wicked as possible, in order that the world might the sooner grow weary of our wickedness. . . . This special sophistry . . . created, and to some extent still creates, a curious ultimate alliance between pacifists and militarists. The militarist must be allowed to be more and more brutal, because the pacifist hopes that this will prove to everybody how very brutal he is.

—May 2, 1936

Pact (Satanic)

Indeed, there is a metaphysical truth rather too subtle to be expressed in this type of tale which the critic thinks too clumsy to be tolerated. When a man clings to one fact, against the tide and torrent of the whole truth, when he sets his feet firmly on one possession or one power, against commonsense and even his own instincts about the nature of things, when he answers everything by saying "I have the bond; I have the promise; I have the formula," it is indeed true that even his own talisman will almost certainly fail him.

—September 19, 1925

Paganism (Neo-)

Shelley invented half a hundred goddesses, but he could not pray to them, not even as well as the old atheist Lucretius could pray to Venus, mother of Rome. All Shelley's deities were abstractions; they were beauty or liberty or love; but they might as well have been algebra and long division, so far as inviting the gesture of worship goes. In this, as in everything else, what is the matter with the new pagan is that he is not a pagan; he has not any of the customs or consolations of a pagan.

—July 5, 1930

Pagans (Modern)

... the modern pagan delights to dance about clad in nothing but vine leaves or ears of corn, without referring them back in any way to the digging of real vineyards or the ploughing of real cornlands. He forgets altogether the foundation of the old Hellenic city state; he forgets that its foundations were outside the city. He forgets that the very word pagan really means peasant. He will talk about being a pagan, without stopping, for twenty years; but he would not like to be a peasant for twenty-four hours.

—April 25, 1936

Pantheism

A man must be outside a thing in order to love it; that is why pantheism will never be a popular religion.

— September 6, 1924

Pantheism may or may not be a good creed for a philosopher; pantheism is certainly in one sense a very good creed for a pagan philosopher. But pantheism is a hopeless creed for a revolutionist. If all things are equally divine, then the tyrant and the bigot are as divine as the tribune and the truth-seeker.

—January 25, 1930

If all things are equally unfolded from one natural root, the worms of oppression are as natural as the flowers of freedom. If they came otherwise, then the universe is not universal; and the worm in the tree of nature is as theological as the snake in the tree of knowledge.

—January 25, 1930

Papacy

It is the oldest, immeasurably the oldest, throne in Europe; and it is the only one that a peasant could climb. In semi-Asiatic States there are doubtless raids and usurpations. But these are of brigands rather than peasants: I speak of the pure peasant advanced for pure merit. This is the only real elective monarchy left in the world; and any peasant can still be elected to it.

—August 29, 1914

Paradox

All my life, or at least all the later part of it, I have been trying to discover the meaning of the word "paradox." It seems to have two meanings—a statement that seems to contain a contradiction or to be intrinsically improbable, and a statement that happens to be different from the catchwords common at a particular moment. Now, as a fact, these catchwords themselves often are paradoxes. These catch-words themselves are often intrinsically contradictory or improbable. So that, by

336

the simple operation of stating the dull and obvious truth, one may gain quite a picturesque reputation for dashing and dazzling paradox.

—August 1, 1925

Parenthood

The parent, whether persuading or punishing the child, was at least aware of one simple truth. He knew that, in the most serious sense, God alone knows what the child is really like, or is meant to be really like. All we can do to him is to fill him with those truths which we believe to be equally true whatever he is like. We must have a code of morals which we believe to be applicable to all children, and impose it on this child because it is applicable to all children. . . . In other words, we must believe in a religion or philosophy firmly enough to take the responsibility of acting on it, however much the rising generations may knock, or kick, at the door. I know all about the word education meaning drawing things out, and mere instruction meaning putting things in. And I respectfully reply that God alone knows what there is to draw out; but we can be reasonably responsible for what we are ourselves putting in.

—July 29, 1922

Parents, Children and Equality

Why should one citizen sponge on another citizen from the age of two to the age of twenty? Why should he or she contract this curious obligation in a world where all are equal? Now the new revolutionists do not denounce the obligation; they do not deny it; they do not propose a definite substitute for it; they have no new *theory* about the relation of parent and child. They simply assume the obligation and then ignore the obligation. They take it for granted that the young person must live on the old person as long as he chooses and then defy the old person as soon as he likes. This may be a rebellious mood, but it is not a revolutionary idea.

—March 13, 1926

Parliament

It is useless to discuss whether the adventurer will enter Parliament: the adventurer has entered it. That is, the financial adventurer has entered it. It is exactly the better sort of adventurer—the intellectual and sincere adventurer, the man who

337

has ideas which he will not sell—who is kept out. The patriot would be content with mere pocket-money if he could get it. It is the pickpocket, the man who wants other people's pocket-money, who is always ready to pay a trifle to get into a crowd of rich people.

—*October* 22, 1910

...if anyone knows what the last Parliament did, he is keeping it to himself.

—*December* 24, 1910

Anyone who has worked in a modern parliamentary election knows that the most lamentable part of it is the person who is elected.

—*October* 11, 1919

What is wrong with Parliament is corruption and cowardice and the failure to punish powerful people for selling titles or taking tips.

—*May* 31, 1924

The best speeches made in Parliament are interruptions of other speeches.

—*April* 4, 1925

The most serious things said in Parliament are the jokes.

—*April* 25, 1925

Parliamentary Government

The one Parliament that really does rule England is a secret Parliament; the debates of which must not be published—the Cabinet. The debates of the Commons are sometimes important; but only the debates in the Lobby, never the debates in the House.

—*November* 10, 1906

Parliaments

Most of us are inclined to think that what is the matter with parliaments is par-
liamentarians. . . . They are only too prone to do the work that's nearest; and also
to assist the person that's nearest—the person symbolically known as number one.

—April 17, 1926

Parousia

. . . "Why should not the earth be paradise? It will be some day. We have not been
long on this earth as conscious beings. We have not been intelligent very long."
Certainly anyone listening to a great many exponents of this evolutionary idealism
would agree that they have not been intelligent very long. He might even be
moved to a distressing doubt about whether they are intelligent yet.

—June 27, 1925

Partisanship

The danger of the modern world, with its doubts and divisions—especially its political doubts and its national divisions—is that each party may grow too partisan,
whether in strategy for its own scheme or in politics for its own state. We must
beware, above all things, of proving ourselves right in small quarrels with our friends,
or we shall never really prove ourselves right in the great quarrel with our foes.

—November 17, 1917

Party Politics

The liberal is no longer shocked if you tell him that the mediaeval guild system was
better than modern industrialism. The conservative is no longer horrified if you
tell him that a democratic peasantry like the Irish is better than the rule of the
squires. Even if they still disagree with you, they are no longer astonished that you
should disagree with them. They both have a subconscious sense of something
having silently collapsed and a space being left for something else. The Tory is
ready to consider a better scheme, however new. The radical is ready to consider a
better scheme, however old.

—October 24, 1925

Party, Political

The Tory has taken a little of the colour of the Liberal, the Liberal a little of the colour of the Socialist, the Socialist a great deal of the colour of the Liberal. To-day the parties are chameleons that have changed colour so often as to be practically colourless.

—*August* 11, 1923

Parvenu

The first luxury of a *parvenu* is a pedigree.

—*February* 23, 1918

Past (Conservers of the)

But the important point is this, that the uneducated are, by their nature, the real conservers of the past; because they are the people who are really not interested in beauty, but interested in interest. The poor have this great advantage over the ordinary cultivated class, that the poor (like a few of the best of the very rich) are not affected by the fashions: they keep things because they are quaint or out of the current line of thought. They keep Old Masters because they are old, not because they have recently been "discovered." They preserve old fashions until the time when they shall become new fashions. For the man who is ten years behind his time is always ten years nearer to the return of that time.

—*December* 16, 1905

The Past

We can imagine King John pointing out that he had never killed his mother like Nero; and Nero saying, with legitimate pride, that he had not murdered so many babies as Herod. . . . Nine times out of ten the man who boasts that he is at least better than his predecessor in some special respect would find that he is also worse than his predecessor in some other respect.

—*September* 5, 1925

Past and Present

It is suggested that men always think the present prosaic and only the past poetical.

—January 10, 1925

Patriotism

Patriotism should be a passion—like first love, or a woman's pride in a baby; that is, it should be special and fastidious in the particular case, but quite vulgar and universal in the general character.

—July 31, 1909

. . . in civilised countries patriotic self-praise is an art, and therefore an exception.

—December 8, 1917

. . . patriotism, so far from being the narrowest, is the broadest of all human emotions. In practice, it opens the very widest of all the gates of brotherhood; and through this gate at least even the unfortunate few may return into the city of fellowship. In such an experience as this, even the snob must discover how much the independence of his country simply means his dependence on his countrymen.

—April 13, 1918

Patriotism (English)

. . . English patriotism has a comparative carelessness that makes it look like cosmopolitanism. This is part of an English element which can be seen in scores of little things—even in food or cookery. We are always giving foreign names to very native things. If there is a thing that reeks of the glorious tradition of the old English taverns, it is toasted cheese. But for some wild reason we call it Welsh rarebit. I believe that what we call Irish stew might more properly be called English stew, and that it is not particularly familiar in Ireland. There is, I think, another sort of savoury called a Scotch woodcock, of which I know nothing except that it is presumably not a woodcock, and almost certainly not Scotch.

—August 2, 1919

Patriots and Poets

The duty of patriots is to make comprehensible the love of country; and the difficulty with poets is that they can only talk their native tongue; which is like a secret language of lovers.

—April 29, 1922

Peace

The modern promoters of peace are always trying to discover the points on which nations agree. They will never really achieve peace until they discover and define the points on which they disagree. There are national peculiarities which will always be preserved, and which, for the variety and interest of our earth, always ought to be preserved. International bitterness, international bloodshed, does not come from recognising these differences. It comes from not recognizing them.

—August 15, 1927

I need not say that it is about as sane to say that I would encourage militarism as that I would encourage cannibalism. To begin with, I am strongly in favour of keeping the peace, not because I am a pacifist, but because I am a patriot, and I know very well that England has everything to lose and nothing to gain by a new war at this particular juncture. I am also, oddly enough, in favour of peace because I am a Christian, and should like to see a fuller reunion of Christendom. I am also in favour of peace because I am not a homicidal maniac, who is the only sort of person I can imagine being normally and in the abstract in favour of war.

—September 16, 1933

Peace and Justice

We cannot always at once preserve peace and preserve justice. That whether we are peaceful depends on whether others are provocative, that we can never arbitrate if we always refuse to act, that if something is to be rescued it can only be done by militant energy and not by neutrality and nonentity, and that even that neutrality may not protect us from those who hold themselves at liberty to attack neutrals.

—May 6, 1922

Peace without Love

For the most bitter thing in the world, the thing most full of intellectual cruelties and a hungry hatred in the heart, the most wholly malignant thing known to our humanity, is peace without love. It is possible to love your enemies, so long as you do not make a treaty with them. If you wish to love your enemy, fight him. If, however, you wish to hate him with a really hellish hatred, surrender to him.

—February 3, 1906

Peace without Victory

A peace without victory is a violation of that very practical thing which is called poetical justice. Victory is the only meaning of war. It is to war what the light is to a lighthouse, or what the brain is to a man. Men will not toil for a century to build a lighthouse a mile high, and then put no lamp in it and say it will do no harm. A woman will not travail to bear a man child, and then dash his brains out because the body will lie more quiet. . . . Peace without victory is a dead thing; it is only level as the grave is level; it is only equal as we are all equal in the dust.

—February 3, 1917

Peasant

It is due to Russia, after all her sorrows, sins, or bewilderments, to say that in Russia was found the reality that could resist them when any politician or professor might have collapsed before them. The reality which thus resisted was . . . the peasant.

—December 20, 1919

In short, the peasant has many bad and good characteristics, but among others this one minor characteristic: that with him there may be liberty and without him there must be slavery. A great many socialists and social reformers, as well as a great many millionaires and trust magnates, honestly desire that there should be slavery. They prefer slavery; and they can give rational and plausible arguments for slavery. Thus Mr. Bernard Shaw says that a few capable men must always govern the masses; and the capitalists agree with him and are ready to provide the few capable men.

—October 29, 1921

343

They call him selfish; yet they blame him at the same time for stinting himself for the remote future of his farm and his family. They cannot see that he is starving for an idea; for a domestic patriotism. The case for the best peasantry, as for the best aristocracy, is that it is the very reverse of individualistic. If only in a narrower sense, it fights not for the individual but for the race. The man is emphatically not fighting half so much for himself as for his father or his children.

—July 12, 1924

Peasants are perhaps the only men who are really equal; and wherever they are there will be theories and ideals of equality. On the other hand, industrial management is in its nature despotic, and can therefore work under an ancient despot.

—April 23, 1932

Property is not capitalism, but the contrary of capitalism—which is the denial of property to the masses of mankind, who are thus compelled to work for a wage. The working model of property is peasantry; and it is with a peasantry that Lenin and his school are finding that their own very mechanical model will not work.

—September 6, 1919

Pedant

... the most pedantic sort of pedant is he who is too limited to be antiquated. He is cut off from antiquity and therefore from humanity; he will learn nothing from things, but only from theories; and, in the very act of claiming to teach by experiment, refuses to learn by experience.

—September 28, 1929

Penitence

Our fathers had this great advantage over us: that they did believe, in theory at least, that men should have a sense of penitence at all times, even in times of prosperity. They did not always live up to their ideals of penitence, humility, self-examination or self-knowledge, any more than we always live up to our ideals of social altruism, disinterested citizenship, communal affection, or care for the poor. But they remembered them even when they forgot them; in the sense that they remembered them whenever they were reminded of them.

—July 29, 1933

Penn, William

... it is a first principle, right or wrong, to go back as William Penn did, to the doctrine of the inner light. For William Penn really was a great man and not merely a seventeenth-century sectarian; his thoughts, whether we think with him or no, have a meaning in the twentieth century or any century; and he founded something much larger than Pennsylvania and much greater than Philadelphia—a faith that has not yet failed.

—January 24, 1931

People

It is a weakness to fail in feeling that a statue standing on a pedestal above a street, the statue of a hero, carved by an artist, for the honour and glory of a city, is, so far as it goes, a marvellous and impressive work of man. But it is far more of a weakness to fail in feeling that a hundred statues walking about the street, alive with the miracle of a mysterious vitality, are a marvellous and impressive work of God.

—February 28, 1931

People (Mad)

... mad people are sometimes more representative than sane ones, because they have a certain nudity of mind which shows many things that the wise know and conceal. It requires a very wise man indeed to teach fools. But he must be a very hopeless fool whom fools cannot teach.

—October 21, 1905

People (Modern)

The glory of modern people is that they do really feel. Their only danger is that they cannot think.

—June 30, 1906

I think that most modern people are much stupider than those in the age of my father, and probably very much stupider than those in the age of my grandfather.

—October 11, 1930

People (Rich)

Something happens to people when they become rich; and what happens generally is that they worry on a large scale instead of worrying on a small one. They haggle with a hundred people, instead of haggling with two or three people.

—September 21, 1929

The People versus Faddists

Kings may have made laws, but mobs made languages. The governors may have made statutes, but the governed made the words of the statutes. It was ultimately the people, and nothing but the people, that decided that *plow* should not be spelt so. Both these matters are human and comprehensible; both these matters might be applied without difficulty to the modern problem of spelling. Take your choice of them; neither will do great harm. Trust the scholar and get the thing settled quickly. Trust the people and get the thing settled slowly. But in the name of all ancestral wisdom, do not trust the faddist and get the thing settled wrong. Do not trust the opinion of every chance person whose name you've heard in the newspapers as being somebody vaguely and irrationally important. Do not trust a man because you have heard of him as a cricketer or a journalist or a prize-fighter or a burglar or a millionaire.

—September 15, 1906

Pepper

I could point out that pepper is actually used by criminals as something to fling in the faces of their pursuers, to blind and choke them. So that the pepper-pot takes its place in the police museum as being both a weapon of crime and an instrument of torture.

—February 21, 1931

Perjury

... we know that this is the charge which parliamentary leaders perpetually bring against everybody, especially each other. Perhaps there is something in parliamentary life that makes a man incessantly break his word and incessantly reproach the other man for doing the same.

—February 9, 1924

The Permanent Things

We should always endeavour to wonder at the permanent thing, not at the mere exception. We should be startled by the sun, and not by the eclipse. We should wonder less at the earthquake, and wonder more at the earth. And on the same philosophical principle, I can say, with the most solid sincerity, that I do not wonder at the impatience of the old lady in knocking the policeman's hat off half so much as I wonder at the patience of all the rest of us in leaving it on. The thought that the world contains uncounted millions of sane and healthy men none of whom have knocked a policeman's hat off overwhelms me with a great tide of mystery, like the multitudinous mysteries of the sea.

—October 21, 1905

A man dying for his country does not talk as if local preferences could change ....When men are making commonwealths, they talk in terms of the absolute, and so they do when they are making (however unconsciously) those smaller commonwealths which are called families. There are in life certain immortal moments, moments that have authority. Lovers are right to tattoo each other's skins and cut each other's names about the world; they do belong to each other in a more awful sense than they know.

—July 2, 1910

A man's soul is as full of voices as a forest; there are ten thousand tongues there like all the tongues of the trees: fancies, follies, memories, madnesses, mysterious fears, and more mysterious hopes. All the settlement and sane government of life consists in coming to the conclusion that some of those voices have authority and others not. The only test I know by which to judge one argument or inspiration from another is ultimately this: that all the noble necessities of man talk the language of

347

eternity. When man is doing the three or four things that he was sent on this earth to do, then he speaks like one who shall live for ever.

—July 2, 1910

...a permanent ideal is absolutely necessary to anything like progress or reform. You cannot reform what is eternally formless; and you cannot march towards what is always moving about.

—March 8, 1924

If we really disbelieve in the permanence of anything, even of the standards of the mind, we ought really to abandon the making of monuments, as we have abandoned the making of mummies.

—April 18, 1925

Ideas like truth and fidelity remain to be judged on their own merits without reference to the external modes of the age, as the multiplication table or the theory of cause and effect remains in spite of any alteration in our taste in hats. A man's head will continue to calculate that two and two make four, and that cause precedes effect, however rapid and varied be the succession of hats on his head.

—March 5, 1927

I picture the miserable face of the man who should have said to Socrates that the idea of immortality or of the highest beauty was appropriate to long tunics in the time of Pericles, but not appropriate to short tunics in the time of Demosthenes. I picture the long-drawn agony of his answers when Socrates "put him to the question."

—August 15, 1931

Permissiveness (Legal)

Actually, it is just now, when the police are most perfect as an organisation, that people feel them most imperfect as an idea. Precisely now, when the prisoner cannot possibly get out of prison, we are most deeply doubting whether he ought ever to have been in prison. Now that nothing can keep his head out of the noose, we are most profoundly sceptical about whether anything should put his head in it.

— August 20, 1910

Personality (Dual)

The psychological phenomenon called "dual personality" is certainly a thing so extraordinary that any old-fashioned rationalist or agnostic would simply have called it a miracle and disbelieved it. But nowadays those who do believe it will not treat it as a miracle — that is, as an exception. They try to make deductions from it, theories about identity and metempsychosis and psychical evolution, and God knows what.

— September 12, 1908

Pessimist

For the real pessimist is not he who is weary of evil, but he who is weary of good.

— May 12, 1923

Pessimist and Optimist

. . . the pessimist is a man who thinks a little and thinks wrong, and the optimist a man who refuses to think at all.

— May 20, 1922

Peter Pan

A very fine problem of poetic philosophy might be presented as the problem of Peter Pan. He is represented as a sort of everlasting elf, a child who never changes age after age, but who in this story falls in love with a little girl who is a normal person. He is given his choice between becoming normal with her or remaining immortal without her, and either choice might have been made a fine and effective thing. . . . But it was the fork of the road; and even in fairyland you cannot walk down two roads at once. The one real fault of sentimentalism in this fairy play is the compromise that is ultimately made, whereby he shall go free for ever, but meet his human friend once a year. Like most practical compromises, it is the most

349

unpractical of all possible courses of action. Even the baby in that nursery could have seen that Wendy would be ninety in no time, after what would appear to her immortal lover a mere idle half-hour.

—August 20, 1927

Pets

The attempt of some romantic cavalier to ride upon a beaver would be (to say the least of it) as dubious as the proposal that a horse should build a dam. Man loves the lonely animal, not the civilised and gregarious animal. You pat a dog; you do not pat a rat.

—March 6, 1910

Philanthropists

Philanthropists too frequently forget that pity is quite a different thing from sympathy; for sympathy means suffering with others, and not merely being sorry that they suffer. If the strong brotherhood of men is to abide, if they are not to break up into groups alarmingly like different species, we must keep this community of tastes in giver and receiver. We must not only share our bread, but share our hunger.

—May 28, 1910

The old philanthropist of the New Testament was warned not to sound a trumpet before him when he gave money to the poor. The new philanthropist of the Insurance Act sounds a trumpet before him when he takes money away from them.

—August 22, 1914

Philosophers

I read the other day in some philosophical magazine or other that some Professor whose name I forget (why not say Posh?) was the most conscientious and thorough investigator of ethical origins; and that Posh had come to the conclusion that the old doctrine of a definite thing called the conscience could not be maintained. If I were to say that I had swum to an island where I learnt that there is no such thing as swimming, you would think it a rather odd remark. If I told you that I had read a book which conclusively proved to me that I could not read, your lips might murmur faintly the word "paradox." If I were to say that I had seen a diagram which distinctly proved me to be blind, it is barely possible that you would not believe me. Yet I wonder how many mild but intelligent modern mortals would have read or have read that phrase in the philosophical magazine, and not seen anything absurd in the idea of a man conscientiously discovering that he has no conscience.

— February 20, 1909

Philosophers (Modern)

When I say everybody, of course I mean everybody except the overwhelming majority; that is simply the modern philosophical use of the term. It is sometimes put in the form, "Everybody who counts"; and modern philosophers refuse to go by counting heads, because they will not even admit that average human beings have heads to be counted.

— January 29, 1910

Philosophising

Human philosophising seems to be about the oldest thing in humanity; probably older than cooking; probably older than ploughing; certainly older than practical politics. Men were certainly philosophers before they were soldiers; and I suspect that men were philosophers before they were men. And if you want a common indication of this it can be found in the fact that the oldest art is never natural art. The oldest art is always very symbolical and intellectual, crowded and coloured with things that mean other things; in a word, allegorical, like Egyptian art.

— October 27, 1906

Philosophy

If you can prove your philosophy from pigs and umbrellas, you have proved that it is a serious philosophy. If you have, let us say, a theory about man, and if you can only prove it by talking about Plato and George Washington, your theory may be a quite frivolous thing. But if you can prove it by talking about the butler or the postman, then it is serious, because it is universal. So far from it being irreverent to

351

use silly metaphors on serious questions, it is one's duty to use silly metaphors on serious questions. It is the test of one's seriousness. It is the test of a responsible religion or theory whether it can take examples from pots and pans and boots and butter-tubs. It is the test of a good philosophy whether you can defend it grotesquely. It is the test of a good religion whether you can joke about it.

—*June 9,* 1906

For philosophy is a democratic thing, depending only on man's reason; while science is almost necessarily oligarchical, since it depends on man's opportunities.

—*August 22,* 1908

Philosophy (Linguistic)

... as the English language was not made by Cambridge Professors, but by poor pot-house fellows like Chaucer and Shakespeare and Mallory, poets and such riff-raff, it seems too late to expect that its words will exactly correspond to the newest philosophical categories.

—*June 20,* 1931

Philosophy (Modern)

The modern experiment of first sneering at logic for not being a practical thing, and then timidly praising it for being a priggish thing, seems to have resulted in the general loss of it as a normal function of the mind. It is as if the same Victorian English had supported their railway-trains by forbidding anybody to walk; and then, when all human limbs were paralysed, had deified two or three athletes as gods because they had the power of walking.

—*June 27,* 1931

The idea of logic is so entirely lost in this phase of philosophical history that even those who invoke it do so rather as the Athenians once invoked the unknown god or the men of the Dark Ages retained a dim respect for Virgil as a conjurer.

—*June 27,* 1931

Philosophy (New)

A new philosophy generally means in practice the praise of some old vice. We have had the sophist who defends cruelty, and calls it masculinity. We have had the sophist who defends profligacy, and calls it the liberty of the emotions. We have had the sophist who defends idleness, and calls it art.

—January 6, 1906

Physicists

... the world now revealed by the physicists is not even physical.

—June 14, 1930

Physicists (Modern)

... most of these intellectual innovators instantly elect to go on talking nonsense; and proclaim to all mankind the good news that all space is crooked, or that a yard is sometimes much more than a yard long. All this pitting of relativity against reason seems to me futile; if only because you cannot even observe relativity except by reason. A man who says that calculations about stars and space have made him doubt all measure and proportion, is really eating his own words. He is like a man who should say he had seen, through a very powerful telescope, that he himself was blind.

—December 13, 1919

Physics (Modern)

It is quite true that in Victorian times (the times in which most men of this school are still living) there was some tendency to oppose material hypotheses to mystical ideas. At this moment the material hypotheses are mystical ideas. They are incredibly and unthinkably mystical; they are much too mystical to be called material. They are certainly not sufficiently material to make anybody a materialist.

—April 12, 1930

353

The science of physics no longer means what it says: for it has become a kind of metaphysics.

—*January 3,* 1931

The materialists may be forced to abandon matter. . . .

—*January 3,* 1931

It was the materialists who destroyed materialism, merely by studying matter. They poked and prodded matter, dug into matter, dissected matter, divided and sub-divided matter; until one fine morning matter blew up with a loud bang and has never been seen since. It seems to have entirely disappeared. To judge by the descriptions given by the scientists themselves, it is either nothing at all or it has turned into something like the square root of ninety-nine. It is rather as if we said that the whole solar system had now turned into Tuesday afternoon; or that the real nature of protoplasm is identical with twenty minutes to five.

—*May 9,* 1931

It will be found hard to hush up the incident of the missing atom, which can now be no more exhibited than the missing link.

—*May 9,* 1931

Pig

The actual lines of a pig (I mean of a really fat pig) are among the loveliest and most luxuriant in nature; the pig has the same great curves, swift and yet heavy, which we see in rushing water or in rolling cloud. Compared to him, the horse for instance, is a bony, angular, and abrupt animal. . . . Now, there is no point of view from which a really corpulent pig is not full of sumptuous and satisfying curves . . . . In short, he has that fuller, subtler, and more universal kind of shapeliness which the unthinking (gazing at pigs and distinguished journalists) mistake for a mere absence of shape.

—*May 8,* 1909

Pillory

Indeed, there is only one real and unanswerable objection to the punishment of the pillory; and unfortunately it so happens that this is also the chief objection to the gallows, the prison, the reformatory, the scientific preventive settlement for potential criminals, and everything else of the kind. The only real objection to the pillory is that we should probably put the wrong man into it.

—January 14, 1922

Pius X

The Pope never pretended to have an extraordinary intellect; but he professed to be right: and he was. All honest Atheists, all honest Calvinists, all honest men who mean anything, or believe or deny anything, will have reason to thank their stars (a heathen habit) for the peasant in that high place. He killed the huge heresy that two heads are better than one; when they grow on the same neck. He killed the Pragmatist idea of eating a cake and having it. He left people to agree with his creed or disagree with it; but not free to misrepresent it.... But there was something more in him that would not have been in the ordinary peasant. For all this time he had wept for our tears; and he broke his heart for our bloodshed.

—August 29, 1914

Plutocracy

The power is neither democracy nor aristocracy; it is plutocracy pure and simple, in so far as we can use the words pure and simple of something that is both complicated and corrupt. The barrier between the people and what the people want is not the barrier of the people not having enough votes, or the elections not including enough candidates, or the candidates giving enough pledges. It is the final barrier hiding what ultimately happens to the votes and the pledges, and for that matter the candidates too. All those outer doors stand pretty well open, the doors leading to the polling-booths where things are voted, or even to the lobbies where they are discussed. It is the innermost door of all that is securely locked; and it is the door of the room in which things are done.

—November 11, 1922

355

Poem (Epic)

All adventure stories, in Stevenson's phrase, begin to end well; and in the greatest of adventure stories Ulysses is obviously meant to get home at last; nor are there many people who need to read to the end of the Iliad to find out what happened to Hector. In the case of longer and more elaborate, not to say more entangled, poems, like those of Ariosto and Spenser, it is legitimate to doubt whether everybody does know what happened to anybody.

—August 2, 1930

Poet

... the poet praised by all other poets must always wear the laurel.

—March 21, 1931

[Poets] set out seriously to describe the indescribable. That is the whole business of literature, and it is a hard row to hoe.

—June 6, 1931

... practically every type of human being has been also a poet, and that Byron was a regency buck plus poetry. Similarly, Goethe was a German professor plus poetry, and Browning was a rather commercial-looking bourgeois plus poetry, and Villon was a pickpocket plus poetry, and Wordsworth was a noodle plus poetry, and Walt Whitman was an American loafer plus poetry—for, in the art of loafing, weary Willie could never have stood up against unweary Walt. I have not yet heard of an American dentist or a shop-walker in a large draper's who is a poet, but I have no doubt that both of these deficiencies will soon be supplied. Anyhow, the general rule is that almost any trade or type of man can be an artist—yes, even an aesthete.

—December 26, 1931

Poet (Abstruse)

He has not performed the full literary function of translating living thoughts into literature. He still needs an interpreter; and a crowd of interpreters has officiously rushed between the poet and the public. The crowd is the clique; and it does do a

356

certain amount of harm, I think, by thus intercepting the true process of the perfecting of human expression. It is not wrong because it encourages the great man to talk. It is wrong because it actually discourages the great man from talking plain. The priests and priestesses of the temple take a pride in the oracle remaining oracular.

—June 6, 1931

Poet (Epic)

I have a dark suspicion that there are many poems, and perhaps prose competitions also, which people think they know when they know only the first few lines. Possibly this might explain the sinister haste and eagerness with which the great epic poets cram into the first few lines a statement of the whole story, which they intend to tell in the ensuing twelve books. They always begin with a summary of this kind, perhaps because they have a craven fear that many of their readers will not read any more.

—August 2, 1930

Poet (Modern)

The breach between the people and the poets has been bad for both: the people have gone without inspiration and the poets without applause. . . . But the error was in the poets as well as the people, and certainly it was . . . to praise inhuman and monstrous things, tyranny and chaos, which the heart of mankind hates for ever—things in the highest and most serious sense incredible. It is partly that which chokes the channel between man and the modern poets. The real poet is the man who says what men cannot say—but not what men cannot believe.

—May 22, 1929

That vast but vague revolution that we call the modern world largely began about the time when men demanded that the scripture should be translated into English. It has ended in a time when nobody dares to demand that English poets should be translated into English. It has ended in a new race of pedants who are only too proud of reading the poet in the original, and merely murmur as they read, in a tantalising fashion, that the original is so very original.

—June 6, 1931

Poetry

From the beginning there have been two kinds of poetry; the poetry of looking out of the window, and the poetry of looking in at the window. There was the song of the hunter going forth at morning, when the wilderness was so much lovelier than the hut. And there was the song of the hunter coming home at evening, when the hut was so much livelier than the wilderness or the world.

—July 31, 1909

Poetry, it has been said, is a criticism of life; but it is not a criticism that need be offered in large quantities at short, and regular intervals. No poet is expected to write an ode to the skylark every morning, even on the improbable supposition that every morning he is up with the lark. No spiritual child of Shakespeare and Wordsworth is expected to unlock his heart with the key of the sonnet every night when he unlocks his house with the latchkey.

—February 9, 1918

Poetry (Bad)

Every now and then, after wading through a hubbub of hundreds of words, we find a word that seems to have gone right by accident. We must not complain; nothing in this mortal life is perfect; not even bad poetry.

—July 18, 1931

... there is hardly a single good poet who had not at some time been a bad poet.

—July 18, 1931

Poetry (Modern)

The mad school of poetry is full of normal things regarded as abnormal; not to be admitted as wonderful, but to be feared and loathed as horrible. It is full of crawling surfaces, of prickly and scaly skins, of obtrusive and repulsive features, of blind and greedy growths of green vegetation; all this sort of language being applied to the grass growing or a man having a nose on his face.

—July 10, 1926

There are individuals . . . like Mr. James Joyce or Miss Gertrude Stein, whose prose may be said to be of doubtful sobriety.

—*May 30, 1931*

Does anybody know why it is now the fashion to be very extravagant in poetry and very sober in prose?

—*May 30, 1931*

It is a very queer feature of current poetry that there is hardly anywhere such a thing as a love poem; though there is really rather too much poetry about love. The truth is that the poetry is not really about love, or even about lust. It is about something that they call sex, which is considered from the outside rather than the inside, being at best a subject rather for science than for literature. At the best, they produced a certain amount of psychology, even when it was not psychopathy; and psychology is not poetry.

—*August 19, 1933*

Poets and Politicians

Only imagination of a quite towering and titanic sort can really see the other side of the moon; the other side of the month or the moment. Only a sort of poet could be practical enough to say, as did one great man, "They cry 'hosanna' to-day; they will cry 'crucify' to-morrow." The practical politician is almost always duped and deluded by the particular sort of practical politics that are at that moment being put into practice.

—*January 18, 1936*

"The Point"

I think I shall try some day to write a huge philosophical and critical work called "The point: its position, importance, interest and place in our life and letters." It would have separate sections on seeing the point; on missing the point; on getting to the point; on wandering from the point, and so on. The subject would be so vast and various that I think it would have to be arranged in the form of a sort of encyclopaedia. Thus we should have: point, the, obvious to born fool; see fool. Point, is it rude to? Points, kindred, of heaven and home; see ornithology. Point of pin, use of, when justified; and so on. Point evaded by Professor Robinson, and all the rest.

—October 30, 1926

Poland

It is quite true that there is a chaos of races and religions in those lands that stretch away towards Asia, and are far from the great civic centres of Europe. But it is much more true that there is in that chaos a corporate, communal, and actual thing called Poland—almost as concrete as an eagle . . . It is, perhaps, the one thing in those wild places that really has this ancient and accepted actuality. It lives; it must be allowed to live; it must have all that is necessary to its life. There is a very simple reason, if there were not even better reasons—its life is necessary to our life. A free Poland is . . . necessary to a free Europe.

—January 11, 1919

The very fact that Poland is an ancient state proves that it is not an ephemeral state.

—January 18, 1919

When the Poles defeated the Bolshevists in the field of battle, it was precisely that. It was the old chivalric tradition defeating everything that is modern, everything that is necessitarian, everything that is mechanical in method and materialistic in philosophy. It was the Marxian notion that everything is inevitable defeated by the Christian notion that nothing is inevitable—no, not even what has already happened.

—July 2, 1927

I remember when anything could be believed against the rule of the Czar, and when anything could be believed against rebels against the Czar. But in all this welter, some things had fallen out well; and, thank God, before I died I have seen Poland free.

—September 27, 1930

Police

The police, of course, are neither the noble fellows that they are made out by their friends, nor the atrociously clever fellows that they are made out by their enemies. Broadly, their faults and merits are the faults and merits of the working-class from which they are drawn. Broadly, their merit is that they are brave, that they are normally good-humoured, that they are, in an elephantine way, even sometimes good-natured, and above all that they are, like all the English proletariat, really humorous. Their vice is that they are, like the whole English people, snobs and respecters of persons. You hear stories of their kindness, but it is always from well-dressed people. You hear stories of their harshness; it is always from the poor. This is not a mercenary plan; it is a religion. Wealth is the romance of the poor. Snobbishness is the poetry of policemen. In this they are not to be denounced for being policemen so much as for being Englishmen. They are hearty, healthy specimens of the English democracy, not much better or worse in themselves than the rest of the democracy. And the democracy has no democratic sentiment.

—June 2, 1906

Politeness and Policemen

Politeness is not really a frippery. Politeness is not really even a thing merely suave and deprecating. Politeness is an armed guard, stern and splendid and vigilant, watching over all the ways of men; in other words, politeness is a policeman. A policeman is not merely a heavy man with a truncheon: a policeman is a machine for the smoothing and sweetening of the accidents of everyday existence. In other words, a policeman is politeness: a veiled image of politeness—sometimes impenetrably veiled. But my point is here that by losing the original idea of the city, which is the force and youth of both the words, both the things actually degenerate. Our politeness loses all manliness because we forget that politeness is only the Greek for patriotism. Our policemen lose all delicacy because we forget that a policeman is only the Greek for something civilised.

—September 29, 1906

Political Cartoon

You cannot bring an action for libel against an allegorical picture.

—May 17, 1924

361

Political Compromise

A political compromise is like two children tugging at a cracker till it comes in two in the middle. One child gets one half, but the other half flies further away. In short, the situation is a paradoxical one, which can only be conveyed in such forms of speech as are mysteriously called Irish. The real objection to taking two bites of a cherry is that you only get one bite.

— August 6, 1910

Political Faith

A political faith ought to have, like a religious faith, a slight element of mortification: it ought either to mortify the flesh or, what is (in the case of prigs) much more important and valuable, to mortify the spirit. And the Liberals of Manchester ought to be saying to themselves: "As teetotallers we disapprove of a brewer, as revolutionists we naturally dislike a rich man, as individuals we loathe the sight of him; as free, abstract, emotional souls we should like to boil him in oil; but as Liberals we cannot deny that he is the Lord Mayor of Manchester."

— October 12, 1907

Political Party

English experience indicates, I fancy, that when the two great political parties agree about something it is generally wrong. The stale and sterile fallacy about the great Napoleon has remained among us very largely because both the two political parties, from two different motives, agreed in falsifying his greatness. The Tories undervalued him because he came from what was called the revolution; the radicals undervalued him because he founded what was called the empire.

— November 15, 1919

Political Terms

It was really ridiculous enough when party politicians used the terms of war in the time of peace. It was absurd even then that comfortable candidates and wire-pullers should talk perpetually about raising the banner and routing the enemy, about storming the breach and breaking the battle-line. It was bad enough when it was said quite hazily and heavily, by political hacks who had never raised anything but taxes or broken anything but promises. It is intolerable that these ridiculous things should be said in the very presence of the real things; that politicians should talk thus about losing their seats to men who have lost their legs and arms. . . .

—December 14, 1918

Political Theory

. . . saying: "We may not understand political theories, but our constitution works well in practice," is a piece of wild paradox and only loved as such, like a nonsense rhyme of Lear or Lewis Carroll. It is exactly like saying: "We cannot add up figures correctly; we are quite content if the result comes out right." It is like saying: "It is true that we got the wrong longitude and the wrong latitude; but what does that matter, when it means that we find the place we are looking for?"

—March 26, 1927

Political Unit

Mr. H. G. Wells believes in a world state to which our direct patriotic service should be due. The Bolshevists believe in a division not between nations, but between classes—that is, they believe not merely in a world state, but in a world revolution. Some people, for all I know, believe in social units much smaller than nations; some certainly did take this view about those Italian cities that were the famous republics of the Middle Ages. Personally, I think that view much more human and sensible than either the world state of Wells or the world revolution of Trotsky. We must have a common principle; it ought to be a religion, but it must be an idea and it must not be a platitude. Above all, it must not be in the hands of anybody so unpractical as a practical politician.

—February 28, 1925

Politicians

. . . what is really intolerable, what is really atrocious, is certainly this—that politicians should venture not merely to deceive the people about the things that the people do care about, but should insolently attempt to oppress the people in the things that the people do care about.

—December 22, 1906

...there are politicians who call themselves "independent" politicians; and who boast that they are not attached to any party. They are not; but they would very much like the party to be attached to them.

—October 16, 1909

It is difficult in these days to escape from the topic of politics even by deliberately talking about something else. For there are a considerable number of people who will at once attribute any disaster, from the weather to the Brighton railway smash, to the particular politicians whom they dislike.

—February 19, 1910

...most politicians are engaged in trying to imitate the other politicians, which cannot be considered as a school of virtue.

—July 9, 1910

It is obvious that a politician often passes the first half of his life in explaining that he can do something, and the second half of it in explaining that he cannot.

—March 30, 1918

When he is in opposition he is an expert on the means to some end; and when he is in office he is an expert on the obstacles to it. In short, when he is impotent he proves to us that the thing is easy; and when he is omnipotent he proves that it is impossible.

—March 30, 1918

We must save democracy from parliaments, or parliaments from politicians.

—June 7, 1924

...the men in whom nobody has any sort of confidence are demanding votes of confidence from everybody.

—June 21, 1924

We hold political meetings to elect politicians; and even at those meetings it is impossible to use the word "politician" except as a term of abuse.

—December 20, 1924

... they leave nothing to be desired in the matter of not meaning what they say, or of saying it as if it meant nothing. Surely they fulfil all our loftiest ideals of meaningless utterance and lifeless accent.

—November 14, 1925

It was a very fortunate day for professional politicians when some reactionaries began to accuse them of being demagogues. The truth is that they seldom dare to be demagogues; and their greatest success is when they talk with delicacy and reserve like diplomatists.... But a politician will be much wiser if he disguises himself as a gentleman. His power consists very largely in getting people to take things lightly. It is in getting them to be content with his sketchy and superficial version of the real state of things.

—June 1, 1929

But if I do dislike a certain particular type of politician, it is not because he resembles a bookie, but because he resembles a welsher. That is, it is because he falls below the standard implied even in his own sport or profession.

—February 8, 1936

Politicians (Practical)

Modern politicians are always trying to be practical; consequently, they never get to the point at all. For the core of life is not practical; the heart of a man desires beatitude, which is a spiritual state.... If once you have seen the life of our English poor even for an instant from the inside you will know that the things which are called sentimental or secondary by politicians are exactly the things which are primary and palpable. For instance, it is a far more really practical question in what *tone of voice* officials speak to the poor than even what they say to them.

—October 17, 1908

... all modern politicians have been taught the deplorable trick of trying to be practical politicians. The practical politician is a man who always takes the notion that lies nearest—not because he is morally prompt, but because he is mentally lazy. One result of this is that they are surrounded by a swarm of quacks, struggling for their wandering attention, like a swarm of hotel touts struggling for a bag.

—February 15, 1917

Politicians and Class

Practical politicians are always cracking jokes about the absurdity of the religious people who want to have in their schools the "atmosphere" of one creed. But these politicians all take care to send their own sons to schools where there is a much narrower thing—the atmosphere of one class.

—October 17, 1908

Politicians and Crowds

Politicians are always by the nature of things the enemies of crowds. There have been dark and tremendous times when the politicians have shot down the crowds. On the other hand, there have been brighter and purer times when the crowds have torn the politicians to pieces. But always the man who cared first and foremost for politics has been essentially separated from the men who made up the people, who ploughed and reaped, and bought and sold, and married and were given in marriage; he is fully as much separated from them as is the professional soldier or the priest.

—December 22, 1906

Politics

... there are only two things in human politics; and they are Power and Persuasion. The proof of a practical politician is that he knows which is which. You convict a man—or else you convince him. You convince him of sin—or you convict him of crime. But no good has been done from the foundations of the world by men merely nagging at men—and still less by men nagging at women.

—April 4, 1914

In politics . . . it is true in any case that the simple are too much influenced by the clever and too little by the wise.

—January 24, 1925

When politics were more local, they were more truthful.

—January 24, 1925

. . . endless lobbyings and more or less corrupt compromises . . . that is the way of politicians all over the world.

—December 20, 1930

. . . the sport of politics has sometimes fallen rather lower than the sport of horse-racing. It is due to particular problems, in a particular period, that some public men remind us rather more of jockeys who pull horses than of knights who ride them.

—February 8, 1936

Politics (English)

It might well be maintained that we have no politics in England; and that is why we were obliged for such a long time to borrow our politics from Ireland. The name of one of the two parties in England, and that almost certainly the larger party in England, actually bore a title that only referred to the discussion of home rule for Ireland. It was called the Unionist party; and it is still called the Unionist party. It is still called by the old name, because English people cannot even invent a new name until some new Irish controversialists invent one for them.

—September 6, 1924

Politics (International)

If we judged the world at present by its professions, we should suppose it was exclusively inhabited by saints of the most sacred innocence and sages of the most serene rationality; by just men made perfect, who desire nothing whatever except the restoration of national rights and the establishment of endless peace. If we judge it by its practice, we know we shall find a world weltering in blood, and becoming more and more bestial in its ways of shedding it.

—*October* 6, 1917

Politics (Practical)

Practical politics are in this world continually coming to grief; for the truth is that practical politics are too practical for this world. This world is so incurably romantic that things never work out properly if you base them on the sound business principle. For instance, it is always assumed in modern social philosophy that ornaments, curiosities, *objets d'art* etc., are things that people add to their lives when they have procured all that is solid and sensible. The actual fact is quite otherwise. The savage wears an *objet d'art* in his nose before he discovers that clothes are of any use at all. Man discovered that dress was a luxury before he discovered that dress was a necessity. It is not only true that luxuries are more noble than necessities; it really seems as if they were more necessary than necessities.

—*December* 16, 1905

In practical politics the survival of the fittest frequently means only the survival of the fussiest.

—*August* 8, 1925

Politics and Technology

Parliamentary reports have occupied a smaller and smaller space even in our newspapers, at the very moment when it is proposed to proclaim them with a trumpet in our homes. There is less and less belief in the politician who thus blows his own trumpet, at the very moment when his trumpet is to become the most tremendous sort of megaphone.

—*April* 4, 1925

368

Polls (Public Opinion)

I have recently seen a compilation by some social settlement, cataloguing all kinds of live men and women of the poorer classes, and classing them as "well equipped" and "badly equipped," and so on. They are classified according to their answers in a sort of examination-paper, about their aesthetic tastes, their knowledge of parliamentary politics, and many other things. I have a strong social objection to people who happen to be poor being thus examined. But my first logical objection is simply that we cannot examine the examiners. We cannot tell how or why they selected their questions; for what reason and in what spirit. They may themselves have been very badly equipped touching certain very important things; such as appreciation of humour and experience of human nature. . . . Also there may be a great many questions which the working people could answer, and the examiners could not answer; and therefore could not ask.

—September 27, 1919

Pollster

It does not seem to have occurred to them, for instance, that when a workman indicated that his expenditure on amusements could be summed up in the word "beer," he may have thought the monosyllable convenient for cutting short the conversation. It did not strike them that when he said he would employ his leisure in smoking, he may have chiefly desired to avoid spending it in answering the psychological question of a total stranger. Nor is it impossible that those who brightened the examiners round, with their taste for Botticelli or the London School of Economics, may have been indulging in irony of a more luxuriant sort.

—September 27, 1919

Polygamy

Profligacy may be made romantic, precisely because it implies some betrayal or breaking of a law. But polygamy is not in the least romantic. Polygamy is dull to the point of respectability. When a man looks forward to a number of wives as he does to a number of cigarettes, you can no more make a book out of them than out of the bills from his tobacconist. Anything having the character of a Turkish harem has also something of the character of a Turkey carpet. It is not a portrait, or even a picture, but a pattern. We may at the moment be looking at one highly coloured and even flamboyant figure in the carpet; but we know that on every

369

side, in front as well as behind, the image is repeated without purpose and without finality.

—July 15, 1922

The Mormons talked about the wives of a man being "stars in his crown" in heaven; so that a latter-day saint would walk about with a specially splendid constellation round his head, in honour of the number of times he had broken the law against bigamy.

— February 2, 1924

Poor

It seems never to have occurred to some people to speculate about what all the work of the world would be really like, if the poor were quite so idiotic or quite so irresponsible as they seem to suppose. Every house we live in would fall down, every train we travel in would go to smash, every chair we sit on would break (this does sometimes happen to chairs in my own experience)...every boat would sink, every flock would stray, every furrow would run crooked—the whole framework of our earthly lives would fall to pieces in an instant.

—April 13, 1918

Popularity

...most modern popularity is negative; it is no more than toleration. Many an English landlord is described as popular among his tenants, when the phrase only means that no tenant hates him quite enough to be hanged for putting a bullet in him.

—May 28, 1910

Pornography

All dignified civilisations conceal sexual things, for the perfectly sensible reason that their mere exhibition does affect the passions.

—January 6, 1923

Possessions

People attached to things they do care about tend to fear for them. People attached to things they do not care about tend to brag about them.

—January 11, 1908

Poverty and Respect

What the poor citizen wants is not merely charity, or even sympathy, still less regulation; it is respect, which is the social soil of self-respect. That is why he is sometimes happier as a soldier, in spite of all the sickening horrors of soldiering; because humanity always has respected, and always will respect, a soldier.

—April 13, 1918

Practicality

Then there is the everlasting nonsense about being a practical man. When will people see the simple fact that practicality is a question of means, not of ends?

—February 22, 1908

Pragmatism

Pragmatism *is* bosh; but the best test of this is the test of the great Pragmatist himself; the appeal to the nature and reason of the ordinary man.

—September 17, 1910

Preacher

. . . the extreme liveliness in the preacher is produced by dullness in the congregation.

—October 11, 1930

371

Predictions

The one really rousing thing about human history is that, whether or no the proceedings go right, at any rate, the prophecies always go wrong. The promises are never fulfilled and the threats are never fulfilled. Even when good things do happen, they are never the good things that were guaranteed. And even when bad things happen, they are never the bad things that were inevitable. You may be quite certain that, if an old pessimist says the country is going to the dogs, it will go to any other animals except the dogs; if it be to the dromedaries or even the dragon.

—April 17, 1926

Prejudices

It is generally only moderate people who have prejudices. Indeed, what is called moderation is generally only a deadlock of prejudices.

—November 29, 1919

It is not only true that, when a man is completely deceived, he does not know he is deceived; it is also true that, when a man has been completely misled, he does not know he has been led at all. We might almost say that when a man has been completely instructed he forgets that anybody ever instructed him. The ideas or prejudices, for good or evil, have passed into the substance of his personality, and he feels as if they had always been part of himself.

—November 18, 1922

Present

We have less chance than any of our ancestors to pause upon and really enjoy the present.

—December 13, 1930

Press

... if you never believe the Press and if you always believe private gossip (within reason) you will probably be right.

—February I, 1908

It is the duty of the Press to expound; occasionally it is its duty to expose. Rarely, very rarely, it is its duty to suppress, though this is almost the only duty which it still performs with gusto. But it can only be right to do one of two things—either to expose a thing because it is bad, or to hide the thing because it is bad. It cannot be right to ruin the thing by shaky allusion and shifty argument, to seek to suggest that it is wicked without even stating what you hold wickedness to be.

—July 18, 1908

The things which the newspapers call startling are things that the real people in the world have long ceased to be startled at. To journalists Darwin is still a novelty, while to biologists he is an antiquity, and even a rather damaged antiquity.

—March 26, 1910

It is a great pity that our headlong and hurried Press is always half a century behind the times. The reason is in no way recondite; it is behind the times because it is hurried and headlong. That which is forced to be rapid is specially likely to be trite. If you have five minutes to write a sentence on a slate, doubtless a man of your talents will produce a polished and yet audacious epigram, exquisite in literary form, and startling in its intellectual stimulus. But if you have five seconds to write it in, you will probably begin to write "Honesty is the best policy.". . . Upon this very simple fact of human nature—that bustle always means banality— the whole gigantic modern Press, the palladium of our liberties, is built.

—March 26, 1910

In short, the Press has ceased to be roughly representative, and become almost solely oppressive. The newspaper proprietors now possess England almost entirely because they are typical rich men, and not because they are typical men who happen to be rich. Of course, I know it is not easy to distinguish to a shade between representation and oppression; that is why all oppressors have managed to succeed.

—June II, 1910

It seems impossible to exaggerate the evil that can be done by a corrupt and unscrupulous Press. If drink directly ruins the family, it only indirectly ruins the nation. But bad journalism does directly ruin the nation, considered as a nation; it acts on the corporate national will and sways the common national decision. It may force a decision in a few hours that will be an incurable calamity for hundreds of years. It may drive a whole civilisation to defeat, to slavery, to bankruptcy, to universal famine.

— September 30, 1922

The very fact that we have seen a remark made a hundred times in the newspapers is normally a very good reason for considering seriously whether the opposite is not true.

— September 8, 1928

Pride

. . . all sins and sorrows spring from a certain fever of pride, which cannot enjoy unless it controls.

— April 9, 1910

I think the instinct of mankind against pride, as the ultimate human evil, can be proved from the most prosaic details or the most babyish beginnings. We do not specially resent a schoolboy being in love with a different girl every week, nor even his being in love with all of them in the course of the same week. Our dim yet divine desire to kick him only comes when he says that they are all in love with him. Even at that early and innocent stage the egoism is more revolting than the appetite.

— August 22, 1914

Prig

The definition of a prig, I suppose, is this: one who has pride in the possession of his brain rather than joy in the use of it.

— June 12, 1909

Prigs and Snobs

But I am no more awed by the flying fashions among prigs than I am by the flying fashions among snobs. Snobs say they have the right kind of hat; prigs say they have the right kind of head. But in both cases I should like some evidence beyond their own habit of staring at themselves in the glass.

—December 12, 1908

Principle

One great advantage of principle is promptitude. This is supposed to be associated rather with that clumsy thing that is called practicality. But practicality by itself cannot decide anything that is worth deciding. The key to every problem is a principle, as the key to every cipher is a code. When a man knows his own principle of action he can act.

—April 7, 1923

Unless we have a moral principle about such delicate matters as marriage and murder, the whole world will become a welter of exceptions with no rules. There will be so many hard cases that everything will go soft. I do not insist on my suggestion of a benevolent millionaire paying off those people who seem naturally designed to be murdered. But I do insist that they will be murdered, sooner or later, if we accept in every department the principle of the easiest way out.

—September 21, 1929

Progress

It is queer that, while some of the most poetic of the scientific prophecies of our fathers are being fulfilled before our eyes, there should be about all the fulfilments an element of the fantastic, which in one case at least verges on the farcical. That men should fly is as legendary and wonderful as that pigs should fly; but the flying-machines have shapes which are almost as absurd as the shape of a flying pig.

—October 9, 1909

Progress, in the good sense, does not consist in looking for a direction in which one can go on indefinitely. For there is no such direction, unless it be in quite

375

transcendental things, like the love of God. It would be far truer to say that true progress consists in looking for the place where we can stop.

—January 28, 1922

It is quite certain that a man in the past revisiting the world at intervals of five hundred years, would very often have found startling changes in machinery without any fundamental change in morality.

—February 23, 1924

The notion that America is advanced only shows how deceptive is the mask of machinery and materialistic science. As a historical fact, those who have been advanced in their machinery have generally not been advanced in their ideas.

—August 2, 1924

... I remember the dear old days when one could get from one part of London to another quicker in a cab than on one's feet. By entering the cab, I found myself privileged to form part of a solid block or fixed settlement of cabs, which remained motionless while some distant policeman tried to coax the whole cross-traffic of London through some little crack between two barricades, blocking the street better than the barricades of a revolution. I did not object to this delay, for I am of a contented and unprogressive disposition. It rather pleased me to fancy that we might remain there permanently.

—October 11, 1924

I have read a vast number of mystery and murder stories; I have even, alas! written a few. And I do not think a detective in one of those stories would be allowed to boast that he had made "enormous progress," merely because he had successively adopted and abandoned a number of totally different clues that came to little or nothing. He does it, of course; but he is not proud of it, and does not call it progress. . . . Such is the morbid mediaeval humility of the policeman as compared with the glorious progressive optimism of the man of science.

—May 9, 1925

Progress is a metaphor taken from the act of walking further and further along a particular road in a particular direction.

—May 9, 1925

Most of us probably know what is meant by a question that begs the question. . . . An American interviewer asked me recently: "What do you consider the greatest proof of the progress of the world in recent times?" So far as I am concerned this is exactly as if he had asked, "What do you think contributed most to the German victory in the recent war?"

—December 19, 1925

Progress may be relative, but it must be relative to a direction, and cannot count in all the steps it has taken in the opposite direction.

—December 31, 1927

When progress has to be whittled down to a process which perpetually undoes everything it has done, and yet somehow "proceeds by trial and error to the truth," it seems to have become rather too thin a thing for all the praises of the Progressives.

—January 28, 1928

All that is best in progress is a simplification. All that is worst in progress is an over-simplification. Now, it is of the nature of an over-simplification that it tends ultimately to a negation.

—October 20, 1928

. . . the world has improved in everything *except* intellect.

—October 11, 1930

Is the present generation better educated than the last generation? Is it more intelligent than any one of any number of past generations? Most of those writing on the subject say "yes." Most of them, by a curious coincidence, belong to the present generation, or some very recent generation.

—October 11, 1930

I am willing to agree, with eagerness and enthusiasm, that the whole world progresses; so long as it is universally admitted that it progresses backwards.

—December 13, 1930

The principle of progress is that we are always in revolt against progress. That is why we progress, in so far as we do. We are perpetually throwing off the accumulations of past progresses, which have always produced a great deal more than we want. In progress, as in more practical things, our real calamity is over-production. It is too easy to produce the fashionable thing.

—December 13, 1930

Not everybody realises how much of what is called progress is really rather procrasti-nation. It is not so much hurrying on towards the ideal state; it is rather hurling the ideal state onwards, far in front of us, that it may be a good long time before we catch up with it. There are a great many meanings in the word "to-morrow"; and it may mean looking to to-morrow, or hoping for to-morrow, or merely putting off till to-morrow. Men in the past did not specially believe in a spiritual ideal in the future different from that in the present, and therefore they felt the instant and continuous pressure of that in the present. They knew it was wrong to be covetous or to oppress the poor, even when they wanted to do it; even when they did do it. There is some danger of their modern counterparts merely looking forward to a happier society, with a healthier psychology, when they will no longer even want to do it.

—January 28, 1933

Progress as Precedent

The fallacy I wish to impugn might be roughly described as the fallacy of Precedent and Progress. It consists in always unintelligently quoting the most recent change as an argument for the next change. . . . The people who say they are pursuing progress are really only obeying precedent. By this system a

378

Conservative means a man who must stop where his grandfather stopped; and a Progressive means a man who may only walk where his grandfather told him to. My own temperament is such that I would rather stand still without knowing where I was than walk on without knowing why I was doing it; the former is not so tiring.

—May 7, 1910

Progressive

The controversialists, with an air of no little candour and audacity, say a great deal that only amounts to saying that the young are young, and the old are not infrequently old. That is the worst of a progressive mind; it never can get any further. Progress has brought it to a standstill; it is stuck and stuffed up, as it were, with this one isolated idea of inevitable change. It amounts to no more than saying that youth is youth. But it is somehow confused with the idea that youth is truth; possibly because the words often rhyme in the verses written in albums.

—June 3, 1922

Progressive Conservatives

Instead of considering a process, and testing it by a principle, he merely considers how far that process has yet gone, and tests it only by whether it is going farther. This is the real irrationality that men have really though obscurely felt in a certain type of Toryism. It is not that it loves the past, but rather that it loves the present—a far more absurd appetite. It is an essentially impossible illusion, for it is perpetually destroying itself. Every step of the progressive becomes a status for the conservative. Every wicked revolution becomes a worthy institution. Every abominable thing that is attempted becomes an admirable thing because it has succeeded— not because it is a successful institution, but solely because it has been a successful revolution. A conservative often means merely a man who conserves revolutions.

—October 30, 1920

Progressives

I have never been able to make out what the Progressive Movement is, except that it is rather like a policeman who always tells people to "move on," without telling them where to go.

—January 1, 1910

379

The truth is, of course, that all that is really pedantic or inhuman in the campaign of Progressives owes its success almost entirely to the fact that it is opposed only by Conservatives. It is not opposed by reasonable reactionaries, who have an alternative ideal of the state, but simply by people who share the same ideal, and only object to the ideal being any further realised. The socialists have one solid and respectable quality—that they know what they want; and they will never be successfully resisted, except by somebody who really knows that he wants something else.

—*October 30, 1926*

The Progressive, generation after generation, does elaborately tie himself up in new knots, and then roar and yell aloud to be untied.

—*July 29, 1922*

It is odd that those Progressives who are always proclaiming that the merits of modernity are wholly modern instantly take refuge in antiquity when dealing with its alleged demerits, and answer hastily that they are quite ordinary and old. After declaring that all their songs are songs before sunrise and that the sunrise will be splendidly new, they abruptly fall back on the defence that there is nothing new under the sun. They announce their victories by saying that boys will soon be men, will soon be supermen, will soon be gods, and then cover their defeats by saying that boys will be boys.

—*December 9, 1922*

What the progressive professor really means, I fancy, is not that his pupils really dislike being told things, but that he has nothing to tell them. It only means that he is the sort of philosopher who looks for guidance to his own followers, as the followers used to look to the philosopher.

—*June 28, 1924*

When men have come to the edge of a precipice, it is the lover of life who has the spirit to leap backwards, and only the pessimist who continues to be a progressive. . . . Every soldier who is really a strategist, and especially every strategist who is really a soldier, knows what is meant by the glory and the triumph of such a retreat. He knows that so to save an army may be far more wonderful than to win

380

a victory. And so to save a society may be far more wonderful than to introduce a reform or even a revolution.

—November 8, 1924

Some fabulist might write an amusing conversation between two or three clocks about the clock-maker or clock-mender. The clocks might exhibit certain interesting variations among themselves, and on their own plane. There might be a conservative clock, regarded as almost a profligate clock, because it was not ashamed of being slow. Presumably this Tory and traditional clock would be a grandfather's clock. I know not what the more promising and progressive time-piece would be, unless it were a cuckoo clock. For the cuckoo is very like the prophet of progress, since he comes to announce something new, and announces it so often that we feel as if it were already old.

—February 21, 1925

...Progressives are always great at misleading metaphors; and very naturally, since progress itself is only a metaphor and the most misleading of all metaphors.

—June 13, 1925

They would be much wiser to prove that there has not been much improvement in the past if they want to startle [one] into improving in the future. Progress yesterday is really the enemy of progress to-morrow. Indeed, in one sense the whole theory of progress is the chief obstacle to our progressing. It does not stir people into any very bustling activity on the staircase to tell them it is a moving staircase.

—June 27, 1925

You can always prophesy what sort of thing one of our progressive prophets will prophesy next. Once we had the telescope and the telephone, somebody was sure to talk about television. Once we had the war and the League of Nations, somebody was sure to talk about the world state. The very things which are offered as provocative are always of one particular type of provocation. Even the man who boasts of being a blasphemer is generally traditional, not only in his blasphemy but in his boast.

—May 14, 1927

381

... why it is that men who seem so keen on reforming the world equip themselves with the worst possible philosophies for doing it?

—February 1, 1930

... what I complain of is the shallowness of people who only do things for a change, and then actually talk as if the change were unchangeable. That is the weakness of a purely progressive theory, in literature as in science. The very latest opinion is always infallibly right and always inevitably wrong. It is right because a new generation of young people are tired of things, and wrong because another generation of young people will be tired of them.

—November 12, 1932

Progressives and the Family

To that type ... the state was everything; that great official machine, which managed the traffic and took over the telephone system, was the very cosmos in which these people lived. For them, the family was a stuffy thing somewhere in the suburbs which only existed to be the subject of problem plays and problem novels. The only question about it was whether its gloom should be brightened up by suicide; or its selfishness exalted by self-indulgence. But the whole of this view, though it is a view very nearly universal in the big modern towns, only exists because the big modern town is an entirely artificial society. . . . In some ways a lunatic asylum or a convict settlement are much better organised, are certainly much more elaborately organised, than the hugger-mugger of human beings doing as they like outside. But it is the human beings outside who are human; and it is their life that is the life of humanity.

—June 17, 1933

Progressives and New Notions

There is a tradition ... that jumping off a high precipice is prejudicial to the health; and therefore nobody does it. Then appears a progressive prophet and reformer, who points out that we really know nothing about it, because nobody does it. . . . He insists that there is seldom a ... continuous procession of persons, filing past Dover up to Shakespeare's cliff with this scientific object; and that there is, therefore, no sufficient number of cases of the needs of induction. At last some highly scientific character does jump off Shakespeare's cliff, and is found dead on

Dover sands. And the other scientists, standing round his corpse in a ring, do not regard it as the remains of a fool or a hero or an example of the ancient human tragedy. They regard it as if it were some entirely new and interesting sea-beast thrown up by the sea. They have made a discovery. They hardly realise that it is merely the discovery that all their fathers and grandfathers and great-grandfathers were right.

—March 9, 1918

Progressives versus Conservatives

The business of Progressives is to go on making mistakes. The business of the Conservatives is to prevent the mistakes being corrected. Even when the revolutionist might himself repent of his revolution, the traditionalist is already defending it as part of his tradition. Thus we have the two great types—the advanced person who rushes us into ruin, and the retrospective person who admires the ruins. Each new blunder of the Progressive or prig becomes instantly a legend of immemorial antiquity for the snob. This is called the balance, or mutual check, in our constitution.

—April 19, 1924

Prohibition

Prohibition is a provision by which a Lord may be as drunk as a Lord, so long as the hall-porter and the cabman are kept artificially sober to look after him.

—November 26, 1921

I do not think even Prohibition likely to lead to all Americans drinking themselves to death.

—October 4, 1924

Prohibition, like every other form of persecution of the poor by the rich, is comparatively easy to engineer in the plutocratic modern state. . . . When it is once started it will never stop prohibiting. In a prohibitionist paper I have just received from the district of Boston, published under the very shadow of the University of Harvard, there is a long list of the things that are to be prohibited next. Smokers will be interested to learn that "wild fear and panic often seizes tobacco-users. . . . The

383

dope that is sending all America to defeat and destruction is nicotine, caffeine, and theine. . . .

—January 3, 1925

Paradoxical as it may seem, there is one thing in the world that is more absurd than Prohibition, and that is the legal position of Prohibition.

—July 28, 1928

Men could survive without ever eating meat. How much more obvious is it that they could survive without sprinkling pepper or splashing mustard on meat. And from this it is but one step, according to the clear logic of Prohibition, to the conclusion that the use of pepper or mustard is a mortal sin.

—May 11, 1929

Men have tried to make drink illegal, and have only succeeded in making murder legal. They have not only given us almost complete immunity to professional murderers, so long as they are also bootleggers; they have given a special and peculiar licence for murdering to those whose official duty it is to prevent murder. It is not surprising that even teetotallers begin to feel doubtful about incessantly pouring out blood to prevent somebody else from pouring out beer, and even then not preventing it.

—December 20, 1930

Of course, no serious person could ever have taken Prohibition seriously. But the only really serious part of it is that it prevents people from taking anything else seriously.

—January 17, 1931

Prohibition (Age of)

In theory this is the Age of Prohibition; in practice it is the Age of Cocktails.

—August 30, 1930

Prohibitionist

... the Prohibitionist, having pride as his special spiritual weakness, can never quite make up his mind whether to brag of never having entered a public-house, or to brag of knowing all about what dark and demoniac dens they are.

—August 1, 1931

Proletarian

... there is all the difference in the world between a poor man and a propertyless man; and the proletarian is often a propertyless man. I do not think that in the cities of the West, with their older traditions of dignity and discipline, he will relapse into anarchy; I think there is much more danger of his relapsing into slavery. Capitalism may break up, and I hope it will—in the sense of a better distribution of capital.

—February 1, 1919

I never can understand why the Bolshevists use the word proletarianism as if it were the perfect condition to be enjoyed, instead of being presumably the unjust condition to be ended. If a man in old Virginia said: "Slaves must be without a god," he would presumably mean that they ought not be slaves, because it is bad for them to be godless. But the only other thing he could mean is that it is good for them to be godless, and therefore they ought to be slaves.

—April 14, 1923

Propaganda

Unfortunately, there can be little doubt that this notion of a mild, but perpetual mutiny has become very widely recognised as a weapon for those who believe themselves rightly or wrongly oppressed. Not to gag an enemy with rope, but to gag him with noise; not to suppress opinion by edict, but to suppress it by confusion; not to cut off the King's head, but to attempt by howling to make him lose it—these expedients are being more and more used. I do not say that there are not peculiar occasions upon which they may be the best expedients. But I object to the general recognition of the method myself, and I object to it for two very strong reasons. First, because it prevents order; and second, because it prevents

385

revolution. As long as you can tell people that it is enough to carry banners, they will never again carry guns. And that will be a horrible pity.

— November 21, 1908

Property

The magic of property can be felt about the foulest hovels, but it could not be felt about modern prisons even if they were palaces. If the warder brought round champagne and oysters, if the beds were of gold and satin, there would be quite as little of the magic of property in a prison as there is now. The simple fact is that there is in property not only an idea of security, but also an idea of self-respect.

— November 14, 1908

If property is a bad thing, nobody should have it; if property is a good thing, everybody should have it — or as many as possible should have it. In the former case, we should work like a socialist state to destroy it. In the latter case, we should work like the peasant states to distribute it.

— November 29, 1919

If we want property to be a part of the commonwealth we must make it common, not in the sense of a communal ownership, but in the sense of a common experience.

— March 31, 1923

Property (Private)

. . . men have in the past almost identified property with liberty. When the wisest of the Tsars trusted the serfs with liberty, he also trusted them with land.

— February 1, 1919

The real economic tyrant does not cease to be a bully when he becomes a bureaucrat. The only real freedom for workmen is to have some reserve of possessions independent of any institutions. The new system will have its own vices as well as the old system; it is only what a man owns that he can use to defend himself against any vices of any system. In a word, the man must own his own stick, especially if he has on rare occasions to use it as a cudgel.

—*October 25, 1919*

... men are happiest when they have personal possessions, and not merely communal possessions.

—*November 29, 1919*

It is normal to man to possess. He may go without possessions because he is a saint, or he may be robbed of his possessions by a bandit; because a man may lose his hand for the sake of the kingdom of heaven or have it cut off by torturers of the kingdom of hell. But while he has a hand, his hand is meant to hold something; not much, but something; not somebody else's, but his own. It is because this sense of property is primary and not artificial that the whole philosophy of communism is fundamentally false.

—*January 5, 1924*

The mediaeval commonsense saw that the millionaire was not the champion but the chief enemy of property. He is the man who makes it certain that most of the shopkeepers shall have no shops. If it be a good thing for men to have private property, he prevents them from having it. If private property is a natural thing, he is an unnatural thing. The purpose of the state, and of all sane social effort, is to resist any process by which the ordinary private person is likely to lose his ordinary private possessions. It exists, in that sense, in order that property may be preserved.

—*February 16, 1924*

Property and Hospitality

I will only say for the moment that one of the many reasons that make me believe in the more equal distribution of private property is the need for expanding domesticity by the much wider practice of private hospitality. That is the normal and dignified manner of mixing with the world; the way which leaves a certain responsibility, at once creative and vigilant, in the maker and master of the feast, and bids him, as in the parables and the nursery rhymes, to call in his neighbours to be his friends.

—March 5, 1927

Prophecies

That which really happened in history can often confirm our principles, though it by no means confirms our prophecies. That is, if we have been so unwise as to utter any prophecies. The particular practical thing predicted hardly ever happens. Indeed, strangely enough, it is generally the thing that is most remote from us that can be calculated, and the thing nearest to us that is quite incalculable. The man of science can prophesy a comet, but he cannot prophesy a shower. Clouds are close to us, and of great practical importance to us; but they remain far more free and fitful and elusive than the remotest star.

—July 17, 1926

Prophet

...it is a matter of fact that Burke has not been very specially denounced or derided, whereas Byron has been incessantly denounced and derided.... If you are a prophet of resurrection and revolution, of the future and of the dawn, your sepulchre is likely to be pelted and defaced even after it has been built. But if you were only a builder of sepulchres, your sepulchre will be left in peace.

—October 17, 1931

It is an eternal truth that the fathers stone the prophets and the sons build their sepulchres; often out of the same stones. For the reasons originally given for execution are often the same as the reasons given later for canonisation. But it might be added that there is often a third phase, in which the grandsons wreck and reduce to ruins the sepulchres that the sons have made.... It is full of ups and downs; even for a dead prophet, who is not generally allowed to remain dead in peace. And nothing is more curious than to note the way in which this change does affect great reputations, and especially revolutionary reputations.

—October 17, 1931

Prophet (Scientific)

The scientific profession of knowing the future seems to accompany the agnostic profession of knowing nothing.

—September 23, 1922

Proportion

Gin does make a man happy; up to a point more gin will make him more happy; but even more gin will make him many other things as well. By a succession of phases not contemplated by the philosopher in his first phase, it will make him first drunk, then dead drunk and then dead to the world, and then very possibly dead altogether. That also seems to be a simple truth, requiring no great subtlety; but the savage cannot see it, and the sex novelist cannot see it. He cannot see, what nearly everybody in history has hitherto seen, that there are certain laws and limits to the mind, as there are certain laws and limits to the body. There is such a thing as concentration; there is such a thing as contrast; there is such a thing as proportion; there is emphatically such a thing as boredom. Above all, there is such a thing as a contradiction in terms; and it is a contradiction in terms to have every moment a crisis, every event an escapade, every fact an exception, every person an eccentric, every day a holiday, or society an endless saturnalia.

—May 18, 1929

Proximity

By a paradox we find that proximity accentuates distance, because it accentuates difference.

—May 24, 1924

Prussians

... the Prussian appeared in history as an enemy, exactly as we see that the Hun appeared in history as an enemy. We know very little about the followers of Attila; and that little, like so much that modern learning has deduced from the Dark Ages, is very probably wrong. But that the glory of Attila was a calamity to society, that the power of Attila was the impotence of society, is the verdict; and it will not be reversed.

—April 14, 1917

I do not maintain that all Prussians are pigs; but I do say that their peculiar disposition to go the whole hog makes them appear, to those opposed to them at the moment, more roundedly and completely hoggish.

—September 23, 1933

Psychiatrist

It is no good telling us that science will give us a world of honest men. It would need a world of honest men for science to be run honestly.

—February 23, 1924

Psycho-analysis

The trend of psycho-analysis is to detect in most things the sexual element. . . . I do not deny that there is an unconscious mind, nor that sex may be an element in it. I merely repeat that to suggest the possible presence of one psychological element is not psycho-analysis. It is pulling one thread out of the tapestry, as an idle child might do; but there are many richer colours and more intricate imagery embroidered on the curtains of the tabernacle.

—January 22, 1921

We are always being asked to accept this or that as science; but we already know that it is as easy to tell lies in scientific language as in literary language. And most of us know that the danger is already present in the very thing Mr. Wells invokes: the new study of psycho-analysis. For one man who adopts it to help mankind, there may be three who adopt it to make money anyhow, and three more who adopt it as a sexual anarchy allowing them to do anything, and three more who only take it up as another new stick to beat the old dog of Christian doctrine.

—February 23, 1924

Psycho-analysts

The psycho-analysts know nothing at all about the Greek tragedies. I gather this from the astounding fact that they talk about the Oedipus-complex, obviously without knowing who Oedipus was. Nobody familiar with the Greek play would

390

ever have used that Greek parallel. It was the whole point of Oedipus that he did not have the Oedipus-complex. It was the whole point of him that he only knew certain things too late which our bright and breezy psycho-analysis would introduce us to much too early.

—October 26, 1929

Psycho-prisons

Considering what a vast amount of solemn nonsense is talked in our time about the advance of psychology and mental experiment, and considering with what a ravenous simplicity it is all absorbed by the reading public, there seems no reason at all why this immense engine of pathological argument and medical coercion should not be put at the service of all the tyrants in the future. Instead of sending a man to prison for blasphemy, they will send him to the hospital for brain fever. If they want to put down Socialism, they will call it Irresponsible Promiscuity; if they want to put down individualism, they will call it the malady of the Exaggerated Ego. This may be the new rule of Humanitarianism; and no tyranny like it has ever darkened the sky for men.

—March 30, 1907

Most readers will remember that some years ago a young woman was actually shut up in a lunatic asylum by her parents and two doctors because she believed in the theory of Free Love. This certainly proved (I think) that she was not a very deep moral philosopher; it may have proved that she was a fool; anyhow she was a fool. But it certainly did not prove that she was mad; and she was not mad. The story is only important, however, as illustrating how this purely medical weapon can be used. These parents were simply using what was meant as a measure of hygienic safety as a tool of religious persecution. And if instead of doing this they had taken the principle of persecution and acted on it frankly, they would have behaved both in a more honourable and a more humane way. If her father and mother had taken a very big stick and beaten the young woman until she abandoned her opinions, they would have been much better logicians, much better philosophers, and much better parents than they were.

—March 30, 1907

Psychological Determinism

On the highest and and hoariest of the ashpits of hell sits the oldest of all the demons, whose name is doom; it is he who has always blighted mankind with superstitions of the destiny and death of race; who told the old Greeks like Oedipus that they were bound to their blind crimes; who told the old feudal tribes that there was a curse on a castle or an abortion that was the burden of a family. And when modern science said "heredity" the old fiend stirred, and saw a new chance of renewing the old bondage. For however we take the symbols, it was a wise instinct by which heaven was symbolised by wings that are free as the wind, and hell symbolised by chains.

—February 15, 1930

Psychologists

They no more expect a will to choose whether it will do right than a wheel to choose whether it will go round. If the wheel does not go round, whether it be a wheel in the brain or in the body, it can only be because the proper conditions and compulsions do not come from outside.

—February 23, 1924

Psychologists (Modern)

The new people are not interested in the child, but in the spoilt child—that is, in the unchildish child.

—August 2, 1924

. . . they have a method of keeping sane, or at least of preventing their own theories from dragging them to insanity.

—July 19, 1930

Psychologists and Testimony

The trouble with nearly all these scientific theorists is quite simple: it is that they have cultivated the art of learning while they have entirely neglected the art of thinking. They find out the most varied and fascinating facts, but they always lose that thread of reason on which alone facts can be strong: their rotten string is always breaking, and their precious beads being lost. This notion of the expert giving evidence on the value of evidence is a very strong example.

—April 17, 1909

Psychology

A science in which there is no prejudice, no pretension, no quackery, no jealousy, no fakes or frauds, would not be the necessary preliminary to a perfect morality for men. It would be a proof that the morality of men was already perfect.

—February 23, 1924

The true meaning of all this talk of psychology is simply this; that those who have failed to improve men by a mechanical method are still trying to improve them in a mechanical spirit. They still think of morality as if it were machinery. It never occurs to them to appeal to will. . . .

—February 23, 1924

In the science of psychology even illusions are facts; just as even dreams are data. And it is true in this sense that every man knows what he wants, and in that degree knows it to be worth wanting. No man was ever in love with a slut, but only with somebody whom others perceived to be a slut. And it is not even true to say that a man gets drunk in sordid surroundings, since it is the very definition of his drunkenness that they cease to be sordid.

—October 8, 1927

Everybody understands by this time, I imagine, that our age is specially the age of psychology and therefore not the age of philosophy. Or, if we prefer to put the point otherwise, it is the age of suggestion and therefore not the age of reason.

—February 13, 1932

Psychology (Child)

In this age of child-psychology nobody pays any attention to the actual psychology of a child. All that seems to matter is the psychology of the psychologist: the particular theory or train of thought that he is maintaining against another psychologist. Most of the art and literature now magnificently manufactured for children is not even honestly meant to please children. The artist would hardly condescend to make a baby laugh if nobody else laughed, or even listened. These things are not meant to please the child; at the best they are meant to please the child-lover. At the worst they are experiments in scientific educational method.

— October 15, 1921

Psychology (Introspection)

Everyone is some sort of psychologist, since everyone has some sort of psychology. Just as real religion concerns everyone born with a heart, so real philosophy concerns everyone born with a head. According to Professor James, psychology was a kind of surgery in which each man must be content to be both the operator and the patient; every man must dig up his own soul like his own garden. But it was above all in his eyes a solid study.

— September 17, 1910

Psychology (Modern Empirical)

The error is in always treating the soul as a product and never treating it as an origin.

— February 23, 1924

Psychology and Testimony

I would rather have the narrowest rules of evidence of the English law-court, which do serve as some sort of protection to the liberty of the subject, than throw the whole thing open to the license of the psychological speculator. We shall no longer be told not to testify to what the soldier said. We shall testify first to what the soldier's subconsciousness said; then to what the soldier's father-complex said; then to what his mother-complex said, and so on. And before very long, when we have gone along that road, we shall hear very distinctly what the soldier's ghost said; what the soldier's gory wraith or spectre said or shrieked or gibbered, brandishing a blood-stained bayonet and dancing in the moon. And it may be left for some of the superstitious slaves of supernaturalism, like myself, to make a last appeal for the liberties of common law and elements of common sense.

—December 31, 1921

Publican

Publicity is rather of the nature of a harmless romance.... In other words, I am concerned with pointing out that the passage from private life to public life, while it may be right or wrong ... is always of necessity a passage from a greater work to a smaller one, and from a harder work to an easier one. And that is why most of the moderns do wish to pass from the great domestic task to the smallest and easier commercial one.... They would rather take the salutes of a hundred soldiers than try to save the soul of one. They would rather serve out income-tax papers or telegraph forms to a hundred men than meals, conversation, and moral support to one. They would rather arrange the educational course in history or geography, or correct the examination papers in algebra or trigonometry, for a hundred children, than struggle with the whole human character of one. For anyone who makes himself responsible for one small baby, as a whole, will soon find that he is wrestling with gigantic angels and demons.

—August 12, 1922

Public House

It is impossible to imagine a more splendid and sacred combination of words, a more august union of simplicity and glory, than this great phrase "a public house." It expresses in one word all that is oldest and soundest and most indestructible in the idea of human society: the house where every man is master; the house where every man is guest. As we should have private ties, so we should have public ties. As we should have private prayers, so we should have public prayers. As we have private houses, so we should have public houses.

—December 9, 1905

... the only way of saving a public-house is by making it more public. If you really want to turn a public-house into something like a den of devils, then I can easily tell you what to do: turn the public-house as much as possible into a private

395

house. Any policeman will tell you, any man who knows the big cities and the small streets will tell you, that the worst places are always the most private. In the long run the best way is not to send a file of police through these places. The right way is to send a file of the public through these places. . . . Either have everybody in public-houses or have nobody in them. Either have public-houses so public that they are like cathedrals, or have them so private that they do not exist.

—December 15, 1906

If the Bishops and the great Nonconformist leaders and the wealthy philanthropists and the presidents of ethical societies and the professors of sociology, if all these important and solemn people really want to improve the public-house, perhaps upon the whole the best thing they can do is simply to go there. I have no doubt that their entry into such a place *en masse* will improve the public-house. It would also improve them.

—December 15, 1906

Public Life

. . . what is called public life is not larger than private life, but smaller. What we call public life is a fragmentary affair of sections and seasons and impressions; it is only in private life that dwells the fullness of our life bodily.

—August 12, 1922

Public School

I do not think the modern elementary school spreads enlightenment. I do not think it spreads anything—except occasionally mumps.

—January 31, 1914

Publicity

Publicity does not mean revealing public life in the interests of public spirit. It means merely flattering private enterprises in the interests of private persons. It means paying compliments in public, but not offering criticisms in public.

—June 30, 1928

Publicity must be praise and praise must to some extent be euphemism. It must put the matter in a milder and more inoffensive form than it might be put, however much that mildness may seem to shout through megaphones or flare in headlines.

—June 30, 1928

Puritan

The Puritan has become the prohibitionist, in the narrow sense of having only one thing to prohibit. In so far as he still prevails, he has concentrated the whole of his old moral indignation on the one isolated infamy of drinking a glass of beer. If the workman can still be prevented from having one glass of beer, it seems to have become a secondary matter whether he has one wife or twenty, or one child or none. We used to complain that the modern Puritan had added a Moslem commandment to the ten Christian commandments. It seem hardly to matter now whether all the Christian commandments are broken, so long as the one Moslem commandment is kept.

— September 27, 1930

. . . while [liberals] still insist that the Pilgrim Fathers were champions of religious liberty, nothing is more certain than the fact that an ordinary modern liberal, sailing with them, would have found no liberty, and would have intensely disliked almost all that he found of religion. Even Thanksgiving Day itself, though it is now kept in a most kindly and charming fashion by numbers of quite liberal and large-minded Americans, was originally intended, I believe, as a sort of iconoclastic expedient for destroying the celebration of Christmas.

—January 24, 1931

. . . the Puritan always insists not that glory is vanity, but that glory is infamy. He thinks this sort of action, this sort of ambition, not only the worst but the most horrible; he thinks there is no smell so foul as the smell of gunpowder. I think the smell of the hair-oil of hypocritical peace-mongering infinitely more offensive.

— February 7, 1931

397

Puritanism

The old theological Puritan had principles. The new enlightened Puritan has only prejudices. Puritans of the earlier type rejected the things they really loved because they thought them wicked. Puritans of the new type reject all the things they happen to hate, and then simply call them wicked.

—July 4, 1908

Pursuit of Happiness

And the whole object of real art, of real romance—and, above all, of real religion—is to prevent people from losing the humility and gratitude which are thankful for daylight and daily bread; to prevent them from regarding daily life as dull or domestic life as narrow; to teach them to feel in the sunlight the song of Apollo and in the bread the epic of the plough. What is now needed most is intensive imagination. I mean the power to turn our imagination inwards, on the things we already have, and to make those things live. It is not merely seeking new experiences, which rapidly become old experiences. It is really learning how to experience our experience. It is learning how to enjoy our enjoyments.

—September 20, 1924

Putting Back the Clock

I have heard a great deal about the impossibility of putting back the clock, especially to the Middle Ages—or, as such critics would call them, the Dark Ages. It strikes me as highly quaint that people should be so fond of this figure of speech for fantastic and impossible reaction, especially just now. For they are now regularly performing, twice a year, a mere trick with time, the second half of which does invariably consist of putting back the clock. They do it, as it happens, because they want a little more daylight, not to mention a little more sunshine. That is why I want to put the clock back to the Dark Ages.

—April 23, 1919

Q-R-S

Quack

...if we want to find quacks nowadays, we shall not find them practising medicine, but theorising about science.

—July 19, 1930

Quarrel

People generally quarrel because they cannot argue.

—March 9, 1929

Quote

I do not complain of his quoting what I said, since, however strange it may seem, I happen to agree with what I said. And, since he honoured me to excess in quoting so much, I naturally cannot complain of his not quoting more. Nevertheless, the passage by itself might be taken as part of a very different philosophy. And it is the paradox of quotation that, while the part can never be greater than the whole, it can sometimes cover and hide the whole.

—August 10, 1918

Race

... what determines the human part of human history is religion and not race ....

—September 20, 1930

Race (Chosen)

The welcome we offer to men of any belief must be in its nature different from that we offer to men of any blood. If only for the simple reason that, if a man may believe anything, he may believe in the badness of all blood except his own blood. You may associate with him and his race, simply considered as a race. But if it is a chosen race, he may not associate with you. His thoughts, whatever they are, must determine everything about his relations with you; whereas the colour of his skin may be in most relations quite irrelevant.

—August 31, 1929

Race versus Religion

A race is that which is narrower than the world, and means that we select, rightly or wrongly, one tribe from among the tribes of men. But a religion is that which is wider than the world; yes, even if it is a false religion, it is still in conception wider than the real world. Instead of selecting or subtracting from mankind, it includes the whole of mankind and a great deal more, with a few angels and devils thrown in.

—September 26, 1931

Racial Theories of Politics

It is, indeed, ludicrous to suppose that, in the chaos of falling Rome, men carefully sorted themselves out according to the shapes of their skulls: they had precious little interest in skulls except to smash them.

—May 14, 1910

Racism and the State

Settled states can respect themselves, and also respect each other; because they can claim the right to defend their own frontiers and yet not deny their duty to recognise other people's frontiers. But the racial spirit is a restless spirit; it does not go by frontiers but by the wandering of the blood. It is not so much as if France were at war with Spain; but rather as if the gypsies were more or less at war with everybody. You can have a league of nations, but you could hardly have a league of tribes. When the tribe is on the march, it is apt to forget leagues—not to mention frontiers. But my immediate interest in this flood of tribalism is that it has since poured into the empty hollows left by the slow drying-up of the great deluge of the Thirty Years' war; and that all this new and naked nationalism has come to many modern men as a substitute for their dead religion.

—February 10, 1934

Radicals versus Conservatives

A radical generally meant a man who thought he could somehow pull up the root without affecting the flower. A conservative generally meant a man who wanted to conserve everything except his own reason for conserving anything.

—July 3, 1920

Radio Broadcasting

When a [wireless] announces, "listening-in to the launching of a ship," it might just as well talk about "smelling a famous statue," or "special seats to view the taste of garlic." It is simply a comic contradiction or inversion of the five senses, not to say the five wits. To listen to the few confused and accidental noises that accompany a great visual spectacle must be about as satisfactory as shutting your eyes and smelling all the oil-paints of the Royal Academy. On the other hand . . . it is really true that broadcasting can be used to bring pleasure to those who are hampered in their ordinary movements by age and sickness; and . . . ought to be recognised as a branch of the very ancient mission of human charity. It belongs to the spirit so nobly noted in one of the oldest books in the world: "Eyes was I to the blind and feet to the lame"; and there is no man in that religious tradition who will say a word against it.

—May 7, 1927

Rationalism

Rationalism was not rationality or reason; it was, in the strict sense of the word, prejudice. But it was prejudice akin to prophecy. It was prejudiced in favour of any materialistic system that should make its appearance, even before that system had appeared. It was waiting for some theory of natural selection as millennarians are waiting for the millennium.

—December 8, 1923

Rationalists

. . . suppose a man lived in a house of mirrors so craftily constructed that he really thought he was alone on an open plain. Suppose a man lived in a church painted inside so splendidly with sky and cloud that he thought he was in the open air under the dome of heaven. He would be in the same position as the typical Rationalist. Instead of being conscious that he stands in a large church, he is simply unconscious that he stands in a small universe.

—April 30, 1910

It is not only true that Rationalists might in their writings on indifferent subjects introduce such a bias against the religious or romantic point of view; but I think it indubitable that Rationalists do. . . . They do not do it meanly or treacherously. They are so bigoted that they do it unconsciously. There is no person so narrow as the person who is sure that he is broad; indeed, being quite *sure* that one is broad is itself a form of narrowness.

—April 30, 1910

The very first use which they made of free thought was to deny the existence of free will. In other words, the very first use they made of liberty was to deny the very possibility of liberty.

—September 15, 1923

Reaction

I have already seen too many reactions to be a reactionary. One of the advantages of the passage of time is that man does learn how much of fashion there is in mere reaction.

—*June* 13, 1925

... nobody who notes the real movements in the intellectual world just now can doubt that there has been the sort of revolution that is called a reaction. In America, the very last place where most people would look for classicism, there has arisen an influential school of classicists. Those who most fiercely denounce the fact most clearly confess the fact, and even their denunciations are witness that it is a universal fact. The enemies of humanism denounce it as intellectual fascism. ... I am talking about the way the world goes round, and pointing out that the moral world does not always go round from right to left. It is, at this moment, most certainly going round from left to right.

—*March* 21, 1931

Reactionary

It would be all right if the innovators really had new ideas they had adopted recently, and the traditionalists really had old ideas that they treasured still. But the reactionary is only clinging to revolutions of which even the revolutionist is weary. He is merely a man one generation behind in the general disillusion about the last discovery.

—*April* 19, 1924

Realism

To warn a man that he will probably be killed if he defends his honour or defies his oppressor is not idealism; on the contrary, it is a sordid but solid sort of realism.

—*December* 1, 1923

Realism (Literary)

A realistic novel is written by stringing together all the tag-ends of human life—all the trains we miss, all the omnibuses we run after without catching, all the appointments that miscarry and all the invitations that are declined; all the wasted half-hours at Clapham Junction, and all the infant prodigies that grow up into stupid men; all the rainy days and all the broken engagements; all the Might-Have-Beens and all the Hardly Weres. Realism is the art of connecting everything that is in its nature disconnected. But to do this properly a man must be a great artist and rather a good liar.

—*March* 12, 1910

Realism (Socialist)

The [Bolshevist] gentleman who announces that he is going to burn Raphael (which might be mistaken at the first glance for a sort of private pogrom) really only serves to remind us of those dusty theologians of the seventeenth century who very nearly did burn Raphael. The great cartoons of Raphael were threatened by the Puritans, and only saved by a certain pagan common-sense. . . . The Bolshevist poet is welcome to have a shot at destroying museums. But he will find the museums full of the broken bits of men who wanted to destroy museums. The past is full of the fanaticism which he seems to regard as the unique and perhaps the only pleasure of the future. He may burn Raphael in the name of his morrow; but his morrow is everybody else's yesterday; and all those yesterdays have lighted fools the way to dusty death.

—*October* 4, 1919

Reality

There is a great deal to be said for rapidity; but it is not especially a good way of grasping reality. People merely going the pace, in any age, have generally missed everything except the most artificial and external costume and custom of that age. Men need to walk a little slower to look at the earth and to face the facts of nature.

—*October* 5, 1929

Reason (Age of)

The Age of Reason was in some ways an age of innocence. It had more illusions than the ages of faith.

—January 31, 1925

Rebel

... there is no sympathy, certainly no continuity, between the old rebel and the new rebel. Swinburne was just as ready to dismiss or despise Byron as all the other people of his aesthetic time and school, or rather readier than the rest. There was no sympathy between revolution and revolution, simply because there was no sympathy between fashion and fashion.... Every novelty has its own nonsense, and never sees that it is nonsense, and always sees that the older novelty was nonsense.

—October 17, 1931

Rebellion

Rebellion is as abnormal as an emetic or an amputation, and it is sometimes as wholesome. But it is only wholesome if it is an abnormality which is intended promptly and decisively to restore the normal.

—November 21, 1908

There is no excuse for any disorder which is not rebellion. It is permissible in extreme cases to smash the State; it is never permissible merely to make it work badly.

—November 21, 1908

Recollection

There are many books which we think we have read when we have not. There are, at least, many that we think we remember when we do not. An original picture, perhaps, was imprinted upon the brain, but it has changed with our own changing minds. We only remember our remembrance.

—February 26, 1910

Reductionist

He tells me that if I had watched a monkey, say, for as many years on end as did an inexhaustible French naturalist, I should see he was in some ways like a man. But that is the whole point. How long should I have to watch a man before I saw he was not a monkey? The man would have managed in the first fifteen minutes to do a whole wonderland of things that exist nowhere in the world except in him. ... Whether he put on his hat, or looked at his watch, or lit a cigarette, or sat down in a chair, or did any other ordinary action, he would be working miracles as compared with the world before he came.

—October 31, 1925

Reformers

What was the matter with most reformers hitherto was that the reformers were never contented or even concerned to reform. They were not satisfied to alter the abnormal in favour of the normal; they were much more eager to alter the normal in favour of the novel. The trick that has tripped up generation after generation of perfectly just reformers is that they were more interested in some particular new-fangled plan than they were in pointing out the old and obvious evil. The removal of every abuse of abomination was always tangled and tied hand and foot with some temporary and trumpery fad.

—October 28, 1922

... when a man comes up to me (whether in official uniform or otherwise) and, after reciting certain statistics about what he calls "alcohol," like a sort of incantation or litany, knocks my glass of claret out of my hand, I am distinctly vexed. I am more vexed when he walks into the public house opposite, where five poor men are drinking glasses of depressingly mild modern ale, and kicks over their table and robs them of their own beer. I am most vexed of all when he knocks over the beer-mugs of my poorer neighbours, but dares not, or, anyhow, does not, interfere with the claret in my cellar, merely because it costs rather more. I think that the fellow, in or out of uniform, is a vulgar fanatic whom some antics of "social reform" have legally permitted to behave like a bully and a thief.

—June 3, 1933

Relativist

There is a certain type of pragmatist or relativist or universal sceptic who, instead of imitating Job and putting his hand upon his mouth, can never for an instant cease to open his mouth, if it is only to proclaim proudly the emptiness of his mind. In the last resort, he has really nothing to say except to declare that it is not worth while to say anything. But even despair has its code of good manners, and Job ought to put his hand upon his mouth, if only to conceal a yawn.

—June 20, 1931

Relativity

If everything is moving there is really no measure of movement; and these relativist reminders are not really relative to anything.

—June 27, 1925

Relic

In the face of all reason the sceptics say that . . . relics are probably deceptive and unreal, because their adorers are superstitious. But even if they are superstitious, that is all the more reason for supposing that their relics are not unreal. The sceptics talk as if, to a Buddhist monk, one bone would be as good as another. But it is exactly because one bone is not as good as another that he troubles to have relics at all. "Are these bones really the bones of Buddha?" may be an interesting question to a scientist, but it is a practical question to a Buddhist. In such a case the devotee will be as realistic as possible; nay, he will be as sceptical as possible. The more he is fanatical, the less he will be credulous.

—September 4, 1909

Religion

Religion is the last reality of man. . . .

—December 24, 1910

Religion

What makes a real religion mystical . . . is that it claims (truly or falsely) to be hiding a beauty that is more beautiful than any that we know, or perhaps an evil that is more evil.

—February 17, 1923

. . . religion is the reality in politics. It is so much so that we can even base our own politics on somebody else's religion.

—September 29, 1928

It is no disgrace to Christianity, it is no disgrace to any great religion, that its counsels of perfection have not made every single person perfect. If after centuries a disparity is still found between its ideal and its followers, it only means that the religion still maintains the ideal, and the followers still need it.

—March 2, 1929

All art is religious, because religion includes both practice and theory, both morality and art. Religion is the sense of ultimate reality, of whatever meaning a man finds in his own existence or the existence of anything else.

—June 15, 1929

Religion (Comparative)

It is absurd to have a discussion on Comparative Religions if you don't compare them. And if the representatives of two energetic Eastern philosophies do begin to compare them, there is, of course, always the possibility that this delicate scientific analysis may be conducted with long curved knives.

—October 10, 1908

Religion (Modern)

. . . modern despotism has come out in the modern religions. If there was one thing reiterated and re-echoed in all our papers, pamphlets, and books, it was that the coming religion must be a "free religion." Whatever else it was (people said), it must avoid the old mistake of rule and regimentation, of dogmas launched from an international centre, of authority sitting on a central throne. No pope must control the preacher—no council, even; it was doubtful whether any church or congregation had the right. All the idealistic journalism of the nineteenth century . . . repeated, like a chime of bells, that the new creed must be the creed of souls set free.

—December 24, 1910

Religion is the sub-consciousness of an age. Our age has been superficially chattering about change and freedom. But sub-consciously it has believed far too much in barbaric and superstitious authority; it has worshipped strong men, it has asked for protection in everything: this can be seen in its two most genuine expressions—its novels and its new creeds.

—December 24, 1910

Religion (Negative)

. . . those who are so innocently confident of the attraction of merely negative religion might realise that a broad-minded parson can be as much of a bore about nothing as anybody can be about anything.

—October 4, 1930

Religion (Organised)

In short, all this modern cant against organised religion is a highly modern result of disorganised reason. Men have not really thought out the question of how much or how little organisation is inevitable in any corporate action, and what are its proper organs. They merely think they can sling any cant at religion, being under the highly comic delusion that it will be dead in a hundred years.

—April 12, 1930

Religion and the Modern World

The modern world was not made by its religion, but rather in spite of its religion. Religion has produced evils of its own; but the special evils which we now suffer began with its breakdown. Nor do I mean religion merely in an ideal, but strictly in a historical sense.

—July 5, 1919

Religion and Modernity

It was never allowed to be enough of a success to be properly called a failure. All the actual causes—colonial expansion, scientific warfare, industrial development, racial theories, even journalism—were all things which the modern mind has made in its reaction from the old religion. In a word, religion may bear the burden of having burnt witches or persecuted Galileo, but it is innocent of having made the industrial system of society. It has not made modernity—it has not that on its conscience. Its only spiritual justification, and its obvious social strategy, is to attack modernity. It ought to show, as it really could show, that social evils have not come from its presence, but rather from its absence.

—July 5, 1919

Religion and Politics

There are many excellent societies, organising debates as well as dances or concerts, which are careful to explain to their lecturers that they must not talk about politics or religion. What else there really is in the world to talk about, I do not know.

—March 22, 1924

Nothing of importance can be separated entirely from its social effect, which is politics, or from its ultimate value, which is religion.

—August 14, 1926

Religion and Riot

Religion and riot are very near, as the history of all religions proves. Riot means being a rotter; and religion means knowing you are a rotter.

—January 11, 1908

Religion versus Philosophy

The real difference between a religion and a mere philosophy is (among other things) this: that while only subtle people can understand the difference between one philosophy and another, quite simple people, quite stupid people (like you and me), can understand the difference between one religion and another, because it is a difference between two different things. The difference between two philosophies is like the difference between two solutions of a geometrical problem. The difference between two religions is like the difference between the smell of onions and the smell of the sea. But nobody requires to be cultured in order to distinguish one from the other. The whole practical working world bears witness to this fact, that ordinary people do not recognise a philosophy as a reality in the same way that they recognize a religion as a reality. There are real people living in real houses who will not have a Roman Catholic servant. I never heard of any people living in any houses who advertised in the newspapers that they would not have a Hegelian servant. People are really horrified if they learn that a man is an atheist; they do shrink from him morally; they almost shrink from him physically. But ordinary people do not shrink from a Hegelian: they merely pity him.

—June 8, 1907

Religions (Great)

The great religions, as distinct from mere mythologies on the one hand and mere philosophies on the other, have a certain fundamental claim. The religions are revelations; that is, they add, or claim to add, something to the sum of things. They utter truths that are not truisms. They at least utter something that we commonly call *ideas.* And there is all the difference in the world between the really creative, constructive, organic things we call ideas, and the weak, washy, wordy things that we commonly call ideals.

—August 9, 1930

Religions (Modern)

... the new philosophies and new religions and new social systems cannot draw up their own plans for emancipating what they regard as the most ordinary reforms without instantly imposing the most extraordinary restrictions. We are to live under a sort of martial law lest we should hear of anything martial. All our children are to be watched by the grimmest of all governesses lest they should be told, even by accident, of a fairy or a fight with robbers. Everybody is to be drilled

411

with an anti-militarist discipline which is quite as stiff and strict as a militarist discipline. All the nursery stories are to be subject to a censor, who shall object if they are too pretty, as the very dullest sort of Victorian or Philistine censor would object if they were too ugly. . . . The new religion, every bit as much as the old religion, will be a persecuting religion. It will be, by its very nature, a thing fighting for its life against the normal forces of human nature; every bit as much as has been alleged of any system of asceticism or self-denial in the past.

—March 11, 1933

Religions (Respect of All)

We do not (at least, I do not) respect any sect, church, or group because of its sincerity. Sincerity merely means actuality. It only means that a man's opinion undoubtedly is his opinion. But if a man's opinion is that he ought to burn dogs alive, I do not respect him because he really feels like that; on the contrary, I should respect him more if I could believe that it was an elegant affectation. . . . I do not respect him any more because he holds it firmly; I should much prefer that he should hold it lightly. I do not think the more of a devil-worshipper because he truly loves devilry. . . . The true doctrine surely is this—that we respect the creeds held by others because there is some good in them, not because they are creeds and are held. In other words, an honest man must always respect other religions, because they contain parts of his religion—that is, of his largest vision of truth.

—October 29, 1910

Religious Festival

This is why religion always insists on special days like Christmas, while philosophy always tends to despise them. Religion is interested not in whether a man is happy, but whether he is still alive, whether he can still react in a normal way to new things, whether he blinks in a blinding light or laughs when he is tickled. That is the best of Christmas, that it is a startling and disturbing happiness; it is an uncomfortable comfort. The Christmas customs destroy the human habits. And while customs are generally unselfish, habits are nearly always selfish. The object of the religious festival is, as I have said, to find out if a happy man is still alive. A man can smile when he is dead. Composure, resignation, and the most exquisite good manners are, so to speak, the strong points of corpses. There is only one way in which you can test his real vitality, and that is by a special festival. Explode crackers in his ear, and see if he jumps. Prick him with holly, and see if he feels it. If not, he is dead, or, as he would put it, is "living the higher life."

—January 11, 1908

Religious Mysteries

The way in which religious mysteries are mixed with merry-making is very shocking to some people—especially. . . . to the people who do not believe in the religious mysteries. Sceptics are so very sensitive on the point of reverence. . . . I could not but smile at the thought of those who have again been trying to prove to me that religion has no function but to make men sad. Those who gradually built up the ancient customs of mankind had a better sense of proportion and decoration. They knew, if only by instinct, how things grave and gay can be combined and distributed, and where flippancy is fitting and where solemnity fits in with it; what contrast will best bring out a real severity, and what is the psychological meaning of that profound phrase "comic relief". . . .

—June 19, 1926

Renaissance Era (The End of)

. . . we have come to an end of that cycle which began with the Renaissance, and which might perhaps be called the romance of rational curiosity. The discoveries will doubtless go on; but they will not really be adding anything to the mind. They will only be bringing something to the eye or the ear. They will not exactly fulfil the implied definition of Bacon at the beginning of the modern movement; they will not be concerned *de augmentis*. It may be that the time has come once more for another kind of curiosity, such as the Greek philosophers felt in their little cities, or the mediaeval mystics in their little cells. Perhaps the time has come for the other sort of pilgrimage; the inward rather than the outward journey. Or perhaps for that tale of travel through the spiritual world, which showed us Ulysses and Aeneas passing through the world of wailing shadows, or Dante walking among the dead.

— September 11, 1926

Repetition

It is an absolutely essential quality in a propagandist. . . . Those who have nothing to say may say it a million times and in a million forms.

—April 11, 1925

Repetition and Reality

As an objective fact, the hundredth blade of grass is as green as the first blade of grass. The hundredth sunbeam is as bright as the first sunbeam. And the hundredth child murdered by King Herod is as pathetic as the first. King Herod may have come to the end of his pleasure; but the mother has not come to the end of her pain. And her pain is a plain fact of nature, absolutely radical and realistic; as solid as a lump of rock. It has every quality of stone—antiquity, universality, simplicity, permanence. And a stone is not any the less a stone because it is not the only pebble on the beach.

—August 20, 1927

Reporters

The man who reports a criminal trial in a modern newspaper seems to have only three quite clear and definite objects. First, in all cases, he desires to conceal the name of the crime. Second, in aristocratic cases he desires to conceal the name of the criminal. And third, in all cases political, religious, or in any way important he desires to conceal the whole course of the argument.

—February 1, 1908

These writers take some painful and delicate matter—such as the limits of exposure in statuary or in dancing—and they talk of it for columns and columns with a sort of sombre allusiveness which is really nothing more or less than an infinite license of libel. An honest man (one would think) would either avoid the subject or tell the truth.

—July 18, 1908

. . . the Man on the Spot is almost always wrong, for he hears only the most intemperate and fantastic accusations from one side, and that without understanding the local and traditional senses of the words, the allowance to be made for atmosphere, the proportion of ritual, or the personal equation of anger.... But the Man on the Spot sees everything spotty: for him all the mud that is thrown sticks.

—April 2, 1910

Representative (Elected)

If a man represents two men, it is obvious that he ought to walk like a quadruped. When he represents a hundred, it is not surprising that he walks like a centipede.

—November 20, 1909

Honestly, I think the priests were nearer to Heaven than the politicians are to England. The common curate may at least be trying to be like the divine ideal, whereas I am sure that the statesman is not even trying to be like his cabman. Yet this is what representative government implies, or ought to imply. It ought to mean men striving to express the mystery of democracy, as priesthoods try to express the mystery of deity. If a man has been elected by a million voters, he ought to walk at once powerfully and doubtfully, as if he were a million men.... If the thought makes him walk a little more heavily and with a slight slouch, so much the better. He is all the more a representative.

—November 20, 1909

Republic

It has long been the custom to sneer at the small republics of America, for reasons that would equally justify us in sneering at the small republics of antiquity. If a state is to be despised for having narrow borders, fierce battles, and frequent revolutions, we can all take our pleasure in despising the Athens of Pericles or the Rome of Regulus; not to mention the Florence of Dante or the Assisi of St. Francis. There are very real evils in the close wrestle of intensive ideals and insane rivalries that tear each other to pieces in such a narrow space; but they are not the only evils in the world.

—March 28, 1931

Revolt

Everybody says that each generation revolts against the last. Nobody seems to notice that it generally revolts against the revolt of the last. I mean that the latest grievance is really the last reform.

—July 29, 1922

Revolution

It is often said nowadays that in great crises and moral revolutions we need one strong man to decide; but it seems to me that that is exactly when we do not need him. We do not need a great man for a revolution, for a true revolution is a time when all men are great.

—October 8, 1910

For in a revolution all men become theorists; because custom has broken down. There can never be a rebellion against dogma; for a return to dogma must always follow the destruction of routine.

—October 15, 1910

Revolution may be a good deed, but it is a bad habit.

—July 21, 1923

Every revolution is a revival.

—October 4, 1924

... practically all revolutions in human history have consisted entirely of turning back.

—April 11, 1925

When the heavenly kingdom becomes an earthly paradise, it sometimes tends to be a hell upon earth. But it sometimes tends to be what is even worse, or at least weaker—a very earthy imitation of the earth. So long as revolution is a failure, we all feel that it holds the promise of success. It is when it is a success that it is so often a failure.

—*June* 16, 1928

... there is no tradition in revolutions; every revolution is a revolution against the last revolution.

—*June* 10, 1933

Revolution (Modern)

The danger of our society is not so much an external revolution as an internal revolution with an external continuity. It is that we may continue to take our hats off to ladies, when we have avowedly abandoned all belief in chivalry; or that we may continue to take our hats off in church when we have avowedly abandoned all belief in churches. In short, the danger is that change may eat out the heart of conviction and leave the shell of convention.

—*November* 27, 1920

Revolutionist

There are two kinds of revolutionists, as of most things—a good kind and a bad. The bad revolutionists destroy conventions by appealing to fads—fashions that are newer than conventions. The good do it by appealing to facts that are older than conventions.

—*April* 30, 1910

All revolutionists are reactionaries; or rather, perhaps, resurrectionists. The only difference is that the most advanced dig up the dead; while the more moderate merely release those that are buried alive. In other words, both the traditionalist and the anti-traditionalist are living by old traditions; but the latter lives by a tradition that is lost. The futurist is so called because of the exceedingly remote past to which he would return. He professes to draw like primitive man instead of primitive mediaeval painters. But mediaeval art is still living art; men still copy its

417

crafts and worship in its cathedrals. Prehistoric art is just old enough to be dead; therefore it is just dead enough to be new.

—*September* 20, 1919

Revolutionist (Old)

Now the old revolutionist, of the early days of Shaw and Wells...discussed different subjects; but he did not apply a different philosophy to each. There was a body, a personality, a whole point of view that was Bernard Shaw; another that was Wells; another that was William Morris; another that was Karl Marx. But it seems to me that the more modern mind is breaking up; sometimes into brilliant fragments; sometimes into merely brittle and futile fragments.

—*August* 29, 1931

Rhetoric

...when people talk about "mere rhetoric" as if it were something artificial, ask them why there always has been rhetoric at very real moments of politics, why there has always been rhetoric when there were bullets and blood.

—*March* 19, 1910

Since the world has discarded rhetoric as something false, it has lost the only natural expression of anything that is true.

—*April* 19, 1930

The Rich

The striking and even startling peculiarity of the present...is the fact that the rich wield a quite new and abnormal power that was never known in the world before. I should say that no rich man in the past ever had anything like the power over humanity possessed by a millionaire or financier to-day. He often had local powers of a more violent or ferocious kind. In old days he could sometimes scourge men to death, where he can now only starve them to death.... But that has nothing to do with the scope and scale of power;

that is simply a difference of ruder manners to be found in any incident on any scale.

— May 29, 1926

I need not add that the rich ruler of today has another new power which he values most of all; the power of remaining nameless. He has the gift of being invisible, or, in other words, irresponsible. The crimes of the Earl of Chester could not be hidden from the people of Chester. But we only see financial conspiracies in their vast, yet often vague, effects, not in their invisible causes.

— May 29, 1926

Rings

When a woman wears rings for pleasure or personal show, the rings are infinitely complicated, they are twisted like serpentine arabesques, they are loaded with complex and often incongruous jewellery. The one ring that a woman wears as a part of a public ceremony is her wedding-ring, which is quite plain. It is quite plain because it is the tendency of all high public ceremony to keep the ring a mere ring, as it keeps the Cross a mere Cross. The one ring that is perfectly simple is the ring that is entirely ritualistic.

— April 14, 1906

The Ridiculous versus the Wise

It is one of the journalist's tragedies that whenever he introduces a thing purely as an impossibility, somebody writes to say that it really occurred. If I use a foolish metaphor at random I generally receive two letters — one complaining that the thing is too violent and absurd, the other saying that it happened to the writer's aunt. My wild phrases are quite tame; they have been domesticated for centuries. This is pathetic and sometimes almost disheartening. Suppose I say (as I most certainly do say), "The statement that wine is wicked is to me exactly as unmeaning as the statement that linoleum is wicked." I suppose that I have made a flippant but at least a clear and emphatic statement of my views; and I go to bed. Next morning I receive a letter from the secretary of the "Young Saints' Anti-Linoleum League," regretting my sneer at the great moral movement which has arisen to destroy a deleterious and unnecessary fabric. Suppose I say (as I think I did say) "To wear an eyeglass in one eye seems to me as ridiculous as to wear a boot on one

419

leg." What is the consequence? The consequence is that "Lady Maudie" in "Bond Street Gossip" says that if I were really acquainted with the latest things and the best people, I should know that our smartly dressed men, this season, *are* wearing a boot on one leg. . . . However wild I make my fictitious examples, the truth is always wilder. It does not seem possible to keep up with the exuberant idiocy of things as they really are to-day. Whatever occurs to me as ridiculous has always occurred to somebody else as wise.

—September 22, 1906

Ritual

Ritualism is more natural than rationalism about these things. It is a living necessity for those who survive; sometimes almost a necessity to enable them to survive. It is almost the first gesture of awakening, by which they show that they have not also been struck by the thunderbolt. Funeral ceremonies are not a tribute to the dead, but to the living.

—December 5, 1925

Ritualism

The only way to stop an ornament becoming infinitely extravagant is to make it mean something. If the Cross, for instance, had no religious meaning, the Cross by this time would have ten arms like a tree. Because it keeps its intellectual meaning, it keeps its simple form. The one effect of what is called Ritualism is to keep human ritual within bounds.

—April 14, 1906

Rockefeller, John D.

If I die worth millions (which again is only a hypothesis) and leave a huge legacy of pots of beer to all the people in workhouses—for that is the form of charity I should choose—then my motives might be considered to be my own affair. . . . But in the case of Rockefeller the motive is relevant, because his philanthropy is . . . offered as a defence or expiation of his alleged commercial methods. If we are to set that philanthropy as a virtue over against his vices, then we have a right to ask if it is really virtuous. The question is about his morality; the question is whether he got his millions by tyranny or fraud; whereas if I died worth millions, it would be quite self-evident that I could only have got them by mistake.

—May 29, 1909

Some men cross Europe to kiss the Pope's toe, and I would willingly cross America to tread on Mr. Rockefeller's toe.

—April 16, 1910

Road to Hell

It is an admirable thing to be humble; and it is often a pardonable though always a perilous thing to be proud. It is always a far stronger and healthier thing to be vain than to be proud. But in any case it is a dreadful and diabolical thing to be proud of being humble. That is, I suppose, the last of the temptations which the demons offer to the saints; the last and the most subtle and therefore the most evil. Perhaps that was what Bunyan really meant when he said that he saw there was a road to hell even from the gates of heaven, as well as from the city of destruction.

—March 28, 1925

Romance

Romance is more solid than realism, and that for a very evident reason. The things that men happen to get in this life depend upon quite shifting accidents and conditions. But the things that they desire and dream of are always the same.

—March 17, 1906

Practically all old romances were built upon a plan of promise or obligation; there was a vow, or there was a quest, or there was, at any rate, a test. . . . For the basis of all such stories was, broadly speaking, that there was a king who sent forth a knight to fight something or find something or rescue something; and by the royal judgment his conduct was ultimately to be judged. And this is, in my judgment, an extremely realistic story, and exceedingly like life.

—April 18, 1931

Romance, in its healthiest sense, is as old as the world; and even in a more special sense it is inspired by that particular intensity of colouring and pointed energy of outline which belonged to the shields, the windows, and the pennons of mediaevalism. Mediaeval romance, which was a sort of pattern for modern romance, came from the vividness of visionary or spiritual experience leaving a sort of glamour or glory around all experience. But it did throw that coloured light especially on the experience of love, and, in some sense, modelled romance on religion; as Chaucer called the legendary lovers the saints of Cupid. In that sense we may say that romance belonged to the Middle Ages; and in a deeper sense that it belonged to any ages.

—*August 27,* 1932

Romanticism

Briefly, I have always meant by romance something that may be stated thus. The belief that the simplified and symbolic version of life, which depicts it, under the image of love and war, as a quest with a prize (especially a princess), is nevertheless a true version of life; that is an enlightening symbol and a legitimate simplification. St. George must kill the dragon, or the dragon will kill the princess; that seems to me a truer picture of the aim of life and the lot of man than any realistic novel. That may fairly be called romanticism.

—*April* 18, 1931

Rome

... the whole foundation of our civilisation is as Roman as its framework of the Roman roads. All modern road-making, for instance, is on a Latin and not a Teutonic pattern. It is a popular proverb that all roads lead to Rome. It is historic and literal fact that all roads come from Rome.

—*March* 22, 1919

Everything was done to take away the Roman character from Rome. The emperor was taken away, but the pope remained. The pope was taken away, but the pope returned. The former could not make a new Rome at Byzantium. The latter could not make a new Rome at Avignon. The former experiment had behind it the great civilisation of the Greeks; the latter had behind it the great civilisation of the French. The Greek emperors thought they could move it easily to the East, and the

422

French kings that they could move it easily to the West. But Rome, especially Christian Rome, is a rock not easily to be moved.

—January 11, 1930

Rousseau, Jean Jacques

Few would picture Rousseau as the manager of a big bank or the controller of a chain-store. But the full theory of freedom did tend to be thinned out into a thin theory of free trade which began to span the world like a spider's web. And the chain-stores do suggest a sort of parody of the very words of Rousseau, for modern democracy was born free, and everywhere it is in chains.

—April 11, 1936

Routine

That is the whole meaning of industrialism, individualism, progress, hustle, and hundred-percent efficiency. That is the meaning of Pittsburg and Chicago, of the skyscrapers and the quick lunches. They want to see wheels go round, more and more wheels go round, larger and larger wheels go round, wheels that go round, faster and faster.... It is the nature of a wheel going round to come back to the same place.

—August 2, 1924

Russian

The element in the Russian character, in which it is most remote from ours, is but roughly symbolised by saying that a Russian is hypothetically always a revolutionist.

—July 21, 1917

Russian Revolution

There was certainly treason in the rapid and quite irrational rot that corrupted the Russian Revolution—the treason of a small minority doubtless, but it is the very definition of such modern and sham democracy that the small minority always rules. What is most needed now is a living impatience, and even a sort of savage laughter, against the thought of all our mountainous labours being undone by a rat or a worm.

—*November* 10, 1917

Men talk of a counter-revolution in Russia; but they forget that the Russian revolution was itself a counter-revolution in Europe.

—*August* 24, 1918

We must all be very much in the dark about what is going to happen in Petrograd. But then, we are all very much in the dark about what has happened in Petrograd for the last five years—possibly for the last two hundred years, or ever since there was such a place.

—*November* 1, 1919

As the Prussians were cowed by militarism, so the Russians were cowed by mentalism, or what the French call intellectualism. It was a minority of this type, a group of bookish Bolshevists, who seized supreme power at the end of the Russian revolution, and attempted to impose upon their brethren all that they had read in their books. They had read that property was theft, that proletarians and bourgeoisie were the two real rivals for the control of the world, that all good was to be found in sharing and none in owning, or even in giving.

—*December* 20, 1919

[There is] the old view that communism is a utopia too good for this world; that it is something very beautiful and ideal which unfortunately cannot happen. As a fact, it is something very real and ugly that did happen. It is not, as the anti-socialists used to say, a thing that may or may not come in thousands of years, when the world is sufficiently good. It is a thing that may come quite suddenly, because the world is quite sufficiently bad. But they do not know why it can come suddenly. They do not know what is bad.

—*January* 17, 1925

Russian Revolution and the Ukraine

And as Lenin goes on to talk about the "bitterness" of civil war in the Ukraine, where the instinct of property in the peasantry will further "modify" his policy, I imagine it will be modified with something even bigger than a stick. It is more likely to be "considerably whittled away" with a big sabre.

—September 6, 1919

Rustic

The rustic is externally stiff with conventions. A ponderous politeness marks all his words and gestures; he recites ritual phrases about beer and the weather; he expects people to keep their places, gentlemen to be gentlemen, parsons to be parsons, ladies to smile, and poachers to poach. He does not really take himself seriously; for Christianity is sunk somewhere out of sight in his soul. He will openly exhibit himself as the village drunkard or even the village idiot; he will tell old tales of fights in which he was beaten, of dreams or bets that did not come true. His soul sings like one little ribald bird in an ivy-covered castle of custom.

—July 23, 1910

Rustic versus Bourgeois

There never were two sets of people more unfit to understand each other than the yokel and the clerk. And all over two or three counties round London yokels and clerks are mixed and jostled together; often sown alternately, like peas and beans in a field. Perhaps one might say like tares and wheat in a field, for the only quite obvious solution is to wait till the harvest and bind the tares into bundles and burn them. But I have not affirmed which are the tares.

—July 23, 1910

... there is not one word that one can say which the other will not certainly mistake; there is not one virtue that either can exhibit which the other will not revile as a vice; they will both offend each other.

—July 23, 1910

Sacrifice

...a very common mistake is made by our modern sceptic in the matter of the phrase "self-sacrifice." Men of the school of Nietzsche or of Mr. Bernard Shaw often talk of self-sacrifice as if it meant the same as self-subordination or self-effacement. To sacrifice a thing is the Latin for making a thing holy. If you sacrifice yourself you make yourself something solemn and important. The old Pagan did not sacrifice his worst beast; he sacrificed his best beast to his gods. He paid it a compliment—with a hatchet. It would be an awful and stimulating thought to imagine this process of selection applied, for instance, to the human fauna of London. It is beautiful to think of the honest cabman being solemnly immolated because of his worthiness, and then of the stockbroker being splendidly and scornfully spared. But in any case, self-sacrifice is for this reason the opposite of self-effacement; and for this reason self-sacrifice is the very opposite of suicide. If you really think yourself a worm you have no right to practise self-sacrifice. Worms (unlike cabmen) are not creatures fit for the altar.

—July 21, 1906

Salesman

The perfect scientist persuades a man that he hasn't got what he has got. The perfect salesman persuades a man that he does want what he doesn't want.

—August 30, 1930

Salt

But salt is not a *pièce de résistance.* It is a corrective. It is the priest, not the man. The meaning of salt is that there exists something which we cannot live on, but cannot live without.

—October 23, 1915

I have always wondered why there is no new religion forbidding the use of salt....

—February 21, 1931

Salvation (Social versus Individual)

... those who talk at large about the unfit do not know that they are arguing on the old simple pagan principle against the old and more subtle Christian principle. What I complain of is that they cannot realise that they are up against another code and creed, which holds that we must not wrong a man, even if he is one man. Very soon, there will be no dispute, for the disputants will be too distant from each other. One man will be left repeating foggily that he represents science, and that the other man only represents sentiment. You cannot settle any moral question in that sort of fog. It is just as much a sentiment to desire social salvation as to desire individual salvation. And science is merely the name of a tool, which could be used equally for either purpose; for saving an individual or saving a society, or blowing a society to hell with dynamite and poison gas.

—November 4, 1933

Satire

... people seem to see everything about a satire except its direction. They recognise the cap and bells, but they never know whom the cap fits.

—April 18, 1925

Modern society is far too much of a burlesque to be burlesqued. The world we know is far too wild a place for satirists to live in. They are perpetually seeing their satires fulfilled like prophecies, and what they meant to be impossible become not only possible but palpable.

—May 2, 1925

Satirists (Modern)

The modern satire is full of one sort of curious certainty: that existing society is insanity. I incline to agree; and perhaps it is rude to reply that the modern satirist himself has doubts about his own sanity. Anyhow, he has doubts about his own definition of sanity. The longer he looks at the modern world, the fewer and fewer people he seems really to think sane. It is an old joke that the satirist should end up by saying that he is the only sane man in the world. But I am not sure that the modern satirist will end up with any very complete confidence even about that. At the best, his ideal solution will be something so eccentric and esoteric and

427

abstruse that the balance will be left rather doubtful between the satirist and the thing satirised. There will be no body of common sense to decide which of the two is really uncommon nonsense. There will be no public opinion, but only a chaos of private opinions.

—February 29, 1936

Savage

We must remember that what savages say can only be a very crude and rudimentary version of what savages think. Their words are few, as is the case with decayed as well as undeveloped peoples; and for the same reason the very act of speaking probably has about it something stiff and unnatural. In any case, they are either trying to speak our language, or we to understand theirs. It is hopeless to expect a Red Indian really to tell us what he means by the great spirit in terms of our own distinction between a ghost and a god, a creator and a demon....But by all analogy we may assume that he means something much more deep and delicate than he says. Savages may or may not be primitive men, but at any rate they are men.

—January 26, 1924

Sceptic

...[his] faith is something contrary to reason, but not superior to it. He merely denies what he cannot destroy. The modern sceptic makes a claim upon credulity more wild and sentimental than was ever made either by the meekest or the maddest theologian. He does not merely ask us to believe in the invisible; he asks us to disbelieve in the visible.

—January 15, 1910

The vague sceptic bred in the modern towns goes wrong in a peculiar way. He is often a sceptic because he is not a realist. He thinks a thing must be a fancy and not a fact precisely because his own vision of the fact is really a fancy. He thinks he is superior to a belief in it, when he is really only ignorant of the evidence for it.

—March 14, 1914

. . . a sceptic is often described as a man relying on his reason. But the real sceptic is the man who will not rely on his reason. The complete sceptic is the man who is as sceptical of reason as of everything else. Some old-fashioned parson might say that the Bible was being questioned by sceptics and rationalists. But nowadays it is the rationalist who is being questioned by the sceptic.

—May 28, 1927

By the sceptic I do not mean the agnostic. . . . I mean the man who is intellectually impatient, and will not listen at all to the low and vague murmur of mankind. He prides himself on being hard-headed; and it is quite true that he is hard of hearing. He actually praises the hardness of his head because it keeps out common-sense, the common atmosphere in which common people have lived and died, and where, if anywhere, their ghosts will return.

—January 12, 1929

The first questions asked by the sceptic sometimes have an air of intelligence; but if the sceptic has no answer, or only a negative answer, the silence that follows soon becomes the very negation of intelligence.

—February 22, 1930

. . . what are we to say of the superior philosophical sceptic, who can only begin the controversy by calling the other controversialists a fool, and in the same moment end the controversy because he need not controvert with fools?

—May 17, 1930

The man who says twenty times a day, or writes in ten different newspapers, always in the same words, that intelligent people can no longer accept The Creed, has quite as little basis either in theory or experience. He not only does not know why it should be so, but he does in fact know that it is not so.

—May 17, 1930

Scepticism

... there is in modern discussions of religion and philosophy an absurd assumption that a man is in some way just and well-poised because he has come to no conclusion; and that a man is in some way knocked off the list of fair judges because he has come to a conclusion. It is assumed that the sceptic has no bias; whereas he has a very obvious bias in favour of scepticism.

—May 4, 1907

Modern scepticism ... is simply a reaction, a turning back. The modern sceptic starts from the twenty-fifth proposition of Euclid and hacks his way back to the axioms. The whole modern adventure is to break one's way past forests and mountain ranges till one finds the way back to the infant-school. As soon as a man feels that he has got anywhere near the end, he begins to know that he must go back to the beginning. A man passes all the most terrible truths before he finds the truisms.

—October 16, 1909

Scepticism can be not only as metaphysical, but fully as mystical, as belief. Only the period is over, during which the case was complicated by a clockwork theory of the cosmos, for that clock has stopped for ever.

—January 3, 1931

Scepticism (Age of)

A man like Voltaire happened to begin asking questions at a moment when men had forgotten how to answer them.... I know of no question that Voltaire asked which St. Thomas Aquinas did not ask before him. Only St. Thomas not only asked, but answered the question. When the question merely hung unanswered in the air, in a restless, worldly, and uncontemplative age, there came to be a vague association between wit and that sort of sneering inquiry.

—February 22, 1930

Scepticism (Modern)

...there is not only doubt about mystical things; not even only about moral things. There is most doubt of all about rational things. I do not mean that I feel these doubts, either rational or mystical; but I mean that a sufficient number of modern people feel them to make unanimity an absurd assumption. Reason was self-evident before pragmatism. Mathematics were self-evident before Einstein. But this scepticism is throwing thousands into a condition of doubt, not about occult but about obvious things. We shall soon be in a world in which a man may be howled down for saying that two and two make four . . . in which people will persecute the heresy of calling a triangle a three-sided figure, and hang a man for maddening a mob with the news that grass is green.

—August 14, 1926

Scholars

...specialist works about the holes and corners of history . . . are almost secrets. The only man who could have criticised the book has been employed to write it. We talk of people who live by taking in each other's washing; but the eminent archaeologists of Europe must surely live by taking in each other's monographs!

—November 19, 1910

Often they never hear the songs, because they are sung in public-houses. Often they never hear of the arts and crafts, because they are not recorded in books. This sort of instruction is indeed ignorance; but it is ignorance in arms, ignorance militant and triumphant, ignorance advancing with all its armies across a conquered land.

—November 6, 1920

They had not the disinterestedness or detachment of gossip. They were not merely mentioning the things they remembered, but remembering only the things they were supposed to mention. Their minds had formed a mechanical habit of recording only the things that were suited to the records, and writing only the records that were suited to the official record office. Some of them were stark liars; some of them, which is much more strange and uncanny, were honest men.

—February 14, 1931

431

Scholars and Guessing

I have often thought there might be a place for intelligent guesswork which admits that it is guesswork.... In the case of history and similar sciences, it might be possible to draw up a rich and flattering analogy to the turf. The Dons of Oxford and Cambridge, the professors and professional historians, who are often, indeed, bookmakers, may be compared to bookies. The dream or fancy thrown out by the mere literary amateur may be compared to the dark horse in the very loose box of his light and irresponsible brain. But the dark horse always gives him a good run for his money. And it is justified, so long as it does not run away with the whole of his money; that is, with the whole of his serious reputation and peace of mind.

—July 2, 1932

Scholarship and Society

... real historical scholarship was Anti-Teutonic even just before the war. Only it was not the mode in Victorian society, nor (I will add) the Victorian court. Therefore, a mere picturesque amateur like Kingsley was made a professor, while a historical student like Belloc would still only be treated as a picturesque amateur.

—June 21, 1919

School

A queer and almost fantastic expression is used about a certain sort of girls' school; it is called a finishing school. But all our schools are finishing schools. They finish what has never begun.

—June 2, 1928

Schoolmaster

Not only does a schoolmaster not exist to teach mere facts, but he exists to prevent people from learning mere facts, to insist on their learning what the facts mean; to insist, that is, on their learning the ideas.

— September 12, 1908

School Sports

Nobody can prove positively . . . whether the strategical excitement of organised games is great enough to outweigh the loss of personal self-determination and adventure. . . . In modern schools for instance, what is called playtime has become a sort of extended work-time, though both have probably been turned into rather more pleasant work. But none of it is so pleasant as playing alone to the sort of child who likes playing alone. Some of it is acutely and painfully unpleasant to that sort of child. Since education permitted more play, it has perhaps permitted less leisure . . . and certainly less liberty.

—July 23, 1927

Science

Science invents conveniences by design and inconveniences by accident.

—September 25, 1909

Physical science is always one of two things; it is either a tool or a toy. At its highest and noblest, of course, it is a toy. A toy is a thing of far greater philosophical grandeur than a tool; for the very simple reason that a toy is valued for itself and a tool only for something else. A tool is a means, a toy is an end. . . . When science tells me that there is a house in Ealing that I can communicate with, I am interested; when science says there is a star in Sirius I cannot communicate with, I am amused. But in neither case can science be anything else except a tool or a toy. It can never be the man using the tool. It can never be the child playing with the toy. It can never, in short, be the thing that has natural authority over toy and tool.

—October 9, 1909

The rationalists of the Renaissance were almost as rapid in inventing poisons as the rationalists of the nineteenth century were in inventing medicines; and some say that the effect of both is much the same.

—August 20, 1910

The truth is that science would be all very well if it could be confined to scientists. But the shadow of science is much darker than science itself; and, what is worse, it is much larger than science itself. The serious students of these subjects adopt

433

hypotheses which they know to be hypotheses—that is to say, guesses. But the best thing about the serious students is that they do not take them quite so seriously. But it is a horrible calamity that crowds of outsiders should get hold of the suggestion when it is half-made—or, worse still, when it is already unmade. For the public does not so much snatch at what science has suggested as pick up what science has actually thrown away. In short, there is truth in what Tennyson said about science—that she should know her place.

—January 10, 1920

The mere word "science" is already used as a sacred and mystical word in many matters of politics and ethics. It is already used vaguely to threaten the most vital traditions of civilisation—the family and the freedom of the citizen. It may at any moment attempt to establish some unnatural utopia full of fugitive negations. But it will not be the science of the scientist, but rather the science of the sensational novelist. It will not even be the dry bones of any complete and connected skeleton of pithecanthropus. Rather it will be the mere rumours of fashionable fiction that will be fixed into a new tyranny; and the lost little finger of the missing link will be thicker than the loins of kings.

—October 9, 1920

The truth is that any advance in science leaves morality in its ancient balance; and it depends still on the inscrutable soul of man whether any discovery is mainly a benefit or mainly a calamity. This is, perhaps, the strongest argument for a morality superior to materialism, and a religion that refuses to be bullied by science. Moral progress must still be made morally; and a modern scientist who has invented the most complex mechanism, or liberated the most subtle gas, has still exactly the same spiritual problem before him as that which confronted Cain, when he stood with a ragged stone in his hand.

—April 1, 1922

Unfortunately science is only splendid while it is science. When science becomes religion it becomes superstition.

—April 8, 1922

... there are far more tiles loose on the hall of science than on the parish church, or even the revivalist's chapel.

—*March* 8, 1924

Science has plenty more blunders before her in her brilliant future.

—*July* 5, 1924

Science is ever moving onward; and we may end up on a flat earth for all I know.

—*May* 30, 1925

There were, indeed, venerable Victorians, of the agnostic sort, who would have been very much surprised to learn that science had not destroyed religion by A.D. 2030. But they would have been still more surprised to learn that science had destroyed the indivisible atom, had broken through the conservation of energy, had cast doubts on the principles of Newton and reacted everywhere against the hypothesis of Darwin. Science is perfectly right to go on changing its mind if it sees reason to do so.

—*April* 12, 1930

If we were only allowed to accept scientific suggestions as jokes, we could sometimes get some serious good out of them.

—*July* 5, 1930

The new scientific theory never does really deny the old religious theory. What it does do is to deny—or, rather, destroy—the old scientific theory. And it was precisely in the name of that old theory that religion was once to have been destroyed. The heretics never attack orthodoxy; the heretics only avenge orthodoxy on each other.

—*July* 5, 1930

Science (Humility of)

The star-gazing mathematician, when he allows for the personal equation, allows for it in his own person, not in some other person living down the road, still less in

435

dead people living long ago, least of all in the very people or things that he is studying. . . . That is what is called the humility of science; and it is an admirable thing when you can get it. In many departments you really do get it; but you do not get it enough in the department of history.

—August 15, 1925

Science (Modern)

An American astronomer has made a suggestion, apparently unsupported, that the world will soon come to an end. But most other men of science talk rather as if it had already come to an end. They are walking about, waving their hands, as if the sun and moon had tumbled from the sky, because of the discovery of a Teutonic professor. It will be well to remember that the world which has come to an end is a world which only very recently had a beginning. It is not the objective world of trees and lamp-posts, but their own theoretic world of certain abstractions about life and light.

—December 13, 1919

To-day the scientific temper is scientific doubt. It is not, as it was, scientific doubt of religion. It is scientific doubt of science. The whole thing is working backwards and destroying itself; and so far as one can guess it will end in that more or less mystical ignorance, in which all the myths arose. The night returns—and the dreams.

—July 3, 1920

Science (Monument for)

Why should we erect a temple to stand even two hundred years if all our conceptions of science and philosophy will be quite different in twenty years?

—April 18, 1925

Science (Sham)

The art of heraldry degenerated because it was turned from a real art to a sham science. A good many modern arts seem to be going the same way. The art of fiction, for instance, seems to be turning from the reality of romance to the affectation of psychology or psycho-analysis. As the heralds cut their lions and

436

eagles in half to fit in with the father's quarterings, or the mother's pales and partitions, so the new psychological novelists are cutting up their human beings into father-complexes and mother-complexes, till they resemble heraldic figures of which only a leg or arm remains in a tangle of bends and chevrons. In both cases the result is a diagram instead of a drawing; and in both cases the spirit is pedantry instead of poetry.

—January 1, 1921

Science (Symbol for)

I can suggest a great many symbols for the vague evolutionary faith and hope which would be much more appropriate. Thus, if I wanted to commemorate the finality and conclusiveness of science, the security with which we can all repose in her conclusions, I should select a weather-cock. If I wished to suggest the firmness with which it can put its foot down in moral matters, I should select a snake.... The essential of the symbol must be that it must be different every day.

—February 21, 1925

Science and Authority

... the speakers stressed Professor Einstein's statement that "If you can get two per cent. of the population to assert in times of peace that they will not fight, you can end war." ... And though these people are not accepting relativity by reason, but blindly and submissively by mere authority, at least they are accepting their pope in a matter on which he is an authority. And then they suddenly let go of this last thin thread of reason, by invoking his authority on a subject on which he is obviously not an authority at all. They admit that they swallow Einstein's science not because it is science, but because it is Einstein; for they swallow a moment later another remark of Einstein's which cannot possibly have any connection with science at all.

—May 16, 1931

Science and Criminals

... I learn from an apparently authoritative paragraph that the men of science ... have at last thoroughly measured and examined the criminal skull, collected statistics about the criminal skull, measured it ... and taken away the number they

437

first thought of. And they have now finally discovered that the criminal skull does not exist. The principal object of examining a thing so closely as that is to discover that it does not exist. Men used to make game of metaphysics by saying it was looking in a dark room for a black hat that wasn't there. But the students of metaphysical science are here much less fantastic and futile than the students of physical science. If the metaphysicians look for a hat that isn't there, the materialists have been looking for a head that isn't anywhere.

—January 10, 1920

Science and Jargon

If somebody (with a turn for original observations) remarks that one swallow does not make a summer, that is a matter depending on special study of such seasons and birds. . . . It could throw no light, for example, upon the fascinating problem of whether one Polar bear would make a winter. Natural History must be unnatural to the extent of using scientific and almost secret terms. So if the scientists choose to call the swallow *hirundo vulgaris*[1] (or whatever they do call it) and if they choose to call making a summer "aestivation," I think they are cheeky, but within their rights. But I object to their using this mysterious language when they are not talking about whether one swallow makes a summer, but only about whether one swallow makes two swallows.

—September 17, 1910

. . . the ultimate study of thought and of the mind ought to be the simplest of all studies; not, I mean, simple in its task, but perfectly simple in its language. If we say something of universal scope we can obviously say it as easily of a plain or comic thing as of any other thing. Technical terms belong to the study of special physical facts—birds or beasts, or stars or stones, or weather. . . . Abstract truths like logic and mathematics can obviously be illustrated as well by common examples as by abstruse ones. And I object to the man who gives the Latin name for the most recently discovered bean-plant when he is only engaged in proving how many beans make five.

—September 17, 1910

---

[1]The more frequently used term is *hirundo rusticae.*

438

Science and Metaphysics

The truth is that, according to the latest science, it is impossible for physics to go any further without fading into metaphysics. The electron is rather a mathematical idea than a material object; it is a principle of energy acting, in the normal sense, upon nothing, or nothing that can be expressed in terms of anything. In fact, about the nearest approach to the very latest speculations of the physicists is the ancient formula that it was out of nothing that God made the world.

—April 12, 1930

Science and Morals

Those great professors of evolution and ethical science, at whose feet I have so meekly sat all my life, have generally said two things about the morals of nations and tribes. First they said that all creeds were the same, because they were the Message of Man. Second, they said that all creeds were different, because they were the Accidents of Evolution.

—October 23, 1909

Science and the Public

. . . when any part of the general public is drawn into a debate on physical science, we may be certain that it has already become a debate on moral science. Mobs are always moral. There never was a mob that rose to demand the squaring of the circle or the closer observation of the transit of Venus.

—February 15, 1930

Science and Race

Take the terrible business of the burning of Negroes. Why, the whole of that sentiment has been and still is justified entirely on grounds of popular science; the sort of science that popular education would make popular. Ask the average American to excuse, or merely to explain, this brutal feeling about the Blacks; and he will quite certainly refer it to biological and anthropological notions. He will say, or at least he will say that others say, that the Nigger is not so much a man as a monkey; that the very form of his skull forbids him to have a human soul. Before the dawn of science the South was ashamed of slavery. In the daylight of science it was ashamed of having been ashamed of it.

—July 5, 1924

Science and Reason

They do indeed claim that some of their own last discoveries go against reason; and they apparently infer that it must be so much the worse for reason. But it will certainly make a great deal of difference to most of us, if these apparent contradictions are not found in the concrete world of which we are certain, but in one of vast scientific visions, of which we may always have been sceptical. If a man tells us that he has measured his window, and finds it is wider than his house, we shall certainly agree that there must be something a little odd about the house, or possibly about the man.

—December 13, 1919

Science and Religion

I mean that the most recent and revolutionary scientific suggestions do not happen to throw any doubt on any religion. The Book of Genesis does not say that God formed the substance of the world out of atoms, and therefore a scientist cannot be rebuked as a bible-smasher if he says it is formed not of atoms, but of electrons. The Council of the Church which laid down the dogma of the co-eternity of Father and Son did not lay down any dogma of the conservation of energy. Therefore Mme. Curie could not be burned as a heretic even if, as some said, her discovery disturbed our ideas about the conservation of energy.

—August 21, 1920

The Athanasian Creed does not say that parallel straight lines never meet, so it would be unaffected by Professor Einstein saying, if he does really say, that they are not parallel or even straight. The prophets did not prophesy that a man would never fly, and are, therefore not discredited when he does fly. The saints certainly never said there was no such thing as wordless talking, and therefore have nothing to retract if there is such a thing as wireless telegraphy. In many ways it would be far easier to maintain that the modern inventions have verified the ancient miracles. Now in these technical and utilitarian examples it is still true to say that, if they do not disturb religious doctrines, they also do not disturb scientific doctrines. But the former class of more theoretic discoveries do disturb scientific doctrines. It is

440

the doctrines about gravity and energy, about atoms and ether, about the very foundations of the purely scientific universe, that have been affected or threatened by purely scientific research.

—August 21, 1920

The mere word "science" has become a mystical and even magical word. The new religions use it as a word of power, even when they are mortally opposed to its ordinary meaning. . . . The very system which would deny and destroy all physiological science, all medical science, all anatomical and surgical science, still calls itself Christian Science.

—November 13, 1920

I have never been able to understand why men of science, or men of any sort, should have such a special affection for disorganised religion. They would hardly utter cries of hope and joy over the prospect of disorganised biology or disorganised botany. They would hardly wish to see the whole universe of astronomy disorganised, with no relations, no records, no responsibilities or the fulfillment of this or that function, no reliance on the regularity of this or that law. Mr. Joad would be mildly surprised if I welcomed inorganic chemistry but forbad organic chemistry, because the latter had organs to organise it.

—April 12, 1930

Science and Scepticism

I know there is a general notion that it was science that introduced scepticism, and the study of material facts that made men materialists. But it is all nonsense, if only for the obvious reason that it is anachronism. It is like saying that the failure of the League of Nations led to the outbreak of the Great War.

—January 3, 1931

Science and Sin

The weakness of all the scientific proposals for helping mankind is that they are doing it behind mankind's back. . . . All the modern talk about environment and the best conditions really means that man will somehow become good without knowing it. It is, perhaps, possible to become good without knowing it; but it is highly impossible to leave off being bad without knowing it; and that is the task before the great part of humanity. The sinner wants his sin to succeed as a sin; apart from that he wants it to be forgiven as a sin: sometimes he even wants it punished as a sin. He never wants it called anything else except a sin. He understands charity; he may want his sin explained. He never wants it explained away. And the horror which common humanity has of modern science is a horror of its horrible mercy. If we were really only lifting burdens which certainly ought to be lifted, humanity would be quite content. But humanity fears that it is denying evils that certainly ought not to be denied.

—December 7, 1905

Science and the Supernatural

... science has profoundly modified the old Victorian view of miracles; science has forced us to accept scores and hundreds of miracles in the manner of the miracles of the scriptures and the saints; miracles of healing, miracles of cursing, miracles of flying without wings, miracles of speaking without speech, miracles of a dual personality like diabolic possession, miracles of thought transference identical with the incredible stories of one who could read men's thoughts. In short, it is quite true that science has changed our views of the supernatural; for it has forced us back on the supernatural.

—July 7, 1923

When I was a boy, people used to talk about something which they called the quarrel between religion and science. It would be very tedious to recount the quarrel now; the rough upshot of it was something like this: that some traditions too old to be traced came in vague conflict with some theories much too new to be tested.

—November 10, 1910

Science versus Religion

To this day this remains roughly true of all the relations between science and religion. The truths of religion are unprovable; the facts of science are unproved.

—November 5, 1910

Scientism

That quite elementary and commonplace principle suffices for all the relations of physical science with mankind. . . . Science is a splendid thing; if you tell it where to go to.

—*October 9, 1909*

The only evil that science has ever attempted in our time has been that of dictating not only what should be known, but the spirit in which it should be regarded. It does not in the least matter whether we look at a lamp-post or a tree as long as we look at it in a certain spirit. . . . We must not ask the telephone what we are to say to it. If we do, we shall find the young ladies at the exchange somewhat sharply insensible to the pathos of our position. Science must not impose any philosophy, any more than the telephone must tell us what to say.

—*October 9, 1909*

The persecution of religion by science has relatively, perhaps, only begun; but it is already at work, in we know not how many obscure cases of pedantry and cruelty. The mystics are very likely to be the martyrs when the psychologists become the kings.

—*March 8, 1924*

It may take materialists and semi-materialists some time to discover that the bottom has fallen out of the old materialist universe. At present the waverers and the doubters are probably still repeating the doubts of the nineteenth century. What they call their search for truth, and their revolt against tradition, is itself merely traditional. It is amusing to think that even religious people may still be driven to abandon religion by a science which scientists have abandoned.

—*May 24, 1930*

Scientism and Dogma

Let anyone run his eye over any average newspaper or popular magazine, and note the number of positive assertions made in the name of popular science, without the least pretence of scientific proof, or even of any adequate scientific authority. It is all the worse because the dogmas are generally concerned with domestic and

443

very delicate human relations; with heredity and home environment; and everything that can be coloured by the pompous and pretentious polysyllables of
psychology and education.

—July 12, 1930

Scientist as Ideologue

So long as he supposed that material inquiry supported materialism he roared and
bellowed at us that we must "accept the conclusions of science." But he is not in the
least inclined himself to accept the conclusions of science if they happen to go
against his own crude and clumsy creed.

—June 14, 1930

Scientists

We constantly say for instance, that So-and-So will certainly be exact, impartial,
and veracious because he is a man of science. But we only remember the word
"science" and forget the word "man." In so far as he is of science he will doubtless
be exact, impartial, and veracious. In so far as he is a *man* of science he will be
loose, partial, and a liar.

—January 27, 1906

There is one very vile habit that the pedants have, and that is explaining to a man
why he does a thing which the man himself can explain quite well—and quite
differently. If I go down on all-fours to find sixpence, it annoys me to be told by a
passing biologist that I am really doing it because my remote ancestors were
quadrupeds.

—January 1, 1910

Scientists (Modern)

Some moderns seek to make Man a mere symbol of the brutes. These old scientists
were only interested in the human side of the beasts. Some new scientists are only
interested in the beastly side of the men. Instead of making the ape and tiger mere
accessories to the man, they make man a mere accessory, a mere afterthought to the
ape and tiger. Instead of employing the hippopotamus to illustrate their philosophy,

444

they employ the hippopotamus to make their philosophy, and the great fat books he writes you and I, please God, will never read.

—November 11, 1905

We are always told that the theologians have grown more liberal; but it is at least as true that the scientists have grown more doubtful.

—August 8, 1931

Scientists (Pseudo)

When a poet walks about, he realises something strange in the fact that he can walk about, and that a tree or a mountain cannot walk about. But the object of the pseudo-scientist is to utter a sort of formula of enchantment which will chill and freeze these wanderers for ever. If their bodies still move about, at least their minds will never move again. He utters the magic words "Man has evolved powers of locomotion"; and man loses them on the spot. Those who were previously walking about remain stuck like statues in the garden of the wizard.

—August 6, 1932

Scopes Monkey Trial

It is impossible to argue at once that the schoolmaster ought to teach everything, and to argue that he will teach nothing that will not please everybody. In practice he need only teach whatever pleases somebody; that somebody being himself. And if his own private opinions happen to be of the rather crude sort that are commonly contemporary with, and connected with, the new sciences or pseudo-sciences, he can teach any of them under cover of those sciences. That is what the people of Dayton, Tennessee, were really in revolt against. And that is where the people of Dayton, Tennessee, were really and completely right.

—August 8, 1925

Scotsman

The Frenchman who said we had a hundred religions and only one sauce was mistaken—at least, partially mistaken, as most foreigners are; as mistaken as the

Englishman in Ireland. . . . The Scotch really did have a hundred religions and one sauce; the sauce being presumably Scotch whisky.

—September 6, 1924

Séance

It is awkward to get hold of the sow by the wrong ear; but it is positively dangerous to get hold of the angel by the wrong wing. Very broadly, the real objection to Spiritualism is that it calls entirely upon unknown gods—that is, upon any spirits that may be strolling about. There is something inevitably vulgar about this universal invitation in things of the soul.

—October 30, 1909

The phenomena of spirit control are far less fantastic than those of food control or paper control. People putting their hands on a bare table and waiting for spirits to descend are no more adventurous than people putting empty plates on a bare table and waiting for prices to fall.

—April 12, 1919

Secret Societies

Healthy human Governments in all ages have always hated and have often crushed . . . secret societies merely because they were secret, because they would not avow their public aims to the republic. Thus the Templars were trodden down; thus the Jesuits became unpopular; thus half the nations of the earth are fighting with Freemasons. The one thing odious to democratic politics is the thing called "tact"—which in public affairs always means conspiracy, and generally bribery.

—February 27, 1909

. . . there is that infinitely dangerous and generally indefensible thing—a secret society. It is perfectly obvious that the method is being used more and more, not merely for crime, but for criminal insanity. . . . A secret society can never clear itself of any crimes, so long as it remains secret. And even the admitted anarchy and atrocity are bad enough.

—September 13, 1924

446

Sects

From time to time, as we all know, a sect appears in our midst announcing that the world will very soon come to an end. Generally, by some slight confusion or miscalculation, it is the sect that comes to an end.

—*September 24, 1927*

I resent this surrender to small sects in the matter of classification. I resent it, for instance, in the discussion about what is "non-sectarian" or "undenominational." We are told, let us say, that it is unsectarian to worship God as a pure spirit. Then a sect springs up in Oklahoma declaring that God has three heads and nine hands; and *then* the view that he is a spirit becomes "sectarian." It is universal human morality to advise a man not to kill his mother; until a new movement arises, in which mothers are offered as human sacrifices from economic motives; and *then* not killing your mother has become a "dogma" or the creed of cryptic priests. I protest against the power of mad minorities to treat the majority as if it were another minority. But still more do I protest against the conduct of the majority if it surrenders its representative right so easily.

—*January 1, 1927*

Secularism

Antiquity was full of scepticism, but not of secularism. The worship of the gods was always conceived as a necessary part of public life, even by some who joked about it in private life. . . . Never until the nineteenth century was it supposed that the church or temple was a sort of side-show that had nothing to do with the state.

—*July 26, 1930*

Secularism (Contemporary)

. . . the secular society of to-day is sceptical not merely about spiritual assumptions, but about its own secular assumptions. It has not merely broken the church window or besieged the tower of tradition; it has also kicked away the ladder of progress by which it had climbed. The Declaration of Independence, once the charter of democracy, begins by saying that certain things are self-evident. If we were to trace the history of the American mind from Thomas Jefferson to William James, we should find that fewer and fewer things were self-evident, until at last

447

hardly anything is self-evident. So far from it being self-evident to the modern that men are created equal, it is not self-evident that men are created, or even that men are men. They are sometimes supposed to be monkeys muddling through a transition stage before the superman.

—August 14, 1926

Self-determination

It is a most extraordinary fact that all the modern talk about self-determination is applied to everything except the self. It is applied to the state, to the empire, to the province, to the parish—quite rightly in my opinion; but it is not applied to the very thing to which its verbal formula professes to apply. I, for one, do believe in that mystical doctrine of democracy, which pre-supposes that England has a soul, or that France has a self. But surely it is a much more obvious and ordinary fact that Jones has a self and Robinson has a self.

—July 30, 1921

Self-interest

If the world were really a world of war, it could not possibly be a world of self-interest. If the thousands who died in the last war were all trying to take care of themselves, their calculation was curious and rather difficult to follow.

—December 1, 1923

Self-limitation

... the eternal interest of the Noah's ark, considered as a toy, consists in its complete suggestion of compactness and isolation; of creatures so comically remote and fantastic being all locked up in one box; as if Noah had been told to pack up the sun and moon with his luggage. In other words, it is exactly the same game that I have played myself, by piling all the things I wanted on a sofa, and imagining that the carpet around me was the surrounding sea. This game of self-limitation is one of the secret treasures of life. . . . If anybody chooses to say that I have founded all my social philosophy on the antics of a baby, I am quite satisfied to bow and smile.

—February 8, 1930

448

Self-pity

A man may quite reasonably regard himself as a jolly good fellow. He may at the same time quite consistently regard himself as a miserable sinner. The evil comes in when he thinks himself too good a fellow for fellowship. The evil comes in when he thinks himself so very miserable a sinner that his misery is more important than his sin.

—July 31, 1909

Self-satisfaction

The distinction in question may be defined as the habit of manufacturing self-satisfaction out of any materials whatever. The deadly danger of this process consists in the very fact that it is facile, and therefore infinite; whatever I happen to be doing, I can always praise myself for doing it. If I walk, it shows my energy; if I sit down, it shows my composure; if I fall down, it shows my fearless acceptation of the risk. This infantile idea is developed with elephantine and laborious thoroughness in the schools of German thought.

— September 29, 1917

Senility

It is a sign of senility for a man to begin to quote himself, especially to quote himself with approval.

— February 28, 1925

Sentiment and Fiction (Modern)

The term, in any case, is always applied in a bad sense. And it is almost always applied exactly where it does not apply. There are apparently some people so constituted that they are sickened by any sentiment concerned with certain simple and popular things, such as the love of mothers or the charm of children. . . . There is nothing weak about showing such feelings; there is nothing realistic about denying such feelings. The feelings are facts; they are even very fundamental facts. We are not the less dealing with facts because we are dealing with a very large number of facts.

— August 20, 1927

449

Sentimentalist

A sentimentalist is a man to whom the pure prettiness of certain emotions (especially the slighter forms of sexual love) is so agreeable that he indulges them, not when they are overmastering and real, but when they are weak enough to be contemplated rather than experienced. He plays with the lion's cubs, but he has never seen the lion. He sees himself in all sorts of half-serious parts. He flirts with fifty women because he wants to be fifty men. He sulks. Just as flirting is a profanation of holy love, so sulking is a profanation of holy hatred. In all cases his spiritual crime is this—that he takes things which God meant to be rare and noble necessities and turns them into perpetual luxuries.

—January 30, 1909

Seriousness

I do not like seriousness. I think it is irreligious. Or, if you prefer the phrase, it is the fashion of all false religions. The man who takes everything seriously is the man who makes an idol of everything: he bows down to wood and stone until his limbs are as rooted as the roots of the tree or his head as fallen as the stone sunken by the roadside.

—January 17, 1914

Sermons

I think it is true that the ordinary Sunday sermon has become rather pointless and sterile. Personally, I should like preaching done by preaching friars; by people trained, and traveling for that particular purpose. But if the sermon has weakened, it is, I think, for the very contrary reason to that commonly alleged. The parson is not dull because he is always expounding theology, but because he has no theology to expound.

—August 27, 1921

Servile State

For the servile state, properly understood, is not something that may come if somebody does something. It is something that is only too likely to come if nobody does anything. It is almost a negative thing, in the sense of being an unconscious drift of modern society.

—September 1, 1923

Sex

The two first facts which a healthy boy or girl feels about sex are these: first that it is beautiful and then that it is dangerous. While all the philosophical Forels go floundering about in a world of words, saying that this is wrong if it disturbs your digestion, or that that is right if it does not disturb your great-grandchild, all plain, pleasure-loving people have an absolutely clean instinct in the matter. Mankind declares this with one deafening voice: that sex may be ecstatic so long as it is also restricted. It is not necessary even that the restriction should be reasonable; it is necessary that it should restrict. That is the beginning of all purity; and purity is the beginning of all passion.

—January 9, 1909

It becomes something that is much worse than mere anarchy, something that can truly be described as *malice;* a war, not against the restraints required by virtue but against virtue itself. The old moral theology called it malice; and there will be no future for the modern psychology until it again studies the old moral theology. Sex is the bait and not the hook; but in that last extreme of evil the man likes the hook and not the bait.

—March 30, 1929

Sex and Love

The later sex writers would refuse to admit that there is any sacred bond between anybody and anybody else. The truth is that this mystical feeling about the love of man and woman was treated so clumsily that it fell between two stools. When it was really mediaeval, it could be preserved for ever in a story like that of Dante and Beatrice. When it was really modern, it simply fell to pieces, into little decaying scraps rather like wriggling worms, the hundred little loves and lusts of the modern sex novel. But the romantics of the nineteenth century held it up in a sort of indeterminate pre-eminence; a . . . toppling idolatry; trying to make it at once as sacred as they thought good and as free as they found convenient. They wanted to eat their wedding-cake and have it.

—August 27, 1932

The Sexes

Every period in which men had any civilisation—that is, any imagination—has always made a difference between the dignity and decoration of the two sexes.

—*April* 25, 1925

Shadows, Age of

For all the apparent materialism and mass mechanism of our present culture, we, far more than any of our fathers, live in a world of shadows. It is none the less so because the prophets and progressives tell us eagerly that these are coming events which cast their shadow before. It is assumed that nothing is really thrilling except a dance of shadows; and we miss the very meaning of substance.

—*December* 23, 1933

Shakespeare and Bacon

. . . it is a queer paradox that Shakespeare was an obscure and almost unhistorical figure; according to some nameless or worthless, according to others impersonal and self-effacing, but anyhow somewhat elusive and secret; and from him came a cataract of clear song and natural eloquence; while Bacon was a public man of wide renown and national and scientific philosophy; and out of him have come riddles and oracles and fantastic cryptograms and a lifelong hobby for lunatics.

—*October* 1, 1927

Shaw, George Bernard

It would be impossible to pay Mr. Shaw a more complete compliment than to suggest that he mystifies the stupid and convinces the wise.

—*March* 8, 1924

I have never been disturbed by his disbelieving the things he does not understand, and I have always been delighted with his disbelieving the things he does understand.

—*February* 7, 1931

I should have no difficulty in admitting him to my list of great men, though perhaps my list might be a little longer, and perhaps a little more liberal, than his. I actually wrote a book about him in the ancient days; and I am happy to say that he reviewed it himself, with the typical opening: "This is the best book of criticism that I have yet produced." And what I said then is very much what I should say still. There is no very fundamental antagonism between Mr. Bernard Shaw and myself except in one fact—that he is a puritan and I am, at least relatively, a pagan. It is true that I have become a Christian, but that is a thing that happened to quite a large number of pagans. Only I never became a puritan; and it seems to me that Mr. Shaw never became anything else.

—*February 7,* 1931

Shaw and Revolution

The youthful G. B. S. laid down the law, but he thought there was a law to be laid down. . . . He was a rebel, but a rebel who wanted to establish or lay down a rule; a revolutionary rule, of course, but still, a rule. Nowadays, the young rebels do not want to lay down a rule, but to lay down exceptions. . . . They want to be exceptions. . . . But they have broken up the scheme of existence into exceptions, which have no real rule to connect them.

—*August* 29, 1931

Shelley's Prometheus Unbound

. . . Shelley, in the rise and fall of those remarkable lines of the Prometheus, is referring to the old pagan conception of the great year. He feels that it justifies him in saying that the world's great age will begin anew and the golden years return. But he does not want to drain the urn of prophecy to the dregs, because the same wheel of fate that has brought round the golden years will bring round also the leaden and the iron years; and we shall all be forced to repeat all the crimes and tyrannies of history. . . . I think I may say that it is not a cheery prospect; and that I am exceedingly proud to observe that it was before the coming of Christianity that it flourished, and after the neglect of Christianity that it returned.

—*August* 2, 1930

Sherlock Holmes

A little while ago I lifted up my voice in this space to offer the belated tribute of a lifetime to Sherlock Holmes, and to that much more fascinating character, Dr. Watson. I think we have never been grateful enough for the fun we have had out of those famous tales. I hope to see the day when there shall be a statue of Sherlock Holmes in Baker Street, as there is a statue of Peter Pan in Kensington Gardens. Those are perhaps the only two figures in fiction who have in recent times really become legends. . . .

—January 15, 1927

Short Cut

Many a man walking across country has found that a short cut has one incidental disadvantage—that it takes a long time. This has even been known to outweigh its higher beauties in the matter of picturesqueness and novelty. If the short cut is a trespass, and damages the fences and fields of many other persons, it has been known to take an even longer time—time in the poetic sense employed by those who find that their private path passes through a public jail.

—February 17, 1917

Silence

Carlyle and other sages have doubtless preached that it is chiefly in silence that something is done. But my own experience is rather that it is chiefly in silence that somebody is done; and the somebody who is done is generally the average British taxpayer.

—July 9, 1910

It is often a strategic mistake to silence a man, because it leaves the world under the impression that he had something to say.

—August 14, 1915

Simplification

And that logical end of all simplification is not sufficiently kept in mind by those who are simplifying our social relations to-day. There is such a thing as removing unnecessary and artificial obstacles and coming to the essence of something. But there is also such a thing as regarding everything as an artificial obstacle, and coming at least to the essence of nothing. There is such a thing as sitting down to peel a peach, and removing the skin so as to get to the peach. But there is also such a thing as sitting down to peel an onion, and throwing away all the skins and never finding the onion.

—October 20, 1928

The modern world seems to have no notion of preserving different things side by side, of allowing its proper and proportionate place to each, of saving the whole varied heritage of culture. It has no notion except that of simplifying something by destroying nearly everything. . . .

—May 2, 1931

Sin

Men do not differ much about what things they will call evils; they differ enormously about what evils they will call excusable. The sins are substantially the same all over the earth. What men fight each other about is the question of which are the venial and which the mortal sins.

—October 23, 1909

For sin, whatever else it is, is not merely the dregs of a bestial existence. It is something more subtle and spiritual, and is in some way connected with the very supremacy of the human spirit.

—September 1, 1928

Slander

During my own life, many . . . lies have rotted; but I regret to say that there were not many men left alive to call them rotten. I will not say that all the work of the lie is done, in the sense that it cannot be undone. But I notice that it was done very

455

noisily and that it is undone very quietly. I notice there is a great row when men stone the prophets; and a great silence while they build their sepulchres.

—August 8, 1931

Slander (Journalistic)

There is one infamous use of the allusive method against which a protest must be made. It consists in gliding gracefully over a subject as if we all knew about it and it was very horrid; whereas, in fact, most of us know nothing about it, and the few who do know may be finding it very nice. Thus, if one wrote: "On the private life of the Mayor of Dulcam we will not dwell"; or, "Of the moral state of East Dudsey little need be said," these would be extreme examples of this wanton and baseless style of slander.

—August 7, 1909

Slavery

It is almost the definition of a slave that he does receive unemployment pay. That is, he receives board and lodging, whether his master wants him to work at that moment or no. The whole point of the servile relation is that the master does undertake the whole support of the slave, idle or busy, but receives in return the right to decide when he shall be busy and when idle. Expressed in modern terms, the slave-owner agreed to give unemployment pay, on condition of getting rid of strikes. To a very large proportion of perfectly humane and intelligent business men to-day, it would seem a very workable compromise. It would also be slavery—or the servile state.

—September 10, 1921

The unconscious combination of our general desire to provide work and food for the poor, with our increasing impatience with strikes and labour quarrels, may lead to a compromise by which the working classes will be fed even when they are not working on condition that they are always ready to work. And if that compromise is enforced by law, it will be slavery, though it will not be called slavery. It will be the pagan condition in which men are forced to serve certain masters and masters are expected to support certain men.

—September 1, 1923

I know of only one real objection to slavery; and that is that it is not freedom.

—September 1, 1923

Slavery in America

It describes exactly a certain double attitude towards the Negro, which is nearly always developed in actual dealings with him. The literature of the old gentry of Virginia or Carolina, for instance, seemed simultaneously to paint the Negro blacker than he was and prove he was not so black as he was painted. He could be a nurse for the children, and yet a nightmare for the men and women. . . . The same society that was in one aspect founded on fear of the Negro was in another aspect full of affection for the Negro.

—February 8, 1919

Slogan

English mobs in the past used to shout short unmistakable remarks that really can be shouted, such as . . . —"No popery!" . . . but . . . learned "democrats" of our day. . . . have evidently entirely forgotten that they were ever meant to be shouted at all. In an American Bolshevist paper called *The Liberator,* for instance, I find the following simple cries from the heart: "Down with the imperialistic conspiracy of capital! Long live the international republic of the proletarian councils!" Can you imagine a maddened rabble rushing in thousands down the street, shattering windows and wrecking lamp-posts, and all saying simultaneously, with correct and coincident articulation, "Long live the international republic of the proletarian councils"? . . . If they had tried to howl all that, even the watchmen and bow street runners of that freer and happier age would have found them in an exhausted condition after the effort, and ready to go quietly with the most inefficient police.

—August 18, 1919

Most modern titles and slogans have to say the precise opposite of what they mean for the sake of brevity.

—January 25, 1930

Sloth

Sloth is a great fault: but we do not necessarily dislike the sluggard. We only dislike the sluggard when he becomes the aesthete—the man who need not do anything, but need only "exist beautifully."

—*August* 22, 1914

Smile

I will only annoy the sceptical philosopher by smiling; which is a sign, not of doubt, but of certitude.

—*January* 31, 1931

Snob

. . . common-sense has been corrupted into mere conservatism by a very vulgar fallacy. It has been only too easy for shallow people, when shown that things should be in a certain proportion, to assume that this point of perfection was the supreme moment when they came into the world. The snob supposes that the perfect proportions of things are simply the proportions which have made him comfortable.

—*May* 31, 1924

One thing that stamps a man as being really among the uneducated is the fact that he has a contempt for the illiterate.

—*July* 26, 1924

Soap

Mr. Blatchford, the Socialist leader, broke out once, I remember, into an extraordinary tirade of scorn against the word "piety"; he ended by saying that what the world wanted was not piety but "soap and Socialism." Here he was wholly under the influence of the aristocratic wave. Piety is always the glory of the poor; soap is the glory of the rich. Soap and Socialism are two things which just now, at any rate, reek only of the over-educated class.

—*July* 20, 1907

Social Darwinism

... they would get into a most horrible muddle if they did really try to apply the Darwinian test to the problem of poverty. They would produce the very opposite of all that is wanted, even by themselves. Suppose that miners began to lose their eyesight through working so much in the dark. From a social standpoint, that is a tragedy. But from a biological standpoint, it is only an adaptation. The miner is, in fact, becoming fit for his environment. ... If a typical slum population is springing up in the slums, they are not the unfit; they are possibly those fitted—for the slums. All this is horrible heathen nonsense, of course; and to me it is a mere denial of human dignity and of the image of God. ... The moral is that it will be as well for most people to leave biology to biologists; to forget the sham science called eugenics, and return to the real science called ethics.

—November 19, 1927

Social Darwinism and War

Wicked men make war for money, or for vanity, or, in slightly more Christian cases, for vengeance. But no modern man, however wicked, makes war because he gets up before breakfast with a thirst for the blood of Germans or Frenchmen, or because a purely animal appetite hurls him upon the bayonets and entrenchments, as it hurls him upon the bacon and eggs. It is simply a part of that silly scientific sentimentalism that takes a vague pleasure in suggesting that an explanation is biological even when it is not logical. It is a confusion that comes from allowing certain more or less tenable though incomplete hypotheses about anthropological origins to colour popular thinking so exclusively that pithecanthropus and sinanthropus seem to some people more real than Hitler or Mussolini.

—December 2, 1933

Social Darwinists

... if they really want the struggle for life to produce their polished and refined types of virtue ... they must make art or truth an evasive and flying thing for fat old gentlemen to run after. They must reverse the modern crusade for making education easy; they must make it difficult. So far from distributing spelling-books among millions of reluctant children, they should stick one spelling-book on top of a greasy pole or a monkey-tree, to be reached only by some child who was eccentric enough to want it.... The meetings of the Ethical Society should be held in the heart of a dense forest, full of wild beasts. Then, perhaps, they might really produce their ethical Superman, refined, exalted, intellectually beautiful: and a very unpleasant fellow I should imagine he would be.

—September 11, 1909

They are always trying to twist out of [evolution] crude and fanciful theories of right and wrong.... They still go blandly boring on, saying that a man's mind must grow and develop in the same sense in which all Nature has grown and developed. They might as well say that a man's head must go round and round, just as the Solar System goes round and round. Some of their heads do.

—April 23, 1910

Social Reform

No one ever really knows how long an experiment will be allowed to last; no one really knows how much sustained public force there is behind any trend of reform, or when it may suddenly give out. It is all very well to talk of revolution as a leap in the dark; but every step of reform is a step in the dark. And we do constantly find in English history that calamity has overtaken these partial proposals before they achieved their final object.

—August 6, 1910

To control family life, for instance, you must have at least one police spy for every family.... Police spies are now a minority (though I fear an increasing minority). ... Once make a thing which any man may do a crime, and every man must have a "shadowing" detective as every man has a shadow. Yet this is precisely the preposterous end to which are directed most modern projects of "social reform" which select things like drink, diet, hygiene, and sexual selection. If men cannot govern themselves in these things separately, it is physically impossible for them to govern themselves in these things collectively. It not only means publicity instead of privacy; it means every man in his public capacity being in charge of every other man in his private capacity. It not only means washing dirty linen in public; it means all of us living by taking in each other's washing.

—June 9, 1917

I believe most of the great social reforms of our time will remain in history as follies.

—May 3, 1919

Social Pressure

Now, in all these matters, which the law can only control very clumsily, the most valuable force is social pressure—the opinion of a man's neighbours and equals: Let there be as far as possible a local inn, and let a man behave there like a decent man—or like an indecent one, if he chooses to lose his friends. But it *is* an evil that he should be served as a decent man in seventeen successive houses and turn up an indecent man at the end of it. It is an evil that the multiplication of the very things meant to make men sociable should tend to make them solitary. It is an evil that while with one tavern you have friendly drinking, with ten taverns you have secret drinking. And it is an evil very typical of our times, for the chief evil of our times is that the social collectivity has increased spiritual solitude. Never were bodies so much jostled; never were souls so much deserted.

—June 6, 1908

Social Science

If we have to discuss the most familiar and fundamental human problems all over again, let us at least take advantage of their antiquity in the fact that the vocabulary of them is fairly popular and clear. Let us realise that marriage is not natural selection but fighting; that wine is not alcoholic stimulation, but wine; that work is not the creation of capital, but work, a very unpleasant thing. It seems that we have a great upheaval and revision in front of us. The discussion will certainly be long, but at least the words might be short.

—June 12, 1909

... there seems to be a curiously bloodless and polysyllabic style now adopted for the discussion of the most direct and intimate matters. The human home, for example, which whether it be comfortable or uncomfortable is, after all, the only place in which humanity has ever lived, people discuss as if it were the nest of some extraordinary bird, or the cell of some occult insect which science had only just discovered. The combination of man and woman may be, and indeed is, a dangerous chemical combination; frequently resulting in an explosion; but

461

the explosion is one to which we might have got pretty well used by this time.

—*June* 12, 1909

That is why every prediction of the future, even by a genius like Mr. Wells, always looks like a long row of noughts. Our fathers were content to say that the future was x, or the unknown quantity. Our futurists are really content to prove that x = 0. The mathematical figure for nought is round and harmonious and symmetrical, and has a fine inevitable curve; but it is also hollow and blank—a face without features. In all these points it resembles the usual utopian or pessimistic prediction about the human race. But history has not been merely a row of noughts. Religious history, at worst, has been a game of noughts and crosses.

—*November* 25, 1922

Mention a number of myths that have some connection with meals; mix them all up like a soup; leave out all the joints and bones of argument; and you can easily leave the reader with a general impression that a meal is a myth. Above all, you must keep on praising the reader, as a progressive fellow superior to his father; and you can easily make him feel superior to meals—until next meal-time.

—*April* 4, 1931

There is no space here for my powerful and cogent exposure of the superstition of sleep. It is set forth (or it might be some day) with all the exact process of thought and careful citation of facts and scientific authorities essential to this sort of work; the footnotes fill up most of the pages and the appendices are in five volumes. The recognised scientific method in such cases consists of two parts. First the writer points out that sleep has a perfectly simple, single, and obvious origin in mythology, and then (second) he proceeds to trace it to about ten totally contradictory mythological origins.

—*April* 4, 1931

If we are to employ the scientific method, while we are actually employing the scientific method let us at least be scientific, and banish from our minds tests that are merely tastes and tastes that are analogous to the aesthetic.

—*December* 5, 1931

Social Scientists

Yet I have scarcely ever known a "modern" and scientific sociologist who did not follow his own likes and dislikes in his social science. I have hardly known one who did not colour it with his party colours; with his taste for the red of communism or his distaste for the black of clericalism. Above all, I have never known such a social doctor who could take a medicine he did not like.

—December 5, 1931

I have never known a man of that kind who could bear to come to scientific conclusions contrary to his philosophical conceptions. . . . Consider the case of all those . . . who would apply science to society in the matter of the prevention of war. If they are socialists, wars are only waged by capitalists. If they are democrats, wars are the result of aristocracy; if they are reactionaries, or claim to be an intellectual aristocracy, wars are only made by mobs. If they are atheists, wars are waged by priests, or the only people who are ever exempt from waging them. If they happen to have a hatred of babies (and some of them seem to have, heaven knows, to judge by their essays on procreation and population) they will probably discover that babies lead us all into battle.

—December 5, 1931

Social experiment differs from chemical experiment, or anything that is really practical in the way of scientific experiment. It differs in this vital respect: that the students of the social science dispute, not only about what will happen, but about what did happen. Two chemists are not left quarrelling about whether there was or was not an explosion with a loud bang. If there was, both will agree that for some reason a state of unstable equilibrium did exist; and that it did happily stabilise itself and return to equilibrium with a loud bang. But two sociologists will continue to argue whether there was really an unstable social equilibrium; whether the social explosion was large or small, artificial or real, accidental or symptomatic, and whether the bang was really loud enough to be noticed.

—August 26, 1933

Social Theorists

... modern theorists seem to me to be strangely lacking in the instinct of what is really great.

— October 2, 1931

Social Theory

It is amusing to notice how these theories pursue each other, and how the last almost always devours and destroys the last but one. Generally, in fact, the last is the flat contradiction of the last but one. Generally they are equally extreme, equally exaggerated, and, so far, equally untrue.

— October 2, 1931

I myself grew up under the gigantic shadow of the Teutonic theory. It was essentially a theory that everything valuable had been done by fair-haired men, which is quite as ludicrous as the same assertion about red-haired men. ... I only remark that such theories, whether true or false, do affect the truthfulness of historians, and more often in the direction of falsehood than of truth.

— October 2, 1931

Everybody knows, or ought to know, that making a universal theory about human society is the easiest thing in the world. The logical weakness in this sort of superficial social theory is this: that the social values are not fixed like mathematical values, and can themselves be moulded to fit the theory. If I say that red-haired men are always the men who sway the destinies of the world, I can always make out a case, by taking all the red-haired men who were important and making them out more important than they were.

— October 2, 1931

Socialism

... the aim of a good citizen should be the equalisation of property; and the equalisation of property is the opposite of the negation of property; just as the equalisation of drinks would be the opposite of the negation of

464

drinks. Mechanical collectivism is a desperate remedy, a Nihilist remedy, like teetotalism.

—November 16, 1907

There are many arguments against Socialism. The only important one is that it is awkward, when you are dealing with grammar, to abolish the possessive pronoun.

—November 16, 1907

I believe there are some people who say that they want Socialism, but do not want bureaucracy. Such persons I leave in simple despair. How any calculating creature can think that we can extend the number of Government offices without extending the number of Government officials and the prevalence of the official mind, I cannot even conjecture. Some people look forward to a splendid transformation of the general human soul. That is a good argument for accepting Socialism—and, when one comes to think of it, an even better reason for doing without it.

—January 2, 1909

I am not satisfied when the Socialist says that Socialism will only come slowly. I am not comforted when the Protectionist says that Protection will be introduced with great tact and care. If the fourth leg of my chair is burning, I would rather be shrivelled at a quick fire than roasted at a slow one.

—July 9, 1910

Officials come round and leave little cards about the hygienic way in which to give children food. They leave the cards: they do not leave the food. Lady scientists come round with bright little essays about milk; they do not come round with the milk. Poor children are told in laundry classes to pass a garment through three waters, but nobody gives them so much as one water. Children are told in cookery classes to pass the viand from a saucepan to a stew-pan; but nobody offers to lend them even the saucepan. . . . Government has already made the ordinary man pipe another tune: only Government has not paid the piper. The officials have already *gained* the right to order the poor man about like dirt. Only they have not yet earned the right. They have not even attempted to earn it, by making him one halfpenny less poor.

—September 10, 1910

Whether one is a Socialist or not, one may well admit that Socialism (like most schemes propounded by people not startlingly above or below mankind) promises some advantages and involves some risks. The strictest Socialist will agree that one pays something for Socialism, just as the firmest Churchman will agree that one pays something to keep up the Church. . . . Suppose we were crushed by colossal taxation for the Navy, while at the same time there was not the tiniest British boat anywhere on all the seas of the world, I think there are discontented spirits among us who would remark upon the fact. Yet this is actually the situation with regard to Socialism.

—September 10, 1910

Obviously, the advantage of Socialism would be that, if the State were supreme everywhere, it could see that everybody had enough money and comfort. Equally obviously the disadvantage of Socialism would be that if the State were supreme everywhere, it might easily become a tyrant, as it has been again and again. To pack the whole matter as solidly as possible, officials could certainly go round and feed the whole people with bread. But it has often been found that in practice they feed the people with insults.

—September 10, 1910

To Socialism, as to any other bargain, there is a good side and a bad side. The good side we may or may not get ultimately and enjoy; but the bad side we have got already. It is useless for the few remaining followers of Herbert Spencer to discuss whether the English, in entering Socialism, will sell themselves into slavery. They are already in the slavery: but they have not sold themselves into it. For they have not got any money for it, nor even the promise of any. It is vain for Individualist orators to adjure the people not to lose their birthright for a mess of pottage.

—September 10, 1910

A doctor descends upon [a] . . . widow, and tells her to take her son to some remote hospital to be examined. She does so (being the meek and broken subject of an already Socialistic State) and most probably she finds she cannot be attended to. She has to travel to the remote hospital again, and perhaps again, spending sums on trams and trains which correspond to a £5 note for you and me. Eventually her son's eyes are examined. That happy youth is told that he ought to have a particular pair of spectacles. . . . There, I repeat heavily and literally, is the entire end of the matter. . . . The poor woman has got everything out of the Government in the way of command and coercion that she could possibly get under the most

466

despotic system. Her child has been forcibly taken from her, forcibly sent to school, forcibly sent to strain his eyes, forcibly overhauled about his eyes, trailed ceaselessly on a tram, hurled ceaselessly into a hospital. In short, he has got everything that is absolute out of the Government—except the spectacles.

—September 10, 1910

It is too impersonal; it proclaims that no one shall be human lest anyone should be inhuman.

—December 24, 1910

Socialism, like teetotalism, is a desperate remedy; that is, it is only a defensible remedy if it is the only remedy. I do not believe it is the only remedy. I believe it is possible to reverse the evil of the excessive concentration of wealth, and that any reform that does not reverse that evil will only exaggerate it, just as the collectivist would remedy the concentration of wealth by concentrating it still further.

—May 12, 1923

It is a tragedy of the consumer, not of the middleman. And the tragedy of the consumer is that for some reason or other he cannot get anything to consume.

—January 5, 1924

It is as natural to provide a hundred huts for soldiers as to provide a hundred hats for soldiers. That is because the hats are, as their name implies, uniform, and because the soldiers are on the march; but they are marching somewhere. The whole modern proletariat is on the march; but it is marching nowhere. When we talk of housing them we only mean finding them huts for the night with no real notion of what will happen next day.

—September 26, 1925

We ought to say: "By the same argument by which you prove Socialism to be a panacea I prove Socialism to be a servitude. It is you who say that it would prevent any unjust agreements, because the state would make all the bargains. I deduce from your own statement that, if the state is unjust, all the bargains will be unjust. It is you who say that nobody will starve, because the state will feed everybody. I

467

deduce from your own statement that anybody whom the state refuses to feed will starve.

—October 10, 1925

Socialism is a tyranny; that it is inevitably, even avowedly and almost justifiably, a tyranny. It is the pretence that government can prevent all injustice by being directly responsible for practically anything that happens.

—October 10, 1925

... [You say] nobody will be able to accumulate capital for private purposes such as exploitation or competition. I deduce from your own statement that nobody will be able to accumulate capital for private purposes such as free criticism of the state or popular protest against the state. It is you who say that the state will buy and sell everything, so that nobody will be cheated. I deduce from your own statement that, if the state cheats, everybody will be cheated.

—October 10, 1925

The mob is meek enough, certainly, when it is thus herded to its pastures by its sociological and educational pastors. It does not really mean that the many sheep, but that the few shepherds, will rule over all the meadows. And when the nomadic shepherd finds himself confronted with the static or domestic peasant, with the man who is actually ruling his own small meadow like a realm, there is always a collision and a sort of civil war in the countryside. In any case, the original paradox remains: that it was regarded as a simple thing that all the meadows should belong to all the men, but a frantic and fantastic thing that any man should own any meadow.

—May 31, 1930

Socialism (German)

The Prussian Socialism is a strict state Socialism; in other words, the Prussians still believe in the divine right, or diabolic right, of the state. The theory remains that the state is the only absolute in morals—that is, that there is no appeal from it to God or man, to Christendom or conscience, to the individual or the family or the fellowship of all mankind. The very theory that was the ethical excuse of all their crimes in the past is the first principle of their political philosophy for the future.

468

The fact is surely very relevant to the problem of any remaining menace from the Germans.

—December 22, 1918

Socialist

Leader-writers on the Yellow Press have a right to hold the opinion that all Socialists are profligates, or the equally rational opinion that all Socialists have tails.

—December 31, 1910

A socialist cannot believe in dividing property, for the simple reason that he cannot believe in property. If he believes in any such thing, he must believe in combining property, in concentrating it in the hands of the State and the statesman— whom lately we have learnt to love so much.

—February 21, 1914

Thirty years ago every intellectual who had any intellect was more or less of a socialist. Everybody was a socialist, except the working-man who was supposed to benefit by Socialism.

—August 9, 1924

If he could trust a poor man with the care of a cow or a cottage, or a common or garden child, I might believe he was sincere in wishing to trust all poor men with the destiny of all cottages and cows. As it is, I suspect that he is not going to trust that destiny to a democracy of poor men, but to an official or oligarch appointed to organise the poor man. Similarly, if the new social philosophies fervently encouraged people to think more about domesticity and less about divorce, I might believe that they really were preferring the future generation to their own.

—May 30, 1931

Socialist State

Now, the theoretic preference for a certain sort of socialist state cannot be put in plain words. It is generally put in preposterously polysyllabic and pedantic words. To suppose that the mass of hard-working men all over the world have spontaneously developed an onward spiritual hunger of "the assumption by the state of all the means of production, distribution, and exchange," is quite wild. It is to suppose that a crossing-sweeper is always talking about his "assumption" of a broom and a badge, that an agricultural labourer invariably refers to the "maximum production" of his kitchen garden in the matter of turnips, or that a rat-catcher in a village public-house is careful to call for the "adequate distribution" of five pots of beer.

—*June* 18, 1921

Society (English)

I should divide our society into its four parts, roughly, as follows—The Governing Class.... The realities that bind it together are two; first, an immense amount of money, which permits a particular and very luxurious kind of life; second, a taste or hobby or ideal of governing other people.... The second class I will call the Ladies and Gentlemen. They include thousands of aristocrats with small or moderate means; relatives of Dukes, who get their living as curates, or as colonels, or as Socialist agitators.... The third class are those whom one may call (in anger) the Clarks, but whom one should also call (in admiration) Citizens. They are the self-respecting, self-supporting men in black coats and bowlers who fill most political and religious meetings.... The fourth class is the People of England, innumerable millions of cabmen, navvies, dustmen, and crossing-sweepers. They are not at all refined: and if ever they begin to talk there will be fun.

—*December* 10, 1910

Sociological Dogmas

... when they tell us emphatically that science declares this and that about the relative wisdom or welfare of different societies, it is obvious that these sociological dogmas are very lax and inconclusive indeed. We have no exact way of testing the proportion of people in any society who really enjoy its social institutions more than they would enjoy other social institutions.... Nobody knows, for instance, whether the noise of modern London is not actually a friction to the nerves which diminishes pleasure even while it drives people on to more pleasure. It is no answer to say that the people are driven to become yet noisier in order to

470

forget the noise. . . . There is no way of measuring happiness in that scientific sense.

—July 23, 1927

Sociologists

The sociologist tells us that all sorts of things under certain conditions must happen, that the obliteration of nationality must happen, that the command of everything by science and scientific men must happen; and all because some particular economic or material fact must happen. "Yuss," we says. "That's one of the things that'll 'appen. Another thing'll be that we shall punch their fat 'eds off at the root for takin' a lib with the moral traditions of humanity." Their evolution will go on exactly until our revolution chooses to begin.

—October 21, 1905

Sociology

Cheap and pedantic prophesying is the curse and the characteristic weakness of the whole of modern sociology. It is allied to materialism, which is allied to the brutes. It is all based on the assumption that man's future can be calculated like the action of a machine; whereas to be incalculable is the definition of being human; it is only because a man cannot be made a subject of science that there is any fun in being a man.

—February 9, 1907

Those who insist most sternly that sociology is a science seem specially incapable of being scientific. I do not say, for my part, that it is enough to be scientific; but they do. They say it is the first, last, and only necessity to be scientific, and then they are unscientific.

—December 5, 1931

Will any scientific sociologist say he had worked out a sociological weather-chart, dating the exact emergence and importance of Hitler? Can we hope, perhaps, that all of us will begin to see what some of us can claim to have seen from the beginning: three great truths or dogmas on which all history hangs? (1) That humanity is far too complex to have such calculations made about it. (2) That

471

humanity is afflicted with Original Sin. (3) That the will of man is free. Granted these three facts, it is obvious that nobody can predict that nobody will start this or that idea, will start it even if it has been unsuccessful, will start it even if it may fail again, will start it even if it is wicked, and its success therefore more wicked than its failure. There are too many men, each with too many moods, each with too many influences on them varying from instant to instant, to predict how the man will jump; for he is much more capricious than that lazy animal, the cat. Let us at least thank all the rioters and brawlers and demagogues and dictators and casual despots for their one good deed in destroying the science of sociology.

—April 15, 1933

Soldier

If it be awful that death should be so deadly in the very house of youth, it is still in a sense, beautiful that youth should be so young in the house of death. . . . If our soldiers seem too young to die in battle, at least they are young enough to live in battle; and death does not find them dead.

—November 24, 1917

Soldier (British)

The British soldier is generally our old friend the British working man. He has lived by trades that are too often treated as merely grimy or grotesque; and in the case of new and almost crude conscript armies, like those we have lately raised, he has generally quite recently dropped those tools and left those trades. It is the plumber, who is charged with pottering about for days before he stops a small leak in a pipe, who has often in a few minutes stopped with his body the breach in the last dyke of civilisation, lest it should let in a sea of savagery. . . . And the purpose of the parenthesis is only to support the general truth, that many refined persons will do well to revise their moral estimate of the masses.

—April 13, 1918

Solemn Occasions

People do solemn things because they think the occasion is solemn; To scatter flowers on a grave is simply a way in which an ordinary person can express in gesture things that only a very great poet can express in words. I decline to believe

472

that those who do it necessarily believe that the dead man can smell. I doubt whether even those who did it in prehistoric times necessarily thought that the dead man could smell. Strange as it may seem, I do not think they were thinking in that vivid vicarious fashion about the dead man's feelings. I think they were relieving their own feelings. "Funeral customs are a tribute not to the dead but to the living," said St. Augustine.

—January 29, 1927

Solipsist

In short, it is the magic of that one trivial phrase, about music and digestion, that it calls up suddenly in the mind the image of a certain sort of man, sitting at a table in a grand restaurant, and wearing a serious and somewhat sullen expression. He is manifestly a man of considerable wealth; and beyond that he can only be described by a series of negatives. He has not traditions, and therefore knows nothing of the great traditional talking that has enriched our literature with the nights and feasts of the gods. He has no real friends, and therefore his interests are turned inwards, but more to the state of his body than of his soul. He has no religion, and therefore it comes natural to him to think that everything springs from a material source. He has no philosophy, and therefore does not know the difference between the means and the end. And, above all, there is buried deep in him a profound and stubborn repugnance to the trouble of following anybody else's argument; so that if somebody elaborately explains to him that it is often a mistake to combine two pleasures, because pleasures, like pains, can act as counter-irritants to each other, he only receives the vague impression that somebody is saying that music is bad for his digestion.

—September 29, 1923

Solitude

I can recall in my childhood the continuous excitement of long days in which nothing happened; and an indescribable sense of fullness in large and empty rooms. . . . I still feel a very strong and positive pleasure in being stranded in queer quiet places, in neglected corners where nothing happens and anything may happen; in unfashionable hotels, in empty waiting-rooms, or in watering-places out of the season. It seems as if we needed such places, and sufficient solitude in them, to let certain nameless suggestions soak into us and make a richer soil of the subconsciousness. Certainly, if there is such a need, it is a need that is now being everywhere neglected.

—May 3, 1930

473

Sophistry

...sophistry, being the silliest sort of intellectual pride, is in itself a sort of intellectual pleasure....

— *October* 13, 1917

Sophists

...sophists [are] the more subtle sort of liars, who are always careful to tell the truth, or the wrong half of the truth. They can always be trusted to point out that there is a green that is very nearly blue and a blue that is very nearly green, applying the argument to men and monkeys, or morals and manners, or anything else that may be convenient to the people who have the money to hire them.

— *January* 6, 1923

Soul

...the soul *soaks* the body like a strong savour, and does not merely inhabit it like a hat in a hat-box.

— *February* 17, 1917

Soviet Union

It looks as if Russia might remain for an indefinite time in the queer congested compromise of decayed communism and alien capitalism, and servile or conscript labour....

— *April* 19, 1924

Soviet Union (History of)

The Russian peasant, of whom so much has been written both by Russians and other Europeans, has certainly played a part here which the world does not yet understand, and probably greatly undervalues. I suspect that, as the darkness lifts from this dark continent, the strange and rugged figure traced by Tolstoy ... will seem all the more gigantic against the dawn. For where so much is uncertain, one thing seems increasingly certain; that the peasant has saved his own land from the communists. While princely land-owners have been butchered like wild beasts and the lords of great provinces murdered as a jest, the small peasant on his small square patch of soil has managed to save it, like a man on a small square raft in a restless and tumultuous sea.

—December 20, 1919

Specialists

The economist does not teach economics; he teaches the economic theory of history. The anthropologist does not talk about anthropology, but about whether mind can exist without matter, in face of the peculiar behaviour of a tallow candle. The anthropologist, by his researches into the habits of anthropoids, has discovered that some of them possess the power of blowing out a candle. After this experiment, the exponent of evolution appears to remain very much where the traditional recipient of the revelation of Genesis remained after the light was similarly extinguished.

—August 4, 1928

Spencer, Herbert

... the youth of Herbert Spencer was emphatically a misspent youth. It was spent over the scientific names of things instead of over the things themselves—Herbert Spencer never saw a thing in his life; if he had seen a thing he would have fled screaming. He misspent his youth merely because he missed his youth; he lost knowledge and found science. He had not one single brick of experience with which to build his enormous temple of opinion. In every single question there is this absolute disparity between the very much he knew and the very little he had known. He knew all about sex; he knew nothing about love. He knew all about the philo-progenitive instinct; he knew nothing about fatherhood. He knew all about religions; he knew nothing about a religion.

—August 25, 1906

Herbert Spencer, in his moral system taken as a whole, was prim and prosaic to the point of Methodism. But in his scheme for the nursery he was audacious to the point of literal insanity. He wanted the poor miserable infants to learn by "experience" and by the punishments of Nature. If a child falls into the fire and is reduced to a delicate, feathery ash, Spencer suggests (very truly) that he won't do it again. Nor anything else.

—January 15, 1910

475

Spengler's Decline of the West

... human history was *not* continuous, *not* a thing presenting points of comparison between one stage and another. According to this new theory, there is only a series of closed cycles of different cultures, so separate that they can hardly be compared. We may say that there is no progress, but only progresses. We might almost say that there is no history, but only histories. . . . Theories of that sort must be rather easy to make up—if you leave out more than half the facts.

—October 2, 1931

Almost immediately after the end of the Great War a German wrote a highly successful or widely boomed book called "The Decline of the West." The most human inference (in the opinion of many) was that the German, having assisted at the spectacle of the decline and fall of the German Empire, naturally wanted all the rest of us to decline and fall with him. He felt it would be obviously a breach of taste and tact for any nation to flourish if Germany had declined; if, indeed, he was even aware of the existence of such fringes of his empire as France or Flanders or England.

—September 3, 1932

For me . . . it was false because it was fatalist . . . unhistoric; and false because it involved a particular falsity about the very spirit of the great culture which the critic criticised. It is the whole point of that culture that it has been continuous; it was the whole point of the critic that it had been discontinuous. . . . He cut up ordinary European history into chunks. . . . He chopped ordinary Christian History in two in the middle, in order to deny that either part of it was Christian. . . . He attributed the first half of it entirely to the Moslem Arabs, because they were not Christian; and the second half of it to people of the type of Faust, because they were rather fishy sort of Christians, and German as well. And he talked about these divisions as if they were like the abysses that might separate a stratum full of primordial crystals from a stratum, aeons afterwards, containing the first fantastic traces of marsupial life.

—September 3, 1932

Spirits

Meanwhile, I fear I shall remain one of those who believe in spirits much too easily ever to become a spiritualist. Modern people think the supernatural so improbable that they want to see it. I think it so probable that I leave it alone. Spirits are not worth all this fuss; I know that, for I am one myself.

—April 14, 1906

I do not, of course, believe that good and evil spirits are merely allegories that stand for abstractions.

—September 19, 1925

Spiritualism

I do not mind spiritualism, in so far as it is fierce and credulous. In that it seems to me to be akin to sex, to song, to the great epics and the great religions, to all that has made humanity heroic. I do not object to spiritualism in so far as it is spiritualistic. I do object to it in so far as it is scientific. Conviction and curiosity are both very good things. But they ought to have two different houses. There have been many frantic and blasphemous beliefs in this old barbaric earth of ours; men have served their deities with obscene dances, with cannibalism, and the blood of infants. But no religion was quite so blasphemous as to pretend that it was scientifically investigating its god to see what he was made of.

—April 14, 1906

. . . the spiritualists are always insisting on the strongest argument against themselves— the parallel with our present life. They insist now, apparently, that because we have golf and whiskies-and-sodas here, we must have golf and whiskies-and-sodas hereafter. Any comparison between these small things, here and hereafter, must suggest a comparison between the large things here and hereafter; and the largest and most obvious things are good and evil. If we look for drink, why are we not to look for poison? And if we have to deal with games, why have we not to deal with cheating?

—March 15, 1919

I am not, like a spiritualist, a man whose religion may be said to consist entirely of ghosts. But I am not like a materialist, a man whose whole philosophy is exploded

477

and blasted and blown to pieces by the most feeble and timid intrusion of the most thin and third-rate ghost.

—May 30, 1936

Sport

In sport a man goes into a wood and mixes with the existing life of that wood, becomes a destroyer only in the simple and healthy sense in which all the creatures are destroyers; becomes for one moment to them what they are to him—another animal.

—January 4, 1908

Sports (Professional)

I entertain a private suspicion that physical sports were much more really effective and beneficient when they were not taken quite so seriously. One of the first essentials of sport being healthy is that it should be delightful; it is rapidly becoming a false religion with austerities and prostrations. . . . This frightful solemnity in sport is the real cause of the corruptions that have arisen in it.

—August 25, 1906

We have not made cricket and football professional because of any astonishing avarice or any new vulgarity. We have made them professional because we would have them perfect. We have dedicated men to them as to some god of an inhuman excellence. We care more for football than we care for the fun of playing football. The modern Englishman cares more for cricket than for being a cricketer. And having taken the frivolous things seriously we naturally take the serious things frivolously. Our Derby is the most important thing in England.

—August 25, 1906

State

. . . my solution is the very opposite of the Socialist solution, for it is that, in so far as the state acts at all, it ought to act for the deliberate erection of barriers against itself. It ought to work for the reconstruction of a multitude of small properties, in which men could live securely while they criticised and even defied the state. For it is based on the philosophy that the state may be wrong, as the other solution is based on the philosophy that the state must be right. And that again comes back to the philosophy that man has a house and not a hive; and that the household gods are more sacred even than the gods of the city.

—February 16, 1924

State (Modern)

The large modern State does not secure genuine unity at all. Many of the large States are simply large anarchies—America, for instance. The United States are essentially disunited States.

—August 27, 1910

Endless denunciations of distant vices, endless defiance of distant dangers; endless exploiting of people who know nothing by people who know too much; endless entanglements between the worst indecency of rabbles and the worst secrecy of oligarchs; the poor rioting for what they do not know, and the rich scheming for what they dare not say; all the facts fourth-hand and all the principles fourth-rate— these, palpable and visible before us, are the actual fruits of Union, of the large, highly organised modern State.

—August 27, 1910

State (Totalitarian)

For nothing is needed, to dispose of the whole preposterous Prohibition stuff altogether, except a little clear thinking about the nature of social evils, and how far they can be regulated by social laws. It is not a question of the evil being very evil. There are a great many evils, intrinsically far worse than intoxication; such as spite, or spiritual cruelty, or crushing depression, or all sorts of things, which do not happen to be things that can be dealt with by any law without the extinction of every liberty.

—August 1, 1931

Statesman

If it were really a question between hearing a statesman talk sense and hearing a clown talk nonsense I think I should sometimes, perhaps often—say once in thirty times—wish to hear the statesman. But it is not that: it is a question between hearing the statesman talk nonsense that I am not allowed to laugh at and the clown talk nonsense that I am allowed to laugh at.

—*July* 10, 1909

Public men are, of necessity, uncommunicative. We might say that public men are, of necessity, private. The one person from whom it will be most difficult to extract a real announcement of national policy will be the man who is set up specially to announce it.

—*December* 20, 1930

Statistician

The real statistician says—"Seven men to four" (in some place or other) "take to drink"; but he does not ask why they take to drink. Taking to drink is a mere external act, like taking breakfast at eleven. Not only can two men take to drink for different reasons; they can take to drink for opposite reasons. Jones takes to drink because he is poor and has no other pleasure. Smith takes to drink because he is rich and has no other occupation. Brown takes to drink because he is prosaic and cannot enjoy anything else. Robinson takes to drink because he is poetical and can enjoy everything else, but thirsts for more enjoyment. Tomkins takes to drink because he is a bold man and anxious for experience. Jenkins takes to drink because he is a coward and afraid of pain. The habit of the modern statisticians is always to get hold of these external acts, which mean nothing, to cut them off from their psychological causes, which mean everything, and then to put them thus detached into the human mind (which has been well called divine), where they produce a wholly false impression.

—*November* 18, 1905

480

Statistics

It is an error to suppose that statistics are merely untrue. They are also wicked. As used to-day, they serve the purpose of making masses of men feel helpless and cowardly. If I choose to light a pipe I am not the less free because ten thousand others are doing exactly the same.

—*November* 18, 1905

The weakness of all statistics is that, even when the numbers are generally right, the names are generally wrong. . . . If somebody says that there is a certain percentage of educated people in Heliopolis, Neb., he will very likely say it as firmly as he would say that there are so many Negroes in that Nebraskan seat of culture. Whereas it is rather as if he were saying that there were so many opinionated people, which is a matter of opinion.

—*July* 23, 1927

. . . when people talk about "educational statistics" and make tables of the condition of culture in Nebraska or anywhere else, there is really nothing in their statements that is exact except the numbers; and the numbers must be inexact when there is nothing to apply them to. The statistician is trying to make a rigid and unchangeable chain out of elastic links.

—*July* 23, 1927

Statue (Modern)

It seems absurd that a thing should not be popular when its whole object is to be public. The most exquisite art may be a puzzle to the mere passer-by; but if it is elaborately erected on a pedestal merely in order to impress him, it seems a pity that it should only puzzle him.

—*November* 3, 1917

If a public statue is only a private taste, it might much more properly be a private statuette.

—*November* 3, 1917

481

Stein, Gertrude

I grieve to say, from what I know of human nature and history, that I doubt whether posterity will even try to understand Miss Stein. So that she will share her little joke with her creator until the end; which may be quite a good joke too. But the theory that has been so common of late, the theory that the evolution of literature branches out into new experiments, seems to me to be flatly contradicted by all the facts of literary history.

—September 12, 1931

Stevenson, Robert Louis

Stevenson was an artist; he was also an aesthete; and it was the age when artists and aesthetes posed in picturesque attitudes all down the street. What was arresting about Stevenson was that he posed in a cheerful and courageous attitude—in a fighting attitude. And he really had something to fight . . . it was really disease and death; which some have thought to be even more depressing things than German officials and Protestant missionaries. It is not strange that he stood out among a number of poets and prose writers (most of them in excellent health) who declared that life itself is a disease of which the only cure is death.

—July 25, 1925

Stevenson's Dr. Jekyll and Mr. Hyde

. . . in the background there are very big ideas, that have been embodied in the images of angels and devils fighting for the soul of man. Now one of the oldest and newest, one of the most subtle and the most sound, of those ideas about the spiritual struggle is this—that the devil is a traitor. It is more dangerous to be his friend than to be his foe. He betrays; and even the bribe he offers is not the bribe he gives. In any number of old legends this is expressed by the idea of the flaw in the deed, the unforeseen disadvantage in the contract.

—September 19, 1925

Strictness

. . . there are two quite different kinds of strictness. We apply the word strict, narrow, bigoted, or intolerant, to two separate states of mind which are not only different but are really quite opposite. To put the point quite crudely, we call a man narrow when he is illogical; but we also call a man narrow when he is logical. If a man has a pure doctrine you call him a bigot. Yet if a man has a mere prejudice (or, if you like, a mere sentiment or instinct), you call him a bigot too. But a man must have something. If he has not got doctrines, he must have prejudices.

—July 4, 1908

Stoic

. . . the cheap Stoic or superior person is none the less as lifeless as a stone, because he generally regards himself as a precious stone, and falls into the not uncommon geological error of supposing that he is the only pebble on the beach. Compared with him, there is something like movement in the mere mass of pebbles that are rolled to and fro by the sea.

—December 5, 1925

Story

. . . no sane author would say that any one story was absolutely and in all aspects the best; indeed, a sane author is more likely to be hag-ridden with the horrid memory of the worst.

—January 25, 1930

I think there is in all literature a sort of purpose; quite different from the mere moralising that is generally meant by a novel with a purpose. There is something in the plan of the idea that is straight like a backbone and pointing like an arrow. It is meant to go somewhere, or at least to point somewhere; to its end, not only in the modern sense of an ending, but in the mediaeval sense of a fruition. Now, I think that many of the less intellectual stories have kept this, where the more intellectual stories have lost it.

—March 8, 1930

Style

... I know in all my bones that the thing we call *style* is not a flourish or a varnish; but is a thing virile and fit for men. Style is in the inside of a man, and not on the outside.

—July 31, 1915

Every new style has arisen because people were tired of an old style, and has generally been followed by a return to a yet older style. The amplification and accumulation of everything drives us on towards the future, and right round the world, till we come again to the past.

—December 13, 1930

Submission

Radicals often speak of the evils of a slavish and panic-stricken submission to the past. ... There is one thing meaner; a slavish and panic-stricken submission to the future.

—February 22, 1908

Sub-conscious

Many young people to-day have probably grown up with the idea that Freud discovered the subconsciousness, just as many of my generation grew up with the idea that Darwin invented the theory of evolution. I am old enough to remember that nearly everybody talked about subconsciousness when nobody had ever heard of Freud. When I was a boy professors were burrowing in it, especially in that tunnel that may or may not connect the psychological with the psychical. The psychological generally called it the subconsciousness. The psychical generally preferred to call it the subliminal consciousness. Even as a modern theory it is older than I am.

—May 30, 1925

Success

All journalists, I suppose, are asked by all sorts of people how to succeed in journalism; even those who have not succeeded. Moreover, even if the success be genuine of its kind, it by no means follows that the successful man is the man who knows most about it. It is one thing to do something, and quite another to know how it is done. But for such a distinction authors and critics would both perish miserably.

—August 21, 1909

... whatever we may think of the boldness and brilliancy of the paradox that nothing succeeds like success, I will make bold to emphasise another and more neglected truth: that nothing fails like success. I mean that nothing can fail so completely, hopelessly, and finally as that which is solely based on success.

—December 19, 1931

Suffragette

They were really very unpolitical women—certainly much more so than ordinary women. But even they discovered this truth by experience, though they never realised it in theory. They began by throwing bricks and bombs at politicians for not agreeing with Female Suffrage. But they soon found themselves throwing bricks and bombs at the same politicians for agreeing with Female Suffrage—and then doing nothing for it.

—July 7, 1917

Suffragette Legislation

If you hold a more decent opinion, that, upon the whole, the tyranny of the world is that of male over female rather than that of rich over poor, then you may welcome Mr. Shackleton's bill as a sort of symbol. If you think (as many do, both rich and poor) that England is on the whole better governed by rich men than by Englishmen, then you should take Mr. Shackleton's bill into your arms like a new-born babe and cherish and strengthen it above all things. But if, by any wild chance, you originally became a Suffragist because you believed in the ultimate rule of the people, then you ought to stamp it down into the mire.

—August 6, 1910

Suggestion

... there is such a thing as suggestion, which is nearly all of modern journalism. ...

—February 15, 1930

Suicide

I admit that murder must be classed among acts distinctly improper and, indeed, morally wrong. But suicide seems to me the supreme blasphemy against God and man and beast and vegetables; the attack not upon a life, but upon life itself; the murder of the universe.

—April 16, 1932

Sun Myth

In my cradle, so to speak, I heard the echoes of laughter at the sun myth, already largely recognised as not so much a myth of the early savages as a myth of the early scientists.

—May 9, 1925

Superman

In short, the great man is a man; it is always the tenth-rate man who is the Superman.

—July 2, 1910

... many earnest evolutionists in our time have written gravely as if the superman was to be expected next week! ... The Superman was simply and solely a phantom called out of the void by the imagination of a lunatic; a quite literal lunatic named Nietzsche. Yet how vivid that utterly unreasonable vision became for many of our wavering and weak-minded generation! And the strangest thing of all is that it was some of the best brains that were thus bewitched.

—March 8, 1924

Superstitions

Superstitions are a sort of sombre fairy-tales that we tell to ourselves in order to express, by random and realistic images, the mystery of the strange laws of life. We know so little when a man will die that it may well be sitting thirteenth at a table that kills him. Superstitions really are what the Modernists say that dogmas are: mere symbols of a much deeper matter, of a fundamental and fantastic agnosticism about the causes of things.

—May 28, 1910

... there are undoubtedly materialists still surviving in the modern world who have some such absurd ideal of rooting out all superstition. Even if they could root out all religion, it is very doubtful if they could root out all superstition. All that the process ever does is to destroy the happier and healthier legends, and leave the darker and more degraded ones. Thus the Puritans largely succeeded in destroying the belief in saints and encouraging the belief in witches. Thus the industrial nineteenth century took away from the funeral the cross and candles, and left only the black plumes and the mutes. And thus the most pagan part of the modern world retains a mass of meaningless omens of misfortune, which once had a relation to happier mysteries. Men called Friday unlucky without remembering why it is called good; and talk about thirteen without thinking of the twelve apostles.

—August 20, 1921

Surrender

We surrender, not when circumstances are miserable, but when we are miserable. As long as a man is not a pessimist it does not matter how much he is a failure. He will survive that strange midnight in which is born the strangest and most awful kind of optimism.

—July 14, 1906

Survival of the Fittest

The theory of the survival of the fittest simply means this: that if there is nothing but dirt, those will survive who will eat dirt. It says nothing about the "height" of dirt-eating people; it does not even indicate that the dirt-eaters will improve the physical universe, let alone the human commonwealth.

—September 18, 1909

This is a very transparent catchword, and yet not everybody could see the catch in it. For it only means that one of the animals, very much of the lower animals, is fit to survive. It does not mean that he is fit to rule, or fit to be admired, or fit to be touched with a barge-pole.

—February 20, 1932

Swastika

Germans have died in millions fighting bravely for real national or imperial symbols, which were historic and human. But these things came, as do our national symbols, from the older culture of Europe; not from the new culture of college professors.... When did any historic German really bother about the crooked cross that is identified with certain ritual ideas in the old civilisations of Asia and the Near East? Did any Bavarian peasant ever make the sign of the swastika? Did any of the Teutonic knights fighting in Poland emblazon his shield with the swastika? Did any of them worry whether they were Aryans or not? No; Christendom is a reality; and Prussia is a reality; and even the notion of a Teutonic race may be more loosely and relatively a reality. But the notion of an Aryan race uniting those who talked Sanscrit with those who talk high Dutch is not a reality; it is a pedantry....

—June 11, 1932

Swearing

We all know that the worst of using strong language is that it produces weak language. Words which were uttered with the best intentions, in the way of violence and abusiveness, are gradually weakened and corrupted into courtesy and amiability. The earnest and eloquent person who has carefully chosen his words with the pure purpose of being blasting and blasphemous finds that by his very exaggeration he has become coldly conventional and polite. He struggles against the creeping paralysis of propriety, but his very struggles increase the stiffness that inevitably follows the abuse of violence. Instead of having strengthened his own case, he has only spoilt a large number of beautiful swear-words.

—August 28, 1926

Swift, Jonathan

The greatness of the great Jonathan Swift grows upon me as I go on through life, like a man travelling nearer and nearer to a mountain.... I liked him for liking Bolingbroke; for despising Marlborough; for showing up the glorious Hanoverian succession in Ireland as a very low and dirty job; for treating the wit of the freethinkers with contempt; for giving the first place to the virtue of honour, which practically disappeared from politics and financial affairs about this time. It is doubtless true that he was too bitter and exclusive, but that is no reason why we should be. And the final phase of true philanthropy is not complete until it can love the misanthrope.

—*October* 15, 1932

Swinburne, Algernon Charles

... I asked myself, "What on earth did Swinburne mean? Or did he mean anything?" It is easy enough, after reading some of the poems, especially the later, longer, and generally lesser poems, to say that he did not mean anything; that he was simply a musician gone wrong; a lunatic with something singing in his head; a creature throbbing with suppressed dancing; a creature who could not help foaming at the mouth with flowers and flames and blood and blossoms and the sea.

—*January* 25, 1930

"Swing of the Pendulum"

Some people have invented a very wicked phrase.... They call it "the swing of the pendulum." But a man ought to be ashamed to be compared to a lump of lead. A pendulum swings because it cannot help it. But if there be a man who is ready to regard himself in the light of a pendulum, I have no use for him. Such a man ought to hang himself. Then he could be a pendulum and swing as much as he liked.

—*November* 18, 1905

Symbol

The most practical thing of all, in that sense, is not to have any decorations at all. If it is too much trouble to symbolise anything, it is too much trouble to have symbols. There cannot possibly be any sense in taking the trouble to have symbols that do not symbolise. If names are not worth troubling about, flags are not worth troubling about; and it is the most unbusinesslike thing in the world to spend money on things you do not want.

—August 2, 1919

Symposium

Cows drink water, and philosophers, at least real philosophers, drink wine. The very word still used in our magazines for a debate among intellectuals about some interesting topic is simply the name of the drinking-bout or wine-party of the old Greek philosophers. When an editor asks me to take part in a symposium, I suppose I am really entitled to assume that he has offered me a drink.

—January 3, 1925

Everybody knows that the old Greek title of a symposium has fallen from its first high classical purity and dignity of meaning, by which it meant drinks all round, and descended—nay, degenerated—until it only means a set of separate printed statements, generally in every sense dry.

—April 2, 1932

T-U-V-W-X-Y-Z

Taste

A dispute about taste is never in any sense settled. But as a fact, men for the most part vastly prefer to dispute about taste, because they do not want their disputes settled. You cannot prove in black and white the superiority of blue and green, but you can bang each other about the head and pretend to prove it in black and blue. Hence we always find that these illogical disputes are the most pugnacious and provocative. They produce a prodigious race of people swaggering and laying down the law. And they lay down the law because there is no law to be laid down. There is no disputing about tastes and therefore there is always bragging, brawling, and rioting about tastes.

—December 17, 1927

Tax

A citizen can hardly distinguish between a tax and a fine, except that the fine is generally much lighter.

—May 25, 1931

Of course, there is a sort of paradox in taxation, anyhow ... there is often the notion of checking something, and yet the hope that it will not be checked. A lover of birds might wish to have a tax on cats, with the idea that there would be fewer cats. But the statesman imposing the tax would presumably hope that the streets would be thronged with thousands and thousands of cats, each bringing its little subscription to the embarrassed exchequer.

—May 25, 1931

Taxes

The Church gives, or ought to give, to the people a religion or revelation they cannot get anywhere else. The inn gives, or ought to give, to the people a quantity of ale or wine that they have not got. But the people can only get out of a pillar-box what they have put into it; and the individual citizen is not even allowed to do that.

—August 9, 1924

Tea

...a lady I know very well, said on first tasting the beverage in its modified American form, "Well, if that's the sort of tea we sent you, I don't wonder you threw it into Boston harbour."

—January 3, 1925

Tea-time

Where there is tea, there is tea-time. Where it really exists as a beverage that can be drunk, it also exists as an institution that must be observed; and the name of it is not merely tea, but afternoon tea. . . . A certain stage in the slow descent of the sun, a certain line in the mathematical map of heaven that is traced in stars, a certain fine shade between afternoon and evening, is made and marked by the ancient human instinct even for the modern institution of tea. Tea is a libation to the sun in that quarter of heaven, to the gods of that condition of earth and sky, fully as much as Easter eggs are proper to Easter or Christmas puddings to Christmas.

—January 3, 1925

Technology

Many modern people . . . worship the means of civilisation instead of the end. There are many ladies and gentlemen I know who would seriously approve of the rack if it were kept quite clean and worked by electricity.

—August 20, 1910

Teetotalism and Temperance

The places where nobody has ever dreamed of Prohibition, the places where nobody has ever heard of Prohibition, these are precisely the places where people have achieved largely, and on a large scale, the practise of moderation in drink. . . . In Bavaria, where nobody ever dreamed that beer could be forbidden, beer is a very light and mild brew shared by husbands, wives and children in harmless picnics. In Chicago, where beer is forbidden, beer has acted as a sort of dynamite of revolution and has turned a racketeer into a dictator. In France, where hardly anybody drinks anything but wine, hardly anybody drinks very much wine. In Scotland, which is scoured by fanatics screaming for Prohibition, every public holiday pours out a rabble, drunk on raw whisky to scream back at them like demons.

—August 1, 1931

Temperance Reform

Temperance Reform generally takes two forms—the limitation of the places of drinking and the limitation of the hours of drinking. I think the first quite useful and the second quite useless. Shutting up three public-houses and leaving the other two would, I think, be good for temperance; shutting up all five an hour earlier would be good for drunkenness, and for nothing else.

—June 6, 1908

Temperance Reformers

. . . temperance reformers . . . (according to some) have water on the brain after another fashion.

—May 21, 1910

493

The Ten Commandments

... the curtness of the Commandments is an evidence, not of the gloom and narrowness of a religion, but, on the contrary, of its liberality and humanity. It is shorter to state the things forbidden than the things permitted; precisely because most things are permitted, and only a few things are forbidden. . . . In comparison with. . . . positive morality, the Ten Commandments rather shine in that brevity which is the soul of wit. It is better to tell a man not to steal than to try to tell him the thousand things that he can enjoy without stealing; especially as he can generally be pretty well trusted to enjoy them.

—January 3, 1920

Teutonic Theories

A man once sent me a book full of these Teutonic theories (now politely called Nordic theories) about the English nation—a book that bore the cheery title of "By Thor, No!" I pointed out to him, at the time, that the very phrase upset the whole of his case. No Englishman in all recorded history ever said "By Thor!" But hundreds and thousands of Englishmen have really said "By Jove!"

—July 16, 1927

Teutonism

The Teutonic view that virility came only from the North got over Napoleon somehow; I really do not know how. Perhaps the Scandinavians had skated all the way to Corsica in the Ice Age.

—December 6, 1919

Theist

It is now universally recognised. . . . that anybody who believes in things called creeds and dogmas is a worm. But there has been considerable consternation of late, because the worm has begun to turn. Now, the worm can turn because it is a living thing. A dead thing, working like a rod or running on a rail, can only go forward; it is limited to one movement and is therefore progressive. But worms, though limited to few movements, are not limited to one movement. They have the power to turn—that is, the power to return; even to return on themselves, which is the sign of life and the beginning of thought. . . . The case of the religious worm [is] beginning to turn when about ten thousand mechanical and monotonous and precisely similar railway-trains of dull materialism have gone over him.

—May 17, 1930

Theologian (Liberal)

. . . these "broad-minded" people are always telling us that belief is not confined in certain forms, but is a certain spirit. To which I answer, "Very well, trot out the spirit; give me a little of it in a liqueur-glass. If religion is only a matter of taste, call the waiter, and let me taste my religion. I shall know whether it tastes right or not." And then the New Theologians bring me something which is made in the shape of a goose and tastes of half-baked beans.

—January 1, 1910

Theologians (Progressive)

The minds of these people work backwards, from effect to cause, and not from cause to effect.

—October 4, 1930

Theology (New)

For instance, I see in the papers persistent talk of something called a New Theology. I am attracted by this, for I could myself with the greatest pleasure make up a number of New Theologies if I did not happen to believe in an old one. I look at the New Theology, however, and find that it is an old Theology, that it is even more than that—that it is something older and duller than Theology itself; that it is the dim and vague cosmogony which men required before they were intellectual enough to require Theology.

—February 2, 1907

The new theologians often say that the old creeds need re-statement; but though they say it, they do not mean it. They mean exactly the opposite. They do not mean that we should find new words to express the exact meaning of the old doctrines. They mean that we should say the old words, but agree that they mean something entirely different.

—July 3, 1920

The statement, repeated in a hundred forms, is in its commonest form something like this: "The world is weary of the creeds; it does not want disputes about dogmas; what it wants is a living church inspiring a Christian life." Now this is quite false. The world wants exactly the opposite. The world *does* want discussion on creeds; it *does* want disputes about dogmas; it proves the fact in every word that is printed and said. And, though a truly Christian life would certainly be far nobler than any newspaper discussion, it is quite doubtful whether it would not bore the average newspaper-reader. It would bore him, perhaps, even if it were real Christianity; it would certainly bore him horribly if it were the sort of healthy, hazy, provincial thing that is often called real Christianity.

—November 25, 1927

Theory and Practise

If anything is new, it is not the ideas which are supposed to belong only to this generation. It is the riots, massacres, wars, military proclamations, and wholesale executions, which were always supposed to belong especially to the past barbaric and superstitious generations. I knew all about the communist theory of Karl Marx before I was twenty-five. What I did not know was that the communist theory would ever make ferocious use of the Russian secret police, or would shoot down workmen by the score for going on strike. I had heard all about Nietzsche and the master mind and the reaction against democracy when I was a young art student. What I did not dream of was that a mob of master minds would ever be able to silence the centrum by force and drive the Jews out of Germany.

—April 7, 1934

Thinking

Mr. Wilson, like M. Poincaré, belongs to the small group of honestly strong men who think before they act, for thinking is the hardest work in the world, and the most repugnant to our nature. Therefore the lazier sort of politician takes refuge in activity. The Superman, the Man of Action, acts before he thinks: he has to do his thinking afterwards.

—September 26, 1914

Slow thinking is accompanied with incessant excitement; but quick thinking is more quiet.

—June 21, 1930

Thought

To come to the conclusion that a divine revelation has been made to man, and treat it as such, is thought; and it is not valid unless it is voluntary; that is, unless it is free. But to have a vague horror of the word Darwin being mixed up with the word monkey-house is not free thought; because it is not thought. It is rather habit; and a very bad habit, too.

—December 8, 1923

The recent decay of thought may be due to the general notion of merely going forward; whereas all thinking is thinking backwards.

—May 17, 1930

Thought (Free)

If free thought means that we are not free to rebuke free-thinkers, it is surely a very one-sided sort of free thought. It means that they may say anything they choose about all that we hold most dear, and we must not say anything we think in protest against all that we hold most damnable.

—June 10, 1922

Thought (Modern)

Have you ever seen a fellow fail at the high jump because he had not gone far enough back for his run? That is Modern Thought. It is so confident of where it is going to that it does not know where it comes from.

—July 11, 1914

497

Not one man in ten throughout the whole nineteenth- and twentieth-century civilisation has had the very vaguest notion that he needed to have any first principles. He often actually imagined that there was something rather scientific and rational and modern about not having any first principles.

—November 21, 1925

... Matthew Arnold put his complaint against a theologian in the form of saying: "The very thing he sets out with he is unable to prove." That description would apply to the best piece of logic in the world. It would also apply to every piece of logic in the world. It would apply to the logic of Arnold's own complaint. ... But to complain merely of a logician setting out with something unproved is itself a disastrous lapse of logic. How could he ever set out at all, if he was always set back and made to prove his own starting-point? What is needed for that starting-point is not that the point should be proved at the start. It is, ideally, that it should be self-evident.

—November 21, 1925

All this that calls itself Modern Thought is a series of false starts and belated stoppages. It starts by believing in nothing, and it ends by getting nowhere. But the point is that, even if it ever gets anywhere, it no longer even tries to get where it originally wanted to go.

—November 9, 1929

Thought Process

They say that second thoughts are best, but I incline to disagree. I think that third thoughts are sometimes best. But I think that first thoughts are much better than second thoughts, and have more resemblance to the real ripeness of third thoughts. In the first stage we act merely on instinct, and are sometimes right. In the second stage we act merely on reason, and are fairly frequently wrong. In the third and truly reasonable stage we use our reason until we understand our instincts. And if we do that with romance we shall come pretty near reality.

—June 27, 1914

Threatening Letters and Civility

I receive these threatening letters by every post; they choke up the front passages; yet it never occurs to us that there is anything funny in the fact that the man begins by describing us as "dear." This is because we never actually read the word "dear" at all. We do not read what the man says; we only read what he means. And what he means when he says "Dear Sir" is not in the least what he says. What he means is, "Because I consider you an atrocious brigand and a disgrace to human society, that is no reason why I, in addressing you, should omit the customary ceremonials of a citizen and a civilised man."

—November 25, 1905

Titles as Façade

There happens to be a mere fashion in the modern world of giving to all sorts of enterprises fancy titles, which are democratic in form. A man will call his party the popular party; though he is no more disinterested than a tradesman who will call his soap the popular soap.... One of them will be called something like the Worshipful Company of Bricklayers, without retaining any very vivid traces of its daily task of bricklaying. Another will bear some such name as the Worshipful Company of Chimneysweeps; and will give the most glorious dinners, at which the presence of a chimneysweep, fresh from work, would be notable, and even unexpected.

—October 6, 1917

Tobacco

For those who sneer at tobacco may be expected, in the same sense, to sniff at snuff, and presumably to snivel over pepper, for a great part of their moral eloquence consists of sniffing and snivelling. Nothing is needed, for most of their moral movements, but a sort of gesture of priggish repugnance and small-minded superiority; and it would be just as easy for a moralist to make that sort of face over a jar of pickles as over a pot of porter.

—February 21, 1931

Toleration

Modern toleration is really a tyranny. It is a tyranny because it is a silence. To say that I must not deny my opponent's faith is to say I must not discuss it; I may not say that Buddhism is false, and that is all I want to say about Buddhism. It is the only interesting thing that anybody can want to say about Buddhism—either that it is false or that it is true.

—October 10, 1908

It is the tragic irony of the progressive position to-day that those who talk most about toleration are exactly those who cannot tolerate the idea of anybody drinking at an inn.

—January 7, 1928

Tolstoy, Leo

Literature, especially good literature like Tolstoy's, is much more reliable than Government reports or journalistic facts. And good literature like Tolstoy's is quite as convincing when you think it wrong as when you think it right. I have never been inside a Russian prison; but I have been inside a Tolstoy novel. And, spiritually speaking, I have sometimes thought that I should prefer the prison.

—January 23, 1909

I hate his philosophy myself; but I almost love him for making it so hateful.

—January 15, 1910

... the last fact is still that he preached a false morality. He did preach, and preach explicitly, courageously, and with a quite honourable clearness, that if you see a man flogging a woman to death you must not hit him. I would much sooner let a leper come near a little boy than a man who preached such a thing.

—December 24, 1910

If Tolstoy had been my friend, I should have boasted everywhere, and boasted with justice, of the intimacy of so original and intense a mind—a man of genius who must have stimulated even when he provoked. . . . But if he had come within twenty miles as a tutor to my children, I would have chased him off the land. I would have let loose a dog. I would have fired off a cannon; anything rather than that children should be taught by Tolstoy. I would have provoked civil war (from which my English temperament is profoundly averse) rather than allow one helpless, top-heavy little infant to learn Tolstoy instead of learning truth.

—December 24, 1910

Tolstoy, Leo (and Education)

. . . what he says is briefly this: Every child must be told that he has a soul and a body, and that all evil comes from obeying his body and all good from obeying his soul. The child is to keep a little notebook, apparently, and recall at the end of the day the occasions on which he has wickedly obeyed his body, and those on which he has wisely obeyed his soul. It is further to be explained to him that in our souls we are all naturally loving and united (a lie) and that it is our animal bodies that delight to bark and bite, for 'tis their nature to. To say that the body begets evil and the soul good is to say that the Publican is worse than the Pharisee; and if that is not un-Christian, what is?

—January 15, 1910

Tory

In short, the Tory of two or three years ago only existed in order to defend what the Tory of two hundred years ago was trying to prevent.

—April 19, 1924

It is highly characteristic of English Tories that they were told never to find a definition of anything—even of Toryism.

—June 7, 1924

Townsman

In short, the modern townsman is only a part of a complicated system—or, as was more unkindly said of the ancient tailor, he is only one-tenth of a man. He does not understand a tenth or a hundredth part of his own life, his own livelihood, his own world. He would certainly be very ignorant if the newspapers told him nothing. As it is, he is only fairly ignorant, for many newspapers tell him lies.

—July 26, 1924

Tradition

Tradition is simply the democracy of the dead.

—January 11, 1908

There are two kinds of tradition; and two kinds of mistake made about it. The first may be called the careless of secular tradition, like that of the Cretan Labyrinth; the second the careful or religious tradition, like that of the bones of Buddha. . . . The first is that when a man tells the tale of the maze of Minos, we actually think him a fool because he points to the maze itself in front of him. The second is that, because three million men would have died in torments to find the real bones of Buddha, we deduce that they have probably put up with the bones of somebody else.

— September 4, 1909

All continuity must be a series of restorations. And all restorations must invariably be revolutions.

—November 19, 1910

Tradition is not a dry and dusty and antiquated affair. Tradition is as vital and dramatic as treason, which is the same word. The silent passing of a scrap of history from father to son is as personal and passionate as the silent passing of a scrap of paper from traitor to spy.

—November 19, 1910

It can be plainly shown, I think, that unconsciously, by a flowing and historic process, men tend to say that things are recent when they are really very ancient. . . . And there is the same tendency to refer everything to the last authority. The tradition, as a matter of fact, has come down through numberless generations; but each person remembers it by the person who had it last. He does not think of it as a thing connected with his first forefathers; but as a thing connected with his father. Hence the

502

tendency (in drink, quarrel, or old age) is to refer everything to the generation just before. And so it is really true that old traditions often declare for new monuments. It is now continually assumed that old men and old legends will describe things as too old. This is not so. Old men and old legends often describe things as much too new.

—November 19, 1910

For it is precisely the poor people, after all, who have preserved . . . traditions, when the rich were often deserting them in pursuit of fashions. Dickens was not only strictly right, but strictly realistic, when he made the penniless Cratchits cling to the tradition of pleasure; while the wealthy Scrooge scoffed at it, in the name of the fashion of utilitarianism. Indeed, Dickens was much more right than he himself knew. He only knew the human debris of the industrial breakdown; he knew nothing of the poor self-organised into a stable and respectable caste, as in the countries of the peasants. But in most places it is the peasants who preserve the historic and even the prehistoric things.

—December 29, 1917

. . . the only truly traditional tradition is one that is still a living thing.

—August 30, 1924

. . . tradition is the truth of the common people.

—September 18, 1926

. . . there is such a thing as tradition, which is nearly half of true history. . . .

—February 15, 1930

A young man grows up in a world that often sounds to him intolerably old. He grows up among proverbs and precepts that appear to be quite stiff and senseless. He seems to be stuffed with stale things; to be given the stones of death instead of the bread of life; to be fed on the dust of the dead past; to live in a town of tombs. It is a very natural mistake, but it is a mistake. The advantage of advancing years lies in discovering that traditions are true, and therefore alive; indeed, a tradition is not even traditional except when it is alive. It is great fun to find out that the world has not repeated proverbs because they are proverbial, but because they are practical.

— March 14, 1931

... in practical experience the human being generally does go back. And he goes back for one of the commonest and most practical reasons ... because he has left something behind. There is such a thing as social wreck, like the wreck of Robinson Crusoe's ship. There is such a thing as social progress, like the progress of Robinson Crusoe's farm. But where the philosophers are wrong and the romancer is right and indeed very realistic is that Robinson Crusoe will have to go back very often to the wreck in order to stock or furnish the farm. When there really is anything like the building of a new civilisation, it means that there has been a great deal of quarrying in the ruins of the old civilisation. When there is only a false start, a half-built farmhouse, a half-baked culture and bankruptcy, it means that the reformers have tried to simplify life too much; they have left behind them all that they wanted most.

— December 30, 1933

Traitor

The man who tells the truth about a detective story is simply a wicked man, as wicked as the man who deliberately breaks a child's soap-bubble — and he is more wicked than Nero. To give away a secret when it should be kept is the worst of human crimes; and Dante was never more right than when he made the lowest circle in Hell the Circle of the Traitors.

— November 7, 1908

Transference (Negative)

Balzac did not become a great novelist because his father had annoyed him with practicality; he became a great novelist because he was a great man. Beethoven did not succeed because his father drank; it is much more likely that he was a composer for the same reason that made his father a fiddler. These are only a few random examples of these random statements which are thrown about everywhere, that the people may learn science from men who have never learnt logic.

— July 12, 1930

Trash (Cult of)

I mean by trash something much more essential and psychological; I mean the tendency to get the mind itself stuffed with rubbish, in the sense of wordy expositions of anything or nothing; or phrases that are only the fragments of philosophies; of dead words used as talismans, like the dead hand. In short, the cult of trash is the contrary of the cult of truth; it means using language, or even learning and literature, without any lively current of curiosity or purpose running in the direction of truth.

—*July 6, 1929*

Travel (Modern)

... travel, in the true sense, has become impossible in the large urban or urbanised districts. There are twenty ways of going everywhere, and there is nowhere to go.... A traveller in simpler times travelled with two legitimate and even estimable objects: first to see strange things in the places he went to; and second, to boast about the country he came from. Both these admirable arts are bound to suffer neglect and negation under existing conditions, when the place he finds is exactly like the place he leaves. All such places are alike, plastered with the same advertisements, blocked up with the same big shops, selling the same newspapers, attending the same schools.

—*October 2, 1926*

Traveller

... travellers' tales are in their nature the very opposite of official reports.

—*May 24, 1924*

Tree-climbing

That great master of romance, the ordinary child, has always attempted to anticipate aviation, with all the ardour of Leonardo da Vinci. There is a strange illusion that boys climb trees for the purpose of birds'-nesting. As a fact, the boy does not climb the tree to rob the birds, but to rival them; and he covets not their eggs, but their wings. Have you never seen a boy in a tree? Have you never been a boy in a tree? If you want to know what he is doing, or if *he* wants to know what he is doing, I can enlighten him; he is trying to invent an aeroplane.

—November 24, 1917

Trollope, Anthony

The really interesting fact to be inferred from Trollope is this. Nineteenth-century England is not a country in which we have a populace led by a liberal middle class on one side, and a powerful Tory nobility led by dukes and earls on the other. The division of the parties is totally different, and unconsciously betrays the real secret, not only of the nineteenth, but of the eighteenth and seventeenth centuries. It betrays the truth about the Glorious Revolution of 1688, and the nature of the new system which it really introduced. The Crown did not pass from James II to William III. Like many stolen treasures, it was cut up: it was cut up into coronets. What the serious historians have disguised, the frivolous novelist has detected. Their histories are fiction and his fiction is history. That is the truth; and that is Trollope's unconscious witness to what the Whigs really did in English history. . . .

—March 15, 1930

Trotsky, Leon

Everything in Russia that Trotsky did not like was bourgeois—in a country where there is hardly any bourgeoisie. The peasant proprietor does not fit in neatly with the Marxian scheme, so he did not figure very largely in the maximalist speeches, though he figures by thousands in most of the European countries about which the speeches were made. At the best, such divisions are curiously crude and external. It is as if a man were to say that England must be divided into upper, middle, and lower classes, because there was a first, second, and third class on the railway.

—February 23, 1918

It is possible that some ladies may have fallen in love at first sight with the features of Mr. Trotsky, flashing past them in the illustrated papers—though, from my own recollections, I think it improbable.

—March 2, 1918

This sort of man always says that peasants cannot read or write, so it is no wonder if they kill their own mothers and eat them. He can be marked out and branded by his black stupidity in always saying something like that; and Trotsky says something very like it. He is always as much cut off from the earth as a dwarf on stilts. He always thinks that a man like a magician, who can conjure live things out of the earth, knows nothing. He always thinks that a man like himself, who can read dead words out of the newspaper, knows everything.

—June 12, 1919

Truth

There is a case for telling the truth; there is a case for avoiding the scandal; but there is no possible defence for the man who tells the scandal, but does not tell the truth.

—July 18, 1908

The whole truth is generally the ally of virtue; a half-truth is always the ally of some vice.

—June 11, 1910

In almost all these liberal and progressive and social evolutionist or revolutionist causes there were great truths which can only be forgotten and can never be falsified. Such truths always return, for there is nothing so formidable and terrible as a fact that is forgotten. But such truths in their exile will only expiate their essential and really evil error, the idolatry of the clock. They are failing because they boasted of being modern instead of being right, and now things more modern claim to be more right. They boasted of being new instead of being true, and now things more new boast of being more true. But in so far as they themselves were true, their truths will remain; and nothing about them will look foolish except their names.

—September 30, 1933

Truth and Philosophy

It would be impossible to pay a more complete tribute to the truth of a philosophy than to say that nobody understands it except the few people who have found it to be true.

—March 8, 1924

Turkey

A turkey is more occult and awful than all the angels and archangels. In so far as God has partly revealed to us an angelic world, he has partly told us what an angel means. But God has never told us what a turkey means. And if you go and stare at a live turkey for an hour or two, you will find by the end of it that the enigma has rather increased than diminished.

—January 4, 1908

Tyranny

Just as it was the mark of old tyranny to stretch the law, so it will be the mark of new tyranny to make a law that can be stretched.

—March 17, 1923

Unity

Human unity is a huge and overwhelming truth in the face of which all differences of continent or country are flattened out.

—January 11, 1931

Universal

It can easily be applied to any other norm as well as the norm of nationality. Is there such a thing as a dog? And if there is, what are its essential characteristics? What is there in common between a mastiff and a minute Pekinese . . . and so on. In one sense the difference is indeed very difficult to ignore, and the identity very difficult to define. In practice we can only say two things about it. First, that we know that all the dogs know they are dogs, and act accordingly. And second that a man who ignores the fact may soon be found trying to teach a pig to be a watch-dog, and to hunt a fox with a pack of cats; and may be found soon after that in a madhouse.

—*March* 15, 1924

Unpractical

There is no such thing as an unpractical aim; though there may be such a thing as a wrong aim. There can be nothing "unpractical" about a serious ultimate desire; though there may be something wrong about it.

—*February* 22, 1908

Unreason (Apostles of)

There really *are* some writers, very modern and fashionable writers at that, who *are* Apostles of Unreason; and say they are. M. Bergson ... really seems to hold that we may find out what we want by trying to get it—without knowing what it is.... Mr. Bernard Shaw ... has maintained that all logic leads to killing oneself; and, of the two, it is better to kill logic. Nietzsche ... said, "We must have chaos within, that we may give birth to a dancing star." The Pragmatists are Apostles of Unreason. Nearly all the Modernists who were condemned in the Pope's Encyclical were condemned for being Pragmatists and Apostles of Unreason.... Oscar Wilde set the fashion of being an Apostle of Unreason when he said that brute reason was hitting below the intellect.... In short, we may really say that nearly all the people who consider themselves specially progressive, advanced, up-to-date, modernist, or futurist, are avowedly Apostles of Unreason. Practically, it comes to this, that the people who are now opposed to reason are practically all the people who are also opposed to religion.

—*March* 21, 1914

Unsectarian ("Objective")

They are discussing, not whether religion can be unsectarian, but whether anything can be unsectarian. I do not mean they would deny that one can teach some things without bias. I suppose one can teach any exact science without a bias—except astronomy.... But these disputants do raise the whole question of whether what is commonly called culture—history, citizenship, literature, and the great languages—can be taught without a philosophy being either implied or assumed. The argument began, of course, in connection with an alleged bias against religion in the State textbooks; but it has developed into an equally animated allegation of a general bias against nationalism, chivalry, and the military virtues.

—April 30, 1910

Utopian

The "world" is already set free, if that is freedom; but is it exactly what the utopians want to demand as freedom? It is undoubtedly an idle society, but is it an ideal society? Is utopia to be found in Belgravia any more than in Bohemia? Are the rich all good or better than anybody else? Are they all clever or cleverer than anybody else? Are they even all free and happy, or all freer and happier than anybody else?

—March 21, 1925

Values

All the modern mystics and pragmatists and popular preachers, and people interested in problems of evolution and ethics, suddenly began to say "Religion is the science of values." They also, I regret to say, began to string words together with hyphens in the German manner, and talk about the experience-value of the immortality of the soul or the survival-value of the disappearance of the tail. There was something about this notion of calling a thing valuable that seemed to make it very vivid and vital and fresh. Doubtless people went about applying it to the psychology of daily life, saying "Mr. Puffin is a man of very vital values." . . . Anyhow, any number of fashionable people had fallen in love with the new word. And some of them never noticed that it was simply identical with an old word, and one of the most tame and tiresome of old words.

—August 28, 1926

Vanity and Pride

Vanity is a desire for praise; even the gods have it, and it exists in heaven. Vanity means thinking somebody's praise important, more important than yourself. But pride (which does not exist in heaven, but at quite an opposite address) is thinking yourself more important than anything that can praise or blame you.

—November 12, 1910

Vegetarian

It has often been pointed out that Cain was an agriculturist and therefore most probably a vegetarian; while Abel kept flocks and killed and ate them. I am sure that somewhere in this fact is to be found the key of that dark and terrible story. It seems so like a vegetarian to kill his brother on strictly altruistic principles.

—July 7, 1906

Vegetarian Menu

... there is the larger and more philosophic riddle of why the vegetarians, or fruitarians, try to make their dishes sound, or even seem, like meat dishes? Why do they talk nonsense about nut-cutlets or tomato toad-in-the-hole? ... It cannot be supposed to take anyone in. We meat-eaters might as well pretend that cutlets grow on trees. We might as well talk about picking sausages in the hedgerows, or growing fish-cakes in our own garden.... It is beneath the dignity of men who ... elaborately mimic the shapes and titles of the system which they seek to dethrone. We expect Food Reformers to be prigs; but they need not be snobs too. If they really think it wrong to eat meat, if they honestly consider it a kind of cannibalism, why should they introduce reminders of the revolting habit they have renounced?

—December 4, 1909

Vegetarianism

The true compromise lies somewhere here. Some people, I believe, adopt the compromise about drink of being teetotalers between meals. Well, I am a vegetarian between meals. From breakfast to lunch not a leg of mutton crosses my lips.... Only four times a day I will eat, like a man; for the rest I will browse happily, like all the beasts of the field.

—December 4, 1909

511

"Venerable"

It is a very patent platitude . . . that a word may be an intrinsic eulogy and still be a tactless compliment. The word "venerable," as it is applied to an abbey, should not in every case be applied to an aunt, any more than it is wise to assign the same date to a friend's wine at dinner and to his eggs at breakfast. . . . But the case is worse when one such word is multiplied unmeaningly in every aspect of life, and when a man is congratulated on his broad-minded hat, his broad-minded boots and his broad-minded umbrella, or perpetually praised for his venerable vote or his venerable visiting-card. And it is worst of all when the word in question is not even so vague as these, but is a very definite and even doctrinal word, only valuable because it distinguishes certain opinions from others.

—*May 5, 1917*

Versaille (Treaty of)

The peace of the world will depend not merely on the facts, but on the German version of the facts. . . .

—*September 29, 1917*

The justice of it, if disputed at all, should be disputed on the ground that a nation cannot be criminal, or that a nation cannot be punished by nations. I myself believe that a nation can be criminal, and can be punished for crime. I believe it because I am a nationalist, and still more because I am a democrat—or, if the phrase be more exact, a republican. That is, I believe a commonwealth has a common will, a corporate spirit which can be loved, and which therefore can be blamed. Those who say that a democratic Germany cannot deserve punishment are denying the first dogma of democracy. But the nation, to do it justice, does not deny that Germans might deserve punishment, or that we in a similar case should deserve punishment.

—*May 31, 1919*

Verse (Traditional versus Modern)

Now, half the current case for free against traditional verse turns simply on that. It consists in calling "I know not where" pompous and theatrical; and calling "I don't know where" natural and sincere. It is not more natural and it is not more sincere; it is only more conversational. And the fact that it is conversational only means that it is conventional. In our time, especially, slang is merely the most conventional mode of address. But it is not a mode of expression, as poetry is a mode of expression, for the emotions and indescribable imaginations of men, for the simple reason that it does not express them. Common speech is not the thing by which men express their emotions; it is only the thing by which they fail to express them.

—April 1, 1933

Victorian Age

Like all great epochs, like all great things, it is not easy to define. We can see it, touch it, smell it, eat it; but we cannot state it. It was a time when faith was firm without being definite. It was a time when we saw the necessity of reform without once seeing the possibility of revolution. It was a sort of exquisite interlude in the intellectual disputes: a beautiful, accidental truce in the eternal war of mankind. Things could mix in a mellow atmosphere. Its great men were so religious that they could do without a religion.

—June 5, 1909

Victorianism

Victorianism was not the beginning of the world. It was rather the beginning of the end.

—June 24, 1922

Victorianism seems to be a virtue that flowers late, and generally after the death of Victoria.

—March 9, 1929

Violence

We have taken the essential responsibility which is involved in war in merely being citizens of a State; we have declared war in favour of certain practices which we approve and against certain practices which we disapprove. It is a dreadful responsibility to declare that burglary is bad for mankind. It is a dreadful responsibility to declare that burglars shall be hurt because we think them harmful. It is a dreadful responsibility; but we have taken it. The decision has all that daring appeal to dogma which is the essence of revolution. Government itself is a revolution. The State itself is a *coup d'état.*

— October 20, 1906

Virginia

It is a commonplace to say that Virginia was the very throne of the authority of the revolution. From Virginia came Washington, its hero, and Jefferson, its prophet. The state was known as the mother of presidents. It was felt as a sort of council chamber of the fathers of the republic. . . . It is enough to say that, in the Civil War, the adherence of Virginia to the side of local patriotism, which happened to be the losing side, was certainly the fact which almost turned it into the winning side. In Virginia, in that dark hour, arose the greatest of American generals; who was, perhaps, the noblest of Americans. I really cannot imagine why a history which begins with Raleigh and ends with Lee, and incidentally includes Washington, should be utterly swept aside and forgotten. . . .

— September 11, 1920

Vividness

Vividness has nothing to do with truth; in fact, truth often tends to look a little misty and atmospheric. It is the lies that glow and glare and impose themselves. Very few things are so vivid as a vivid dream. The reason is obvious: we can take waking things lightly, but the nightmare on the chest is always heavy. A man walking about in the daylight can shut his eyes to many things, and wink at the rest. But this is the whole horror of a man being asleep: that he cannot shut his eyes; something has got inside the brain and is burning it.

— December 3, 1910

Vivisection

In vivisection a man takes a simpler creature and subjects it to subtleties which no one but man could inflict on him, and for which man is therefore gravely and terribly responsible.

— January 4, 1908

Vivisection (Anti-)

... I am a strong anti-vivisectionist. That is, if there is any vivisection, I am against it. I am against the cutting-up of conscious dogs for the same reason that I am in favour of the eating of dead turkeys. The connection may not be obvious; but that is because of the strangely unhealthy condition of modern thought. I am against cruel vivisection as I am against a cruel anti-Christmas asceticism, because they both involve the upsetting of existing fellowships and the shocking of normal good feelings for the sake of something that is intellectual, fanciful, and remote.

—January 4, 1908

Voting

... voting ought to mean arguing for hours and hours in a public-house and interrupting people and hitting the table. It ought to mean elbowing in great crowds and roaring and singing and rising in rebellion, and killing men over barricades. In short, voting, if it means anything, means doing all the things that males have always done—notably, fighting, drinking, and talking about everything and nothing. In other words, it means doing all the things that women have always hated, that children (who are the kingdom of heaven) have always hated; for all children loathe long conversation, just as all children loathe the taste of wine. Also it means doing all the things that saints have always hated, and which archangels probably hate. But they are the things that men as men love; and the man who does not love honest liquor and honest argument and all the things that make the coarse camaraderie of men, is a man who has failed to be a man and not risen to be a woman.

—March 16, 1907

I have always believed in "One Man One Vote"; and I believe in it still. But for all that, a great many different voters go to make up a man. The same, I believe, has been alleged of tailors; I do not know why. But, politically, the average man is not all of a piece: he is not the same colour all the way through. Various human qualities will make him vote or not vote. Show me a supercilious young Socialist terrorising timid yokels with terms like "inevitable" and "solidarity," and I sympathise with the yokels against the Socialist. Show me a vulgar millionaire, with a bought coronet and a coarse mouth, saying that such Socialists should be "put down" or "shot down," and I sympathise with the supercilious Socialist against the millionaire. Nor is this fickleness; but a quite clear and fixed principle of proportion.

—July 25, 1914

Vox populi

One genuine point of resemblance between the voice of the people and the voice of Heaven is that they are both very often rather difficult to understand.

—November 20, 1909

It is the peasants who preserve all traditions of the sites of battles or the building of churches. It is they who remember, so far as anyone remembers, the glimpses of fairies or the graver wonders of saints. In the classes above them the supernatural has been slain by the supercilious. That is a true and tremendous text in Scripture which says that "Where there is no vision the people perish." But it is equally true in practice that where there is no people the visions perish.

—July 30, 1910

Vulgar

When somebody tries to impress us, either with his wit or assurance, or knowledge of the world, or power, or grace, or even poetry and ideality, and in the very act of doing so shows he has low ideas of all these things—that is vulgarity. In other words, a thing is only vulgar when its best is base.

—June 8, 1929

Vulgarities

A queer quality of this queer age is that it is impossible even to launch a curse without it turning into a compliment. There have been so many paradoxes against common morals that there is no longer safety and satisfaction even in vulgar abuse. You lean back comfortably in your armchair, content with the thought of having thrown out some remark which will be thoroughly offensive to somebody, and you are grieved to observe that it has become almost a form of flattery by the time it reaches him. . . . If you tell him that his evil ways are beyond all toleration, he may look at you with the calm insanity of Nietzsche and say: "Of course, they are beyond everything; for they are beyond good and evil." . . . Vulgar abuse, like every other really popular thing, depends upon popular beliefs and popular traditions. . . .

—May 16, 1936

Vulgarity

Vulgarity is no longer a rare and distinguished and striking thing; vulgarity has become vulgarised. It is as if every man in the street had a large red nose and a little hat like a music-hall comedian. It is now really common to be common.

—December 20, 1924

. . . the perpetual implication that everybody is going nowhere except to the best restaurants is vulgar. For vulgarity is a thing of visions and even ideals; and men are judged by their dreams.

—June 8, 1929

War

. . . there is really a great deal to be said against war, especially modern war, with its huge scientific engines and huge conscript armies. It is merciless, it is mechanical; it uses or destroys man and nature for its own purpose. It is anti-domestic like a press-gang, and often secretive like a conspiracy. It makes things depend on small rings of statesmen and diplomatists, often corrupt and always cynical. It has aspects nobody can be proud of, such as the institution of spies. It necessarily interferes with that fundamental carelessness which is akin to kindness and is the wisest of the customs of mankind. It gives the mere scientific expert a more dangerous power than he has in any other department even of the modern world. Also it kills people. Every one of these objections is a real objection, great or small; but we, objecting to these things as much as older men born of women, repeat that in a certain clear case and just cause we think it right to endure them.

—October 17, 1914

. . . war is not "the best way of settling differences"; it is the only way of preventing their being settled for you.

—July 24, 1915

But while the statement that God is on our side is merely another way of saying that we are justified in having a side, there is another and more special sense in which we can use so transcendental a phrase. Those primary and pre-human elements whose work we are uphold us against the cocksureness of the kingdom of

517

clockwork. God is on our side because Man is on our side; and a man is one of the things that men cannot make.

—*October 23, 1915*

War is a consequence of some men being tyrants. Some man or men read a request for arbitration; some man or men tear it up, and take the full responsibility for tearing it up. In doing so they take the full responsibility of every pang that torments the pacifist imagination, of every ruin that is lamented by the pacifist rhetoric. And one thing is absolutely certain—that if such men are not held answerable for doing such things, such men will do them again; and myriads of such men will do myriads of such things, again and again until the crack of doom.

—*September 28, 1918*

... the greatest wars are religious wars, and ... the most incalculable wars are revolutions.

—*April 5, 1919*

If we merely forget and forgive in the matter of who began the war, are we not plainly telling the next aggressor to begin a war and all will be forgotten and forgiven? If we merely distribute the blame for the sin on all parties, are we not obviously encouraging the next man to commit the sin in the hope of distributing the blame?

—*May 5, 1923*

When will people leave off talking about satirising war, or denouncing war, or defending war, or being for or against war? War is not a proposal; it is the refusal of all proposals. War is not an institution; it is the breakdown of all institutions. It is not something that we all agree to have; it is something that we do have when we do not agree. It is idle to talk of it at all in terms of the collective and co-operative action of two parties; it is by definition the condition in which they have to consider themselves separately. It is not the problem of two men and how they shall act together; it is the problem of one man when the other man will not act with him. They do not agree to have war; if they could agree to have war, they would probably agree to have peace.

—*May 17, 1924*

...if Christianity is to be called a failure because it has not abolished war, Buddhism can hardly be a certain and solid guarantee that we shall abolish war. The truth is, of course, that all such talk of abolishing this and that, among the recurrent misunderstandings and temptations of mankind, shows an essential ignorance of the very nature of mankind. It does not allow for the hundred inconsistencies, dilemmas, desperate remedies, and divided allegiances of men. A man may be in every way a good man and a true believer, and yet be in a false position.

—March 2, 1929

It would be a horrible thought, as I have said, that any men should want a war to enlighten them. But though it is hardly probable that any of us would pray for such enlightenment, it is only too probable that, if we blind ourselves to foreign facts, we shall be so enlightened.

—August 3, 1929

Properly speaking, the only rational wars are the religious wars. If a man may be asked to die for anything, it may well be for his whole reason for living, his whole conception of the object of life and death.

—September 26, 1931

...nobody but a lunatic needs to be told that all wars are horrible, and that the next war will be the most horrible of all wars. Indeed, it is a quaint and ironic fact that it is rather specially the progressives, the meliorists and evolutionists, the futurists, the hopeful humanitarians who tell us that humanity is always improving, and every day and in every way growing better and better—oddly enough, I say, it is these people especially who tell us that the next new scientific war will be something worse than the world has ever known in ruder times. But whoever says it...it is true...war will be worse because it will be more cold and calculated, more remote, more impersonal, more indifferent to the individual. In short, war will be worse because it will be more like peace, as some very cold-blooded sociologists would like to make it.

—December 2, 1933

War (Aftermath)

It is, in the real sense, a matter of conscience to show generosity to the defeated, so long as it is consistent with justice to the oppressed.

—May 24, 1919

War (Defensive)

It is always quite easy to forget the advantages gained by a defensive war. A defensive war is always the most defensible and the least easy to defend. The reason is obvious enough. If a man goes out to knock another man down and takes his watch, and if he succeeds, he will at least have the watch to show. But the other man, if he successfully defends himself, will have nothing to show; except perhaps a black eye or a broken umbrella.

—April 6, 1929

War (Holy)

The cheapest and most childish of all the taunts of the Pacificists is, I think, the sneer at belligerents for appealing to the God of Battles. It is ludicrously illogical, for we obviously have no right to kill for victory save when we have a right to pray for it. If a war is not a holy war, it is an unholy war—a massacre.

—October 23, 1915

War (Just)

For a good cause releases the nations. It does not merely deliver them from slavery at the end of the war; it delivers them from sameness at the beginning of it. A bad peace does indeed obliterate boundaries and bind all races in the bonds of imitation: imitation, which may be the sincerest, but is none the less the basest, flattery. But a good war (that is, a war *ex justá causá*) gives every nation a chance to be national without being narrow.

—June 26, 1915

In both cases destruction may be essential to the avoidance of destruction, and also to the very possibility of construction. Men are not merely destroying a ship in order to have a shipwreck; they may be merely destroying a tree in order to have a ship. And the deepest and most democratic of all destructive revolutions was the Great War itself, which destroyed the whole elaborate and laborious machinery of Prussianism which would otherwise have destroyed all the normal liberties and humours of humanity.

—January 3, 1920

War (Modern)

And this appalling scale of slaughter has risen stage by stage, with what we call modern organisation and modern centralisation and modern science. I am not blaming the physical science that happens to be powerful in this age. But I do object to somebody else blaming the clericalism that happens to be almost powerless. The broad truth about the matter is that wars have become more organised, and more ghastly in the particular period of materialism.

—July 26, 1930

Warfare (Cultural)

Invasion may be a sword; but peaceful penetration is a poison. . . . To attack the culture is to attack the country, but it is to attack it from within. It comes from the sort of culture that has already contrived to get inside another culture; the sort unpleasantly suggested by bacteria-culture. Anybody who really loves a national tradition would rather it were attacked from without than eaten away from within. And the national traditions of this country, in landscape, architecture, manners, and domestic comfort, are being silently supplanted by the very inferior ones that go to make up an American hotel. But the trouble is that they are not being vanquished; they are being sacrificed.

—April 9, 1927

Way of the World

It was Matthew Arnold, if I remember right, who invented or popularised the phrase "the way the world is going"; a motto for social reformers only too easily adapted into a motto for snobs. . . . The world seems to be going all ways at once.

—August 23, 1930

Weapons

On every sword that is made by man, while the workshops of the world turn out
that terrible kind of cutlery, ought to be graven the two mysterious phrases which
were on the fairy sword of King Arthur. On one side was written "Take me," and
on the other "Cast me away." If no more than this dim fable recalled the doubtful
hero of Camelot, we should know that he defended Christendom against the
heathen. For the highest mark of Christian civilisation is this capacity for feeling
that the sword is at once noble and unnatural; and the more unnatural it is, the
more noble it is.

—*November* 21, 1914

Weariness

... whatever spirit ought to settle the war of the world, plainly such a problem
ought not to be settled by the spirit of weariness. Weariness is not a principle of
action at all.

—*August* 25, 1917

... weariness ... is the enemy of all noble things.

—*October* 13, 1917

Weather

It is truly astounding, properly considered, that the weather should ever have
come to be called a commonplace topic. Weather, the machinery of all the
mythologists, the mother of gods and demons, the background and often the
subject matter of all poetry and art, ought to be a conversational topic as dramatic
and sensational as any good news or bad. There are whole poems of Shelley that
amount to no more than saying it is a fine day. There are vast canvases of Turner of
which we can only say, with the proverbial frown of the weather prophet, that it
looks like rain. But nothing that looks like rain can be so overwhelming as rain
itself, let alone the ancient terrors of storm and flood.

—*March* 19, 1927

Weather (Hot)

The chief gift of hot weather to me is the somewhat unpopular benefit called a conviction of sin. All the rest of the year I am untidy, lazy, awkward, and futile. But in hot weather I *feel* untidy, lazy, awkward, and futile.

—June II, 1910

Wedding

Heaven knows what has happened to these two antiquated commemorative conceptions in the course of the casual experiments that are now called weddings. ... If the symbols of silver and gold are now unfashionable, those metals are certainly not disliked because of their costliness, but presumably because of their durability. In these days there must be commemorations at shorter intervals, symbolised by more flexible substances. Those who have managed to remain married for a week will celebrate a paper wedding.... At what intervals should occur the very rare festivals known as the plasticine wedding, the india-rubber wedding, and the quaint old gutta-percha wedding I will not venture to speculate. It would seem idle to dwell in detail on merely exceptional types, or the strange and stubborn survivors who manage to remain married for more than a month.

—September 27, 1930

The Welfare State

... the state cannot decide when everybody is to get up in the morning, how late anybody is to sit up at night, how many windows shall be opened in the bed-room, how many visits are to be paid to the garden, when and where every man shall take a walk—the state cannot enforce all this without destroying the last remnants of self-respect and liberty that make life worth living. It is quite true that men can ruin themselves, and even that men in community can ruin the community; but in these cases there is nothing to be said except that if men cannot save themselves by commonsense, they cannot save each other by coercion; and that it is useless to chain them up like maniacs and then command them to save the state.

—August I, 1931

Wells, H. G.

He is also the victim, I think, of the weakness already described—the lack of something which may be loosely described by the theological term of final perseverance. Even his most successful novels fail only at the last moment. They end, but they do not conclude; the writer seems resolved to escape from a conclusion. They do not end in mere negation or despair, but only in an oblivion of their original object—as if the writer had just caught sight of something else that had nothing to do with it.

—January 26, 1918

... he assumes that the mediaeval idea of education was inferior to ours, simply because it involved the teaching of a positive philosophy. But there is something to be said for the idea of teaching everything to somebody, as compared with the modern notion of teaching nothing, and the same sort of nothing, to everybody. For what we force on all families, by the power of the police, is not a philosophy, but the art of reading and writing unphilosophically.

—October 2, 1931

Well's "Outline of History"

I have never ceased to regret that when Mr. H. G. Wells struck off that one splendid and expressive title, "An Outline of History," he immediately forgot all about it, and went off to make an outline of something else; something that began as the outline of a highly doubtful skull in Biltdown or Java, and ended as an outline of the swelled head of a modern prophet of peace.

—March 1, 1930

Westernization

We can at least learn from history what does and does not necessarily civilise barbarism. And I think it the plain fact of history that the mere ballot-box does not—that mere voting in that sense is already sufficiently mechanical to be easy for savages. In any case, it is always easy for the outsider to adopt our fashions, though not our customs; and this is equally true of philosophical fashions.

—February 8, 1919

Whitman, Walt

It is exactly because Whitman tried to be too original in style that the world does not know how original he really was in spirit. This is what the American critic does not see.

—June 13, 1925

Walt Whitman remains largely a rude and half-hewn statue in a studio, to be appreciated only by artists. He remains an almost indecipherable inscription, to be read only by antiquaries. Wishing to be the poet of many, he has remained the poet of the few. Appealing to those to whom no poet had yet appealed, he has been read only by those who specialised in poetry. And even those who understand his mood do not generally share it.

—June 13, 1925

Walt Whitman had his faults, artistic and other, but he did lead the democracy of the "Leaves of Grass" against the oligarchy of "The Green Carnation." He did set the thousand common things against the two or three perverted and exotic things that had been set up as the idols of that age. He had, whatever else he had, the American virtue of thinking things worthwhile. Nay, he did sound like the voice of a new nation; like the voice of many million men. He did not seem entirely absurd when he claimed to be America; to be, in a new sense, a father of the republic.

—April 21, 1928

Wicked Acts

Why on earth do the newspapers, in describing a dynamite outrage or any other political assassination, call it a "dastardly outrage" or a cowardly outrage? It is perfectly evident that it is not dastardly in the least. It is perfectly evident that it is about as cowardly as the Christians going to the lions. The man who does it exposes himself to the chance of being torn in pieces by two thousand people. What the thing is, is not cowardly, but profoundly and detestably wicked. The man who does it is very infamous and very brave. But, again, the explanation is that our modern Press would rather appeal to physical arrogance, or to anything, rather than appeal to right and wrong.

—November 24, 1906

Wilson, Woodrow

... there used always to be a certain detached intellectual distinction about his ideas. In his last message to the Senate it was his ideas that seemed suddenly to have stopped working.... For instance, what can be said of his idea, generally considered as an idea, of peace without victory? Peace without victory is war without excuse. And, if he believes in the idea, would he apply the idea to the quarrels after the peace as well as to the quarrels before it? He wishes to establish a league of peace to prevent wars; obviously it could only prevent them by waging war, or threatening to wage war, with any Power that broke the peace.

—February 3, 1917

Window

A window, however much painted, is a more enlightening and wholesome thing than a mirror. For the most private window is in a sense public, while the most public mirror is in its immediate uses private, not to say personal.

—February 18, 1922

Wine

Obviously one indisputable thing that can be said for wine is that it is made entirely from vegetables. Even more obviously the one thing that can be said for vegetables is that they can be made into wine. Whatever are the crimes of the carnivorous animals, they are all solid and convinced teetotallers. We have heard of an ox in a tea-cup; but nobody has yet heard of an elephant in a liqueur-glass. Tigers have not been trampled into any horrible wine. Bacchus trod his grapes, but he never tried jumping on his leopards. On strictly logical principles it seems obvious that vegetarians ought to urge alcohol as one of the few really inspiring arguments for vegetarianism. The crushed body of a bird or a beetle cannot be made to live a second and celestial life, as does the crushed body of the golden or the purple grape.

—December 19, 1908

Wisdom (Rejection of)

... the man who once leaves the home of human wisdom must go all round the world to get back to it. If he cannot believe what he sees, he must see all that there is to be seen before he can test it truly. Memories and instincts may be mere hints, and still be useful. But an incomplete logical process always leaves off in the wrong place.

—February 17, 1917

Witness

The spirit of our law is that the prisoner must be protected by the rules of the game; if he can be caught and killed in accordance with those rules, no one has the slightest pity for him. The person whom we badger and pursue is the witness, the man who is merely helping human society; but such happens to be the rule of the game.

—July 17, 1909

Woman

... it is obvious that the Victorians were as familiar as anybody else with the idea of a woman having a strong personality; and, if not all the women have it in literature, it is because not all the women have it in life. But manifestly it was not made impossible for a woman to be a power, merely on the ground that she was a woman.

—April 25, 1925

Woman as Judge of Character

... I have just read an enthusiastic essay by a lady suffragist which says (to put it shortly, which she is far from doing) that man has always been a faultless being in the eyes of his women-folk, but that under the influence of the modern movement his women are beginning to find him out. What does it all mean? I never met a woman who had not found out the man long before he was her husband. I never met a wife who did not know all the weaknesses of her husband and count on them as calmly as she counted on sunrise or the spring. I never met the woman who regarded the man as incapable of moral error. Did you?

—August 29, 1908

Women

For the average woman is at the head of something with which she can do as she likes; the average man has to obey orders and do nothing else. He has to put one dull brick on another dull brick, and do nothing else; he has to add one dull figure to another dull figure, and do nothing else. The woman's world is a small one, perhaps, but she can alter it. The woman can tell the tradesman with whom she deals some realistic things about himself. The clerk who does this to the manager generally gets the sack, or shall we say (to avoid the vulgarism), finds himself free for higher culture.

—April 7, 1906

Women (Modern)

... the Bearded Lady at a fair represents the masculine advance of modern woman....

—September 24, 1910

She wishes to remain independent, which seems to mean eating the dinner and then indignantly refusing to pay the bill. Whether or no this be a true definition of independence, it does not seem to me a good definition of generosity. On the contrary, it seems to me to be taking a rather despicable advantage. The dinner has disappeared irrevocably inside the diner. It cannot be recovered at law; it cannot be extracted even by torture.... To refuse the responsibilities that follow on having once consumed your Christmas pudding seems to me a course not particularly courageous, but rather cowardly....

—March 6, 1926

We hear a great deal of the evil passions of class war and the suggestion that the master and man must of necessity be natural enemies. But surely there is a far more perverse implication pervading the modern world; that the wife and the husband are natural enemies. They are, apparently, such mortal enemies that it is enough for one of them to be freed from the other, even in one trumpery particular, though she is not freed from anything or anybody else.

—November 28, 1931

Women (New)

The New Woman says, indignantly: "Yes, you think women are slavish and hysterical." I reply: "Not in the least. I think New Women are slavish and hysterical; I think ordinary women are responsible and vigorous." The Suffragette says, with a withering smile: "For you a woman is weak, imitative, and dependent." I reply: "Far from it. A Suffragette is weak, imitative, and dependent. She repeats stale catch-words, and lives on infectious emotions. A woman is particularly original and unpedantic; a woman almost always thinks for herself." The point is not that woman is foolish; but that she can, if she likes, put herself in a particular position in which she looks foolish, just as a man does when he tries to hold the baby.

—February 27, 1909

Women (Working)

It is in the cold economic sense a waste; it is uneconomic in the full sense of being thriftless. For, obviously, such a neglect of family feeling is the neglect of a natural force, which must be replaced by an artificial and, therefore, an expensive force. If the mother must not take an interest in her children, somebody else must be paid to do what she alone could have a particular pleasure in doing.

—May 3, 1919

Women and Football

I think tennis for women normal, and football for women quite abnormal; and I am no more inconsistent than I am in having a wooden walking-stick and not a wooden hat.

—January 28, 1922

Women and Independence

Independence is not made the ideal of the normal man. It is only suddenly and abruptly introduced, in one particular relation, in the case of the exceptional woman. She is only independent of her husband; not independent in any other real relation of life. She is only independent of the home—and not of the workshop or the world. And it is supremely characteristic of this confusion that one well-meaning individual should make a yet finer distinction, and resolve to be independent in the dressing-room, but not in the dining-room.

—November 28, 1931

Women and Love

If you had said to Deborah the mother in Israel, or Hypatia the Platonist of Alexandria, or Catherine of Siena, or Joan of Arc, or Isabella of Spain.... that Byronic love was "woman's whole existence," they would all have been very indignant and most of them flown into a towering passion. They would have asked in various ways whether there was no such thing as honour, no such thing as duty, no such thing as glory, no such thing as great studies or great enterprises, no such thing as normal functions and necessary labours; incidentally, we may add, no such thing as babies.

—May 2, 1931

Women Despots

The average woman, as I have said, is a despot; the average man is a serf. I am for any scheme that anyone can suggest that will make the average woman more of a despot. So far from wishing her to get her cooked meals from outside, I should like her to cook more wildly and at her own will than she does. So far from getting always the same meals from the same place, let her invent, if she likes, a new dish every day of her life. Let her be more of a maker, not less.

—April 14, 1906

Women, Fellowship and Politics

When we say that women are deficient in a casual habit of fellowship, it is only an accident that we put the matter in a verbal form unfavourable to them. It would be quite as easy, and perhaps more correct, to put it the other way round. It would be much truer to say that men are deficient in intensity and a responsible devotion. The truth of the matter is that women have no comradeship because women will not be induced to waste time; and the very essence of comradeship is wasting time. And for the same reason (I fancy) women will not really be interested in Parliamentary politics; for the essence of Parliamentary politics is wasting time.

Men do not wish to govern well, but merely to govern; they like the atmosphere of citizenship. To women I think it appears as futile as all other very long conversations. It is not that women are not practical enough for politics. It is that politics are not practical enough for women.

—May 26, 1906

Women's Rights Movement

But there is no worse case of the plutocratic influence than in this ordinary phrase used for Woman's Rights, this phrase that men are rulers and masters and women menials. To hear these people talk one would think that every woman's husband was a Cabinet Minister. "Men," they say, "go out to sway the sceptre and to rule, while women sit at home." Men, as a matter of fact, go out to be shouted at and ordered about like niggers all day. Women, as a matter of fact, sit at home either shouting at and ordering about other people, or else in a god-like liberty and solitude. Everybody knows that women have a hard time, a quite indefensibly hard time. But it does not arise from being denied any powers or rights. It does not arise from being given no authority. As a fact, it arises chiefly from being given too much authority. And if there is a person in the world who, in comparison to the woman, can really and calmly be called a slave, it is the ordinary man. The ordinary man (the extreme woman's advocates will be surprised to hear) is not a pirate captain, nor a Prime Minister, nor the head man in an American trust, nor the Pope, but merely the servant of a business.

—January 27, 1906

Women's Rights (Progress of)

The very prominent and wealthy women will be quieted and will silently strengthen their position, as all their class has done for the last four hundred years. And the working-women will remain like the working-men—full of faith, hope, charity towards a race of politicians very much lower than themselves.

—August 6, 1910

Wonder

. . . it will be found that the real psychology of wonder depends on some return to simplicity and even to slowness. We must go back to primitive conditions again and again, if we wish to realise even the scientific inventions, if we wish to feel them wonderful and not merely to call them wonderful. And I do mean that we are merely heaping up boredom so long as we are merely heaping up novelty; and that the notion of merely going faster and faster means to this mortal life what it means in motoring—the incapacity to see anything at all, even our own speed.

—*March* 19, 1927

Work

. . . though there are good and clever and free and happy people among the idle rich, as there are among the idle poor, not to mention the industrious poor, I think it is broadly true that most of us have found that the most sincere and sensible people were people who earned their own living.

—*March* 21, 1925

I am entirely at one with the Socialists in wishing to give most men less work and some men more work. But the abstract question propounded here is not that question; it is whether, if we could, we would give nobody any work.

—*March* 21, 1925

Worker (Independent)

It is not made the ideal of the proletarian or wage-earner, either by the communist or the capitalist system. Both the communist and the capitalist are alike in not thinking of the individual worker as independent. They will discuss whether he is well paid, whether he is well treated, whether he works under good or bad conditions, whether he is dependent on a good or bad business or a good or bad government; but *not* whether he is independent.

—*November* 28, 1931

Worker (Servile)

It is the very mark of the servile worker to forget why he is working. It is the definition of a tool that it does not know why it is a tool.

—March 17, 1917

World (Modern)

Some people complain of the rationalism of the modern world; surely it is the irrationalism that is mostly to be complained of. We are too rapid to be reasonable. It is a common saying that the modern world is too hurried to dream, to picture, or to pray. But, in truth, it is too hurried even to think. Nay, it is too hurried even to doubt, as vigorous sceptics would understand doubting. Modern men have to swallow their dogmas as they swallow their lunch. The eighteenth century was an age of reason, because it was an age of leisure. But we have passed out of the *câge des philosophes,* the age of philosophers, which was necessarily an age of sceptics. We have come into the age of company promoters, which is necessarily an age of faith, of simple faith. Moreover, our modern hurry prevents our doing well, even the things that we want to do.

— September 21, 1907

World State

... the whole world in which Christianity originally rose was a cosmopolitan world. It was the world of the Roman Empire. It was practically what Mr. Wells calls a world state; and it is curious that Mr. Wells should so fondly desire a world state and so furiously hate the only world state there has ever been.

—April 12, 1924

I have lived through the times when many intelligent and idealistic men hoped that the world war would be an introduction to the world state. But I myself am more convinced than ever that the world war occurred because nations were too big, and not because they were too small. It occurred especially because big nations wished to be bigger, or, in other words, because each state wanted to be the world state.

—November 7, 1931

World War I

If we say that this war was everybody's fault, everybody will know that any war he makes will be called everybody's fault—that is, nobody's fault. Every man will know that he can at any moment commit a crime which will be called an accident. Every ruler will know that he can, whenever he pleases, perform an act of aggression which will be called an act of God. Or rather, it will not even be called anything so mystical and disputable as the act of god—it will actually be called the act of humanity. We shall be solemnly told that "all nations are equally to blame" for something which one nation does whenever that nation may choose to do it.

—September 28, 1918

Historians hundreds of years hence will judge the whole nature of what happened in these four fearful years by what happens to Alsace-Loraine.

—October 19, 1918

Its most fashionable form may be summed up in the phrase, "It will be all the same a hundred years hence." I have read pacifist poems and essays in which the old rhetorical flourish to the effect that the corn will grow on the battlefield, or the ivy on the ruined fortress, is seriously used to suggest that it makes no difference whether the battle was fought or whether the fortress fell. We should not be here at all, to moralise about the ivy on castles and the corn on battlefields, if some of the great conflicts of history had gone the other way. If certain barbarian invasions had finally swept certain civilised districts, men would very probably have forgotten how to grow corn, and would certainly have forgotten how to write poems about ivy.

—November 23, 1918

The war was not a scheme elaborately constructed to make things better. It was the successful beating on of besieging barbarians who wanted to make things worse. It did not make things better than they were, but better than they would have been.

—May 5, 1923

Most of the heroes of legend and history have been great because they saved society. The Great War was great because it saved society. It could not have been waged by pessimists who did not think society worth saving.

—May 5, 1923

The fundamental fallacy was the fashion of regarding it as a war between the British empire and the German empire. . . . It would be far more like the fact to go back a thousand years and call it a rivalry between the Roman Empire and the Huns. It was a war between England as a part of Europe and Prussia as the leader of the barbarism that has always existed on the border of Europe.

—January 19, 1924

I do not agree with Mr. H. G. Wells (or Clissold) that the Great War was a war that settled nothing, any more than I agreed with Mr. H. G. Wells that it was the war that would end war. It was quite enough for me, from the first, that it was the war that would end Prussian prestige; and it did. Humanity will go on talking nonsense till the crack of doom, but it will be some other sort of nonsense, and not the sort which regarded a certain very dull North German as if he were not so much the god from the machine as the machine and the god as well.

—April 14, 1928

World War I (American Entry)

. . . the entry of America, which may truly be described as the entry of mankind. It is even, as I say, like the entry of unborn mankind.

—April 14, 1917

World War I and German Victory

. . . there most certainly *will* be no more international law. There will also be no more respect for women in war, no more respect for prisoners of war, no more scruples about torture or slavery—in short, no more European civilisation, which they will have done everything to deny and we shall have done nothing to reaffirm. History will simply say that the barbarians conquered, if history says anything at all. But the subsequent history would not be worth writing; and very probably would not be written.

—August 25, 1917

World War II

I am quite certain myself, for instance, that a great European war could be prevented to-morrow, if the British government had the moral courage to threaten Prussia with British support for France and Poland the moment they were attacked. I am equally certain that the last great war would not have happened at all, if we had done the same thing openly and from the beginning, instead of half secretly and too late.

—December 2, 1933

World War II, Prophecy of G. K. Chesterton and

We are already drifting horribly near to a new war, which will probably start on the Polish border. The young men have had eighteen years in which to learn how to avoid it. I wonder whether they do know much more about how to avoid it than the despised and driveling old men of 1914. How many of the young men, for instance, have made the smallest attempt to understand Poland? How many would have anything to say to Hitler, to dissuade him from setting all Christendom aflame by a raid on Poland? Or have the young men been thinking of nothing since 1914 except the senile depravity of the old men of that date?

—September 24, 1932

Worries

Theoretically, I suppose, everyone would like to be freed from worries. But nobody in the world would always like to be freed from worrying occupations. I should very much like (as far as my feelings at the moment go) to be free from the consuming nuisance of writing this article. But it does not follow that I should like to be free from the consuming nuisance of being a journalist. Because we are worried about a thing, it does not follow that we are not interested in it. The truth is the other way. If we are not interested, why on earth should we be worried?

—April 7, 1906

Worship

Pagans worshipped the powers because they were powerful and had a god of wealth like a god of water or wind or fire. But the snob and the sneak, who are lower than the pagan, were produced by the habit of worshipping worldliness as a power, and then being ashamed of it as a weakness.

—October 12, 1929

"Worth So Much"

It is a mark of the materialistic and servile spirit in the whole social process that language has been twisted to refer to the property-owner as if he were merely the property. The master himself is ticketed with a price like the slave; he is credited not so much with ownership as with value like that of a chattel; and the millionaire merchant ends by being treated like one of his own bales of cloth or bottles of whisky. But that is only a by-product of this very undesirable branch of production.

—September 10, 1932

Writer (Modern)

I can recall, in the decadent days of my youth, the wonder with which I read that Ibsen, or somebody of that sort, had suggested a doubt about whether "two and two may not make five in the fixed stars." It was my immediate impression that Ibsen, if it was Ibsen, might unquestionably know how to write, but most certainly did not know how to think. And that is the chief feature of current fashions, the number of people who do really know how to write, but who certainly do not know how to think.

—December 13, 1919

Writers and the World

The wildest writer cannot make this world out wilder than it is.

—June 28, 1919

Writing

. . . writing, like fighting, deals with things. Unless we know those things, in each particular case, it is perfectly futile to give general advice.

—February 16, 1918

All this talk of waiting for experiences in order to write is simply a confession of incapacity to experience anything. . . . A paralytic of this deaf-and-dumb description . . . announces himself ready to drink poisons, that they may stimulate him like drugs. But it is futile for him to suppose that this sort of quackery will teach him how to be a writer, for he has been from the first admittedly blind to everything that is worth writing about.

—March 7, 1931

The Young

We always think of the rising generation as if it were rising early. It is well sometimes to remember that the rising generation always rises too late.

—November 12, 1927

Young, Brigham

. . . We think the grand Turk sitting in his harem with his turban and scimitar an extravagant or grotesque figure, precisely in that sense Mr. Brigham Young, with his chimney-pot hat and his chin-beard, was really far more extravagant and grotesque.

—February 2, 1924

Youth

I do not believe that young people are incapable of respecting conviction. I do not believe that they prefer weak and wavering teachers, or want everything submitted to them in this apologetic and agnostic fashion. I doubt whether they really wish to be told in a tentative manner that two and two make four subject to their better judgment. I doubt whether they prefer a teacher who tells them that a triangle has three sides for the present. That sort of hopeful hesitation is not likely to arouse enthusiasm in any young persons I have ever known.

—*June 28, 1924*

It is now the custom to condemn youth as too frivolous. But youth is always too serious; and just now it is too serious about frivolity. The conservatism of youth is a good thing; and it is not even necessary to conserve it.

—*October 27, 1928*

Youth is a period when the wildest external carelessness often runs parallel to the most gloomy and concentrated internal cares. An enormous number of normal youths are quite abnormal for a time. Their imagination is working inwards, and on nothing more commonly than on imaginary maladies. To throw a medical encyclopaedia at the head of a young man in this condition is simply to provide him with a handbook of one thousand ways of going mad.

—*August 10, 1929*

There is only one thing which the new generation cannot possibly or conceivably be. It cannot be the best judge of what is new.

—*January 20, 1934*

One of the many fallacies in what the newspapers love to call the appeal to youth is that youth, with all its beauties and benefits, is actually more credulous than old age in accepting things that are old. Youth will quite naturally accept things that are old, believing them to be new.

—*January 20, 1934*

Yuppieism

There is nothing about which men talk so earnestly as about trifles. . . . The tricks of the time seem to be discussed for a sort of eternity; while the things of eternity are generally dismissed in a very short time. Great and grave problems of ethics and politics are only touched on lightly; but flying details of fashion and convention are examined with an enthusiasm and thoroughness which is a marvel of human virtue. . . . A group of talkers will generally drop the subject of Bolshevism, when there begins to be a dark adumbration or shadowy threat that somebody may ask what it is. . . . The same conversational gentleman who hastily drops the subject of Bolshevism when he reads in the eye of another gentleman that he is beginning to wonder what it is, will take up a point about one particular stroke, on one particular putting-green, in a golf match of five years ago, and return to it again and again with the vigilance and passion of valiant armies repelling an invader.

—July 23, 1921

Yuppies

People are taught to say that they have grown indifferent through over-familiarity with the creeds of the past. But, as a fact, when they are indifferent, it is generally through complete ignorance of the creeds of the past. They are represented as rebelling against the theology in which they were brought up, when they were generally brought up without any theology. . . . The truth is that, whether the old theologies are valuable or valueless, a great part of the rising generation has not suffered from too much of them, but quite the reverse. It is not to be pitied for its subjection to historical religions; it is to be pitied on its ignorance of religious history. So far from having been taught these things as theological dogmas, it has not even been taught them as historical events.

— September 18, 1920

The present generation is not revolting against the views its fathers hold; it is making up legends about the views never understood, to suppose that their grandfathers were all lunatics. Perhaps our ancestors have to be made out very silly indeed in order to be sillier than we are. Perhaps this is what is really meant by progress and evolution. But one thing at least is certain—that none of these people talking about evolution and progress have the most remote notion of what their ancestors really did believe.

— September 18, 1920

I am sure that, in so far as there is any sort of social breakdown, it is not so much a moral breakdown as a mental breakdown. It is much more like a softening of the brain than a hardening of the heart. . . . The old abstract revolutionist would have had the star-defying audacity to ask who it is who really runs the trams or controls the tubes. Most of the young rebels of to-day are content to ask whether they will not soon be made a little bigger or a little quicker or a little more convenient. In other words, the individual has indeed a certain kind of independence but I am not sure that it is the kind of independence, which requires much intelligence.

—March 13, 1926

The difficulty is not so much to get people to follow a commandment as to get them even to follow an argument. It seems to tire their heads like a game of chess when they are in the mood for a game of tennis. And in truth their philosophy does seem to be rather like a game of tennis, with the motto of "love all." . . . It seems to me that this modern mood does not mind anything being arbitrary so long as it is also easy. It does not inquire into the authority or even the origin of any order which it has come to regard as ordinary. It only asks to move smoothly along the grooves that have been graven for it by unknown and nameless powers— such as the powers that organise the tubes or the trams.

—March 13, 1926

Zionism

I myself, for one, have been twice in my life rebuked for being a Zionist; originally, because it was a disparagement of the Jews, and recently because it is a defence of the Jews. As a fact, it is neither, but merely a recognition of the Jews, or a desire to recognise them, if not in Palestine, then somewhere else. But the point here is that people are now talking Anti-Semitism in the present, while they are still claiming a superiority to the Anti-Semitism of the past. And while they are already crying out about the Jewish peril, it never occurs to them that it may be their own fault for having refused to discuss the Jewish problem.

—September 4, 1920

I have always held the Zionist or Jewish nationalists' position. . . . I would give special and secure privileges to the Jews.

—September 4, 1920

INDEX OF TOPICS

This index includes only those topics in an excerpt other than the topic under which that excerpt is listed in the text.

545

George J. Marlin is a vice president and partner in Vigilant Advisors, a fixed-income mutual fund and investment advisory company. Born in 1952, Mr. Marlin, a general editor of *The Collected Works of G.K. Chesterton,* resides in New York City.

Richard P. Rabatin, a professional musician, resides in Stony Brook, New York. Born in 1950, Mr. Rabatin received his undergraduate degree in political science from the State University of New York at Stony Brook. He received his Masters Degree at Fordham University in political science, and he studied musical composition at Berklee College of Music in Boston. Mr. Rabatin is also a general editor of *The Collected Works of G.K. Chesterton.*

John L. Swan is a partner in the community relations firm, Institutional Planning and Development Corporation. He was formerly associated with the National Broadcasting Corporation and the American Cancer Society. Mr. Swan, a lifelong resident of New York City, is also a general editor of *The Collected Works of G.K. Chesterton.*

George W. Rutler is a priest of the Archdiocese of New York. A noted preacher and author, Father Rutler's latest book is *The Curé D'Ars Today.*